Planet Auschwitz

Planet Auschwitz

HOLOCAUST REPRESENTATION IN SCIENCE FICTION AND HORROR FILM AND TELEVISION

Brian E. Crim

RUTGERS UNIVERSITY PRESS

New Brunswick, Camden, and Newark, New Jersey, and London

Library of Congress Cataloging-in-Publication Data

Names: Crim, Brian E., author.
Title: Planet Auschwitz : Holocaust representation in science fiction and horror film and television / Brian E Crim.
Description: New Brunswick : Rutgers University Press, [2020] | Includes bibliographical references and index.
Identifiers: LCCN 2019037919 | ISBN 9781978801615 (hardback) | ISBN 9781978801608 (paperback) | ISBN 9781978801622 (epub) | ISBN 9781978801639 (mobi) | ISBN 9781978801646 (pdf)
Subjects: LCSH: Holocaust, Jewish (1939-1945), in motion pictures. | Holocaust, Jewish (1939-1945), on television. | Science fiction films—History and criticism. | Science fiction television programs—History and criticism. | Horror films—History and criticism. | Horror television programs—History and criticism.
Classification: LCC PN1995.9.H53 C75 2020 | DDC 791.43/658—dc23
LC record available at https://lccn.loc.gov/2019037919

A British Cataloging-in-Publication record for this book is available from the British Library.

www.rutgersuniversitypress.org

Manufactured in the United States of America

To Aunt Karen

CONTENTS

Planet Auschwitz

Introduction

This is a chronicle of the planet of Auschwitz. I was there for about two years. Time there was not like it is here on Earth. Every fraction of a minute there passed on a different scale of time. And the inhabitants of this planet had no names, they had no parents nor did they have children. There they did not dress in the way we dress here; they were not born there and they did not give birth; they breathed according to different laws of nature; they did not live—nor did they die—according to the laws of this world. . . . I believe with perfect faith that, just as in astrology the stars influence our destiny, so does this planet of the ashes, Auschwitz, stand in opposition to our planet Earth, and influences it.
—Yehiel Dinur

First impression: the camp is another planet.
—*Night and Fog* (1955)

The 1961 trial of SS functionary Adolf Eichmann a year after his dramatic capture in Argentina by Israeli agents received daily international press coverage, helping to expose the details behind the Final Solution to a largely ignorant or indifferent global audience. Political philosopher Hannah Arendt attended the trial briefly and coined the phrase *banality of evil* after observing the disheveled bureaucrat sitting behind bulletproof glass. Eichmann was not a monster, she observed, but frighteningly normal to the point one could imagine a little of Eichmann in all of us. Arendt's reflections influenced generations of scholars struggling to reconcile the scale of industrialized murder with the rather ordinary men responsible for its implementation.[1] Yehiel Dinur, the Holocaust survivor and controversial author better known by his pen name Ka-Tzetnik, testified at the trial on June 7, 1961, and introduced the world to another enduring concept during his riveting appearance on the witness stand: planet Auschwitz. Dinur's testimony, along with dozens of others in the Jerusalem courtroom during the fifteen-week trial, revealed the interminable trauma of survivors burdened by a secret most believed could never be communicated. Time, space, and transformative events like the Eichmann trial unleashed a compulsion among survivors to bear witness after years of self-imposed silence.[2] The world was unprepared for the torrent of testimony, especially since the voices truly seemed to come from another planet. If Arendt believed perpetrators of genocide were legion, both historically and in the post-Auschwitz world, Dinur seemed to articulate the opposite view when it came to survivors. He was part of a special breed, neither hated nor pitied, just remote. Dinur testified he was "fall-out" from "that planet" of Auschwitz and after struggling to answer simple questions, he collapsed on the stand and never returned.[3] Survivors, he feared, were practically an alien race speaking a language no one could understand. Raul Hilberg, who wrote the first comprehensive history of the Holocaust soon after the trial, believed survivors had special knowledge grounded in their experience and used expressions like *planet Auschwitz* to accentuate the insurmountable gulf in experience between those who were there and those who were not.[4]

The notion that Auschwitz is a black hole defying description, representation, and therefore understanding derives from prominent intellectuals and survivors declaring it so. Elie Wiesel claimed "We speak in code, we survivors, and this code cannot be broken, cannot be deciphered, not by you no matter how much you try. A novel about Treblinka is either not a novel or not about Treblinka. A novel about Majdanek is about blasphemy. Is blasphemy."[5] In his foreword to Annette Insdorf's influential book on Holocaust film, Wiesel reluctantly agreed media was necessary to inform, educate, and sensitize future generations, but cast doubt on how effective representation could be by once again invoking the incommensurability of experience: "Auschwitz and Treblinka seem to belong to another time; perhaps they are on the other side of time."[6] For Wiesel, Tim Cole notes, Auschwitz was "a kingdom of night which is so other as to be beyond imagination."[7] Dan Stone notes historians often begin their studies by stating "the Holocaust signals the downfall of western civilization and culture, and then go on to write about it with terms, methods, and implied beliefs unquestioningly inherited from that civilization and culture."[8] The resulting scholarship can be aloof, methodical, and may inadvertently normalize genocide as just another historical episode to record and integrate into the corpus of knowledge. Visual media, however, can subvert the historical narrative by offering complex and creative representations of this great rupture, recognizing the Holocaust as the template for all subsequent trauma and suffering.[9] The Holocaust's cultural legacy is so prevalent, French philosopher Jacques Derrida opined, "that today nothing at all can be burnt, not even a love-letter, without thinking about the Holocaust."[10]

Irrespective of Wiesel's objections, Auschwitz is *constantly* imagined, reimagined, and depicted in every conceivable medium and genre to the point that its historical context is subordinated to the cultural moment. Auschwitz is an actual place with a concrete past, body count, and paper trail itemizing extermination in excruciating detail, yet we are constantly told it defies understanding and tests the limits of representation. Cole traces Auschwitz's evolution from a historical site to what it has evolved into—another Graceland, "a prime spot of Holocaust tourism." "Not only is the word Auschwitz virtually synonymous with Holocaust," Cole continues, "but the word has become virtually synonymous with generic evil. . . . Auschwitz has become so much more than simply a place, it is a place of mind, an abstraction, a haunted idea."[11] Auschwitz is simultaneously everywhere and nowhere, a paradox reflected rather pointedly in the film *The Memory Thief* (2008) in which the character of Lukas, a socially alienated youngster who lives an anonymous existence as a tollbooth collector, immerses himself in Holocaust culture to the point he reinvents himself as a Jewish survivor. After fueling his obsession with survivor testimony as a volunteer at a local Holocaust organization, Lukas begins to blur the lines between witness and spectator in ever more disturbing ways. Nonetheless, Lukas preaches an obvious truth apparent to many of us who witnessed the Holocaust emerge as the universal symbol of evil across the globe, greeting passersby with the refrain: "Didn't you hear? Auschwitz isn't just for Jews anymore."[12]

This book explores the diverse ways in which Holocaust representation influences and shapes science fiction (SF) and horror film and television by focusing on notable contributions from the last fifty years, with a special emphasis on the last two decades. I believe the supernatural and extraterrestrial are rich and wonderfully complex spaces in which to examine important Holocaust themes: trauma, guilt, grief, ideological fervor and perversion, industrialized killing, and the dangerous afterlife of Nazism after World War II. Yehiel Dinur did not intentionally infer the supernatural in his testimony, but his notion of a planet of the ashes influencing Earth from afar is an evocative metaphor for scholars interested in analyzing compelling post–World War II SF and horror. What else but the Holocaust could set the standard for horror in the modern era? If the Holocaust is imaginable here on Earth, at least by those who perpetrated it, why not in a galaxy far, far away? And if our reality is one of many infinite possibilities in time and space, how many also have a Holocaust? The universe of the concentration camp and death camp is so infused with unthinkable horrors it is literally fantastic. Indeed, testimony, memoirs, or "art from the ashes" produced by survivors is awash in gruesome and apocalyptic visions the inexperienced reader could easily mistake for fiction.[13] *Planet Auschwitz* presents representative case studies revealing how the Holocaust of history and the mediated Holocaust influences our culture in provocative and often disturbing ways.

The Holocaust casts a long and deep shadow over our collective imagination. The pervasive use of Holocaust imagery and plotlines in horror and SF reflects both our preoccupation with its enduring trauma and our incessant need to "work through" its many legacies. Terence De Pres's claim that the image of the Holocaust is always with us "at some unconscious level" and remains "a sounding board for all subsequent evil" is undeniable. The Holocaust resides permanently "in the back of the mind . . . for all of us now living: we, the inheritors."[14] As a historian I do not need to approve of a cultural phenomenon to realize it deserves scholarly attention, nor am I a self-appointed gatekeepers determining under which circumstances the Holocaust can serve as a backdrop for someone's artistic vision. Focusing on the fantastic and horrible is not a meaningless or trite exercise. On the contrary, historian Omer Bartov argues, "The more one concentrates on horror, the more one is likely to appear to be engaged in a sincere attempt to expose 'what actually happened.'"[15]

SF and horror often express profound historical fears and desires that resonate with audiences in different eras. "SF is the mind, horror the body," writes Barry Keith Grant, noting a fundamental difference between the genres. "In horror, creatures are monstrous violations of ideological norms, while in science fiction monsters are simply a different life form." Grant cites prominent film scholar Vivian Sobchack's observation that "horror monsters threaten the disruption of the moral and natural order, while those in science fiction address the disruption of the social order."[16] The distinction between genres is not always clear, but horror intends to elicit emotional and physical reactions from the body and SF entertains alternate possibilities and futures grounded in science. SF is not always dystopian, certainly, but I argue some depictions purporting to be utopian conceal a dark side. The works discussed here ostensibly transpire in times and settings disconnected from our immediate reality, if not Earth altogether, but the unsettling truth about Auschwitz is that it happened here on Earth. Nothing we can imagine in horror and SF approximates the concentrationary universe. As Günter Grass declared in 1990, "We cannot get by Auschwitz. We should not even try, as great as the temptation is, because Auschwitz belongs to us, is branded into our history, and—to our benefit!—has made possible an insight that could be summarized as, 'Now we finally know ourselves.'"[17] SF and horror appeals to us because they provide insight into the disruption of the social order and what Freud termed the returned of the repressed, where monsters embody forbidden desires and fears. On a visceral level, SF and horror terrify and fascinate us because they reflect who we are, what we might become, and ultimately what we deserve.[18]

Horror and SF's Complex Relationship with the Holocaust

Many contemporary filmmakers, scholars, and critics argue the Holocaust fundamentalism governing past cultural representation obscures the Holocaust's deeper moral implications and deters serious engagement with its legacy in the contemporary world.[19] Philosopher and sociologist Gillian Rose invented the term *Holocaust piety* to describe overly sentimental and self-righteous approaches to the Holocaust that "mystify what we dare not understand, because we fear that it may be all too understandable, all too continuous with what we are—human, all too human."[20] Rose argues such piety seemingly endorses the "human and metaphysical optimism that lies behind certain forms of Holocaust representation" to the point meaningful representation is suppressed altogether.[21] Inspired by Rose's critique, Matthew Boswell promoted Holocaust impiety as an antidote to decades of pretentious and conservative depictions in film and media especially. Boswell argues that hyperrealistic and surrealistic treatments of the Holocaust, while aesthetically shocking, ensure the Holocaust's continued relevance as a cultural touchstone in modern society. Holocaust impiety, he writes, "attempts to use aesthetic shock as a formal mechanism to induce a deeper ethical engagement with their subject matter."[22] Impiety does not equate to trivializing the Holocaust or commending works that constitute "Nazisploitation";[23] rather, it recognizes working through the relationship between historical atrocity and contemporary culture necessitates the freedom to offend with often brutal and deeply uncomfortable representations. Some SF and horror films and television denigrate the Holocaust's legacy and exploit its imagery of pain and violence for commercial success, but others attempt sincere engagement with the Holocaust despite making impious creative choices. Artists may construct powerful allusions to the Holocaust unintentionally, highlighting the extent to which the Holocaust permeates culture.

The farther removed we are from the Holocaust and as the last survivors pass away, the more susceptible we are to either normalizing it as just another historical episode or reifying it as a sacred event in which the normal rules of historical inquiry somehow do not apply. The Holocaust's unique horrors fade with time and decades of anodyne representations more invested in redemption narratives than substantive engagement with the underlying ideologies and communal violence responsible for the atrocity. Gavriel Rosenfeld's fascinating and measured scholarship addressing how the Third Reich, and Hitler's persona in particular, is normalized through the popularity of alternate history and the digital media revolution raises important questions concerning SF and horror's use of Holocaust and Nazi imagery.[24] Rosenfeld is convinced, as am I with regard to SF and horror, that alternate history deserves scholarly inquiry because "tales of what never happened can help us understand the memory of what did."[25] Rosenfeld distinguishes between the communicative memory of historical events, such as oral histories and testimony like Yahiel Dinur's, and their cultural memory expressed in films, novels, monuments and museums. "Whatever their form," he writes, "the dialectical relationship between official and counter-memories helps to define the overall character of a society's historical consciousness." Normalization occurs when a culture loses interest in moralizing a particular legacy, either through the organic passage of time or cultural and political figures deliberately aestheticizing it for artistic, commercial, and political reasons.[26] Rosenfeld asks us to consider the consequences of this twenty-first-century wave of normalization. What is lost when the Nazi past and its crimes are indiscriminately used as empty signifiers for cultural productions? Is the Holocaust's legacy diminished if the Nazi era is no longer exceptional, or at least governed by "morally grounded restrictions on how it can be aesthetically represented?"[27] Not necessarily, I argue.

Historians like Rosenfeld and myself are understandably wary of tendentious comparisons to the Holocaust and Nazism.[28] It may be Rosenfeld regards Holocaust impiety apprehensively because unorthodox aesthetic choices often contribute to normalization regardless of authorial intent. I believe integrating Holocaust imagery and storylines into horror and SF helps engage audiences that are normally alienated or intimidated by the Holocaust of history.[29] Moreover, Libby Saxton argues, articulating "moral limits or interdictions on representation can become a strategy for evading a properly ethical confrontation with the event."[30] This is not to say every provocative work of art, film, or literature utilizing Holocaust imagery qualifies as a form of ethical confrontation. Many of the iconic images repeatedly cited in SF and horror derive from seminal Holocaust films, not historical materials recovered from the killing fields or the archives. Just as Steven Spielberg employs familiar scenes and imagery from films like *Night and Fog* (1955), *The Last Stop* (1948), and *Shoah* (1985) in *Schindler's List* (1993), so too do the creative teams behind *The Walking Dead* (2010–), *The Leftovers* (2014–2017), and *The Strain* (2014–2017) reference the same films to communicate their characters' trauma, grief, and sense of foreboding.[31]

If cinema is a medium "through which the event can speak," French philosopher Gilles Deleuze claimed, and somehow gives "voice to history," we must be mindful of how cinema alters the history and perceived truth of the event in profound ways.[32] Maybe horror or SF is not a way to escape history and bury trauma, but a useful forum with which to engage it.

Referencing the Holocaust in genres like SF and horror can, and often does, dilute the Holocaust's historicity and moral legacies, but it does not have to. "Film begets film," avant-garde filmmaker Jay Leyda remarked. The diffusion of Holocaust images in horror and SF is partly a consequence of circulating footage and photography acquired during liberation of death camps and concentration camps.[33] The public's inability to grasp the scale of the industrialized killing provoked an inevitable crisis of witnessing that bled into cinema. French director Jean-Luc Godard believed cinema failed to testify to the camps in a meaningful way: "Modern cinema was born out of those images, which have been ceaselessly at work in it, resurfacing in other forms . . . those specifically cinematographic figures that testify to the obsessive presence of the concentrationary palimpsest."[34] The trauma of witnessing the first visual evidence of the Holocaust, whether captured by the Red Army's camera crews, the British Army at Bergen Belsen, or American GIs who stumbled upon abandoned concentration camps as they swept across Germany, permanently altered notions of horror and the fantastic.[35] The Eichmann trial later helped disseminate this imagery in the public sphere, underscoring media's potential to either shock audiences or act as the shock absorber, blunting the trauma with normalizing narratives and judicious editing.[36]

Susan Sontag meditated on the ethics of witnessing trauma in a mediated age, especially images from the Nazi concentrationary universe: "Being a spectator of calamities taking place in another country is a quintessential modern experience."[37] Sontag notes that "after the event has ended, the picture will still exist, conferring on the event a kind of immortality (and importance) it would never otherwise have enjoyed." The responsibility to reflect on images of atrocity belongs to civilization, but their ubiquity renders us either spectators, that is to say voyeurs, or cowards unable to look.[38] How does one negotiate these extremes without succumbing to either cold indifference or, like Lukas in *The Memory Thief*, unhealthy identification with the victims? Using a traditional linear narrative or simple documentary style to describe the unrepresentable risks fetishizing the event and deflecting from the trauma. There simply is no opportunity to mourn.[39] Writing about genocide from the perspective of a historian's detached analytical lens or depicting it on screen in simplistic narratives prevents us from coming to terms with our own complicity in replicating the ideological worldviews that facilitated the Holocaust and more recent genocides.[40]

Theodor Adorno, a leading member of the Frankfurt School of critical theory, famously declared that to write poetry after Auschwitz is barbaric. Adorno's oft-cited (and misunderstood) maxim condemned the notion Western civilization could simply proceed as if the Holocaust never happened. Using the same modes of representation to produce knowledge and culture replicates "the basic principle of bourgeois subjectivity, without which there could have been no Auschwitz."[41] Literary theorist Walter Benn Michaels states the fundamental challenge for contemporary representation: "What the Holocaust requires is a way of transmitting not the normalizing knowledge of the horror, but the horror itself."[42] Is film expected to redeem historical trauma, that is, somehow make it imaginable and reconciled, or is it equally valid for film to communicate the impossibility of redemption?[43] Perhaps insisting time and time again that somehow the Holocaust offers lessons for succeeding generations contributes more to normalization than integrating Holocaust imagery and plot points into unorthodox genres like horror and SF.

Michael Rothberg's concept of traumatic realism articulates an approach to Holocaust representation that conveys both the specifics of the historic event and the trauma experienced by victims, survivors, and civilization after Auschwitz. Rothberg first restates the conflict between realism, or the notion that the Holocaust is knowable through familiar modes of representation, and antirealism, which claims the Holocaust is only knowable via "new regimes of knowledge" and radical representational schemata.[44] Rothberg identifies three demands for traditional Holocaust representation: the need for documentation, reflecting on and honoring formal limits of representation, and evaluating the risk of publicly disseminating discourses relating to the Holocaust.[45] It is possible to bridge the divide between treating the Holocaust as an abyss defying representation and the banality of evil mentality expressed by Hannah Arendt and find a productive middle ground.[46] "By focusing attention on the intersection of the everyday and the extreme," Rothberg writes, "traumatic realism provides an aesthetic and cognitive solution to the conflicting demands inherent in representing and understanding genocide. I maintain traumatic realism mediates between the realist and antirealist positions in Holocaust studies and marks the necessity of considering how the ordinary and extraordinary aspects of genocide intersect and coexist."[47] Rothberg's interpretive framework bridges disciplinary gaps between Holocaust and cultural studies. Traumatic realism has relevance to SF and horror since some of the more profound depictions of trauma belong to these genres. Effective horror accentuates the presence of extremity in the everyday and portrays the traumatic effects violating our reality. Many of the works I discuss here achieve a level of traumatic realism by representing the Holocaust in ways both literal and allegorical.

From survivors navigating the grey zone in *The Walking Dead* (2010–) and Nazi vampires battling a Jewish pawnbroker in *The Strain* (2014–2017) to Catholic priests debating the nature of evil in *The Exorcist* (1973), the Holocaust is the primary referent for horror, trauma, and evil in post-World War II culture. Some films and series aspire to greater understanding of the Holocaust and its indelible shadow; others are decidedly exploitative.

Using Third Reich and Holocaust imagery in horror films is a "dubious proposition" given the ethical concerns raised by survivors and other scholars, Steffen Hantke notes, but the horror genre is "devoted to the sensation with which we must regard the Holocaust." Still, the horrors of history are not the same as horror on screen. "Is not the idea itself," Hantke asks, "to use the Holocaust as a source of cinematic horror, frivolous and tasteless at best, morally reprehensible at worst?"[48] To use the Holocaust cynically as an unimaginative cliché laced with pornographic violence and brutality is all of those things, but the intimate connection between horror and the Holocaust is unavoidable. Why not accentuate horror's potential for allowing nonwitnesses to relate to the Holocaust? One can condemn vulgar and trivial abuses of Holocaust representation while highlighting genuine and often inspired horror and SF films and series.[49] Examining the complex relationship between these genres and the Holocaust reveals the extent to which Nazi film and Weimar film before it depicted Jews and other undesirables as monstrous or otherworldly. Furthermore, eminent Holocaust films celebrated for their realism and positive role in promoting awareness, empathy, and knowledge often rely on the same horror frame used in iconic films like *Psycho* (1960) and *The Silence of the Lambs* (1991).[50] In 1992, *New York Times* critic Caryn James lauded the movement away from documentary realism in Holocaust cinema by artists too young to remember World War II, arguing works infused with fantasy and pop culture can be poignant and respectful. One way to avoid the lurch toward normalization and confront the unique evil of the Holocaust is to acknowledge and accept that each generation will reimagine the event on its own terms.[51]

Disparaging the inevitable blending of horror and the Holocaust ignores their pre-existing relationship and impedes serious engagement with a popular culture format popular with millions globally. After World War II, the horror genre transitioned from a universe populated by Gothic monsters who threaten violence on screen to the all too human fiends who slash, stab, and murder in the most graphic manner possible. This transition is likely a cultural response to the traumatic impact of World War II, especially when one considers that nations who waged it avoid representing that trauma on screen or as part of their commemorative practices.[52] For example, Linnie Blake argues German cinema by and large fails to "evoke the horrors of the past" because the "disgusting viscerality of the Shoah's annihilation of millions was not a subject for graphic depiction." Blake suggests "horror cinema can be seen to fulfill a significant socio-cultural and psycho-political function" by enabling audiences to reflect on historical trauma in ways mainstream culture inhibits.[53] Horror can communicate the traumatic realism Rothberg delineates precisely because the genre evolved in response to the Holocaust and World War II. Adam Lowenstein writes that deeply painful historic shocks like the Holocaust, the atom bomb, or the Vietnam conflict represent powerful "allegorical moments" signifying the "shocking collision of film, spectator and history where registers of bodily space and historical time are disrupted, confronted, and intertwined."[54] Horror is ripe for staging allegorical moments related to genocide and other traumas, and if so-called high culture regards such representation taboo, low culture in the form of SF and horror will inevitably fill the vacuum, for better or worse.

SF may seem to be farther removed from the earthly horrors of genocide, positing alternate possibilities and situating stories within existing scientific knowledge, but Susan Sontag argues SF revels in the aesthetics of destruction and betrays our acute cultural fears.[55] SF allows us to imagine our own death, and worse, the destruction of humanity itself, with no consequences. Sontag sees SF's popularity as evidence of callousness and our inability to respond because audiences emerge from theaters unscathed, physically and emotionally.[56] SF can be sterile and detached, but the imaginative links between violence and destruction on Earth, past and present, and the extraterrestrial are instructive and revealing.[57] Post-Holocaust SF tends to revolve around isolation, survival in extreme environments, and the destruction and rebirth of civilization after an apocalyptic event. Alien contact is a natural metaphor for dehumanizing racism and extermination fantasies.[58] SF constructs worlds and scenarios analogous to past genocides, subtly evoking historical memories and iconic imagery that encourage audiences to contemplate these signposts and perhaps perceive our world differently.[59] Together horror and SF conjure the Holocaust in part because it forever changed our perspective on what is possible, imaginable, and understandable. Moreover, the genres owe much of their early iconography to a German culture transitioning from a beleaguered republic living in the shadow of one total war to an aggressive totalitarian regime preparing for the next one.

Weimar Cinema's Monsters and Cyborgs

Nineteenth-century Gothic horror featured monsters disrupting reality and contaminating the purity of institutions and bodies. These monsters embodied narratives of difference: race, class, gender, and sexuality. "Within the traits that make a body monstrous," Judith Halberstam writes, "that is, frightening or ugly, abnormal or disgusting—we may read the difference between an other and a self, a pervert and a normal person, a foreigner and a native."[60] Gothic horror addressed that most enduring fear of the modern nation: the disintegration of a precarious national community by parasitic outsiders. The popularity of racial science and Gothic horror, specifically the vampire, fed existing antisemitic stereotypes portraying Jews as monstrous contaminants of the nation-state, foreign and perverse.[61] Halberstam demonstrates how horror contributed to what she terms *Gothic antisemitism*, which was obsessed with Jews' perceived intractable hold on modernity's bewildering array of political, cultural, and financial institutions: "The Jew . . . is Gothicized or transformed into a figure of almost universal loathing who haunts the community and represents its worst fears. By making the Jew supernatural, Gothic antisemitism makes Jews into spooks and Jew-hating into a psychological inevitability."[62] Racial antisemitism was already a potent force on the cusp of the twentieth century. Film, another confounding modern invention, translated Gothic fiction and its attendant fears about race, class conflict, and changing gender definitions onto the screen. It was only a matter of time before film popularized Gothic antisemitism as well.

The Third Reich deployed film as a weapon in its war against the Jews. Propaganda Minister Joseph Goebbels understood visual media was more effective for disseminating Nazi ideology than crude broadsheets like *Der Stürmer* or ruffians chanting slogans in the streets. The already robust and respected German film industry, which was second only to Hollywood in the number of films produced and its audience, lent its considerable talents and resources to forging the Hitler myth and depicting Jews in the most monstrous forms possible.[63] Goebbels understood the best propaganda is disguised as entertainment. "Even entertainment can be politically of special value," he wrote in 1942, "because the moment a person is conscious of propaganda, propaganda becomes ineffective." Of the 1,100 films produced during the Third Reich, just twenty percent constituted overt propaganda.[64] The rest were popular genre films commonly shown during the Weimar Republic, such as costume dramas, biographies, comedies, historical dramas, literary classics, and melodramas aimed at women. One would be hard pressed to discern a stylistic break between Weimar and Nazi film. This continuity only strengthened the medium's ability to promote Nazi messaging to an audience conditioned to frequent films for entertainment.[65] Weimar expressionism influenced the Third Reich's tendency to depict racial enemies as monstrous and supernatural. If film begets film, so too did early depictions of Jews flourish beyond the confines of Weimar and Nazi culture and seep into our own.

As the horrors of the Third Reich came to light in the immediate postwar period, the frantic search for answers to the question of how this happened in Germany consumed political and cultural figures. Two important film critics and writers with roots in Germany—Siegfried Kracauer and Lotte Eisner—analyzed Weimar expressionist films for possible insights into Germany's collective soul before the Third Reich. German expressionism permeated visual art after the war and encouraged filmmakers to experiment with technology and special effects meant to probe suppressed desires, subliminal fears, and deranged obsessions.[66] Kracauer and Lotte introduced persuasive and enduring close readings of films by Weimar's greatest directors, but many of their arguments about the supposed connection between expressionism and Nazi ideology are now considered reductive and superficial. Kracauer analyzed iconic Weimar films and believed he discerned imagery, symbols, and metaphors that might explain the unexplainable and perhaps provide insight into the ideological mindset capable of imagining the Holocaust.[67] Kracauer argued films can reveal mass behavior because they are produced by a studio system, not one individual; they appeal to the anonymous multitude; and cinema reflects the inner turmoil of the population when political and psychological systems decompose.[68] Kracauer believed film blurs the line between myth and reason in industrialized nations, and the Weimar Republic, beset by external and internal forces, provided the perfect stage for screening fear, dysfunction, and dark longing.[69] Lotte Eisner read expressionism as an apocalyptic doctrine proving the German soul instinctively preferred twilight to daylight.[70] Eisner peppers her analysis with sweeping generalizations popular in the early postwar years: "The weird pleasure the Germans take in evoking horror can perhaps be ascribed to the excessive and very Germanic desire to submit to discipline, together with a certain proneness to sadism."[71] Unsubtle as their arguments seem, Kracauer and Eisner's influential interpretations of the legacies and influence of Weimar cinema encouraged closer examination of such seminal films as *The Cabinet of Dr. Caligari* (1920), *The Golem* (1920), *Nosferatu* (1922), and *Metropolis* (1927). These films profoundly influenced both Nazi culture and contemporary SF and horror.

The Cabinet of Dr. Caligari

Kracauer and Eisner viewed Weimar film through the lens of foreshadowing the Third Reich, not the consequence of World War I. However, the horrors of total war—the piles of corpses, shattered and dismembered bodies, rats, and apocalyptic landscapes—so pervaded postwar cultural representation it is difficult to distinguish between what was real and what was imagined. World War I served as the primary referent for horror and trauma before the Holocaust.[72] Robert Wiene's *The Cabinet of Dr. Caligari* is the artistic rupture one anticipates after enduring a horrendous and catastrophic defeat.[73] Ostensibly the story of the mad hypnotist Dr. Caligari (Werner Krauss) who uses a somnambulist named Cesare (Conrad Veidt) to commit murder, the film is a layered psychological thriller in which the narrator Francis (Friedrich Fehrer) recounts to a stranger his fiancée Jane's (Lil Dagover) trauma and the details of several murders. We are drawn into a world of nightmares and question both Francis's and Dr. Caligari's sanity and true identity. Francis comes to believe Caligari is replicating the crimes of an eleventh-century Italian mystic named Caligari who also deployed a hypnotized somnambulist to murder people. Just when we think Caligari is discovered and the murders resolved, the film ends with the revelation Francis, Jane, and Cesare are all patients in a mental asylum and Dr. Caligari its director. Is Caligari legitimately seeking to cure his patients or is he the evil mastermind Francis imagined all along?

Caligari is an early expressionist masterpiece with a dark visual style emphasizing radical and deliberate distortions in perspective, narrow and spiraling streets and buildings, and deceptive shadows. The settings are outward manifestations of inner turmoil and menacing urban environments. Early expressionist films are inextricably linked to the trauma of World War I. "The loss of the dead combined with the inability to mourn and forget them, lurked in the shadows on the screen," W. Scott Poole writes.[74] Surveying the ashes of the old German empire and its now defunct façade of law and order, Weimar culture foregrounded the imposter—hypnotists, wizards, gangsters, mad scientists, cyborgs, grifters, and women of the night.[75] Dr. Caligari is both an eminent doctor, Eisner notes, and "the fairground huckster."[76] Produced so soon after the war, *Caligari* references military psychiatry, shell shock, and the legions of shattered veterans wandering the streets of Germany's larger cities with little or no state assistance. Are they insane, or are those who ignore them and their incommunicable secret living in an asylum? "Using motifs borrowed from Gothic fiction," Anton Kaes writes, *Caligari* "rejects traditional cinematic realism by adopting a form that mimics the physical and mental wasteland left behind by the first technological war."[77] Siegfried Kracauer interpreted metaphorical Hitlers throughout pre-Nazi cinema, such as the soulless and vengeful title character *Homonculus* (1916). Kracauer focused on Dr. Caligari's hypnotic power to enact his will—"a technique foreshadowing, in content and purpose, that manipulation of the soul which Hitler was the first to practice on a gigantic scale."[78] Kracauer compared the haunted sets of *Caligari* to the Nazi aesthetic he fled in 1933, noting both overflowed with "sinister portents, acts of terror and outbursts of panic."[79] Retrospectively interpreting *Caligari* as an omen of future evil diminishes the film's obvious artistic and commercial accomplishment.[80] *Caligari* is an audacious assertion of cinema's narrative possibilities and its potential to communicate emotions on screen. A product of total war's devastating aftermath and perhaps a symptom of a deeper psychosis yet to surface, *Caligari* significantly influenced the psychological thriller and horror genres.

The Golem

Carl Boese and Paul Wegener's *The Golem* resurrects the sixteenth-century legend of the golem of Prague in a postwar world contending with an urgent "Jewish question." Eastern European Jews fleeing the ravages of war and the chaos of the Bolshevik Revolution poured into central European cities, provoking a combination of fascination, empathy, and rabid antisemitism. The golem, a clay giant with magical capabilities to protect and destroy the Jewish people's enemies, was popularized in post-Enlightenment literature as both a symbol of Jews' historic need for protection in a hostile Christian world and the dangers of assimilating into the modern nation-state, a fraught and incomplete process for central and eastern European Jews.[81] The film begins with Rabbi Loew (Albert Steinrück), the patriarch of Prague's Jewish quarter, auguring a great disaster after consulting the stars. The next day the emperor (Otto Gebühr) demands Jews leave the city and sends the knight Florian (Lothar Müthel) to enforce the decree. Florian instantly falls in love with Loew's daughter Miriam (Lyda Salmonova), prompting a love triangle between Miriam, Florian, and Loew's assistant (Ernst Deutsch). Seeking a way to protect his community, Loew fashions the golem out of clay and summons a spirit to breathe life into it, turning the golem into Loew's obedient servant. Loew brings the golem to a palace festival and impresses the emperor with feats of strength. Loew then projects the history of the Jews on a magical screen, including the Wandering Jew Ahasuerus, who is mocked so mercilessly by the court the palace begins to crumble. The golem rescues the emperor and noble elite from certain death, an act that saves the Jews from banishment. With Prague's Jews spared, Loew decides to render the golem lifeless. Loew fears a further loss of control after interpreting omens from Ahasuerus indicating the golem could turn on his creators. Order seems restored until the young temple assistant finds Miriam and Florian in bed together. Enraged, the assistant summons the golem to banish Florian from the ghetto, but the golem is unruly and murders Florian, sets the synagogue on fire, and drags an unconscious Miriam into the streets. Ravaging the ghetto the golem was created to defend, Loew rids the golem of Ahasuerus's invasive spirit. In a scene reminiscent of Frankenstein, the golem leaves the ghetto gate and encounters a sweet gentile girl who innocently removes the amulet giving the golem life. The clay giant collapses amid the natural beauty outside the ghetto's walls. Miriam, Loew, and the assistant are reunited and Prague's Jews carry the inert golem back into the sealed ghetto.

Director Paul Wegener, who also plays the golem, made propaganda films for the Third Reich and received the honorific title Actor of the State.[82] While *The Golem* is not an overtly antisemitic film featuring racialized Jewish bodies who control the moral and financial lives European Christians, Wegener's recreation of the medieval ghetto using expressionist set design and his depiction of the golem as a mindless and malfunctioning automaton alludes to Jews' conflicted relationship with modernity and the failure of assimilation. The city in *The Golem*, like *Caligari*, *Metropolis*, *M* (1931), and other expressionist classics, is an ominous character in its own right. Rabbi Loew acts less like a medieval sorcerer than a Weimar industrialist bending nature to his will and catering to his "Jew-Republic," a theme popular with postwar antisemites intent on linking Jews with the beleaguered Weimar Republic and its cities' apparent cultural and moral decadence.[83] In *The Golem*, transgressing boundaries between Jewish and Christian worlds is catastrophic for both groups: Florian is killed for daring to court a Jewess and the golem collapses only after leaving the ghetto walls.[84] Wegener implies these boundaries are not meant to be traversed.

Weimar films often exhibit unmistakable signs of Jewishness without communicating explicitly antisemitic themes. *The Golem* references the strange world of the *Ostjuden* (eastern European Jews), from their supposed unique physiognomy, rituals, and ghetto and shtetl lifestyle, but also the assimilated Jews' perceived domination of science, capitalism, and affiliation to postwar revolutionary chaos.[85] Wegener subtly reminds his mostly German audience of these inherent differences, specifically by having Rabbi Loew evoke the Wandering Jew in his own film screened for the emperor. Intentional or not, *The Golem*'s depictions of Jews foretell the Nazis' own elaborate construction of the Jew in propaganda: The Jew as malevolent outsider; the conniving insider who hides behind the mask of modernity; and the seducer of youth, both men and women, poisoning the blood and defiling the German race.[86] The golem's demise outside the ghetto infers the Jews will always be a state within a state, harboring dangerous forces that are both mystical and modern, and ultimately beyond their control.

Written during World War I and filmed in its aftermath, *The Golem* is a harbinger of Western civilization's infinite capacity for self-destruction. Polish Jewish writer Isaac Bashevis Singer described modern war as "a gigantic global golem . . . that has risen on clay feet and set out on its path, knocking down everything that stands in its way." Singer condemned "everyone of us" for becoming "a small bit of clay in the large golem."[87]

Numerous postwar writers and cultural critics exhumed the figure of the golem from its Jewish roots, seeing the medieval clay monster transformed into a steel warrior from which there is no redemption or protection, just rage and destruction.[88] Author Maya Barzilai delineates the modern incarnations of the golem, from the post-Holocaust Jewish avenger in popular culture to the more common lumbering metaphor for military technology's relentless march toward Armageddon. Paul Wegener's ghetto and Robert Wiene's cityscape in *Caligari* resemble the mazelike trenches carved into European soil like an indelible scar. After World War II, Barzilai notes, the golem "continued to be linked with mass destruction and the threat of nuclear weapons, as well as with cybernetic systems, both disembodied computers and hybrid cyborgs."[89] The golem's symbol as a cautionary tale concerning humanity's fraught relationship to war and technology inspired classic SF films like *The Day the Earth Stood Still* (1951), *Godzilla* (1954), the *Terminator* films, *Battlestar Galactica* (2004–2009), and *Westworld* (2016–).

Nosferatu

F. W. Murnau's brilliant reimagining of the Dracula legend is also influenced by the specter of World War I. However, it was not the technological battlefield *Nosferatu* evokes but the devastating Spanish flu epidemic of 1918 that killed more civilians than the war itself.[90] The story begins in 1838 with the introduction of the young couple Hutter (Gustav von Wangenheim) and Ellen (Greta Schröder) enjoying nature before Hutter goes to his office job working for Knock (Alexander Granach), a real estate mogul. Knock dispatches Hutter to deal with a mysterious client in Transylvania named Count Orlok (Max Schreck), who is interested in acquiring property in their small German town of Wisborg. Before venturing east, Hutter situates Ella with his friends Harding (Georg H. Schnell), a wealthy ship owner, and Hutter's sister (Ruth Landsoff). Hutter encounters fearful villagers who regale him with tales of werewolves and vampires. He devours a book at the local inn about Nosferatu, a nocturnal creature who lives in caves filled with soil dating from the Black Death. The next day Hutter journeys to Orlok's decrepit castle where the two share a meal and hours of conversation deep into the night. At one point Hutter cuts himself on a knife and excites Orlok with the sight of "precious blood." When Hutter awakes the next morning he detects two small marks on his neck. Conducting further business that night, Orlok sees a picture of Ellen and immediately agrees to buy the house next to Hutter's. Hutter investigates the castle and finds Orlok asleep in his coffin, frightening Hutter so much that he falls from his window and is knocked unconscious. Meanwhile, Orlok arranges to send a stack of coffins to Wisborg, including his own. While loading the cargo, dockworkers break one open and see rats swarming inside the black soil. Ellen anxiously awaits Hutter's return from a Transylvania hospital while Knock, Orlok's coconspirator, is consigned to an insane asylum where he learns a plague is ravaging major seaports in Europe, leaving victims with strange marks on their necks. Knock begins screaming, "Blood is life!" over and over again.

Sailors on Orlock's ship fall ill and soon only the captain and first mate remain. The two decide to destroy the cargo, but Orlok rises from his coffin, kills them, and pilots the ship to Wisborg. Ellen, seemingly under Orlok's spell, sleepwalks while Knock becomes increasingly agitated inside his cell. Hutter and Orlok arrive in Wisborg simultaneously, while Harding, who owns the ship Orlok commandeered, fears the plague-ridden rats are loose in Wisborg. Bodies and coffins stream in and out of houses as Knock runs wild through the streets, taunting the townspeople. Hutter attempts to comfort Ellen after she recognizes Orlok from the book Hutter brought back from the inn. Surrounded by death and terrified of their new neighbor, Ellen discovers the only way to defeat the Nosferatu is for a virgin to sacrifice her blood and expose the creature to sunlight. Ellen feigns illness to get Hutter out of the house and lures the eager Orlok to her room with an open window. In a terrifying sequence, Orlok appears at her bedside and envelops the cowering Ellen, drinking her blood. So consumed by the act, Orlok forgets he stayed out past dawn and is obliterated by sunshine piercing the bedroom window. With his master dead, Knock is captured and returned to the asylum and Ellen and Hutter are reunited.

Nosferatu depicts the young and naïve Hutter being deceived by elders to undertake a mission that will likely lead to his death, a direct World War I allusion. Murnau and producer and production designer Albin Grau, both veterans, sought to link vampire lore to the ceaseless death of total war. Grau called World War I "a cosmic vampire" that drank the blood of millions.[91] Like the generation sent to the trenches and sacrificed for an ignoble cause, Hutter returns traumatized by his close encounter with death to a homeland permeated by fear and disease.[92] Furthermore, the East, which is depicted as a threatening and backward land in *Nosferatu*, was more than just a battlefield for Germany during World War I; it represented an ambitious colonial fantasy dating back to the twelfth century. Unlike the Western Front, which devolved into immobile trench warfare by the fall of 1914, German armies in the east occupied swaths of Poland, the Ukraine, and the Balkans long after the armistice. German military and civilian administrators worked diligently to Germanize their conquered space only to see their gains disappear at the hands of an international military coalition and the specter of Bolshevism.[93] Furthermore, eastern European Jews, who were initially regarded as pro-German collaborators in Germany's civilizing

Fig. I.1. Count Orlok (Max Schreck) looms over Ellen Hutter (Greta Schröder). *Nosferatu* (1922) reimagined Dracula for the twentieth century and unintentionally created antisemitic imagery for future Nazi propaganda. (Credit: Photofest.)

mission at the beginning of the war, were soon castigated as literal carriers of typhus and metaphorical carriers of communist insurrection. Stemming the tide of both diseases consumed the disintegrating German empire and fledgling republic built on its ashes.[94] *Nosferatu*'s arcane story of a vampire from the East laying waste to an idyllic German town assumed greater significance for postwar German audiences.

Nosferatu the vampire seems to embody the modern antisemite's nightmarish conception of Jews. French antisemites compared Jews to vampires soon after the film's release.[95] With an exaggerated hook nose, thin fingers, sickly body, and incredible wealth, Orlok leaves his eastern stronghold with a swarm of rats to prey on a beautiful and pure German woman.[96] It is unlikely F. W. Murnau harbored antisemitic beliefs or promoted the sort of völkisch nationalism taking hold of the German Right after the war, especially considering Murnau's close friendship (and likely sexual relationship) with a young Jewish poet.[97] Furthermore, Murnau was politically radical and apparently defended Jewish colleagues in the film industry from insults and discrimination.[98] The talented Murnau emigrated to Hollywood in 1926 and died in a car crash in 1931. *Nosferatu*'s association with antisemitic imagery is not the product of authorial intent, but Nazi propaganda's deliberate and consistent depiction of Jews, particularly eastern European Jews, as monstrous and diseased sexual predators. The Third Reich's propaganda machine often only had to recast existing images from literature and film to convey its own grotesque portraits of Jews as corrupters of German blood and history's eternal parasite. Unfortunately, Murnau did not live long enough to contradict the Nazis' perverse propaganda.

Metropolis

Fritz Lang's *Metropolis* is set in 2026, but German audiences certainly understood that behind its revolutionary special effects fetishizing the marvels of technology was a plot that spoke to their contemporary fears of economic collapse, communist insurrection, and the depersonalization of the individual in the modern city.[99] *Metropolis*'s society is divided between the planners, the elite who live in luxury on the surface, and the workers who toil listlessly underground to maintain the inequitable status quo. The city father is Johann Fredersen (Alfred Abel), whose son Freder (Gustav Fröhlich), an aimless playboy immersed in Metropolis's pleasures, falls for the beautiful and kindhearted Maria (Brigitte Helm). Maria is a representative of the working class and assures the workers a mediator will appear one day and unite their stratified society. Freder descends into the workers' underworld to pursue Maria and is confronted with the workers' plight, witnessing a terrible explosion claiming several lives. Freder commits himself to the workers' (and Maria's) cause. Fredersen, who senses unrest after coming into possession of Maria's rousing speeches, consults his old colleague and rival Rotwang (Rudolf Klein-Rogge), a veritable mad scientist who lives in a distinctly premodern dwelling. Fredersen and Rotwang both loved a woman named Hel, but she married Fredersen and died giving birth to Freder. Rotwang built a gynoid he intended to model after Hel, but Fredersen persuades him to make it resemble Maria so that Fredersen can use it to manipulate the workers. The embittered Rotwang agrees, not to enable Fredersen's scheme but to enact his own revenge fantasy. Rotwang sends robot Maria to kill Freder and destroy Metropolis's fragile social order.

Setting the plan in motion, Rotwang imprisons the real Maria and unleashes the gynoid on the young men of Metropolis. Robot Maria resembles Weimar's archetypal New Woman and performs a memorable exotic dance, provoking a riot among the rich playboys. She then travels to the workers' dwelling, inciting them to rebel and destroy the Heart Machine powering the city. Freder and his new comrades are unable to stop the workers from causing the city's reservoirs to overflow and submerge the underground city, but Freder and the real Maria, who escapes Rotwang's lair, save the workers' children from certain death. The workers mistakenly believe they inadvertently killed their own children and chase the real Maria to the surface, but capture robot Maria instead. Freder watches in horror as the workers burn robot Maria at the stake, unaware that the real Maria is alive and imperiled. Rotwang pursues Maria to the top of the cathedral overlooking the city with Freder giving chase. Rotwang and Freder struggle as Maria, Fredersen, and the workers come to realize their complicity in the unfolding chaos. Rotwang falls to his death and Freder and Maria return to the city streets, seemingly empowered to unite Fredersen with the workers in their quest to forge a utopia. The prophecy is fulfilled—Freder is the mediator Maria promised all along.

Fritz Lang's *Metropolis* is a masterpiece marking the birth of science fiction as a filmic genre. Lang's visual style, special effects, and monumental set design influenced portrayals of the future to this day. Moreover, the film is a fascinating window into Weimar Germany's turbulent political and economic landscape as well as its ambiguous relationship with technology. Providing a comprehensive analysis is beyond the scope of the book, but it is important to highlight the ways in which *Metropolis* intersected with and informed postwar ideological struggles and the aesthetics of an ascendant fascism. Discerning authorial intent is complicated by the fact that Lang's wife and frequent collaborator, Thea von Harbou, embraced Nazism, while Lang emigrated to Hollywood. Still, for nearly two decades the couple brought German mythology to life as Lang expertly translated von Harbou's often ponderous scripts into compelling films appealing to an international audience. German film reviewer and author Rudolf Arnheim was a harsh critic, noting Lang and von Harbou "love to train politics and science for the circus ring, to Wagnerize topical problems."[100] Lang claimed Hitler and Goebbels admired *Metropolis*, specifically the choreographed crowd scenes and fantastic architecture. Goebbels certainly recognized talent and, according to Lang, asked the director to head the German film studio UFA (Universum Film AG) soon after informing him his 1933 film *The Testament of Dr. Mabuse* was banned for political content.[101] Lang and von Harbou's politics aside, *Metropolis* resonated with Germans because it dramatized the struggle for an elusive national harmony and envisioned a proverbial world in which humanity and technology struggled to coexist.

Metropolis's seductive vision of the future channels Italian futurism, which inspired fascist ideology and cultural aesthetics, and the writings of World War I veteran Ernst Jünger. In stark contrast to Erich Maria Remarque's pacifism, Jünger reveled in the violence, destruction, energy, and technological wonders associated with total war. Jünger considered technology exquisite, writing in 1925 that the front generation will "reconcile itself to the machine" and "see in it not only the useful but the beautiful as well."[102] Jünger marveled at the speed and discipline of wartime mobiliza-

Fig. I.2. Fritz Lang's *Metropolis* (1927) profoundly influenced the science fiction genre and inspired the fascist aesthetic. (Credit: UFA/Photofest, © UFA.)

tion, specifically soldiers' subordination to technocratic planning. Scenes of workers in uniform lumbering in formation to service the great machines powering Metropolis evoke images of soldiers marching to the mechanized front.[103] Freder's hallucination of workers calmly walking into the fiery, gaping mouth of the Moloch machine is eerily reminiscent of the industrialized killing one associates with Auschwitz. When the workers neglect the machines, the explosions spew liquids and poisonous gas.[104] Humanity's ambivalent relationship to technology is a staple of the SF genre thanks in part to *Metropolis*. From the *Terminator* franchise to *Battlestar Galactica* and most recently *Westworld*, the prospect of the cyborg servant becoming the master reflects visceral fears, but also endless fascination with technology's promise.

Jünger's essay "Nationalism and Modern Life," written the same year *Metropolis* was released, describes cities the same way Romantics glorified nature: "In the big city, between automobiles and electric signs, in political mass meetings, in the motorized tempo of work and leisure . . . it is necessary to stand like a person from another world . . . and say: All this has its meaning, a deep meaning, which I felt also in myself."[105] In his lengthy 1932 treatise *The Worker*, Jünger envisioned a future class of worker-soldiers reminiscent of Lang's legion of workers tied to the great machines. Jünger was not ignorant of technology's murderous potential; it was a natural consequence of humanity's great leap forward.[106] The human–machine symbiosis is not to be feared, but celebrated. Jünger would concur with Rotwang's assessment of the gynoid, which Rotwang proclaimed proudly is "made in the image of man, never tires or makes mistakes."[107] When the workers rebel and try to destroy the Heart Machine, a foreman exclaims, "Who told you to attack the machines you fools! Without them we'll all die."[108] Both Jünger and Lang aestheticize the fusion of technology and the potential of the Nietzschean will to power, a worldview analogous to what Joseph Goebbels termed "steely romanticism" (*stählerne Romantik*).[109]

Like Rabbi Loew in *The Golem* and Count Orlok in *Nosferatu*, Lang introduced characters in many of his Weimar films easily coded as Jewish. Thea von Harbou's script for *Metropolis* leaves little doubt about who Rotwang is supposed to represent. Consider this excerpt from the script describing Rotwang's abode in light of the modern antisemitism's conviction that Jews are inherently other and an obstacle to national unity:

> There was a house in the great Metropolis which was older than the town. Many said it was older, even, than the cathedral. . . . Set into the black wood of the door stood, copper red, the mysterious seal of Solomon, the pentagram. . . . It was said that a magician who came from the East (and in the track of whom the plague wandered) had built the house in seven nights. . . . Parchments and folios lay about, open, under a covering of dust, like silver-grey velvet. . . . Then came a time which pulled down the antiquities . . . but the house was stronger than the words on it, was stronger than the centuries. It hardly reached knee-high to the house-giants which stood near it. To the cleanly town, which knew neither smoke nor soot, it was a blot and an annoyance. But it remained.[110]

Rotwang is an anachronism, David Desser contends, living in a medieval house and embodying the characteristics of eastern European Jews. This imagery "would be reinstitutionalized in Nazi propaganda" and "bring forth associations of racialized conflict."[111] Metropolis is primed for unity only after Rotwang is eliminated, enabling Freder to perform his intended role as the mediator. Lang's depictions of the licentious nightclub Yoshiwara, the sexualized gynoid Maria, and the decadent lifestyle of the city reflected contemporary antisemitic themes. In Lang's earlier film, *Dr. Mabuse, the Gambler* (1922), the mercurial con artist and hypnotist Dr. Mabuse (Rudolf Klein-Rogge) is practically a shape-shifter, donning and discarding masks and costumes to further his sinister plots. The film begins with Mabuse manipulating the stock market for his own benefit, ruining countless others. His physical characteristics, costumes, and the nature of his plots are coded as Jewish.[112] Lang returns to Mabuse in his last film produced in Germany, *The Testament of Dr. Mabuse* (1933), but in this instance the sinister and scheming hypnotist with a talent for mind control is ostensibly Adolf Hitler, not a Jewish archetype. Goebbels banned the film and Lang fled Germany soon after.

Lang and von Harbou did not create *Metropolis* in anticipation of a Hitlerian figure capable of forging an enduring national community, but viewed in retrospect the film seemingly endorses Hitler's vision for a classless, racially unified nation. Hitler considered himself the architect of a new society, planning his own metropolises with protégé Albert Speer. He also portrayed himself as the great mediator between capital and labor, destined to perform the role: "I move forward with the infallible accuracy of the sleepwalker," he wrote.[113] Freder, too, is seemingly entranced, arms outstretched soon after learning of his destiny from Maria.[114] The figure of the mediator, both Hitler and Freder, is prophesized and welcomed by the masses. The mediator is a myth reinforced by the power of film, one a popular SF feature and the other propaganda. In the final scene of Leni Riefenstahl's *Triumph of the Will* (1935), Rudolf Hess takes to the podium and introduces Hitler as the embodiment of the national community: "The Party is Hitler, Hitler is Germany, and Germany is Hitler!"[115] Hitler and Freder are fated to unify the heart and mind; the modern technological state with an eternal spirit.

Nazism and the Supernatural Imaginary

Representations of Jews originating in Weimar and Nazi cinema are resurrected, reconfigured, decontextualized, and disseminated in contemporary popular culture. Cinematic depictions of Jews, according to Omer Bartov, constantly inform each other, "creating a kind of treasure house or arsenal of representations that can be drawn upon irrespective of the ideological or artistic predilections of the filmmaker and the social, political, or cultural context in which the film is made."[116] Some of the more notorious and effective antisemitic films produced during the Third Reich borrowed existing imagery from the films discussed above. Veit Harlan's infamous *Jud Süss* (1940) and Fritz Hippler's vile "documentary" *The Eternal Jew* (1940) appropriate the horrific physical traits of Nosferatu and the golem along with the perceived immorality and criminality of Rabbi Loew, Rotwang, and Dr. Mabuse. Jean Paul Sartre famously said, "it is the anti-Semite who makes the Jew" and Nazi film committed the symbolic murder of Jews as a necessary step toward enacting their actual murder.[117] "Put crudely," Claire Sisco King argues, "such propaganda films worked to make the Jewish 'monster' in order to warrant his murder, to 'confront the abject' in order to justify the ejection of Jews from Nazi society."[118]

Jud Süss and the antisemitic drama *The Rothschilds* (1940) resonated more with audiences than the vulgar and tedious *The Eternal Jew.* Hippler took cameras into Polish ghettos, lingering on scenes of human misery while a bleating voice relates every antisemitic fable from the medieval era combined with bizarre racial pseudoscience linking Jews to criminality, corruption, and dull intelligence. The film "proves" Jews, like rats, are rootless parasites who spread all manner of disease. The film famously includes close-ups of rats, the ultimate symbol of abjection and otherness, swarming the ghettos in a crude metaphor for the eastern Jews overwhelming the Aryan nations of Europe. One is reminded of Count Orlok infesting the idyllic Wisborg with diseased rats from his eastern lair. Joseph Goebbels understood Hippler's approach was flawed and issued a press release on April 26, 1940, regarding the imminent release of *Jud Süss* and *The Rothschilds*, ordering that the "publicity campaign for the films . . . should not refer to them as anti-semitic films" and should simply show "Jewry as it really is."[119]

Set in eighteenth-century Stuttgart, *Jud Süss* is an expensive costume drama in which the charismatic and devious Joseph Süss Oppenheimer (Ferdinand Marian) ingratiates himself with a bumbling duke (Heinrich George) to enrich himself and the Jews of the ghetto. Oppenheimer uses money, seductive Jewish women, and trickery to bring ruin to Stuttgart and rape the pure Aryan beauty Dorothea (Kristina Söderbaum). The film ends with Oppenheimer condemned and hanged, and the city banishing Jews for eternity. The links to *Nosferatu* are unmistakable and, I maintain, deliberate. Director Veit Harlan imagined Oppenheimer a latterday Dracula who contaminates a pure society, lusting after virginal German blood.[120] *Jud Süss* was a masterpiece in its own right, an instrument of murder as evidenced by the fact the SS repeatedly screened it for killing units in the east and non-Jewish populations on the eve of deportations. SS functionary Stefan Baretzki admitted he showed concentration camp guards *Jud Süss* to instigate abuse of prisoners.[121] If Jews are phantoms, inhuman fantasies, or simply rats—how difficult is it to conceive exterminating them?

From its inception, the Nazi movement regarded Jews as monstrous, inhuman, and supernatural. Historian Eric Kurlander argues persuasively that Nazism consciously appropriated and consistently drew upon what he calls the "supernatural imaginary."[122] Borrowing sociologist Charles Taylor's concept of the social imaginary, which explains how people imagine their own existence and relate to others, Kurlander demonstrates how Nazism employed supernatural and occultist ideas to create "a space in which existing views—be they liberal, socialist, or traditionally conservative—

could be overturned, displaced, or elided to produce a sense of ideological coherence where none otherwise existed." Associating Jews, Communists, Roma and Sinti, and asocial categories of unwanted people with vampires, zombies, demons, and other supernatural phenomena justified implementing the most extreme measures to excise them from the national community.[123] In *Mein Kampf*, for example, Hitler vividly describes Jews in vampiric terms, anticipating the central themes in *Jud Süss*: "With Satanic joy in his face, the black-haired Jewish youth lurks in wait for the unsuspecting girl whom he defiles with his blood, thus stealing her from her people. With every means he tries to destroy the racial foundations of the people he has set out to subjugate."[124] Nazi "scholars" later harnessed the links between vampires and antisemitism to dehumanize Jews in preparation for their destruction. Examples include a 1939 article entitled "Jew and Woman: Theory and Practice of Jewish Vampirism and Infection of Upright Peoples" and a 1943 Nazi Party Regional Education Office pamphlet "The Jewish Vampire Brings Chaos to the World—A World Infected by Jewry or a World Free of Jewry."[125] In Nazism's supernatural imaginary, Jews are simultaneously preternatural enemies possessing great power and harboring malicious intent and an inferior race, a biological disease, but in no sense are they viable members of the human race.[126] The Nazi method for dispatching what they perceived as monstrous involved creating an otherworldly killing ground so infernal that its survivors believed they were on another planet.

1

From Muselmann to *The Walking Dead*

Holocaust Imagery in the Zombie Genre

> Their life is short, but their number is endless; they, the Muselamänner, the drowned, form the backbone of the camp, an anonymous mass, continually renewed and always identical, of non-men who march and labour in silence, the divine spark dead within them, already too empty to really suffer. One hesitates to call them living: one hesitates to call their death death, in the face of which they have no fear, as they are too tired to understand.
>
> —Primo Levi, *Survival in Auschwitz*

The zombie haunts history. Whether it is the enslaved peoples of the Caribbean and their descendants forced to endure the grueling sugar plantations, the golem who protects vulnerable Jews only to turn against them, or vengeful colonial subjects menacing their imperial overlords, the zombie is a victim, perpetrator, and witness to humanity's worst crimes and instincts. Zombies reflect social anxieties and act as the ultimate "meaning machines," Jeremy Strong writes, "as metaphorically cannibalistic as they are literal," invading every genre and cultural milieu.[1] The zombie is a herald of the apocalypse, humanity's demise, and a spectator to the physical and metaphysical destruction of civilization. Zombies bear witness to human survivors dismantling the moral and ethical infrastructure that brought order and meaning to life, reverting to the brutal survival of the fittest code of prehistory. Zombies torment, stalk, and consume humans, but they also unnerve humanity by transgressing the boundary between life and death. When a character in George Romero's *Dawn of the Dead* (1978) asks about the origins of the ghouls menacing them, another responds, "They're us, that's all."[2] Zombie narratives reinforce Friedrich Nietzsche's timeless epigram conceived on the eve of the horrific twentieth century: "Anyone who fights with monsters should make sure that he does not in the process become a monster himself." The second part of the epigram applies more to those of us who voraciously consume zombie narratives: "And when you look for a long time into an abyss, the abyss also looks into you."[3]

Reflecting on the state of Holocaust cinema after Claude Lanzmann's masterpiece *Shoah*, French film critic Jacques Mandelbaum wrote "of all the ghostly creatures depicted onscreen, the zombie . . . is the one that demonstrates with the most acuity the effect of the return of the genocide in the history of cinema."[4] This chapter first explores how zombie narratives integrate historical trauma and speak to great crimes and injustices. Second, it examines the relationship between the Muselmann, by which I mean the culturally constructed figure derived from literature, film, memoirs, and historiography, and the zombie of pop culture.[5] Third, there is a close reading of arguably the most profound zombie narrative in recent years—AMC's long-running series *The Walking Dead* (*TWD*). Partially inspired by iconic Holocaust representations, *TWD* uses Holocaust imagery and themes to depict its postapocalyptic universe and contextualize its characters' search for meaning in an empty world.

News of the concentration camps and death camps trickled out of Europe in early 1945 accompanied by photographs and now infamous footage of traumatized and skeletal survivors. The camps' liberators used terms like *walking dead* and *zombies* to describe what they saw. Years later Primo Levi introduced Muselmann to the lexicon, the prisoner whose humanity the camps systematically and deliberately eradicated. In recounting his years at Auschwitz, Levi revealed that the Muselmann was pitied at first, then reviled, and eventually forgotten. The "anonymous mass" of broken bodies and spirits was the more authentic witness, the "complete witness," as philosopher Giorgio Agamben argues, to modernity's assault on the citizen.[6] Zombie narratives like *TWD* meditate on the meaning of survival and interrogate survivors' moral choices in ways reminiscent of actual Holocaust survivors. Moreover, *TWD* encourages viewers to contemplate the humanity of the walkers hounding characters in unexpected ways. Are zombies corpses to be discarded on the ash heap of history, or are they too close in body and spirit to humans to be dispatched gleefully and without remorse?

Zombies and the "Deep, Dark Ocean of History"

The horror of the zombie stems from what Freud termed uncanny (*unheimlich*) and Julia Kristeva the abject, that which "disturbs identity, system, order. What does not respect borders, positions, rules. The in-between, the ambiguous, the composite."[7] Freud and later Jacques Lacan argued strangely familiar experiences can be deeply unsettling and provoke intense anxiety or disorientation about the world around us. Monsters that assume human form, such as vampires, humanoid aliens, and zombies, are especially disquieting precisely because they resemble us, and not just physically.[8] For Kristeva, horror resides in impurities and pollution that threaten the dissolution of both the physical body and the body politic. Indeed, twentieth-century totalitarian regimes conflated social and racial hygiene with horrific results. "The abject has only one quality of the object," Kristeva writes: "that of being opposed to I."[9] The corpse represents "the utmost of abjection. It is death infecting life. It is something rejected from which one does not part, from which one does not protect oneself as from an object. Imaginary uncanniness and real threat, it beckons to us and ends up engulfing us."[10] The zombie is a walking corpse—unearthed, unclean, oblivious to social order and custom, and, most disturbing, a premonition of what awaits us all. The walking dead bear secrets the living would rather forget. Zombies force humanity to confront their own mortality, yes, but also its murderous crimes against the other. "Corpses *show me* what I permanently thrust aside in order to live," writes Kristeva. "These body fluids, this defilement, this shit are what life withstands, hardly and with difficulty, on the part of death. There, I am at the border of my condition as a living being."[11] Zombies truly are meaning machines, but they are equally voracious memory machines devouring those who forget and compelling the living to come to terms with the past.

One of the earliest manifestations of the zombie concerns the thirteenth-century tale of the Wandering Jew (sometimes identified as Ahasuerus), who taunted Jesus on the road to crucifixion and was condemned to walk the Earth until the Second Coming. The Wandering Jew was a powerful antisemitic myth in medieval Europe intended to inscribe eternal guilt on Jews for the death of Christ. However, the legend endured and served as a powerful rhetorical tool for ethnic nationalists seeking to repudiate arguments in favor of assimilation and emancipation in the modern nation-state. Portraying Jews as stateless specters and interlopers in an otherwise homogenous state resounded with proponents of ethnic nationalism. Karl Gutzkow, a leader of the Young Germany movement, resurrected and modernized the Wandering Jew myth in *Plan of a New Ahasuerus* (1838) to undermine Jewish participation in any future German state: "Ahasuerus is the tragic consequence of Jewish hopes . . . only Ahasuerus stays on, a living corpse, a dead man who has not yet died."[12] From myth to metaphor, the Wandering Jew appealed to antisemites seeking to create an indelible image of Europe's Jews as parasites incapable of true national belonging. The Wandering Jew featured prominently in *The Golem* and is referenced in the title of Nazi Germany's notorious propaganda documentary (*Der Ewige Jude*). The notion that Jews walk among Europeans but do not belong to Europe predates the Wandering Jew myth, but conflating Jews with supernatural beings implied Jews posed an existential threat to the nation-state in the modern era.

World War I shattered European hegemony and plunged the continent further into cultural despair, but the rupture prompted a burst of feverish creativity and invigorated the cinematic arts. The obsession with visualizing war's traumatic effects on the human body challenged filmmakers, many of whom endured the "storm of steel."[13] Filmmakers struggled to translate the incommensurability of the experience to Europeans anxious to recast the war in ideological terms, if not forget its terrible toll altogether. French director Abel Gance's brilliant film *J'accuse!* (released in 1919 and remade with sound in 1938) is an unvarnished portrayal of wartime suffering from the perspective of the poilu (French conscript). Filmed in 1918 using French soldiers on the battlefield, Gance, himself in uniform at the time, envisions the millions of fallen countrymen as avenging ghosts, the walking dead bearing the message "Never again." W. Scott Poole argues Gance "ventured to make the first and most explicit effort to connect the story of war to the emergence of horror" by linking the return of the dead to an expression of social criticism.[14] Susan Sontag credits Gance's disquieting climax with allowing viewers to empathize with pain far removed from their own experience. She describes the final scene vividly in *Regarding the Pain of Others*:

> "*Morts de Verdun, levez-vous*!" (Rise, dead of Verdun), cries the deranged veteran who is the protagonist of the film, and he repeats his summons in German and in English: "Your sacrifices were in vain!" And the vast mortuary plain disgorges its multitudes, an army of shambling ghosts in rotted uniforms with multifaceted faces, who rise from their graves and set out in all directions, causing mass panic among the populace already mobilized for a new pan-European war. "Fill your eyes with this horror! It is the only thing that can stop you!" the madman cries to the fleeing multitudes of the living, impassive ghosts overrunning the cowering future combatants and victims of la guerre de domain. War beaten back by apocalypse.[15]

J'accuse!'s haunting conclusion is even more poignant when one considers most of the actors were actual French soldiers who died just months after filming.[16] French media scholar Mari-Jose Mondzain claims *J'accuse!*'s walking dead are connected to filmic representations of the Holocaust because "the cinema has always been a ghost-making machine. How is what happened with Nazism, and in particular the Shoah, touched in detail by this art of ghosts?" Mondzain values both versions of *J'accuse* because Gance in 1918 enables the dead to "say something about history" and, in the case of the 1938 film, he summons the ghosts "to warn us of what may happen" if we fail to heed their warnings.[17] *J'accuse* "became a paradigm of the need to produce horror," W. Scott Poole suggests, "the need to scream a demand that the memory of the war's horror not disappear."[18]

The notion of dead soldiers haunting the battlefield and those who so cavalierly dispatched them to their deaths is an ancient trope, but no conflict had yet approximated World War I's death and destruction.[19] The war normalized industrialized slaughter in Europe, inspiring, and perhaps guaranteeing, its repetition a generation later by veterans drawn to ideologies claiming inheritance to the trenches.[20] The trauma inspired the shell shock cinema of the interwar period, particularly in nations suffering the worst casualties and political chaos. *J'accuse*'s antiwar message is replicated in Hans Clumber's 1930 film *Wunder am Verdun* (*Miracle at Verdun*) in which German and French soldiers rise from the dead many years after the horrific battle, forcing families and politicians to acknowledge their sacrifice and prevent another slaughter. However, the living moved on and the sacrificial dead are deemed useful only in graves and memorials where they belong. How can a nation erect a comforting myth about the war dead if the dead can confront the living with the truth?[21] Paul Bäumer, Erich Maria Remarque's narrator in *All Quiet on the Western Front*, describes himself and his comrades as "dead men with no feelings, who are able by some trick, some dangerous magic, to keep running and keep on killing."[22] Postwar Europe did not fear the reconstituted armies of the dead bursting through fresh graves and marring the landscape, but shattered veterans besieging the capitals and bringing the war home, in some cases demanding the reins of power from those who were not there.

Early cinema kindled interest in the traditional zombie narrative and its roots in Haitian folklore. The plight of enslaved Africans toiling in the Caribbean inspired the first horror films featuring zombies, specifically *White Zombie* (1932) and *I Walked with a Zombie* (1943). Kyle Bishop notes these early portrayals reveal "imperialist anxieties associated with colonialism and slavery. By allowing native voodoo priests to enslave white heroines, these inherently racist movies terrified Western viewers with the thing they likely dreaded most at the time: slave uprisings and reverse colonization."[23] The legend that zombies were slaves condemned to labor in the sugar cane fields for eternity—soulless, mindless, and tireless—intimates a symbiotic relationship between slavery, colonialism, and capitalism. Zombies are "the 'human face' of capitalist monstrosity," Gerry Canavan posits, and "all that remains of human nature . . . in the immense and unimaginably complex of network economy."[24] Zombies help us understand how capitalism creates wealth for some and misery for others.[25] If Western civilization, particularly North America, is built on the corpses of millions of the enslaved, why would those corpses not exact their revenge on successive generations? Zombies incite great fear in Westerners cognizant of their historic crimes.

Scholars similarly note the ease with which zombies are allegorized as "Orientalized enemies"—Asians, Muslims, and refugees ready to storm the gates of fortress Europe and North America.[26] Danny Boyle's *28 Days Later* (2002) depicts zombies as infected, enraged, and uncharacteristically fast and agile. Boyle considered it important to set the film in Britain because of its "deep, dark ocean of history."[27] Boyle affirms the belief that zombies, or any monster, are forms of retribution. America perpetrated great crimes in its short history, but Britain, Boyle adds, lives in "that dark abyss of the past. And it makes Britain, as a location, very fertile ground for horror."[28] Frantz Fanon issued this dire warning to the colonial and postcolonial powers continuing to subjugate the "wretched of the Earth": "Now, at a respectful distance, it is you who will feel furtive, nightbound and perished with cold. Turn and turn about: in these shadows from whence a new dawn will break, it is you who are the zombies."[29]

George Romero, affectionately known as the Godfather of the Dead, combined racial commentary with a critique of capitalism in his trailblazing zombie trilogy *The Night of the Living Dead* (1968), *Dawn of the Dead* (1978), and *Land of the Dead* (2005). Set in rural Pennsylvania, *Night of the Living Dead* pits seven randomly assembled people against a horde of zombies converging on an isolated farmhouse. Romero's zombies are slow, plodding, relentless, seemingly diverse racially and socioeconomically, and leaderless. The hero of the film, Ben (Duane Jones), is black and portrayed as calm and capable compared to white characters who display cowardice and hysteria. The sole survivor of the night, Ben is mistaken for a zombie and shot in the head by a posse who then toss his body onto a pile of burning corpses. The subtext of this ending was all too clear in 1968, a year of intense racial violence in a decade characterized by racial violence. Gregory Waller notes the truly remarkable aspect of the film is the ease with which "legions of the undead seem capable of overrunning a deeply flawed, perhaps irredeemably corrupt America."[30] Furthermore, Waller writes, "the murder of Ben, extermination of the zombies, and the disposal of corpses in a bonfire do not so much resolve the confrontation between the living and the undead as attempt to render it insignificant, even routine."[31] George Romero's influence on horror and the zombie narrative in particular cannot be overstated. Romero's zombies are baser versions of ourselves. Romero echoes Nietzsche, asking us to consider how one vanquishes monsters without destroying oneself in the process.

Horror master Guillermo del Toro marvels at the zombie genre's malleability, even if he is critical of its current flagship—*TWD*: "We saw [the genre] change from the anarchic iconoclastic threat that George Romero had, and turn into an almost post-apocalyptic redneck fantasy world, you know? That genre alone was anticipating what we're living right now. It turned into a red state subgenre."[32] *TWD* exemplifies the postmodern horror genre, defined by Isabel Cristina Pinedo as "the cumulative outcome of repetitive historical stresses including the Holocaust, the Cold War, Vietnam, the antiwar movement, and the various liberation movements of the 1960s."[33] Horror is obviously inspired by the Gothic, but postmodern horror emphasizes the "violent disruption of the everyday world," transgressing and violating boundaries, irrationality, and the repudiation of linear narrative and closure.[34] *TWD* is set in a world in which science and government are ineffectual and corrupt. Not only are institutions powerless to stop the zombie apocalypse, their actions (or inaction) exacerbate this spontaneous extinction-level event. There is no beginning or end to *TWD*'s narrative as survivors amble from one failed refuge to another, subconsciously mimicking the herds of walkers (the word *zombie* is never used) populating the series' blighted landscape. The characters are also intimately connected to the walkers in ways other zombie narratives are not, transgressing and violating the body, human and zombie, in every episode. Characters watch helplessly as loved ones are torn to pieces and turn into walkers they then must dispatch; they routinely plunge knives and axes into walkers' chest cavities to cover themselves in gore to pass among them; they mimic walkers' behavior, resorting to cannibalism; and, on a few occasions, characters assign walkers human features and identities. The walkers are abject, but so too are the humans who rather quickly cast aside taboos to survive the end of history. *TWD* portrays the post-apocalypse as a fantasy of liberation for self-styled cowboys like the principal protagonist Rick Grimes (Andrew Lincoln). "The intrepid pioneers of a new world trek through the shattered remains of the old," writes Shelley Rees, "trudging through the shells of buildings and the husks of people."[35]

Jacques Mandelbaum's observation that zombies represent a return to genocide in cinema is explained in part by the zombie's status as the ultimate other. Exterminating zombies is an absolute good and a necessary goal for humanity. "Since the audience knows that the zombies are usually not sentient and in most cases do not feel pain," Peter Dendle notes, "it is free to enjoy the spectacle of wanton destruction of human bodies rather than human beings." The exaggerated Otherness of the zombie encourages the enthusiastic goriness common to modern zombie narratives like *TWD*.[36]

It is worth exploring how the exhaustive and creative annihilation of zombies in popular culture relates to the systematic subjugation and genocide of colonial peoples, Jews, and other historic victim groups. As Gerry Canavan writes, zombies allegorize "the racial forms of exclusion and extermination that already surround us" while simultaneously providing the motivation for unleashing "total violence."[37] Michel Foucault's conception of the modern state's biopower was written in the shadow of the Holocaust, but it is applicable to the underlying theme in zombie narratives: "In the biopower system . . . killing or the imperative to kill is acceptable only if it results not in a victory over political adversaries, but in the elimination of the biological threat to and the improvement of the species or race. . . . In a normalizing society, race or racism is the precondition that makes killing acceptable."[38] The zombie apocalypse is not a normal society, but for survivors seeking either to rebuild the old world (usually a fool's errand) or usher in a postapocalyptic utopia—extermination is a prerequisite.

The Muselmann and Zombie as Complete Witness

As a historian of the Holocaust and Germany's tumultuous twentieth century, I share Sara Simcha Cohen's belief that aligning the Muselmann with the zombie of pop culture represents an "uncomfortable interplay of historical reality and cultural representation," but scholars should feel confident in doing so because pop culture is also a response to historical trauma. Moreover, she writes, "the Muselmann blurs the boundary between the living and dead, and in an oeuvre that itself underscores the intersection and overlap between history and popular culture." Both the Muselmann and zombie reflect "an underlying fantasy of genocide, order, and violence."[39] Zombie narratives produced after World War II and the Holocaust are undoubtedly inspired by liberation footage, photographic evidence produced in concert with war crimes trials, and the increased interest and knowledge of the Holocaust after the Adolf Eichmann trial. The Muselmann and zombie speak to the horrors of modernity on a historical and cultural level, particularly the state's unfettered control over the body and the erosion of the concept of death and mourning. Moreover, both figures exist outside what Primo Levi termed the grey zone.

The Muselmänner are what is left of human beings after approximately four months inside the concentrationary universe. The term was used at Auschwitz, but other camps employed their own language, including donkeys, cretins, cripples, swimmers, camels, tired sheikhs, and Muselweiber (female Muslims).[40] They are starved, beaten, and suffering from dysentery, fevers, broken bones, and the absence of a discernible past and future. They exist only in the present. The devolution of the prisoner is described in detail by sociologist Wolfgang Sofsky in *The Order of Terror*. One is struck by the similarity between this vivid description and the cinematic zombie:

> In the final stage of emaciation, their skeletons were enveloped by flaccid, parchmentlike sheaths of skin, edema had formed on their feet and thighs, their posterior muscles had collapsed . . . their noses dripped constantly, mucus running down their chins. Their eyeballs had sunk deep into their sockets; their gaze was glazed. Their limbs moved slowly, hesitantly, almost mechanically. . . . Action lost its somatic prerequisites: physical strength and bodily mobility. Gestures became nervous and uncoordinated. . . . They could no longer lift their legs to walk, and slowly shoved their feet forward. In the end . . . they were no longer the masters of their own bodies.[41]

The sight of the Muselmänner horrified American soldiers who liberated concentration camps in early 1945. Soldiers resorted to cultural references like zombie in relating their stories. In one case, a soldier in 1946 wrote his hometown newspaper that concentration camp prisoners "looked more like zombies than humans."[42] Henry Golde recalled confronting the walking dead as a liberator: "They were the people that were dead, they looked like skeletons, but apparently, their body didn't lie down yet. Their minds were gone. They wandered around blindly. They actually were dead, but they still walked around."[43] General Omar Bradley wrote regarding his visit to Dachau: "Starving prisoners had torn out the entrails of the dead for food."[44] HBO's acclaimed World War II drama *Band of Brothers* (2001) devoted an episode entitled "Why We Fight" to the liberation of a subsidiary concentration camp near Dachau in which the Muselmänner were featured prominently. The soldiers expressed a combination of disgust, horror, and empathy for the shambling hulks swarming them at the gates. Interestingly, scenes from "Why We Fight" are replicated in *TWD*.

The etymology of *Muselmann* and how its usage spread from Nazi officials to the general camp population is difficult to discern, but survivors who wrote or provided testimony about camp life generally disparaged the Muselmann even if they, at one time, counted among them. Zdziław Ryn and Stanisław Kłodziński published an extensive study of the Muselmann phenomenon in 1983 based on surveys disseminated to Auschwitz survivors. Using the detached language of social scientists, the scholars conclude "quantitative and qualitative malnourishment, excessive physical labor, harmful effect of the clothing and unsanitary living conditions" turned prisoners into Muselmänner.[45] Ryn and Kłodziński also determined that most of those surveyed felt little compassion for the Muselmann: "The other inmates, who continually feared for their lives, did not even judge him worthy of being looked at. For the prisoners who collaborated, the Muslims [Muselmänner] were a source of anger and worry; for the SS, they were merely useless garbage. Every group thought only about eliminating them, each in its own way."[46]

Holocaust survivors who took pen in hand and conveyed their experiences the best they could to a world incapable of comprehension often denigrated and dismissed the Muselmann as ancillary to their own experience. They were either insignificant, albeit pitiful creatures, or a cautionary tale for the *real* survivors who emerged from the Holocaust intact spiritually and physically. Jean Améry, who survived Auschwitz, Buchenwald, and Bergen-Belsen, wrote that the "so-called Muselmann . . . no longer had room in his consciousness for the contrasts of good or bad, noble or base, intellectual or unintellectual. He was a staggering corpse, a bundle of physical functions in his last convulsions. And as hard as it may be for us to do, we must exclude him from our considerations."[47] The Muselmann is not a witness, not anything in fact, just part of the anonymous mass hovering between life and death and a source of anxiety for prisoners who began to see themselves in the Muselmann's rapidly deteriorating mind and body.[48] Another survivor wrote about being led to the baths "accompanied by a large group of Muselmänner, as we later called them—mummy men, the living dead. They [guards] made us go down the stairs with them to show them to us, as if to say, 'you'll become like them.'"[49]

Several survivors juxtaposed their own remarkable journey to planet Auschwitz and back with the legions of Muselmänner who never left. The walking dead animating so many memoirs and representations of the Holocaust are portrayed as inherently weak and perhaps even deserving of their fate. This perspective is reinforced by Holocaust studies scholars and educators who adopt a redemptive approach to the victim experience, emphasizing the spiritual strength of survivors who endured the most extreme situation. The redemptive model infers victims can resist their own spiritual decline no matter the circumstance. Moreover, Lissa Skitolsky argues in an article on Holocaust pedagogy that the redemptive worldview reinforces "our moral categories and Western worldview," which considers the Holocaust an aberration, an attack on Western civilization, not its logical consequence.[50] Psychoanalyst Bruno Bettelheim, an Austrian Jew who survived Dachau and Buchenwald, tacitly judged the Muselmann: "Only active thought could prevent a prisoner from becoming one of the walking dead whom he saw all around him—one of those who were doomed because they had given up home and thought and hope."[51] Similarly, survivor and Viennese psychoanalyst Victor Frankl argued in *Man's Search for Meaning* that "only the men who allowed their inner hold on their moral and spiritual selves to subside eventually fell victim to the camp's degenerating influences."[52] Holocaust scholar Terence de Pres deemed the survivor "evidence that men and women are strong enough, mature enough, awake enough, to face death without mediation, and therefore to embrace life without reserve."[53] Does this mean the Muselmann was weak, immature, asleep, disinterested in life? Consigning the Muselmänner to planet Auschwitz, a distant world caught in the "deep, dark ocean of history" denies their existence on planet Earth.

Primo Levi both reinforces our image of the Muselmann and redeems him as the complete witness to the Holocaust. Levi concedes the Muselmänner were faceless presences without thought, reason, moral judgment, or a divine spark, but they nevertheless constitute the most authentic Holocaust testimony. In his 1946 memoir *If This Is a Man* (later published as *Survival in Auschwitz*), Levi was desperate to convey what it means to be a hollow man in the unfathomable world of the extermination camp. He asks us to imagine a man shorn of everything he loves and possesses, beginning with what makes him human. What is left? Only if one commits to this thought experiment, he writes, "one can understand the double sense of the term 'extermination camp,' and it is now clear what we seek to express with the phrase: 'to lie on the bottom.'"[54] Of course, no one could truly understand, a truth that haunted Levi for decades. Writing in *The Drowned and the Saved*, his last work before his death in 1987, Levi notes the history of the camps "has been written almost exclusively by people who, like me, did not plumb the depths. The ones who never returned, or if they did their capacity for observation was paralyzed by pain and incomprehension."[55] Levi expressed the survivor's guilt that would ultimately take his life, writing "those who survived were the worst: the egotists, the violent, the insensitive, the collaborators . . . the informers. . . . Those who survived were the worst, that is to say, the fittest. The best all died."[56] Levi believed decades of memoirs and the explosion of recorded testimony following the Eichmann trial pushed a redemption narrative at the expense of the Muselmänner. A troublesome notion, he sought to correct the imbalance by speaking directly to the negligible minority of Holocaust survivors: "We are the ones who, because of our transgressions, ability, or luck, did not touch bottom. The ones who did, who saw the Gorgon, did not come back to tell, or they came back mute. But it is they, the Muselmänner, the drowned, the witness to everything—they are the ones whose testimony would have had a comprehensive meaning. They are the rule, we are the exception."[57] The Muselmann cannot be forgotten if he is the reigning symbol of modernity, the twentieth century's perfect creation. Writing in 1946, Levi considered the Muselmann paradigmatic of modernity: "If I could enclose all the evil of our time into one image, I would choose this image which is familiar to me: an emaciated man, with head drooped and shoulders curved, on whose face and in whose eyes not a trace of a thought is to be seen."[58]

Primo Levi introduced the world to the grey zone in *The Drowned and the Saved*, defining it as a category of existence "with undefined contours, which both separates and connects the two opposing camps of masters and servants. It has an incredibly complicated internal structure, and harbors just enough to confound or need to judge."[59] Levi used the infamous Chaim Rumkowski, the head of the Jewish Council (Judenrat) in the Łódź ghetto accused of corruption and collaboration as a case study. He asks readers to consider what you would do if "offered a chance for survival: you are given a proposal, or rather an order, to perform a gruesome but unspecified job."[60] Do you collaborate, or commit suicide by snubbing the order, knowing full well someone else will gladly take your place? Levi rejects any comparison between someone like Rumkowski, who acted under brutal coercion and the threat of immediate death, and the Nazis who justified their actions with the pitiful excuse that they were only following orders. Rumkowski was ultimately sent to Auschwitz on the last transport and beaten to death by members of the Sonderkommando whom he helped deport after an SS ultimatum. Levi states candidly that anyone still alive at the end of the war mastered the grey zone, citing Ella Lingens-Reiner's *Prisoners of Peace*: "How was I able to survive Auschwitz? My principle is: I come first, second, and third. Then nothing. Then me again and then all the others."[61] Virtually every zombie narrative invokes some version of the grey zone to explore the ethics of survival. Unsurprisingly, those who survive the apocalypse are often the ones who take Lingens-Reiner to heart.

If Primo Levi resurrects the Muselmann as a true and authentic witness to the Holocaust, Italian philosopher Giorgio Agamben exalts the figure as the ultimate form of bare life, the logical product of modernity's "sovereign sphere . . . in which it is permitted to kill without committing homicide and without celebrating a sacrifice, a sacred life."[62] The Holocaust normalized and systematized the routine devaluation of bare life in the modern era, from prisoners, the destitute, refugees, or any perceived biological enemy. Agamben asserts, "Today it is not the city but rather the camp that is the fundamental biopolitical paradigm of the West."[63] Agamben deliberates on Levi's representation of the Muselmann and his paradoxical statement "the Muselmann is the complete witness," which implies some intriguing contradictory positions: (1) "the Muselmann is the non-human, the one who can never bear witness," and (2) "the one who cannot bear witness is the true witness, the absolute witness."[64] Agamben considers the Muselmann a special kind of meaning machine, a "site for an experiment in which morality and humanity themselves are called into question."[65] "Levi, who bears witness to the drowned, speaking in their stead," Agamben continues, "is the cartographer of this new terra ethica, the implacable land-surveyor of Muselmannland."[66] Like the zombie, the Muselmann is "unbearable to human eyes" because it obliterates the boundary between life and death, operating on a "third realm."[67] Agamben goes further, suggesting the Muselmann "marks the threshold between the human and the inhuman."[68] The Muselmann embodies Kristeva's abjection and Freud's uncanny, forcing humanity to acknowledge the Muselmann as part of the species even if he, by all appearances, is barely human.

Giorgio Agamben attributes enormous power to the Muselmann. "He is truly the larva that our memory cannot succeed in burying, the unforgettable with whom we must reckon," he writes, noting the Muselmänner calls into question "the very humanity of man, since man observes the fragmentation of his privileged tie to what constitutes himself as human, the sacredness of death and life."[69] The Muselmann is the abyss we all look into. The walkers inhabiting *TWD* also serve as constant reminders that in the apocalypse, there is no sacred death, no mourning, no distinguishable divide between life and death, just the seemingly endless production of corpses. The Muselmann's third realm is a site of resistance precisely because it cannot be defined or categorized even by the perpetrators of the crime that made the Muselmann conceivable. The camp's creation, the Muselmann, is "the emergence of something like an absolute biopolitical substance that cannot be assigned to a particular bearer or subject, or be divided by another caesura."[70] The Muselmann has no nationality, race, gender, political identity. Biopower stripped the Muselmann of all distinguishing features, but what is left paradoxically defies sovereign power. "If, in the jargon of Nazi bureaucracy," Agamben notes, "whoever participated in the 'Final Solution' was called a Geheimnisträger, a bearer of secrets, the Muselmann is the absolutely unwitnessable, invisible ark of biopwer."[71] French author and Resistance fighter Robert Antelme spoke to the invisible power of the prisoner whose "instincts are canceled along with his reason." Agamben used Antelme's experiences in a concentration camp to illustrate the Muselmann's furtive power:

> Antelme tells us that the camp inhabitant was no longer capable of distinguishing between pangs of cold and the ferocity of the SS. If we apply this statement to the Muselmann quite literally ("the cold SS"), then we can say that he moves in an absolute indistinction of fact and law, of life and juridicial rule, and of nature and politics. Because of this, the guard suddenly seems powerless before him, as if struck by the thought that the Muselmann's behavior—which does not register any difference between an order and the cold—might perhaps be *a*

> *silent form of resistance.* Here a law that seeks to transform itself entirely into life finds itself confronted with a life that is absolutely indistinguishable from law, and it is precisely this indiscernibility that threatens the lex animate [law embodied in a living entity] of the camp.[72]

What do you do when the paradigm shatters, when you cannot even rely on the certainty of life and death? What happens when your creation no longer needs you, defies you, or turns against you? Like the anthropomorphic monsters of horror, the Muselmann inspires true existential dread. Jean Améry claimed the only way he survived the camps was to deny reality and maintain faith in a transcendent reality outside the barbed wire. In other words, Lissa Skitolsky concludes, "after Auschwitz we affirm our moral world only if the Muselmann remains for us what he was back then; a specter who cannot be seen."[73]

The portrayals of the Muselmann on screen, both in documentary footage and feature films and television, is important for understanding how zombie narratives reflect the anxieties of the modern age. Shows like the *TWD* and recent horror films like Eli Roth's *Hostel* franchise, which also exhibits Holocaust imagery, are often criticized for their excessive gore, brutality, and nihilism. The degree to which culture after Auschwitz is obsessed with Auschwitz, reflexively replicating the earliest representations of this real-life twentieth-century horror, intrigues scholars across disciplines. Libby Saxton raises a profound question relating to this premise in *Haunted Images*: "If the progressive defacialisation or destruction of the face on film is related to the aftermath of the Holocaust and other historical traumas, to what extent might it also be seen as a reflection of the violation, both physical and symbolic, of the face in the camps, to which the 'faceless presences' of the Muselmann and the Sonderkommando bear witness?"[74] *TWD* creator Robert Kirkman concedes the comic book and the series is inspired "a little bit" by Holocaust film. It is interesting that Kirkman emphasizes not history, but the representation of the Holocaust on screen. However, Kirkman is more interested in examining how people "deal with horrible things happening to them" than replicating a Holocaust aesthetic.[75] Zombies are incarnations of bare life and witnesses to genocide, environmental disaster, manmade plagues, predatory capitalism, structural racism, and neocolonialism.

The first depictions of the Muselmänner are those captured in the grainy, raw liberation footage from Allied camera crews. Edited into newsreels meant for a disbelieving German public, domestic audiences, and ultimately as evidence in war crimes trials, the footage unwittingly further dehumanizes and revictimizes both those who perished in the Holocaust and the survivors. The films "de-Judaize" atrocities, denying the centrality of Jewish victims.[76] Omer Bartov argues the footage helps perpetuate the Jew as "the dehumanized body and featureless corpse, which was precisely the goal of the Nazis." Bartov concludes, "by becoming the victim par excellence, the Jew ceases to be a human being."[77] The images are incessantly reproduced and incorporated into museums and films, most notably Alain Resnais's *Night and Fog*, which feature close-ups of mummified faces "stripped of everything that the Western imagination associates with meaningful human existence: individuality, personality, reason, dignity," argues Joshua Hirsch.[78] The long shots show piles of bodies bulldozed into open pits, stacked like cordwood, or thrown together into one amorphous mass. Susan Sontag famously wrote about her experience encountering atrocity photos in a bookstore in Santa Monica in July 1945. She was twelve years old: "Nothing I have seen—in photographs or in real life—ever cut me as sharply, deeply, instantaneously. . . . When I looked at those photographs, something broke. Some limit had been reached, and not only that of horror; I felt irrevocably grieved, wounded, but a part of my feeling started to tighten; something went dead; something is still crying."[79] Sontag articulates the paradox at the heart of Holocaust representation—empathy turns to inurement, even indifference because the images are so pervasive.

Most Holocaust films fail to present survivors as three-dimensional figures with full lives as opposed to simple vessels of memory existing solely to authenticate the past. Claude Lanzmann's *Shoah* is arguably the greatest and most influential film on the subject, but it is not without controversy. Lanzmann needed his interview subjects, the majority of which are survivors, to recount their experiences extemporaneously and without pretense. Lanzmann cajoles his subjects to remember by placing them at the scene of the crime, or, failing that, constructing an environment designed to elicit past trauma. Stuart Liebman credits Lanzmann with "restoring this sense of immediacy of the Holocaust for contemporary viewers" and presenting the past "without adulteration, and with its ironies and horrors intact in all their grisly complexity."[80] We are drawn to Mordechaï Podchlebnik, for example, one of the few survivors of the Chelmno death camp. His permanent smile during his interview, Gertrud Koch believes, "covers the petrified inner world of the former Muselmann, who could survive in the concentration camp only by adopting an expression that anticipated rigor mortis."[81] *Shoah*'s parade of witnesses attest to the degradation of men and women, the erasure of gender altogether and their transformation into Muselmänner. In his dramatic interview concluding the nine-hour documentary, Jan Karski, the Polish courier who infiltrated the Warsaw Ghetto in a vain attempt to bring news to the world, tearfully recalls, "It was not a world. . . . There was no humanity. . . . Women with their babies, publicly feeding their babies, but they have no . . . no breast, just flat."[82] Dominick LaCapra criticizes Lanzmann for being "more interested in victims, especially dead or shattered victims, than in survivors—except for survivors who remained close to their experiences as victims."[83] Maybe so, but Lanzmann freely admitted to prioritizing the testimony over the subject. Most cultural productions about the Holocaust, fiction and nonfiction, seek the survivor look and the Muselmann tends to meet the audience's expectations.[84]

Soon after liberating camps, Allied soldiers and news accounts employed terms like *walking dead, living dead*, and *zombies*. Pop culture soon followed suit, especially in the world of underground comics where censorship was minimal. Postwar horror comics, Sara Simcha Cohen writes, "deal with both torture and brutality, boldly addressing realistic depictions of assault, rape, and murder, much like the artwork produced during and around the Holocaust."[85] As early as the 1940s famed comic book artist Jon D'Agostino depicted victims of the Nazis as avenging monsters resembling a combination of the zombie and the Muselmann. Comic book scholar Jim Trombetta concludes "the zombies of the fifties are also the ones who didn't make it out of Auschwitz, Buchenwald, the entire Nazi 'concentration universe.'"[86] The surge of zombie films in the 1960s and 1970s continued to evoke Holocaust imagery. The trailer for George Romero's *Dawn of the Dead* promised viewers they would be taken "into the darkest day of horror the world had ever known," a phrase most would associate with the Holocaust.[87] In a memorable scene zombies shamble through the shopping mall swaying to Muzak, which William Graebner compared to Primo Levi's description of Auschwitz prisoners marching to music every morning "like automatons." Levi writes "Their souls are dead, the music drives them, like the wind drives dead leaves, and takes the place of their wills. There is no longer any will: every beat of the drum becomes a step, a reflected contraction of exhausted muscles . . . the dance of the dead men."[88] The zombie of the twenty-first century continues to evoke the Muselmann and the Holocaust. How can you depict the end of the world without referencing the event that came closest to ending it?

The Walking Dead and the Twisted Road to Terminus

In a November 2015 essay in *Jewish Currents*, author Lawrence Bush explained why he is drawn to watching the *TWD* each week: "If, twenty or thirty years from now, I were tasked with introducing a young person to the subject of the Holocaust, and particularly of resistance to Nazism, I might well throw into the assignment: Watch a few episodes of *The Walking Dead*." Bush is fascinated by "a world suddenly and grossly changed to one in which death lurks" and the complete collapse of civilization, along with its attendant rules and ethics. Starvation filth, "choiceless choices," and paranoia stalk survivors through their nasty, brutish and short postapocalyptic lives. "There is no end to the horror or the danger in sight; there is no sanctuary that can be counted on for long. There are comrades who help you and abusers who abuse you."[89] Robert Kirkman acknowledged the influence of Holocaust films on the graphic novel, and *TWD* writers were apparently given copies of Viktor Frankl's *Man's Search for Meaning* to better understand the mind-set of individuals who endure extreme situations.[90] Like many Holocaust narratives, *TWD* is at heart a melodrama centering on an extended family of survivors facing dissolution at the hands of a powerful external force.[91]

TWD raises questions about the moral status of both the walkers and the cast of characters. I argue the walkers, like the Muselmänner, are witnesses to our heroes' descent into the moral abyss, the grey zone each character grapples with individually. And like the Muselmänner, the walkers are feared, reviled, and, after a certain point in the narrative, practically forgotten. Humans are monsters; the walkers are white noise. How characters treat the walkers, whether killing them dispassionately or with vicious glee, reveals much about the characters' mental and moral health. Kirkman always intended the audience to recognize the survivors as the walking dead, not the zombies. We learn this is literally true when Rick is told by a Center for Disease Control (CDC) doctor that all humans carry the virus and will turn soon after death. "The zombie plague doesn't just rob the survivors of the protection and resources of society," George Hagman writes, "but more horribly it attacks the human soul itself, transforming our fellow men (and even ourselves) into nonhuman things, without feeling, consciousness, or love."[92] The overwhelming urge to give in to the despairing violence all around them is a constant source of dramatic tension in *TWD*, but it is not always clear if choosing one way or another makes any difference.

TWD begins with Sherriff Rick Grimes waking up in a suburban Atlanta hospital weeks after the zombie apocalypse ravaged the planet. Rick has no idea what happened, and neither do we as we share Rick's hellish journey through the discarded wreckage of civilization. Rick encounters survivors and is eventually reunited with his wife Lori (Sarah Wayne Callies) and son Carl (Chandler Riggs) after a harrowing interlude in downtown Atlanta. Rick assumes a leadership role along with his former partner Shane (Jon Bernthal), who we learn has forged a romantic relationship with Lori after convincing her Rick was dead. The eclectic group of survivors are drawn from every race and socioeconomic group, held together only by the understanding that there is safety in numbers. Somehow the band has time to indulge in racism, domestic abuse, adultery, and misogyny while walkers pick them off one by one. Once bitten, humans turn and join the walkers' endless number, terrorizing the ones they loved. Rick eventually kills Shane in self-defense, marking one of many existential challenges to Rick's leadership and self-identity. Indeed, Rick is our surrogate. When he breaks, we assume all hope is lost. When Rick re-emerges from the darkness, resolute and righteous, so does our faith in a meaningful survival. *TWD*'s primary story line is Rick's desperate quest to find a sanctuary for the improvised family cobbled together after the apocalypse. Every potential haven is either destroyed by walkers or ruthlessly conquered by competing bands of survivors. Set in rural Georgia for the first four seasons, the story moves to the greater Washington, DC area where veritable kingdoms, each as eccentric and twisted as the next, occupy the once great seat of power. Frustrated by zombie films limited to two hours or less, Robert Kirkman envisioned a zombie narrative with no clear ending. How can there be an end to the end of the world? Each season is a different trek through the inferno as our heroes, who appear less heroic with each passing episode, contend with heretofore unimaginable pain and brutality. As the character Morgan (Lennie James) puts it, "The weak people. The people like me. We have inherited the Earth."[93]

The walkers in *TWD* continue George Romero's tradition of zombies inspiring both fear and pity.[94] We pity them because they were us; our fear derives from knowing how easily we could join their ranks. If zombies embody the enslaved, the soldiers butchered in the trenches, the Muselmänner, the refugees, the dispossessed and other incarnations of bare life, *TWD*'s walkers certainly continue this trend into the twenty-first century. Gerry Canavan argues that in *TWD*, like previous zombie narratives, "the tools and technologies of empire are continually borrowed for the purpose of priming . . . violent colonialist fantasy." Characters who express empathy and pity for walkers do so in a way that "merely recapitulates the colonial gaze by recoding it into a new, less objectionable form."[95] *TWD*'s postapocalyptic world is ostensibly free of racial difference, a world where humanity trumps race, but as Dawn Keetley observes, killing zombies is the "thinnest sublimation of the violence against the racialized colonized subject."[96] Sara Simcha Cohen sees in the zombie not just a witness, but "an emblem of hope," which she admits is "an easily overlooked characterization amid the destruction and chaos of the apocalypse." If the apocalypse is a space for survivors to act out all manner of fantasies, like cowboys on the frontier, zombies are the agents of destruction inciting regeneration. "Zombies," she writes, "like the Muselmänner, bear witness to a fraught past, to a history, to a Holocaust. And zombies in twentieth-century film and fiction forcibly destroy broken institutions to allow for rebirth. The messianic, the autoimmune, the witness, and the familial hope: the zombie is not the cause of the apocalypse, but rather the solution to the apocalypse."[97] The *TWD*'s walkers afflicting the twenty-first century can also be read as agents of creative destruction.

The first walker Rick kills after leaving the hospital is a little girl holding a doll who lunges toward him snarling like a rabid dog. Soon afterward he comes across a walker cut in half, inching across a field. The scene is not frightening because the walker is utterly helpless and pathetic, reminiscent of Jean Améry's description of the Muselmänner as a "bundle of physical functions in his last convulsions."[98] The rest of episode 1 ("Days Gone Bye") concerns Rick's encounter with Morgan and his son Duane (Adrian Kali Turner). Morgan has had weeks to acclimatize to the zombie plague, but every day he must watch his wife shuffle back and forth in the cul-de-sac and realize she is no longer human. Morgan struggles with the decision to shoot her from a distance, but he cannot bring himself to pull the trigger. Later we learn she bites Duane, forcing Morgan to destroy them both. When Rick encounters a walker he identifies as a former deputy, he briefly eulogizes him before shooting. In episode 2 ("Guts"), Rick and other survivors trapped in Atlanta disembowel a walker and cover themselves in its guts, but not before determining his identity and eulogizing him as well. This little ceremony is cast aside as time passes. "Days Gone Bye" ends with Rick loaded to bear, intent on finding Lori and Carl, but not before seeking out the severed walker he first encountered in the field. Rick leans over the creature and says plaintively, "I'm sorry this happened to you" and shoots it in the head.[99] "Days Gone Bye" dramatizes the anguish of dispatching walkers who so recently counted among the living—wives, mothers, and innocent children. The characters are never as conflicted about the walkers as they are in the first episodes. Walkers are still considered former people, but their otherness combined with their endless number harden survivors, turning even the most docile human into an efficient killing machine.

Psychiatrist Aaron Hass wrote that Holocaust survivors are often unable to grieve because they are so "inundated with death that they were unable to mourn their losses."[100] Rick's group insists on maintaining certain rituals from the old world, specifically honoring the dead. After a walker attack, Glenn (Steven Yeun), one of the more steadfast and decent characters, chastises those trying to dispose of their fallen alongside the walkers. "Our people go over there," he says pointing to a makeshift graveyard, "We don't burn them. We bury them." Lori urges the group to pause and reflect on the lost, even in the face of escalating danger and constant death: "We need time to mourn. We need time to bury our dead. It's what people do."[101] This determination to maintain a certain level of preapocalyptic humanity waxes and wanes depending on circumstances, but the resolve to at least try distinguishes the protagonists from the villains in the series, men like the

Governor (David Morrissey), the nihilistic Wolves who desire a whole world of walkers, and the incomparable Negan (Jeffrey Dean Morgan) and his Saviors. Andrea (Laurie Holden), an original member of Rick's group who finds refuge in the Governor's community of Woodbury, delivers an impassioned speech to residents shaken by outside violence and walker break-ins. "We don't even have funerals anymore because the death never stops," Andrea laments, not yet realizing the Governor is indifferent to both the living and the dead. Beth (Emily Kinney), a gentle young woman who previously attempted suicide, is consistently humane and devoted to recovering the good in the world. On the run in season 4 with Daryl (Norman Reedus), the self-styled redneck survivalist, the duo hide in a funeral home for a night and come across carefully prepared corpses. Daryl scoffs at dressing up "these things" in suits in a farcical ceremony, but Beth reprimands him: "Whoever did this cared. They wanted these people to get a funeral. They remember 'these things' were people. Before all this. They didn't let it change them in the end."[102] Beth, like so many noble characters in *TWD* who fight against humanity's worst instincts, dies a martyr, but she dies nonetheless.

All *TWD* characters suffer from moral injury, a form of post-traumatic stress disorder common in extreme situations like warfare or genocide. "Moral injury," George Hagman notes, "implies that one's experiences are not just inconsistent with previously held moral expectations, but have the power to negate and possibly pervert them." The truly frightening and tragic realization in *TWD* is that moral injury "is a legitimate and understandable adaptive response to real experiences of moral collapse, or worse, the perpetration of ethically nihilistic acts, or outright evil."[103] Those who take pleasure in killing walkers or use them for any number of unorthodox purposes are portrayed as abnormal and dangerous. The Governor deployed walkers in gladiator games meant to amuse Woodbury's residents; he kept severed walker heads in fish tanks so he could watch his enemies suffer in eternity; and he hid his walker daughter in a secret compartment, feeding her raw meat. Negan also uses walkers as weapons against the living and as depraved decorations. An educated audience surely recognizes similarities between this abhorrent behavior and the horrific stories of Nazis collecting trophies from murdered Jews, displaying human skin lampshades, extracting gold teeth, and forcing Jews to perform or compete in twisted games for the SS's pleasure.

Rick's group tends to dispatch walkers quickly and dispassionately, sometimes resorting to smearing gore on their clothing to pass among them unmolested. When individuals stray, like Daryl out in the forest collecting walker ears for a necklace, they are quickly corrected and brought back into the interim moral order the group enforces. Michonne (Danai Gurira), the consummate survivor who rescues Andrea and eventually joins Rick, walks confidently through the apocalypse toting two walkers in chains, jaws removed. This seemingly cruel and eccentric detail is actually an effective form of camouflage, but it is personal for Michonne since, we learn later, the two unfortunates were responsible for her son's death. Protagonists who depart from the group's prevailing modus operandi and mutilate walkers out of rage or excessive nihilism verge on sharing the worldview of the show's most malevolent archenemies.

The effects of moral injury in *TWD* are most dramatically manifested in children, especially Lizzie (Brighton Sharbino). Lizzie is disconnected from the old world and its attendant rules and ethics; the only life she knows is the zombie apocalypse. Consequently, Lizzie and her younger sister Mika (Kyla Kenedy) sympathize with the walkers, seeing them as pets or a different incarnation of people they once knew. Traumatized concentration camp prisoners, George Hagman writes, similarly experienced "an almost fatal state of desensitization accompanied by identification with death and the dead."[104] Hagman argues convincingly that Lizzie, a vessel of the values and ethics signifying the new postapocalyptic world, "may be the most terrifying person in the series."[105] We first encounter Lizzie and Mika behind the fences of the prison Rick's group has transformed into a functioning society, complete with gardens, livestock, an improvised school, library, and hospital. Carl catches them waving and naming the walkers pressed against the perimeter fence. "They're not dead," Lizzie says, "they're just different." Carl, who bears the scars of his own moral injury, admonishes the sisters, "They're not people, and they're not pets."[106] Carol (Melissa McBride), who begins the apocalypse a cowering housewife before becoming one of the shrewder and more resourceful characters, adopts the girls as her own after their father is killed by walkers. Carol is intent on preparing them for life's harsh realities. When Lizzie tells Carol the walkers are just people who come back, Carol is slow to grasp how delusional Lizzie has become. Carol assures her, "People aren't who they were." Lizzie is adamant, "Yeah, but they're something. They're someone. We all change. We don't say the same as we started."[107] For Lizzie, walkers are part of the circle of life, a rite of passage for all of us.

Months after the Governor destroys the prison and scatters Rick's group to the four winds, Carol, Tyrese (Chad Coleman), Rick's baby Judith, and Mika and Lizzie fend for themselves in the Georgia countryside. Lizzie is getting worse. We see her contemplate smothering Judith to keep her from crying. One evening Lizzie asks Carol about her daughter Sophia (Madison Lintz), who is killed soon after the apocalypse. "She didn't have a mean bone in her body," Carol says. Lizzie is perceptive, but chilling in response: "Is that why she isn't here now?"[108] Lizzie later entices a walker to the farmhouse they are residing in temporarily, dressing it in flowers and playing tag on the lawn. Carol destroys it, sparking another outburst by Lizzie, who again will not accept that the walkers are dead. In her mind Carol killed the walker. Lizzie commits arguably the most horrific act in the series when she plunges a knife into her sister Mika to bring her back and prove to Carol and Tyrese that being a walker is natural, better. Carol and Tyrese discover Mika's white corpse and Lizzie with knife in hand, ready to murder baby Judith next. Carol knows there is no recourse. Carol walks Lizzie into a grove of flowers, offering her soothing and comforting words, and shoots her in the back of the head. Hagman writes that the "combination of loving support and murderous intent in this scene is terrifying."[109] Lizzie is irretrievably damaged in a world populated by the damaged, but we are also stunned by Carol's decisiveness. Carol realizes Lizzie violates the boundaries between the living and the walking dead by inviting the walkers into the broader postapocalyptic community.

Like the millions inhabiting the concentrationary universe, the sealed ghettos, and the dense woods of Eastern Europe, the survivors in *TWD* encounter ceaseless choiceless choices inconceivable to the ordinary person. The postapocalyptic world of the *TWD* is marked by unending nihilism occasionally interrupted by fleeting normality and intimacy between characters. Alicia Clark (Alycia Debnam-Carey), a principal character in the companion series *Fear the Walking Dead* (2015–), invoked her own version of Adorno's maxim about poetry after Auschwitz, stating coldly, "I used to love all this poetry, art. But now . . . what's the point?"[110] For characters in both series the journey involves rediscovering the point or fighting to build a new world in which nihilism is the aberration, not the will to live. George Hagman's thoughts on why audiences are drawn to *TWD* apply to many of us working in the field of Holocaust studies and others compelled to learn about the subject: "*The Walking Dead* is about a fantasy of trauma and the escape from trauma. We are drawn in through identification with the characters and their travails. We experience vicariously and in an attenuated fashion, the terror and emotional damage they suffer, and then we work through it with them, escaping and healing, and eventually achieving a feeling of competence and acceptance, which is often precarious and short-lived. And then we do it again."[111]

TWD delves into the science of the zombie virus in the sixth episode, "TS-19." Desperate for a haven after a series of lethal walker attacks, Rick convinces the group their best bet is the CDC located in Atlanta. The sole doctor left, Edward Jenner (Noah Emmerich), reluctantly lets the group inside, where they quickly avail themselves of food, wine, hot showers, and all the trappings of civilization. Jenner squashes any hope of a cure and shows the group footage of a brain infected with the zombie virus. The healthy brain is alight, like fireworks, but then it goes dark until reanimation. Jenner explains, "In all those ripples of light is what makes you you, what makes you unique. What makes you human." When the brain goes dark from the fever, Jenner narrates the change on screen, "Everything you ever were or will be . . . gone."[112] After a few minutes, minimal sparks radiate from the stem, marking the change to a walker. Seconds later a bullet rips through the brain. Jenner later reveals Test Subject 19 was his wife, a far more talented scientist than he who may have been the one to decode the virus. Jenner's account of brain activity is pointedly similar to Primo Levi's description of the Muselmänner. Levi thought the legion of walking dead in the camp had "the divine spark dead within them."[113] The ripples of light Jenner identifies as a human being's genius are nowhere to be found in the walker, like the Muselmann. Jenner pleads with the group to stay at the CDC as it counts down to self-destruction. There is no hope, just a violent and painful death outside its walls, he reasons. Some in the group agree and die with Jenner in a fantastic explosion.

Primo Levi's grey zone governed the camp universe. In *TWD* the entire planet is a grey zone in which characters struggle to find their bearings. The audience reflexively designates good guys and bad guys, but even the most beloved characters negotiate the grey zone in unpredictable ways. Furthermore, Rick's enemies—the Governor, Negan, the cannibals who operate Terminus—erect structures and codes of conduct that actually make sense in the apocalypse. Who are we to judge? What would we do if the world ended? The show's villains are no less protective of their communities than Rick is of his.[114] Levi asks us to imagine our own complicity under extreme circumstances, and so does *TWD*. From the outset Rick and his group contend with diametrically opposed courses of action. Shane preaches survival of the fittest: abandon the weak, the unstable, the reckless, and the idealists who endanger the group by clinging to obsolete morals. Rick dons his sheriff's uniform in episode 1 for a reason—he is restoring order one day at a time—but should he? Rick risks all to retrieve the violent racist Merle (Michael Rooker) from atop an Atlanta high-rise; he orders everyone to search for Sophia in woods crawling with walkers; and he submits to Herschel's (Scott Wilson) rules in exchange for living on his farm, even when Herschel forbids destroying walkers for some of the same irrational reasons Lizzie did. The list goes on.

Rick issues a moral directive that is quickly abandoned once he comes to realize the nature of the grey zone: "We don't kill the living."[115] When Rick and Herschel encounter a scouting party for what we sense is a particularly vicious group of survivors, one of the ruffians utters a profound truth Rick is reluctant to accept: "Ain't nobody's hands clean in what's left of this world. We're all the same."[116] A firefight ensues and Rick takes a wounded member prisoner, a move that incites a moral crisis within the group. In an episode entitled "Judge, Jury, Executioner," the group debates whether to kill the prisoner or release him knowing he may bring the rest of his gang to Herschel's farm. Shane and Andrea want him dead. "Who says were civilized anymore?" Andrea argues. Dale (Jeffrey DeMunn), the elder statesman of the group and consistent moral center, is appalled, claiming he cannot live in a world where the survival of the fittest supersedes all. "The world we know is gone, but keeping our humanity? That's a choice." Although he opposes killing the prisoner, Glenn stays silent. Dale confronts him: "Not speaking out. Or killing him yourself. There's no difference."[117] Dale is killed soon after the deliberations, the first of many moral voices silenced by the new world order. Rick ultimately decides to spare the prisoner, but Shane kills him anyway. The resulting chaos leads to Rick killing Shane and the collapse of Herschel's bucolic haven. Rick's maxim to protect life seems like a distant memory. As much as everyone will grow to hate the Governor, the audience included, his code is clearly more suited to the apocalypse: "In this life you kill or you die. Or you die and you kill."[118]

The grey zone forces individuals to reassess basic assumptions about life's inherent value and the ethics of bringing new life into the world. Rick modifies his view about killing and adopts three questions he asks any potential new group member: Have you ever killed anyone? How many? Why? The last answer is crucial, but it is not altogether clear the core group would pass its own test. Postapocalyptic existence is so terrifying that previously taboo thoughts become routine. When Carl is accidentally shot by a hunter in the forest and is hanging on by a thread, Lori talks openly about letting Carl die. "This isn't a world for children anymore," she says calmly.[119] If Carl dies in a bed, she might not have to see him perish the way Dr. Jenner predicted they all would. Lori learns she is pregnant soon after Carl's recovery, instigating another bout of existential despair. Dale is elated, telling Lori she can still find joy, but Lori rejects bringing a baby into a world of pain and misery. The anguish of pregnancy in an untenable situation is a common trope in Holocaust representation as well. The miniseries *Holocaust* (1978) foregrounds the struggles of the young couple Inga (Meryl Streep) and Karl (James Woods). The conversation between the two tormented lovers thrown into the abyss mirrors the dilemma plaguing Lori:

INGA: Your child is in me.
KARL: You mustn't have it. . . . If you love me, end its life before it ever sees this wretched place.
INGA: I will not. Karl, please, I want your blessing for our child.
KARL: I want no child.
INGA: The rabbis say that every life is sanctification, a holy spark.[120]

The holy spark takes us back to Primo Levi and Dr. Jenner's observations on what makes one human versus the walking dead. Enabling life in the face of horror, Omer Bartov argues in the case of *Holocaust*, "is the essence of heroism."[121] Lori dies in childbirth, forcing Carl to shoot his own mother before turning, but the baby Judith binds the group together and saves Rick from utter despair. Judith also reminds us of differences between Rick's group and the primitive clans outside their circle, but caring for her comes at a price. When Tyrese overpowers Martin (Chris Coy), a cagey cannibal from a community called Terminus, Tyrese is unable to kill him despite the obvious need. Tyrese cares for Judith while guarding the brute. "Horrible shit just stacks up day after day. You don't get used to it. I haven't gotten used to it," Tyrese explains, hoping to reason with Martin. Martin senses Tyrese's weakness. "Of course you haven't. You're the kind of guy who saves babies. Kind of like saving an anchor when you're stuck without a boat in the middle of the ocean."[122] Tyrese spares Martin, who predictably returns to wreak more havoc. Tyrese, the gentle giant, soon joins Dale and Beth as heroic martyrs to a bygone era.

TWD's depictions of walkers and the group's interminable struggle to retain its humanity are evocative of the Holocaust, but the Terminus storyline is an explicit and prolonged Holocaust metaphor incorporating the most iconic imagery in the canon. At the midway point of season 4, the Governor returns with a tank and dozens of heavily armed followers to take Rick's prison community. The ensuing bloodbath scatters the group into several parties, each left to their own devices and following divergent paths. Several survivors begin following train tracks and notice handmade signs advertising Terminus with encouraging messages like "Those who arrive, survive" and "Sanctuary for All. Community for All." Maggie (Lauren Cohan) studies one map of Terminus closely: "all these tracks in different directions heading to the same place."[123] The tracks are the only unifying element in seven episodes after the prison disaster. Our heroes are dispersed and vulnerable, but so long as they follow the tracks we have hope. Carl and Michonne play games on the tracks; group members sleep on the tracks; long tracking shots linger on the tracks penetrating a deep, dark forest; and our expectation is that if all the bands follow the tracks, eventually they will be reunited. However, the show's history conditions us to be skeptical of any true sanctuary. When Sasha (Sonequa Martin-Green) and Bob (Lawrence Gilliard Jr.) are bonding on the journey to Terminus, philosophizing about keeping a positive attitude, Sasha says something we remember when Terminus's true nature is revealed to us: "If you are so happy to be alive, why are we walking into the heart of darkness?"[124] Carol and Tyrese find other survivors near the tracks, one bitten and near death. The mortally wounded man was also seeking Terminus and offers final words of advice: "Trust me . . . follow the tracks."[125] Shortly before arriving at Terminus the groups reconstitute and sneak into the compound, understandably wary of

Fig. 1.1. *The Walking Dead*'s Carl (Chandler Riggs) and Michonne (Danai Gurira) play games on train tracks leading to Terminus.

any new situation. Garreth (Andrew J. West), the de facto leader of Terminus, is flummoxed, but graciously shows them around. He confides innocently, "It was instinct, follow a path . . . they all wound up here."[126]

Terminus is a giant railroad junction eerily (and deliberately) reminiscent of Auschwitz. When the group arrives, they realize within minutes Terminus is a ruse. The Terminites wear clothes and accessories belonging to Rick's friends, prompting Rick to draw hidden weapons and initiate a standoff he cannot possibly win. Suddenly all of Terminus's welcoming signs are ominous. The steaming bowls of stew set before them are human flesh and the plentiful supplies, orderly gardens, and task-oriented staff are part of a grand design to strip newcomers from head to toe before literally devouring them. Rick's group is trapped. Garreth orders them to stand in a line outside a single red boxcar. They pass a mountain of bones, a series of other boxcars, and messages scrawled in enormous letters on a brick wall—"Never again. Never trust. We first always." They enter the blackness one by one, shivering with fear. The one saving grace—the missing members of Rick's group, along with new friends, are already in the boxcar. Rick plans to resist, fashioning weapons, mapping a plan of attack. Just as the boxcar opens, gas canisters are dropped from above, incapacitating them. Rick, Glenn, and Bob are marched into what can only be described as a slaughterhouse assembly line. Garreth oversees the process with a ledger in hand, dutifully filling in columns, asking for shot counts and any other details from this most recent round up. Rick and half a dozen other men are bound and gagged and bent over an enormous steel basin. One Terminite carries a long knife;

another, a baseball bat. We watch as the two work in concert to stun and slit the throats of three men, blood draining into the basin. Rick and company are spared by a tremendous explosion initiated by Carol, who stages a breakout from Terminus. Carol is smeared in walker guts and armed to the teeth as she sows chaos inside the death camp. She encounters a storage room filled with personal items—watches, children's toys and stuffed animals, clothes, shoes, and weapons. Carol encounters Mary (Denise Crosby), Terminus's matriarch, who justifies her scheme while pleading for her life. "We heard the message," Mary tells Carol. "You're the butcher, or you're the cattle." With Terminus ablaze and overrun by walkers, Glenn urges Rick to release other captives trapped in other boxcars: "We got to let those people out. That's still who we are. It's gotta be."[127] The group escapes into the forest, embraces new members, and Rick and Carl reunite with Judith.

The Terminus episodes are, in one reviewer's words, "a mythic reworking of the Holocaust."[128] "Auschwitz's gate, train tracks, the skeletal forms of the living dead, and the mound of corpses have become imprinted in our mnemic reservoir over the last six decades," writes Eric Kligerman, "they help form our postmemory narratives of the Holocaust."[129] The twisted road to Terminus is replete with historical markers signifying the Holocaust. The Terminus signs reference the infamous false markers indicating the existence of an actual town called Treblinka. Claude Lanzmann underscores the Nazi practice of deceiving Jews until their final moments in *Shoah*. No Jews believed a camp offered sanctuary, but they were conditioned to believe they might survive the ordeal. *Shoah* belongs to a lengthy cinematic tradition of equating train tracks to extermination, a trope *TWD* evokes in exquisite detail. The tracks pierce a primordial forest, not unlike the lush and disconcertingly quiet woods in Poland and the Ukraine Lanzmann films so beautifully. Scenes with Carl, Lizzie, and Mika playing on the tracks are unsettling to viewers knowledgeable of Holocaust representation. Terminus itself is constructed to resemble Auschwitz, complete with a brick chimney, an arcane red boxcar resembling the one currently on display at Auschwitz-Birkenau, and poison gas. The slaughter room is vile but well ordered. One is reminded of SS functionary Franz Suchomel's surreptitiously filmed interview with Claude Lanzmann about his experiences at Treblinka. Suchomel called the killing process "a primitive but efficient production line of death."[130] Terminus's storage room filled with teddy bears and shoes belongs to practically every Holocaust film and documentary ever made. The fact that Terminites appropriate "Never Again" to vindicate cannibalism and industrialized slaughter is also striking. "We first always" mirrors Ella Lingens-Reiner's answer to how she survived Auschwitz, "I come first, second, and third. Then nothing. Then me again and then all the others."[131] The Terminites are the Nazis in this Holocaust metaphor, but they were once

Fig. 1.2. Rick (Andrew Lincoln), Daryl (Norman Reedus), and Michonne (Danai Gurira) await an uncertain fate in a boxcar inside Terminus.

victims themselves. We learn Mary, Garreth, and his family were themselves stuffed into the same boxcar, but they escaped and made Terminus their own. Hence, "Never Again." Are the Terminites just surviving in the grey zone? Can we judge them? There was certainly no shortage of Nazis who justified the Holocaust as a deranged pre-emptive measure against perceived enemies. The Terminites' savagery is self-evident because they are cannibals, but are they so far removed from Rick? A few days before arriving at Terminus, Rick ripped out a man's throat with his teeth to free Carl, Michonne, and Daryl from certain death. You're the butcher, or you're the cattle indeed.

What resonates for *TWD*'s audience is the group's determination not to rebuild civilization, but fashion a new one without the vices of the old. The walkers enable this. Are the survivors worthy of this gift of rebirth? If there is one scene that can answer this question, it is Rick pleading for an accommodation with the Governor as he stands before the prison fence armed with a tank and an army of walkers. The Governor has Michonne's samurai sword pressed against Herschel's neck, but Herschel is at peace because he listens to Rick and understands he is morally strong despite the world around him, that Rick will build something worthwhile after Herschel is gone. Rick has seen and lost so much, yet he has the strength to reach out to the Governor with an offer to share the prison: "Everyone's made it this far. We've done the worst kind of things just to stay alive. But we can still come back. We're not too far gone. We can come back." The Governor simply whispers "Liar" and decapitates Herschel.[132] The act is predictable, and these traumas will repeat themselves for as long as *TWD* continues its long run, but Rick's words endure: "we're not too far gone."

2

Silent Screams

Representing Trauma and Grief in The Pawnbroker *and* The Leftovers

No, No, Mrs. Birchfield, I am not bitter. That passed me by a million years ago. I'm a man of no anger, no desire for vengeance for what was done to me. I've escaped from the emotions, I am safe within my myself. All I ask for is peace and quiet.
—Sol Nazerman, *The Pawnbroker*

We are living reminders of what you so desperately try to forget.
—Patti Levin, *The Leftovers*

Sidney Lumet's *The Pawnbroker* (1964) is a searing portrait of a Holocaust survivor immersed in the desolation of an East Harlem pawnshop in the early 1960s. Approaching the anniversary of his wife's murder in a concentration camp brothel, Sol Nazerman (Rod Steiger) is flooded by debilitating memories of his trauma as events force him to confront his complicity in the seedy underworld of crime and prostitution. Nazerman's only human connections outside the endless stream of pathetic creatures unloading what is left of their lives for a few dollars are Jesus (Jaime Sánchez), his enthusiastic and idealistic Puerto Rican employee, Tessie (Marketa Kimbrell), the beautiful but broken widow of Sol's deceased best friend with whom Sol carries on a passionless relationship, Mendel (Baruch Lumet), Tessie's decrepit and dying father-in-law, and the kindly Marilyn Birchfield (Geraldine Fitzgerald), a social worker who tries to befriend Sol amid his spiraling crisis. Sol's American relatives live in a faceless Long Island suburb and bicker excitedly over planning a trip to the same old country that murdered their family. Living off of Sol's ill-gotten wealth, the family is oblivious to his turmoil, let alone the incommensurable horror of the Holocaust. Sol is in "a self-imposed exile in a soulless graveyard of memory," to quote one discerning review.[1] Once a professor of literature in a verdant and welcoming Germany, Sol lives out his days in the ghetto channeling two millennia of antisemitic stereotypes. A pawnbroker, the Wandering Jew, Sol agrees to teach Jesus gold and crushes the youth's spirit when he exclaims bitterly that money is the only thing that matters in the world. Sol's body is still here, but his spirit, his humanity, died in the camp. *The Pawnbroker* explores the post-traumatic degradation of the individual measured against the wider degradation of society. The film is not about the Holocaust, but about the walking dead who shuffle through the ruins of the world left behind, not unlike Primo Levi's Muselmann inhabiting a planet called Auschwitz.

HBO's *The Leftovers* (2014–2017), created and produced by *Lost* (2004–2010) co-creator Damon Lindelof and novelist Tom Perrotta, presents a universe in which God is dead. One October 14 in the twenty-first century, 140 million people worldwide suddenly disappeared—babies, the elderly, the pope, Gary Busey, four out of the five cast members of *Perfect Strangers* (1986–1993), even fetuses in the womb. The shock, horror, and trauma of what became known as the Sudden Departure left no one untouched, sending survivors into their own spiral of guilt, self-incrimination, anger, hedonism, and feckless search for answers. Some believe it was the rapture, while others, especially the faithful, argue the opposite. As Sophie Gilbert notes in *The Atlantic*, "the question that Perrotta and Lindelof seem to be occupying themselves with isn't how it happened so much as what happens next? How does humanity respond to a universe in which everything is meaningless?"[2] Initially set in a fictional New York suburb called Mapleton, *The Leftovers* revolves around the family of police chief Kevin Garvey (Justin Theroux) and Nora Durst (Carrie Coon), a woman who lost her husband and both children in the Sudden Departure. Nora's brother Matt Jamison (Christopher Eccleston) is a pastor who spends his days revealing the sordid pasts of those who departed to disprove the notion the event was the rapture. Kevin's family is still on Earth, but they are lost to him. His wife Laurie (Amy Brenneman), who lost a pregnancy in the Sudden Departure, joins a cult called the Guilty Remnant (GR) founded by Laurie's former psychiatric patient Patti Levin (Ann Dowd). Kevin's son Tom (Chris Zylka) follows a mystic named Holy Wayne (Paterson Joseph) who supposedly takes people's pain away with a simple embrace. Kevin's teenage daughter Jill (Margaret Qualley) lives at home with Kevin, but she is as cold and distant as the departed. Kevin's father, Kevin Sr. (Scott Glenn), resides in an insane asylum and pushes Kevin to stop pretending nothing happened and embrace his yet undetermined role in the mystery of the Sudden Departure. Seasons 2 and 3 center on Kevin's path of self-discovery and his relationship with Nora amid the continuing mystery of the Sudden Departure.

There are compelling similarities between the protagonists in *The Pawnbroker* and *The Leftovers*. Both Lindelof and Perrotta admit to creating a post-9/11 atmosphere in the series, but *The Leftovers* also uses Holocaust imagery ranging from the industrial processing of corpses, consumption by fire, piles of clothes and personal items left in warehouses, and the GR's spartan and regimented lives, marked by eating one bowl of gruel a day. More significantly, both productions explore the effects of trauma, guilt, unspeakable loss, and a pervasive crisis of faith. The worlds depicted are divided between those who choose to forget and those who will not let them. This chapter examines how historic trauma like the Holocaust confounds representation and influences the depictions of survivors. I examine four intriguing commonalities between *The Pawnbroker*'s and *The Leftovers*'s representations of trauma and grief; First, characters exist in a state of numbness and hide behind carefully constructed walls; second, the protagonists struggle with the incommunicability of experience when confronting others; third, both *The Pawnbroker* and *The Leftovers* have confessors, guides to the inner torment of key characters who provoke existential crises and force the protagonists to feel again, for better or worse; and fourth, there is a comparison of the journey to the protagonists' silent screams signifying utter despair in the face of traumatic memories.

By the early 1960s, Judith Doneson writes, American culture had inscribed the Holocaust as a "watershed event to which future disasters and persecutions, minor or major, would be compared. The Holocaust was becoming part of the vernacular of tragedy."[3] The Holocaust is a powerful and pervasive allegory in any cultural production meditating on grief and trauma, partly because iconic films like *The Pawnbroker* influenced future representation. *The Pawnbroker* joins a grand repository of Holocaust imagery, a "mnemic reservoir" Eric Kligerman calls it, which deviates from redemptive historical narratives and instead probes the inner life of victims, survivors, and those who experience the trauma as post-memory.[4] A film like *The Pawnbroker*, which some critics accused of flippantly comparing the Holocaust to America's systemic socioeconomic inequalities and injustices, is infinitely more honest in how it portrays the survivor of historic trauma than films attempting to replicate history, or serve as a visual document like *Schindler's List*. Claude Lanzmann similarly avoided, Omer Bartov writes, "the inevitable distortion and kitsch of conventional films dependent on plots and actors, sets and scripts."[5] Similarly, *The Leftovers* is powerful because it ponders the human carnage of a horrific rupture—grief, personal trauma, and all-consuming guilt. The fact the series is fictional reinforces the argument that authentic representations of historic trauma do not always have to be embedded in history.

Before and After

One unifying theme in *The Pawnbroker* and *The Leftovers* is how individuals from different walks of life contend with a traumatic event. "The Holocaust . . . constituted a 'tremendum,' an event of such awful transcendence that it cleaved history into a before and after," writes Alan Mintz. "That we view the present through a profoundly altered lens goes without saying, but we also cannot escape viewing the past through the medium of this terrible knowledge."[6] Holocaust representation addresses the before and after through style, content, and medium. Sophia Wood's analogy of the Holocaust as a "massive cataclysm that distorts everything around it" explains artists' varied approaches to representation. Wood also seems to describe the mystery of *The Leftovers*'s central event, the Sudden Departure: "Physicists sometimes speak of gravitational masses as twistings and distortions of even the geometry of the surrounding physical space; the greater the mass, the larger the distortion. The Holocaust is a massive and continuing distortion of the human space."[7] The Holocaust at least had known perpetrators, and while many victims disappeared in the killing fields of central Europe, their fate was never mysterious. The Sudden Departure confounds everyone, including the army of physicists trying to determine what happened and where hundreds of millions of people went. Nothing in humanity's collective knowledge prepared civilization for the Holocaust or the Sudden Departure. One is reminded of Jean Francois Lyotard's simile comparing Auschwitz to "an earthquake [that] destroys not only lives, buildings, and objects but also the instruments used to measure earthquakes directly or indirectly."[8] The fictional town of Jarden, Texas, reportedly the only town on Earth not to suffer a departure on October 14, undergoes an inexplicable earthquake that drains all the sacred water and saves Kevin from drowning himself during a hallucinatory episode. The earthquake also coincides with the disappearance of three local girls, shattering the illusion Jarden deserved its nickname, Miracle, for remaining departure free. Neither the Holocaust nor the Sudden Departure were natural disasters, but they produce expansive and unpredictable aftershocks in their respective civilizations. *The Pawnbroker* and *The Leftovers* evade traditional narrative structures in part because they are wholly inadequate for depicting the human cost of enormous cataclysms.

Theodor Adorno's oft-cited and misinterpreted dictum, "to write poetry after Auschwitz is barbaric" may be interpreted as a rejection of the entire Enlightenment project—ethics, the architecture of knowledge, modes of representation, and even time itself.[9] Our civilization gave us the Holocaust, so how can we go along pretending it still exists after Auschwitz? As Adorno's Frankfurt School colleague Walter Benjamin wrote insightfully, "there is no document of civilization which is not at the same time a document of barbarism."[10] Michael Rothberg rightfully notes the two-word sound bite "after Auschwitz" is as meaningless a slogan as "Never Again!" but contextualizing Adorno's admonition is useful for describing the relationship between representation and trauma. "The message of 'after Auschwitz' is not one of nostalgia for a glorious culture where language approximated light and music, but of the necessity of a new relationship to the future," Rothberg writes.[11] Rothberg's interpretation of Adorno is critical for understanding films like *The Pawnbroker* and profound meditations on grief like *The Leftovers*. "Auschwitz does indeed rupture history's continuity," Rothberg argues, "but not simply in order to divide it into two symmetrical pieces, before and after. The world 'after Auschwitz' becomes a kind of palimpsest in which pre-Holocaust traces continue to exist in the postnarrative world as so many reminders of what has been destroyed."[12] Sol Nazerman's present is haunted by the past, piercing his daily existence with traumatic signs of cruelty and barbarism. He is triggered not by memories of a world before Auschwitz, but by the realization that his present is essentially the same world that took his entire family and left him a hollow man. Post–Sudden Departure society looks and feels like that of pre–Sudden Departure, but the indelible traces of the departed cannot be erased no matter how hard the protagonists try. In both cases the insistence of memory, like history prematurely buried by faux commemoration or denial, ruptures the personal and collective psyche like an earthquake.

The Pawnbroker is set in a society ignorant and indifferent to the Holocaust, which is itself a source of trauma to survivors, while *The Leftovers* is a meditation on massive collective trauma and survivor's guilt. Sol Nazerman is alone with his suffering as the anniversary of his wife's brutal rape and murder approaches, prompting traumatic memory flashbacks and uncharacteristic emotional outbursts. Kevin Garvey and Nora Durst are part of an entire civilization traumatized by the Sudden Departure in which cults, holy men, and packs of wild dogs roam the suburbs assuring no one can go on living like nothing happened. Based on their sophisticated depictions of trauma, I believe the two productions qualify as Joshua Hirsch's post-traumatic cinema and Michael Rothberg's traumatic realism. Hirsch considers trauma inextricably linked to a crisis of representation. If we accept the Holocaust undermines the pillars of Western civilization, including modes of representation, the question remains how we portray the Holocaust "to embody that rupture for the audience, perhaps even to assist in mourning that rupture."[13] Presenting images of atrocity, whether they are fictional, authentic photos and footage, or even the absence of atrocity images (as in *Shoah*), leaves the spectator numb or simply repelled. Post-traumatic cinema is "the attempt to discover a form of presenting that content that mimics some aspects of post-traumatic consciousness itself, the attempt to formally reproduce for the spectator an experience of suddenly seeing the unthinkable."[14] Sol's flashbacks and Kevin's sublime dream sequences in the afterlife are brilliant examples of post-traumatic representation. Traumatic realism is "a hybrid of artistic styles . . . to bridge the chasm between the factual basis of the event and the inconceivability of something like it happening in an advanced industrialized society," Lawrence Baron writes.[15] Viewers are forced to acknowledge their own relationship to a culture replete with trauma while still (hopefully) gaining an understanding of the historical event responsible. Both the Holocaust and the Sudden Departure were inconceivable in their respective civilizations, but once they happened they had to be reckoned with, commemorated, their victims mourned, and their survivors succored.

The protagonists in *The Pawnbroker* and *The Leftovers* are trauma survivors. Previous depictions of Holocaust survivors in films and television influences our understanding and expectations of the survivor on screen and in reality. Lawrence Baron traces the evolution of the Holocaust survivor "from that of traumatized victims dependent on assistance from others to paragons of endurance and moral integrity."[16] Seldom were survivors viewed as complex, deeply scarred, and flawed individuals with permanent moral injuries. Culture can only mirror society and the psychology of trauma was in its infancy in the 1950s and 1960s. Cathy Caruth notes the "singular possession by the past . . . has become a central characteristic of the survivor experience of our time," while Jeffrey Prager writes "trauma indicts in memory the victim's intimate community—principally mother, father, or other caregivers—who, at the time of such overwhelming experience, is felt to have failed to protect the victim."[17] Sol Nazerman is both possessed by the past and traumatized by his failure to protect his family. Likewise, the Sudden Departure transformed every survivor into helpless bystanders and, worse, impotent victims in waiting for the next Sudden Departure no one can predict or stop. "While we may readily acknowledge that we inhabit a world in which nothing is certain, not even our psychological survival," psychologist Doris Brothers writes, "trauma appears to expose us to this truth in a way that we experience as unbearable."[18]

Post-traumatic cinema visualizes survivors' trauma to communicate the dissolution of the self and the unbearable state of being. Narrative memory, according to Caruth, is "linguistic, coherently structured, comprehensive, and highly constructed," while traumatic memory is "characterized by a rejection of the literary and a corresponding turn to the visual."[19]

French author and survivor Charlotte Delbo crystallized the experience of the survivor inhabiting the post-traumatic universe with her inner dialogue: "'Auschwitz is so deeply etched on my memory that I cannot forget one moment of it.' 'So you are living with Auschwitz?' 'No, I live next to it. Auschwitz is there, unalterable, precise, but enveloped in the skin of memory, an impermeable skin that isolates it from my present self.'"[20] As spectators observing the shattering of one's identity in the wake of a traumatic event on screen, we may believe we are witnessing some historical truth about the Holocaust or similar historic trauma, but Dominick LaCapra argues we are not just passive observers since the trauma "unsettles narcissistic investments and desired self-images, including . . . the image of Western civilization itself as the bastion of elevated values if not the high point in the evolution of humanity."[21] The stunning climax of *The Pawnbroker* features Sol Nazerman mouthing a silent scream, unable to voice his torment. Similarly, Nora Durst comes down the stairs one morning to find replica dolls of her departed family sitting at the kitchen table. She, too, can only scream silently. Historian and survivor Saul Friedlander's "first act of communication" after liberation was a scream, writes Susan Derwin. "It takes him out of his isolating 'delirium' and places him on the threshold of 'a community of empty mouths,' that is, of individuals who partake in compensatory sharing of loss through language."[22] Post-traumatic cinema intimates that while we as spectators did not suffer the historic or fictional trauma, we live next to Sol Nazerman and Nora Durst. Post-traumatic cinema shines a light on our own teetering civilization and challenges the naïve sentiment that it cannot happen here.

The Insistence of Memory

Jean Baudrillard wrote, "Forgetting extermination is part of extermination, because it is also the extermination of memory, of history."[23] The Nazis not only desired the physical extermination of Jews, but also the eradication of the Judeo-Christian foundations of civilization. Eliminating Jewish knowledge, places of worship, and the Torah itself constituted a complete mastery of the past and was an integral part of the extermination process.[24] "The forgetting is as essential as the event," writes Baudrillard.[25] Baudrillard did not lament the legacy of Nazi destruction so much as comment on postmodern society's inclination to destroy itself and replace history with simulacra. "We forget too easily that the whole of our reality is filtered through the media, including tragic events of the past," Baudrillard writes. In addressing the controversy surrounding philosopher Martin Heidegger's collaboration with the Nazi regime, Baudrillard believed much greater issues were at stake: "It is really only because we have disappeared politically and historically today (and therein lies our problem) that we seek to prove that we died between 1940 and 1945, at Auschwitz or in Hiroshima—which at least makes for a strong history. We are like the Armenians, who wear themselves out trying to prove that they were massacred in 1917—a proof that is unattainable, yet in some sense vital."[26] Baudrillard is not engaging in Holocaust denial; his intention is to lay bare the unintended consequences of our mediated reality, especially cinema and television, which he hopes will "place all its talent, all its technology in the service of reanimating what it itself contributed to liquidating. It only resurrects ghosts."[27] Survivors on screen appear often as ghosts, or Muselmänner, caricatures of what we imagine and expect from those inhabiting another universe.

Baudrillard insists on preserving memory since "forgetting is . . . too dangerous, it must be effaced by an artificial memory (today, everywhere, it is artificial memories that efface the memory of man, that efface man in his own memory)."[28] Media can both dilute memory and conserve it, a truth Primo Levi expressed shortly before his death: "It is also true that a memory evoked too often, and expressed in the form of a story, tends to become fixed in a stereotype, in a form tested by experience, crystallized, perfected, adorned, installing itself in the place of raw memory and at its expense."[29] The loss of this raw memory complicates authentic representation of historic trauma. Films like *The Pawnbroker* sacrifice the perfect and adorned memory for creative attempts to evoke painful raw memories in Sol Nazerman. *The Leftovers* similarly explores the insistence of memory in its dynamic, fully realized characters by eschewing a formulaic plot. "These are stories that respect the incoherence of the subconscious," critic Emily Nussbaum notes in a review of *The Leftovers*. "They are less about narrative and more about the power of the uncanny image—the symbol that reverberates but refuses to spill its secrets."[30]

The Pawnbroker and *The Leftovers* revolve around key anniversaries and the mounting tensions inside the characters. In the case of *The Leftovers* we experience the collective sense of foreboding that the Sudden Departure could happen again. Troubled souls like Kevin, Nora, and Sol Nazerman float through the days seeking only to suppress the insistence of memory permeating their lives. Sol cannot even bring himself to remove the calendar page, as if leaving the calendar intact will hold his imminent flood of memories at bay. Sol's descent into post-traumatic memory is visualized by Sidney Lumet's innovative use of flashbacks, specifically the brutal rape and murder of his wife, his son suffocating to death in a boxcar while Sol looks on helplessly, and his friend, Tessie's husband, being torn apart by guard dogs. Joshua Hirsch credits *The Pawnbroker* for "demonstrating the possibilities for extending post-traumatic narration into the realm of the fiction film, through its contribution of the post-traumatic flashback."[31] Hirsch writes that in post-traumatic memory "linear chronology collapses. Time is experienced as fragmented and uncontrollable. The past either becomes too remote or too immediate. It remains inaccessibly in the past (amnesia), or presents itself uninvited, seizing consciousness (hyperamnesia)."[32] Sol desperately tries to keep the trauma inaccessible, but as the plot unfolds and Sol is drawn further into the criminal underworld of which he is a part, the human suffering around him shatters his carefully prepared defenses. Sigmund Freud believed flashbacks imply "a domination by an internal psychical reality over the reality of the external world."[33] Sol is enslaved by his internal psychical reality and the flashbacks start to degrade his own indifference to the miserable souls passing through his pawn shop. The cinematic flashback plays a role in acknowledging and representing a historic trauma without surrendering to the stifling and dishonest norms of linear redemptive narratives. Hirsch sees great potential in the flashback, asking "In what ways might the cinematic flashback be an analogue for the psychological flashback as a signifier in this impossible history? How might it be a cultural symptom of historical trauma?"[34] Walter Benjamin acknowledged montage and other film techniques induced shock in viewers, but this "has a productive dimension . . . in that it 'routinizes' the spectator for the staccato sense-perceptions that are so pervasive in late industrial culture, thereby serving as a sort of 'training' for the new tempo and quality of experience in late capitalist urbanism."[35] Sidney Lumet links the trauma of history—the Holocaust—to the contemporary trauma of 1960s urban America.

Sol's environment is ostensibly far removed in time and space from the concentration camp, but Lumet's use of flashbacks conflates the two in Sol's mind. Sol exiles himself daily to the impoverished ghetto community of East Harlem as if subconsciously seeking out an American variant of the human misery he left behind in Europe. Sol's American relatives badger him into loaning them money for a European vacation, desiring the sights, sounds, and smells of old Europe. Sol quips bitterly, "Rather like a stench, if I remember."[36] But the stench is not in the past, on another continent; it is his present as well. Sol toils amid pervasive violence and crushing poverty as his clients wander into the pawnshop hawking anything and everything while he impassively absorbs their sad stories. Lumet, Frank Cunningham observes, "visually reveals both the pawnbroker and the street youths as similar victims of their social and psychological environment." Lumet films Sol and his wretched customers as if trapped behind the bars of the pawnshop. Sol is as much a prisoner of his circumstance as the creatures he trades with, although he has the means to escape. "The cage of Nazerman's experience is visually reinforced at several places in the film's

Fig. 2.1. Sol Nazerman (Rod Steiger) is a Holocaust survivor overcome by traumatic memories on the anniversary of his wife's rape and murder in a concentration camp. *The Pawnbroker* (1964) was a groundbreaking film for its unvarnished portrayal of a survivor.

narrative," Cunningham concludes.[37] The first sequence in the film is a flashback to a joyful Sol and his extended family basking in nature's beauty. There is a picnic, sunshine, children running through a field of flowers, and Sol's beautiful wife Ruth (Linda Geiser), radiant and pure. We focus on Sol's smiling face, which we never see again, as he suddenly turns to stone, dropping his young daughter's embrace. This is the end, the moment Sol's family is entrapped by the Nazi apparatus, and the origin of his debilitating trauma.[38] Sol awakens in a nondescript Long Island suburb surrounded by relatives who know nothing about his turmoil, and care even less. Sol rejects the natural world for the pawnshop, the subway (which stands in for the boxcar in another flashback), the piles of shoes in the window of a thrift store on his commute, and the chain link fences imprisoning the black and brown people of the inner city. How can Sol maintain the walls barring the insistence of memory in an environment as evocative as the one he chooses to inhabit? Perhaps on some level he knows it is only a matter of time before the walls crumble, prompting a catharsis, even if the catharsis is death at the hands of the criminals with whom he associates.

Sol is not entirely cut off from humanity. Aside from his hapless relatives, Jesus Ortiz, and the gangster Rodriguez (Brock Peters) for whom he launders money earned from prostitution, Sol supports Tessie and Mendel in an apartment. He dutifully visits, dispensing money and medicine for Mendel, and engages in sad sexual encounters with Tessie. Unlike Sol, Tessie is a survivor immersed in her sorrow. She longs for connection, weeps when Mendel finally dies, and is surrounded by symbols of Judaism, indicating she stubbornly clings to some elements of faith despite her ordeal. Mendel looms over Sol and Tessie like a specter, judging their languid couplings not as a betrayal of his dead son, but the promise of life after Auschwitz. When Tessie closes Mendel's bedroom door to be with Sol, Mendel utters contemptuously, "Shut me off from the land of the dead."[39] Mendel is closer to death than anyone, but in his view Tessie and Sol truly inhabit the land of the dead. Mendel sees right through Sol and judges him harshly but precisely in one of the film's pivotal scenes. As Sol sits at Mendel's bedside giving him spoonfuls of medicine, Mendel eyes him carefully, sensing Sol's oncoming breakdown as memories intrude on Sol's reality. "I was in Auschwitz, too and I came out alive," Mendel says. "You came out dead." Sol brushes him off, but Mendel is not done, accusing Sol of caring for him out of guilt.

> MENDEL: So you wrap yourself in a kind of shroud and feel you share the dignity of death with those who really died. Tell me, does blood ever flow through you, Sol Nazerman? Can you feel pain?
> SOL: [sits, slumped in a chair, exhausted] No.
> MENDEL: You are a fake. You breathe, you eat, you walk, you make money, you take a dream and give a dollar. You have no hope.
> SOL: [stands, indignant] I survive.
> MENDEL: Survive? A coward's survival, and at what a price. No love, no passion, no . . . no pity. [Sol walks out of the room.] Dead! Sol Nazerman, the walking dead![40]

The allusion to the Muselmann is telling and accurate given what we have seen from Sol thus far. Mendel dies soon after the outburst, but his stinging condemnation for how Sol lives resonates, helping propel Sol closer to an inevitable breakdown.

While Mendel castigates Sol and Tessie for avoiding emotion and living life despite past trauma, the GR cult in Mapleton denies the possibility of a meaningful existence altogether. The Sudden Departure exposed the bankruptcy of all accepted knowledge, religion, love, reason, family, morality, the entirety of what makes humanity human. Led by Laurie Garvey's former patient Patti Levin, the GR devote their entire existence to inciting traumatic memory. The GR take a vow of silence, dress in plain white clothes, live communally, eat simply and sparingly, and smoke incessantly. The use of *remnant* in the cult name is significant. The Jewish notion of the *sh'erit ha'pletah* (surviving remnant) implies forging a Jewish identity based on religious practice. Jews after the Holocaust, like humanity after the Sudden Departure, were left wondering if there is a God, and, if so, why he had forsaken his chosen people. Omer Bartov identifies the existential question facing the surviving remnant of Jews: "Did the Holocaust prove that religion was the fortress of Jewish continuity or that it was its tomb?"[41] *The Leftovers* depicts numerous collisions between the faithful and those who conclude God is dead. By the final season, even Matt Jamison, the devout pastor, surrenders to the mystery and meaninglessness of the Sudden Departure.

In *Remnants of Auschwitz*, Giorgio Agamben explains the concept of the remnant in reference to the messianic event: "Just as the remnant of Israel signified neither the whole people nor a part of the people but, the noncoincidence of the whole and the part, and just as messianic time is neither historical time nor eternity but, rather, the disjunction that divides them, so the remnants of Auschwitz—the witnesses—are neither the dead nor the survivors, neither the drowned nor the saved. They are what remains between them."[42] Agamben calls the remnant "a redemptive machine allowing for the salvation of the very whole whose division and loss it had signified."[43] The GR are not ones to self-aggrandize because they reject any possibility of redemption or salvation, nor would they call themselves survivors or the walking dead, although they emulate them in some ways. The GR believes everyone left after the Sudden Departure is guilty of forgetting, of refusing to acknowledge the world is over. Not unlike Claude Lanzmann, Patti Levin stages traumatic memory because she believes it is the duty of the remnant to testify to loss no matter the pain to themselves.

We are first introduced to the GR on the eve of the third anniversary of the Sudden Departure. As the town readies itself for Heroes Day, Mayor Lucy Warburton (Amanda Warren) dismisses any potential for violence resulting from the GR's stunts. "Everyone is ready to feel better," she tells Kevin. "Not the Remnant," he responds. Damon Lindelof and Tom Perrotta conceived of the parade as just another meaningless American holiday that "you put in a box and move on," but with an event as catastrophic as the Sudden Departure, "you can't."[44] When the anniversary arrives and the maudlin ceremony begins, the GR stand en masse carrying signs reading "Stop wasting your breath."[45] The GR engages in what might be called political theater—following their marks, accepting horrific abuse, and ultimately staging mass break-ins to steal photos of the departed only to replace them with life-sized replicas.[46] When the GR stone to death one of their own as a means to a greater end, Matt Jamison is questioned as a possible suspect. He tells Kevin, "Killing these people is pointless because they don't care. They're already dead. What I want to do is bring them back to life."[47] Matt's insistence the GR should and could mourn their own is derided and mocked by Patti.

The consuming trauma in Kevin's life is not that he lost someone in the Sudden Departure, but that Laurie joined the GR and abandoned the family.

Laurie recruits other tormented souls ready to embrace the GR's nihilistic worldview. The GR insists the rest of the world remember, but Laurie struggles with forgetting her children. On Laurie's birthday, a meaningless day for the GR, Jill gives her mother a cigarette lighter with the inscription "Don't forget me."[48] By season 2 Laurie has left the GR and keeps the lighter. Patti is dead by the end of season 1, but she stalks Kevin's hallucinations and occasional trips to the afterlife, including one memorable encounter in which Kevin is an international assassin ordered to kill Senator Patti Levin before she can become president. In this dreamscape the GR is on the cusp of power with a literal mandate to destroy the family. Kevin poses as a wealthy contributor to get a meeting with Patti, who proceeds to tell him a hypothetical story of a child raised in an orphanage, arguing that the boy will be strong despite problems being loved and accepting and giving love. "It is a survival mechanism," Patti proclaims, "Because on October 14 attachment and love became extinct. It became cosmically and abundantly clear that you can lose anyone at any time."[49] The tension in *The Leftovers* resides in characters deciding whether to embrace this truth or salvage something worth living for in the aftermath of humanity's greatest cataclysm.

Kevin is at the heart of the Sudden Departure's mystery and cannot avoid it, whether he is in Mapleton, New York, Jarden, Texas, and finally the Australian outback. While he personally lost no one in the event, his hallucinations combined with his father's insane theories and voices suggest Kevin is close to acquiring some deeper knowledge of the Sudden Departure's origins and meaning. The fact that Patti will not leave Kevin alone, even in death, underscores this potentiality. In a scene reminiscent of Sol and Mendel's bedside conversation in *The Pawnbroker*, Kevin is urged to accept certain truths about the Sudden Departure from Patti after he kidnaps and drives her to a secluded cabin. The scene is even staged similarly to *The Pawnbroker*, with Kevin slumped exhausted on the floor. Patti explains the GR's purpose and why nothing else matters but contemplating the Sudden Departure:

PATTI: Do you ever think about the 14th, the 14th of October? The great vanishing, the Sudden Departure, the clusterfuck of the modern era? When's the last time you really thought about it?

KEVIN: [shrugs] I don't.

PATTI: Me? I think about it every single fucking waking moment. I mean, c'mon, what else is there to think about?

KEVIN: So, you know where they went . . . what happened?

PATTI: [raises voice] It doesn't matter what happened. But the difference between you and me is that I accept that it did. And

> while you push it aside, you ignore it, we strip everything that distracts us from it. We strip away the colorful diversions that keep us from remembering. We strip away attachment, fear, and love, and hatred, and anger until we are erased, until we are a blank slate. We are living reminders of what you so desperately try to forget.[50]

Moments later Patti slits her own throat, but she haunts Kevin for years to come as a manifestation of his psychosis, which stands in for the collective psychosis that overcomes the planet after the Sudden Departure. Patti's insistence on memory is not intended to provoke Freud's *Trauerarbeit* (work of mourning) as part of some necessary catharsis, but rather to demonstrate that in the wake of the Sudden Departure all emotions are farcical. Patti's utterances would resonate with survivors of a true cataclysm like the Holocaust. The world may want them to move on, commemorate the trauma with a nice ceremony, but the impulse to meditate on nothing but the trauma is very strong.

The Incommunicability of Experience

Gary Weissman's provocative *Fantasies of Witnessing* argues non-witnesses such as educators, scholars, and artists are consumed by fantasies of experiencing the Holocaust vicariously. Weissman "explores how . . . fantasies express a desire for the Holocaust to feel more real than it does today in American culture."[51] Visual culture, America's preferred medium for conveying knowledge, plays a central role in this project. Weissman writes: "The story of boy meets Auschwitz is a form of existential romance, suggesting that the magnitude of the Holocaust and its implications for humanity are most dramatically and effectively conveyed through a lone male figure's existential crisis."[52] Most notably, *Schindler's List* chronicles a gentile's existential crisis and redemption, consigning the Jews to extras and interchangeable stereotypes. Sol Nazerman's crisis occurs decades removed from the event, undermining the very notion of liberation. His life is something to be "endured after death," writes Bartov, not a life to be lived to the fullest because he experienced the darkest moment: "Nazerman is never liberated and the universe he inhabits is as cruel, violent, and crooked as the one he left behind in Europe."[53] While we understand on a superficial level Sol's trauma, his true torment is the incommunicability of experience. Whether it is the youthful and ambitious Jesus, the callous Rodriguez, or the good-hearted Marilyn Birchfield, Sol is imprisoned by the inadequacies of language. All Sol can do is detach himself emotionally and withdraw from society, a state of being that starts to disintegrate once the human misery he is partly responsible for causing overwhelms his carefully prepared defenses.

The guilt of surviving the Holocaust, Theodor Adorno wrote, "is irreconcilable with living."[54] *The Pawnbroker* explores survivor's guilt without resorting to a predictable catharsis or redemption. Sol is the embodiment of the lingering effects of trauma and atrocity, which include the almost subconscious desire to persecute others in return. Once an assimilated university professor enjoying Germany's beauty with his family, Sol now, according to Bartov, "plays the 'Jew' that he never was, the 'Jew' of antisemitic fantasy, the product of centuries of persecution, the figure into which the Nazis had made him."[55] Sol has rejected the entire Enlightenment project as well, launching into an angry, antisemitic interpretation of history when Jesus asks guilelessly, "How come you people come to business so natural?"[56] Why else would Sol become a pawnbroker other than to act as "a contemporary Kapo," Annette Insdorf notes, "controlling the poor clients who barter with him, but also controlled—and imprisoned—by his superiors."[57] Sol's trauma erased one version of himself and replaced it with another, the caricature he self-fashioned which somehow seems more approachable and understandable to the cross section of Americans with whom Sol interacts daily. This too is a part of the incommunicability of experience. Jesus, Rodriguez, and maybe even Marilyn know the pawnbroker as a cultural code, but how could they possibly recognize the Sol before the Holocaust, the professor? He is just another ghost. Alan Mintz notes a figure like Sol is "an extreme case of endemic social ailment" and the "moral disfigurement that results from oppression."[58] Rather than condemn Lumet for such an unsympathetic portrait of a survivor, he manages to generate understanding for the suffering of others and the moral injuries resulting from persecution.

Sol's interactions with Marilyn Birchfield demonstrate the incommunicability of experience in several heartbreaking scenes. Stuart Liebman notes *Birkenau*, the portion of Auschwitz dedicated to extermination, is *Birchfield* in Polish. Given this, it is perhaps understandable that Sol is repelled by Marilyn from the moment he sees her.[59] A traditional narrative might employ Marilyn as a redemptive foil meant to help Sol come back to life and pursue a fulfilling relationship with another lost soul. We first encounter Marilyn entering the pawnshop seeking donations for community improvement. She senses Sol's sorrow and maintains a cheery disposition despite his curtness. Marilyn recently lost her husband and seems to believe Sol is a potential soulmate because of their shared tragedy. Refusing to take no for an answer, Marilyn cajoles Sol into meeting in the park for lunch where the gulf between them is pitilessly laid bare by Sol. After recounting her loss, Marilyn explains she believes "loneliness is the normal state of affairs . . . for most people." Sol, weary and frustrated, responds:

SOL: My dear Mrs. Birchfield, how touchingly naïve you are. *You* have discovered loneliness. *You* have found out the world is unjust and cruel. [Raises from the bench and stands over her, quivering.] But let me tell you something my dear sociologist that there is a world different than yours, much different than the people in it are of a different species. Now, I ask you a question, what do you know?

MARILYN: [shocked] I guess I'm out of my depth.

SOL: Oh, I would say so.

MARILYN: But what happened to me . . . .

SOL: is nothing.

MARILYN: No! That's not so! What makes you so bitter?

SOL: Bitter? No, no Mrs. Birchfield, I am not bitter. That passed me by a million years ago. I'm a man of no anger, no desire for vengeance for what was done to me. I've escaped from the emotions, I am safe within my myself. All I ask for is peace and quiet."

MARILYN: Then why haven't you found it?

SOL: Because people like you won't let me. Mrs. Birchfield, you have made the afternoon very tedious with your constant search for an answer. And one more thing. Please, stay out of my life.[60]

Sol's use of "a world different" and "different species" evokes the planet Auschwitz testimony from the Eichmann trial, which predates *The Pawnbroker* by just a few years. One critic argued perceptively that Birchfield "personifies the naïve liberalism of a benevolent kind that has any tragedy surmountable and prone to a happy ending." Moreover, "her ineffectual attempts to bring serenity to Sol's life are indicative of the incurable wounds paining the survivor and the untold void surrounding them."[61] Sol seeks Marilyn out during his most traumatic series of flashbacks, sitting on her patio framed against smoking chimney stacks and train cars. He finally attempts to verbalize his bitterness:

SOL: Today is an anniversary

MARILYN: What happened?

SOL: I didn't die. Everything that I loved was taken away from me and I didn't die. . . . There was nothing I could do.[62]

Marilyn and Sol sit together silently. She can do nothing for him, let alone comprehend him.

No character in *The Leftovers* approximates Sol's torment and alienation from the world more than Nora Durst, whose entire family disappeared while eating breakfast at the kitchen table. After the Sudden Departure,

Nora becomes Mapleton's totem: the obvious choice to speak at Heroes Day; the woman everyone furtively observes, questioning how she can go on and judging her when she appears to do so. Nora is consumed by survivor's guilt, but she also must contend with the expectations of others. Is she too sad, or not sad enough? Nora must play the role of a survivor as her own trauma manifests itself in unexpected ways, most notably by hiring a prostitute to shoot her in the chest with a handgun after donning a bulletproof vest. The desire to feel anything at all and punish herself for perhaps causing her family's departure, or simply because she is left behind, compels Nora to behave erratically. She engages in more traditional work of mourning as well, buying the same type and volume of groceries as she did with four people in the house (e.g., kids' breakfast cereal) and keeping their rooms pristine. Like Sol leaving his calendar unchanged, Nora maintains her house exactly as it was on October 14. Behind her veil of control and occasional attempts to move on is the persistent fear it will happen again. How can Nora get close to Kevin or anybody again? When scientists from MIT offer Nora three million dollars for her house because of its unique location in the topography of departures, she is understandably angry, but intensely curious.

> SCIENTIST: The richest data can be gathered where multiple departures have occurred in the same proximity. People want to protect them from a recurrence.
> NORA: [shaking] You think it's going to happen again?
> SCIENTIST: Why wouldn't it?[63]

Is that not every survivor's fear?

Like Sol choosing to be a pawnbroker in a depressed neighborhood, Nora's job as a benefits specialist for the newly created Department of Sudden Departure immerses her in the sorrow and traumatic memories of other poor souls. Nora interviews the families of the departed using a nonsensical questionnaire about diet, vices, sexuality, and hygiene. Nora records every interview. The practice of systematically videotaping survivors and compiling the metadata into a giant media archive is similar to Holocaust testimony projects like the Visual History Archive housed in the University of Southern California Shoah Foundation or the Fortunoff Video Archive for Holocaust Testimonies. Critics of these archives note the artificiality of the testimony resulting from hiring volunteer interviewers with only a cursory knowledge of history. To simplify the task, volunteers use uniform protocols and assign a narrative structure to the survivor interviews (before the war, during the war, and life afterward), which contributes to an inauthentic memory of the Holocaust.[64] Nora provokes painful emotional responses from her subjects, perhaps because she is seemingly incapable of it herself. In season 2 the tables turn on Nora as Erika Murphy (Regina King), her neighbor in Jarden and the mother of one of the girls who disappear the night Kevin and Nora arrive, takes the clipboard away and begins asking Nora the slate of questions about her own departed children. Nora breaks down, suddenly aware of her effect on people and the fact her own losses are open wounds.

Nora wavers between nihilism and the promise of happiness with Kevin, but she remains intensely skeptical of faith in anything until the final season when she is tempted by the possibility of joining her children via a reported scientific breakthrough. Her brother Reverend Matt Jamison, in stark contrast, redoubles his faith. *The Leftovers* portrays Matt as a contemporary Job, constantly beset upon and challenged at every turn, starting with his wife Mary (Janel Moloney) going catatonic at the moment of departure. Angry and fearful the Sudden Departure might have been the rapture, Matt spends his day passing out inflammatory fliers defaming the departed, proving they were not angelic candidates for salvation, but adulterers, crooks, physically abusive, or addicts. Consequently, he is regularly assaulted. Matt sees himself as the anti-GR, which makes it especially painful when he loses his church to Patti Levin after the bank forecloses. Matt and Nora love each other, but spar over faith, the meaning of the Sudden Departure, and how to proceed after. In one conversation, Nora tends to Matt's fresh wounds from another row with an angry departure relative:

NORA: Do you know where my family is?
MATT: It was a test. Not for what came before, but for what came after.
NORA: If it was a test, I think you may be failing it.[65]

Matt and Nora's opposing worldviews mirror the intimate debate between two Holocaust survivors in Eli Cohen's film *The Quarrel* (1991). Hersch Rasseyner (Saul Rubinek) and Chaim Kovler (R. H. Thomson) were yeshiva students together before the war, but lost track of each other. They unexpectedly meet in a Montreal park twenty years later and speak for hours about each other's drastically different life paths. Hersh is a rabbi and Auschwitz survivor, but Chaim escaped the Nazis and lost his faith even before the Holocaust. Chaim channels Nora's outlook and even her personal experience, plaintively telling Hersch, "One day you come home and your family is no longer there." Later in the conversation Chaim, whose family perished, asks Hersch, "Where was my wife's miracle?" Hersch, like Matt, resorts to an infuriatingly reductive mantra, "There is an explanation for everything. We are all responsible."[66] Hersch and Chaim's conversation concerning their lost loved ones is suggestive of Matt and Nora's ongoing discussions about the broken world around them. Omer Bartov writes the underlying context of films about survivors is that "the dead were always present and always absent. The memory of the utter helplessness of the time fused with the complete inability to put together again what had been so irreparably shattered."[67] *The Quarrel* ends with no clear resolution, but there is at least warmth and mutual respect. Matt and Nora fail to reconcile their intellectual disagreements, but they are never so close as the moment Nora enters a metal canister that will either send her to another dimension or incinerate her, but she does so knowing she has her brother's unconditional love.

In a scene reminiscent of Sol's exchange with Marilyn Birchfield, Nora confronts someone she believes is a charlatan in a hotel bar during a conference for Sudden Departure affairs. Earlier in the episode we glimpse Nora's rituals and routines, including the nonfatal gunshots and grocery shopping. By the time she reaches Manhattan and discovers somebody stole her identity to enter the conference, Nora is close to breaking. Sitting at the bar working on multiple martinis, Nora watches as people congregate around Patrick Johansen (Curtiss Cook), the author of a book entitled *What's Next*, the saccharine musings of someone who lost family in the Sudden Departure. Nora feigns politeness, but like Sol chatting with Marilyn on the park bench, she can scarcely contain her rage:

NORA: Why no question mark? What's Next period. No offense, but it's not like you know what's next.

PATRICK: Exactly. No one knows. But we can't spend our lives waiting around for something that might never come.

NORA: Back.

PATRICK: Sorry?

NORA: Never come back.

PATRICK: You lost someone?

NORA: I did.

PATRICK: You know my daughter, about a year ago, she's out backyard chasing around some of her friends . . . she was laughing. She saw me watching her and she looked guilty, like she wasn't sure it was okay to be happy. But this, what we've experienced . . . it isn't grief, it's never ending. Ambiguous loss. If my eight-year-old can find happiness again, why can't the rest of us?

NORA: Bullshit.

PATRICK: I'm sorry?

NORA: No, you're not sorry. Sorry people don't write fucking books.

PATRICK: If I offended you in any way . . .

NORA: Ambiguous loss? What is ambiguous about your family being gone? Well, you must know, you lost what? Four? You count your parents in that? What were they, in their seventies? You sit there and tell me a story about your daughter. I lost everyone. I lost everything, you fucking fraud, you fucking liar, you're not in pain! Because if you were in pain you would know there is no moving on. [Patrick rises and tries to walk out, Nora following him.] There is no happiness. What's next? What's fucking next? Nothing is next! Nothing![68]

It appears Patrick Johansen, like Marilyn Birchfield, is out of his depth. Their good intentions notwithstanding, although Patrick might be more motivated by profit than empathy, Sol and Nora are islands unto themselves because their experience is incommunicable to the frauds and busybodies surrounding them.

Magical Negroes

Films featuring a magical or spiritual black character whose sole purpose seems to be aiding white protagonists are a staple in Hollywood. While some view the magical Negro as an example of black and white characters engaging each other in substantive ways, it is more accurate to suggest the construct resurrects and reinvents negative stereotypes.[69] *The Pawnbroker*'s Rodriguez is not representative of the stereotypical magical Negro by any means, but he performs a familiar function by badgering and threatening Sol to the point he finally breaks down and comes to grips with his guilt and complicity in Rodriguez's criminal enterprise. Rodriguez is coded as a villain, not a spiritual guide like Wayne Gilchrest (Holy Wayne). *The Leftovers* acknowledges the magical Negro motif with humor. In season 2, long after Patti commits suicide, her ghost mocks Kevin for seeking guidance from Virgil Murphy (Steven Williams), the exiled grandfather of John Murphy (Kevin Carroll). Virgil wants to send Kevin to the afterlife to kill his demons, starting with Patti. "What if I told you the solution to all your problems was a magical black man at the outskirts of town?" Patti scoffs, "That's borderline racist is what that is."[70]

Sol Nazerman's pawnshop helps launder money from Rodriguez's criminal enterprise, principally prostitution and theft. Sol presumably knows this, but he is indifferent to this reality until his traumatic memories begin to intrude. Sol's wife was raped repeatedly by SS officers in a concentration camp brothel before succumbing. In one flashback Sol is forced to watch. When Jesus's girlfriend (Thelma Oliver), a prostitute, tries to seduce Sol, disrobing and asking for money, Sol's trauma sends him reeling. He loses himself in a city whose collective misery he finally begins to see and feel. Summoning some semblance of courage, Sol goes to Rodriguez's pristine white apartment and confronts him about their arrangement. Rodriguez is a cultured, wealthy, homosexual criminal dressed in a tailored white suit who seems to know and admire Sol despite the unequal relationship. Rodriguez insists on addressing Sol as professor, which makes Sol wince every time he hears it, a painful reminder of a past life. Rodriguez clinically and cruelly dissects Sol's sudden burst of moral righteousness.

RODRIGUEZ: Professor, you don't know it, but the lecture is over. Now you're going to listen to me. Where do you think the money you live on comes from, professor? Money you use for an old Jew's keep [Mendel], money you give Tessie, money you use to pay for a nice fat house on Long Island, and the nice fat family you support there? Oh, I know all about you, and how and where your money comes from. Me. One of the places I get it most is from whorehouses . . . and bowling alleys and parking places and hotel linens and tenements. [Rodriguez stands and leans over Sol, staring him directly in the eyes.] Now tell me where you thought it was coming from.

SOL: [Grimaces, turns away in tears] I . . . don't . . . know.

RODRIGUEZ: That makes you stupid, professor. You're living right in it, right in the middle of one big whorehouse, right in the bosom of the world. How do you say it? Filth! Horror! Right in the middle of if it and you don't know it. Or maybe something else, maybe you don't want to know. Are you that kind of man, professor, the kind who doesn't want to know about things, feel about things, are you that kind? That makes you nothing! A ton of nothing! You give me a front and I give you money, so don't hang up on me professor. Not again. [Rodriguez grasps his face.] Look at me. Look at me! [Sol opens his eyes wide and stares back.] That's it.[71]

In a perverse sense, Rodriguez is Sol's spiritual navigator by virtue of demolishing what is left of his heretofore impenetrable wall. It is not the kindly Marilyn Birchfeld or the eager protégé Jesus who returns Sol to the land of the living—it is the icy gangster Rodriguez.

Unsurprisingly, the world post–Sudden Departure is filled with religious fanaticism, doomsday cults, and itinerant preachers like Holy Wayne, a charismatic healer whose power seems to be hugging people's pain away. Wayne amassed great wealth and lived on a ranch with several underage Asian girls with whom he fathers at least two children before the government raids his compound. Clearly, he has an effect on people; he intuits their pain and discerns their deepest wishes, but his storyline dies with him and we are left wondering if he was anything but a charlatan. On the run, Holy Wayne is hiding in a dank hotel room when he encounters a desperate Nora Durst. Shortly after hiring a prostitute to shoot her, drunkenly kissing a replica of a departed man in a hotel suite, and just moments after screaming at the author of *What's Next* in a hotel bar, Nora stands before Holy Wayne seeking an end to her pain.

> HOLY WAYNE: Nora, I don't give a shit about you. I already got your money, and I'm fucking exhausted. You've lost someone, yes? [He pauses, gets closer, suddenly interested.] Someones. And you believe you will always feel their pain. And when it starts to slip away you . . . you seek out it again, don't you? You won't let it kill you and you won't . . . kill yourself. [Quoting Ecclesiastes 9:4] "For whoever is joined with all the living there is hope. Surely, a live dog is better than a dead lion." Hope is your weakness. You want it gone because you don't deserve it. [Nora is weeping.] Nora, you do deserve hope. I've seen my own death and it is coming upon me very soon, so this is your one chance, your only chance, and the question remains the same—do you want to feel this way?
>
> NORA: No.
>
> HOLY WAYNE: No. [His arms outstretched, ready to receive her.] Then let me take it from you.
>
> NORA: Will I forget them?
>
> HOLY WAYNE: Never. [She embraces him, wailing.][72]

Like Ecclesiastes, Holy Wayne essentially delivers an existentialist message—life is short, so enjoy what you can and accept how fleeting it is.[73] Nora and Sol are closely aligned in their grief, guilt, and feelings of helplessness in the face of the incommunicability of experience. While Sol seldom sees survivors other than Mendel and Tessie, Nora lives among thousands of them. However, Nora's loss is so extreme and devastating that even the experiences of other survivors seem far removed. Rodriguez and Holy Wayne fulfill parallel functions, each inciting the protagonist to confront their pain head on. Sol's crisis deepens after the encounter; Nora, on the other hand, may feel more settled, but Holy Wayne's embrace is a temporary salve.

Silent Screams

Jean Cayrol's script for *Night and Fog* (1955) linked the Holocaust to contemporary events, specifically France's brutal campaigns in Algeria and Southeast Asia. *Night and Fog* was more of a warning than a rumination on the past: "There are those of us who look at these ruins today as though the monster were dead and buried beneath the ruins, who take hope again as the image fades, as though there were a cure for the scourge of these camps, those of us who pretend to believe this only happened at a certain time and in a certain place, and who refuse to look around us, and who refuse to hear the endless cry."[74] *The Pawnbroker* depicts an environment where human misery and injustice often slip into easily identifiable markers of the concentrationary universe. Elie Wiesel observed politicians and protesters who used words like *occupied* and *ghettos* and compared the Watts and Harlem riots to the Warsaw Ghetto uprising, revealing the degree to which the Holocaust informed the present, however inadequately.[75] Jacob Neusner wrote that America's social and political problems in the 1960s and 1970s transformed Auschwitz into a code word "for all things everyone was talking about, a kind of Judaic key word for the common malaise."[76] *The Pawnbroker* may be situated in a deeply flawed urban American environment, but the story is rooted in the personal trauma and grief of a survivor deeply haunted by an incommunicable past. Sidney Lumet does not suggest the Holocaust is directly analogous to East Harlem's endemic problems, but pain, grief, and trauma on some level are timeless and universal. No one hears Sol's endless cry because he is unable to voice it; it is that no one listens.

Sol's relationship to Jesus is fraught with heavy religious symbolism, specifically during the film's emotionally devastating conclusion. Throughout the film Jesus's and Sol's lives are contrasted. Sol shuffles through the days without connection and feeling; Jesus is wildly optimistic, a loving son, and a passionate lover. Jesus wants Sol to teach him gold, viewing Sol as a mentor; Sol is repelled by Jesus's good nature and naivete. When Jesus approaches Sol for another lesson in the art of appraisal, Sol is at his lowest point, having just returned from Rodriguez's searing lecture and the depressing visit at Marilyn Birchfield's apartment. Sol somberly tells Jesus that the only thing that matters in life is money. The harshness of the encounter leads Jesus to make a fateful decision to help his former criminal associates rob the pawnshop, which Jesus knows has five thousand dollars of Rodriguez's money in the safe. When Jesus sees Sol still in the shop during the planned robbery attempt, he intervenes to save Sol's life and is shot by an assailant. As Jesus lays dying on the street outside the pawnshop, Sol kneels beside him, cradling his head. Sol looks to the heavens and tries to scream, but he is mute. Sol wanders back into the shop, flooded by traumatic memories of the previous days—Jesus's wide-eyed smile, the prostitute, Marilyn, Rodriguez, Tessie and Mendel, and the pitiful creatures in his pawnshop. Sol stares at the spike holding the receipts and proceeds to run his hand through. With one hand soaked in Jesus's blood and the other bleeding from stigmata, Sol wanders aimlessly into the streets as the credits roll. Annette Insdorf notes Sol turns his body into a receipt with the impalement: "Nazerman's self-inflicted wound makes concrete one of the film's central themes: survivor guilt."[77] The dramatic action is also Sol's return to feeling, but we are left unsure where it will lead because Sol is clearly marked as a modern-day Wandering Jew.

Nora Durst's silent scream comes after a similarly traumatic event unleashes a torrent of memories relating to the Sudden Departure. Nora is seemingly on a path to normalcy after Holy Wayne's cathartic hug, dating Kevin, forgiving the schoolteacher with whom her husband had an affair, shopping for one instead of four, and ignoring the GR members standing outside her door night and day. But the GR have something planned designed to incite everyone's traumatic memories. As Memorial Day approaches the GR use photographs they stole from every house that experienced a departure to order hundreds of replicas of Mapleton's departed men, women, and children. We see Patti stand over piles of clothes and personal items (not unlike every Holocaust film portraying Jewish goods taken by the Nazis), carefully preparing the cruelest hoax imaginable. Although Patti is stuck in a cabin with Kevin the day of the action, her minions, including Laurie Garvey, execute the plan and position the replicas exactly where the departed were on October 14. When Nora comes down the stairs and sees her husband and two children sitting at the kitchen table, she is overcome. In a scene reminiscent of Sol's final moments with Jesus, Nora tries to let out an anguished cry, but we just hear the piercing numbness reverberating in her head. Damon Lindelof revealed that Carrie Coon actually screamed during filming, but the sound was edited out deliberately to create the silent scream effect.[78] The rest of Mapleton is in shock as well, turning on the GR, murdering some, setting fire to their houses, and burning the replicas alongside the GR in a great bonfire. When Kevin returns from the cabin, the town is ablaze. He sees GR member Meg Abbott (Liv Tyler) bloody and tied to a lamppost. He sets her free and asks what happened. She smirks and writes on her pad, "We made them remember." Meanwhile, Nora calmly sits down at the table with her replica family and pens a letter to Kevin. It is a beautiful reflection on grief in the wake of an unimaginable rupture like the Sudden Departure (or Holocaust). One imagines Sol writing something similar if circumstances were different.

> NORA [voiceover]: I want to believe I'm not surrounded by the abandoned ruin of a dead civilization. I want to believe that it's still possible to get close to someone. But it's easier not to. It's easier because I'm a coward. And I couldn't take the pain, not again. I know that's not fair, Kevin. You've lost so much, too, and you're so strong. You're

Fig. 2.2. Nora Durst (Carrie Coon) in HBO's *The Leftovers* (2014–2017) contends with traumatic memories, unrelenting grief, and survivor's guilt in the wake of a horrific supernatural event known as the Sudden Departure.

> still here. But I can't be, not anymore. I tried to get better, Kevin. I didn't want to feel this way, so I took a shortcut. But it led me right back home. And do you know what I found when I got back there? I found them, Kevin. Right where I left them, right where they left me. . . . I'm beyond repair. Maybe we're all beyond repair.[79]

On her way to leaving the letter with Kevin and driving away forever, Nora finds an abandoned baby, one of Holy Wayne's offspring, on Kevin's doorstep. Kevin has just saved his daughter from the GR-inspired chaos and arrives home to Nora holding the baby. "Look what I found," Nora says, beaming.[80] For all the truth and clarity in her letter, it is now moot. Season 1 ends on a note of hope, which Holy Wayne said Nora absolutely deserves.

For the remainder of the series Nora walks a tightrope between being OK and drowning in the sorrow of the original loss. In the final episodes she discovers the existence of a purported breakthrough in physics that allows people to transport to wherever the departed went. The process is underground, expensive, and only available to properly screened individuals. Outraged at first, Nora is intent on exposing the fraud in her role as an investigator with the Department of Sudden Departure until she watches the videotaped testimony of those who supposedly made the journey. Suddenly she is intrigued and realizes she never has and never will move on from the loss of her family. Kevin senses this too and they follow their separate destinies on the eve of the seventh anniversary of the Sudden Departure, leaving each other in a Melbourne, Australia, hotel room. The penultimate episode witnesses the passage of the anniversary without incident. Kevin's trip to the afterlife did not save the world because it apparently did not need saving and Nora goes forward with the journey into the great unknown, taking the ultimate leap of faith. Kevin asks Laurie, who is now free from the GR and a friend to Kevin, if Nora is gone. She responds simply, "We're all gone."[81]

The final episode never resolves the mystery of the Sudden Departure. *The Leftovers* is, despite the supernatural elements pervading it, a story of love and relationships. "The Book of Nora" occurs fifteen years after Nora's journey, but she is alive and well right where we left her in Australia. Kevin finds her in a remote cabin raising pigeons. He has never stopped looking for her. The two sit down and tell each other their life stories, reanimating the spark between them. Nora proceeds to narrate her journey to the land of the departed, which is an amazing story with a profound truth. "Over here we lost some of them," Nora says. "Over there, they lost all of us."[82] The world was understandably traumatized beyond repair by the mysterious loss of 140 million people worldwide, approximately two percent of the population. Imagine what happens when ninety-eight percent of the world's population disappears. Now in a virtually empty alternate universe, Nora recounts her long journey back to Mapleton to find her family. Afraid to simply knock on the door, Nora observed her now-teenage children and her husband from afar. A woman lived with them, and they all seemed happy. "In a world full of orphans, they still had each other. And I was a ghost," Nora says. "I was a ghost who had no place there." Whether her story is true or not is irrelevant. What matters is Nora and Kevin are reunited and embrace the love that never departed, content to live out the rest of their fleeting and unpredictable lives together.

The Leftovers is one the more impressive series in recent years, and although it does not explicitly reference the Holocaust like *The Walking Dead* or *The Strain*, for example, *The Leftovers* is a truthful and genuine interpretation of collective grief and trauma. Moreover, *The Leftovers*'s themes emulate those found in important Holocaust films and historiography. Many viewers wanted a thorough accounting of what happened, where Nora went, the mystery resolved, but David Lindelof preferred a Claude Lanzmannesque approach to his subject. "Lanzmann's almost obsessive tendency to dwell on the absences left behind the apparatus of mass murder," Karyn Ball writes, translated into a "negatively sublime repudiation of redemptive and identitarian affirmations."[83] By focusing on what is left behind, the leftovers, the series underscores Jean Améry's summation of survivors' lives after the Holocaust: "We, the victims, will appear as the truly incorrigible, irreconcilable ones, as the anti-historical reactionaries in the exact same sense of the word, and in the end it will seem like a technical mishap that some of us still survived."[84] German director Edgar Reitz, whose *Heimat* (1984) chronicled a small German town's history without mentioning the Holocaust or Jews, responded to the criticism by describing Jews as "since time immemorial 'people who go away.'"[85] For Reitz, the Jews were the absence he chose not to represent. Someone watching *Heimat* could assume the Jews simply vanished one day. Nora is convinced, like so many others, that the Sudden Departure was a capricious cataclysm, and maybe recurring. It is a technical mishap of the universe. The departed are the people who went away, but their absence is haunting.

In one of many comically bizarre instances on the show, actor Mark Linn-Baker, the sole cast member of the sitcom *Perfect Strangers* who did not depart, is the one who meets Nora to tell her about the machine designed to send people to the departed's alternate universe. Linn-Baker is traumatized by being the only remaining cast member. "It wasn't my fault," he tells Nora, words she needs to speak herself. "I didn't do anything to deserve this."[86] The Sudden Departure is not the tragedy, the departed's absence from our world is. Being a leftover is the cosmic joke. Nora's obsession with arranging her own departure to be with her family is akin to Gary Weissman's "fantasy of witnessing." Weismann argues "nonwitnesses are haunted not by the traumatic impact of the Holocaust, but by its absence—by a sense that the Holocaust is not enough with us, the popularity of Holocaust museums and Holocaust museums notwithstanding."[87] All the Heroes Day parades, replicas, nonfatal shootings, hugs from holy men, and substitute families cannot fill the void. If we believe Nora, that she did travel to an alternate universe, she found that she did not belong. She was a ghost. Auschwitz survivor Charlotte Delbo traveled between two worlds and found the experience incommunicable: "All of those I met since I came back do not exist. . . . They belong to another universe and nothing will allow them to rejoin ours. Sometimes it seems that they're about to rejoin us. Then they utter one of these superficial words, one of their empty words, and they plunge headlong into their world, that of the living."[88] Nora, whether she traveled to an alternate universe or hid in the Australian outback for fifteen years, chose to rejoin the world of the living, nihilistic despair and all.

3

Nazi Monsters and the Return of History

What has disappeared has every chance of reappearing.
—Jean Baudrillard

Pulitzer Prize–winning historian and Holocaust survivor Saul Friedlander ruminated on the reasons for Western culture's persistent fascination with Nazism in *Reflections on Nazism*: "Is such attention fixed on the past only a gratuitous reverie, the attraction of the spectacular, exorcism, or the result of the need to understand; or is it, again and still, an expression of profound fears and, on the part of some, mute yearnings as well?"[1] I think it is fair to say producers and consumers of popular culture featuring Nazi imagery and storylines fall into one or more of these categories. Horror revels in the spectacular, expresses profound fears, and secretly yearns for proximity to pain and terror in a consequence-free environment. What does it say about the horror genre and its audience that Nazis and their victims are fodder for often fleeting cultural products of dubious quality? Friedlander wrote at the height of the Nazisploitation phase, when the horror and pain of the Holocaust transformed from "subdued grief and endless meditation" to "voluptuous anguish and ravishing images, images one would like to see going on forever."[2] The Nazi monster stalks twenty-first-century horror as remorselessly as it did the twentieth, often with little regard for taste, ethics, or responsible representation. Friedlander's rhetorical questions endure as well: Do we want to understand? Exorcise our historical demons? Or is our fascination evidence of mute yearnings to experience terror and misery unmoored by the weight of history?

Nazism's persistent cultural presence is a legacy of the Third Reich's own prolific film industry and the trove of imagery Nazi citizens and functionaries left behind—from slickly produced propaganda and feature films to the atrocity photos compiled both by perpetrators and the Allied liberators overrunning Germany during the regime's death throes. Like Hollywood blockbusters, Nazi films impressed viewers with their monumental scale, massive sets, armies of extras, and often brilliant direction and editing.[3] Nazi film also prepared for a world in which victory was certain and the regime's enemies—peoples, cultures, and nations anathema to the Nazi worldview—were erased. Filming the ghettos not only implicitly justified extermination, suggesting that the filth and disease so pervasive in these enforced enclosures was endemic to Jewish life, but films like *The Eternal Jew* (1940) and *Das Ghetto* (1942) retroactively invented the history of a race that would soon no longer exist.[4] The notion of a world without Jews went beyond physical extermination; the Nazis wanted cultural, historical, and metaphysical traces removed as well. The Nazis imagined a world with an alternative history and used genocide to achieve it in reality.[5] Nazi film obviously created an attractive self-image for the Reich—heroic soldiers, dedicated youth, and virtuous and fertile women—but it also mobilized media to eradicate and define a monstrous enemy. Nazi aesthetics, Eric Rentschler notes, "amount to emotional violence, stunning and captivating beholders so strongly that they literally become captive audiences."[6] No one is captive today, yet the aesthetics, even if defrocked of obvious Nazi signs and signifiers, influence contemporary culture. The physical ruins of the Third Reich serve as cautionary tales, reconfigured for pedagogical needs and disaster tourism. However, the cultural legacy may endure a thousand years in the mediated universe, where judgment, context, and the weight of history and historical scholarship seldom figure into representation.

Another source of our perennial fascination with the Third Reich is the popular notion the twelve-year episode signified a radical break from Western civilization grounded in Enlightenment ideals. Destroying or testing faith in reason, science, and our institutions is at the root of most horror and SF.[7] Nazism is the embodiment of evil in the modern era, populated by monstrous figures who seemed to vanish mysteriously during the chaotic final months of the Reich. The regime's total defeat combined with the disappearance of its most villainous personalities continually stoke our imagination.[8] Americans remain traumatized by the encounter with Nazism, filling screens with actual Nazis or monsters coded as such. If we accept the premise monsters are political entities reflecting our collective ideas about good and evil, then we must ask ourselves why contemporary culture is replete with the Nazi menace seventy-five years after its defeat. Aaron Kerner believes the Nazi monster is both "tawdry" and "deeply dangerous. It is dangerous because it is too easy to dispense with—neutralizing history and foreclosing any possibility for the contemporary spectator to consider our possible affinities with the Nazi character."[9] Nazi zombies, vampires, and mad scientists are sufficiently frightening, but they also provide a comforting veil of otherness. We cannot possibly be like them, we tell ourselves, so let us enjoy the carnage without critical self-reflection. Putting a stake through the heart of a Nazi monster does not free us from our own responsibility for Nazi crimes because the ideology those monsters serve is still present, constantly evolving, and all too human. "If there is to be any appreciation that the Nazi-disposition is not wholly alien to us," Kerner writes, "then, in all likelihood we need Nazis with whom we can identify."[10] Creating believable cinematic Nazis is easier to do in historical dramas than horror films, but the principle still applies. Even if the monster is beyond salvation, too grotesque to engender empathy or understanding, its origins and the reactions of those confronting it reveal continuities between a distant past and a complacent present.

This chapter argues horror films and television featuring Nazi themes, imagery, and characters, both Nazisploitation trash and enduring classics, represent the collision of history, trauma, memory, and national identity.[11] Productions mining Nazis haphazardly contribute to morbid normalization and are often evidence of lazy writing and direction. The Holocaust denotes pain, torture, and nightmarish scenarios that do not have to be imagined, simply replicated. Substantive films and television use Nazi and Holocaust imagery to illuminate an open wound, or perhaps an inability to mourn. These productions demand audiences confront their own history or risk dismemberment, disintegration, and madness. The works discussed in this chapter demonstrate continuity between the horrors of the Third Reich and our own time and place, usually postwar America. There are Nazis in the attic, small towns, big cities, and even in the halls of government. Whether we choose to fear them, laugh at them, or heed the warnings they are meant to communicate depends on the filmmaker's perspective and audience reception.

"Eins! Zwei! Die!": Nazi Zombies and the Military Horror Film

Nazi zombies are a popular subgenre of the broader zombie phenomenon, but they differ from the slow, plodding walking dead and the quick and nimble zombies infected by a modern plague. Nazi zombies are intentional in their violence, demonstrably evil, organized, led either by a zombified commander or malevolent humans still loyal to the defeated ideology, and militarized. Nazi zombies are the super soldiers Nazi propagandists created in media laboratories to intimidate numerically superior enemies.[12] Like their less willful brethren, Nazi zombies judge and confront the living with a past they struggle to forget and embody the perversion of science by the state. Nazi scientists performed horrific experiments on human subjects, devised terrifying wonder weapons like Wernher von Braun's V-2 missile, and tested chemical and biological weapons on concentration camp inmates. Nazi scientists mirror the mad and depraved figures haunting Weimar cinema, or even Dr. Frankenstein himself, driven by the art of the possible and indifferent to consequences. Notorious figures like Josef Mengele, whose fictional exploits in *The Boys from Brazil* (1978) approximated his actual crimes, inspired the archetypal villain in the horror genre—the charismatic and deviously cruel professional, Hannibal Lecter in a uniform.[13] The Nazi zombie film often features mad scientists hard at work facilitating the merger of man and machine, transforming soldiers into what they are destined to become in the twenty-first century—a subservient cyborg.[14]

The spate of Nazisploitation films in the late 1960s and 1970s offer some insight into how audiences remembered the Third Reich and Holocaust a generation removed from the event. Both fascinated and appalled by its extraordinary atrocities, audiences were drawn to Nazi themes in horror that played into increasing Cold War anxieties about nuclear war and science run amok. It was not too far-fetched to portray Nazi scientists alive and well given many remained gainfully employed throughout the world serving new masters, the United States above all.[15] *Shock Waves* (1977) is an early example of the subgenre. The low-budget thriller follows the familiar formula of placing an eclectic group of tourists in peril, stalked by a mysterious force dispatching them one by one. Set in the Caribbean, a hoary ship captain (John Carradine) regales his passengers with the strange history of the area, speaking cryptically, "The sea spits up what it can't keep down."[16] When engine trouble stalls the ship, passengers explore a deserted island and its dilapidated estate. The only sign of life is classical music emanating from an old phonograph. Upon further investigation the passengers discover a Nazi flag hanging over the balcony and a lone inhabitant, an elderly German (Peter Cushing) who explains the passengers' perplexing disappearances. Cushing's nameless character is a former SS commander responsible for creating a "Death Corps" of super soldiers capable of fighting in any environment. The unit was composed of reanimated dead soldiers ("not dead, not alive, somewhere in-between") who quickly developed a reputation as the "most vicious and bloodthirsty SS division."[17] With the Reich collapsing around him, the SS commander escaped by sea with the unit, but the zombies could not be controlled, broke free and sank the ship, leaving the commander exiled on the island. With the Death Corps reanimated by the lure of fresh tourist blood, the commander is killed trying to destroy his own creations while the sole remaining passenger, Rose (Brooke Adams), escapes the island. The film ends with Rose in a hospital, delirious and unsure of how to communicate her ordeal.

The Death Corps' underwater resurrection is a memorable scene imitated by subsequent films in the genre, including *Dead Snow* (2009), *Zombie Lake* (1981), and the viral trailers for the unmade Richard Raaphorst film *Worst Case Scenario* (2008). Lying dormant for thirty years in tropical waters, half a dozen figures rise to the surface, uniforms intact (now including sunglasses), and work in concert to kill the young interlopers. The Death Corps was built to serve evil, but with the Reich consigned to the dustbin of history, their resurrection is a symbol of science's unintended consequences. These zombies have outgrown their ideological purpose, roving the oceans and far removed from Europe's historic killing fields. The Death Corps is analogous to a natural disaster, like a nuclear meltdown or, more appropriately for the film, the Bermuda Triangle, indiscriminately taking lives. Aside from Cushing's cursory explanation, there are no references to history or contemporary politics. Cushing's character, like his more famous portrayal the same year as Grand Moff Tarkin in *Star Wars: Episode IV* (1977), evokes nonchalant villainy with a crisp British accent. He is not consumed by hate, grandiose visions of a Fourth Reich, or an obsession with racial purity. Cushing is the consummate technocrat who lost control over his masterpiece. If anything, we are supposed to empathize with Cushing, the only substantive character in *Shock Waves*. James Ward interprets Cushing's supermen as defective weapons, "the equivalent of V-2 rockets that fell short of their targets or of experimental jet fighters that downed more German test pilots than Allied bombers." Ward argues Cushing could just have easily been Wernher von Braun, coddled and lionized by former enemies so long as he delivered for the Americans the same way he did for the Nazis. "Instead he drowns in a swamp," Ward writes, "a victim of the same narrowly focused command mentality that led the . . . engineers to create SS super soldiers in the first place. Nazi habits of mind, like Nazi zombies, die hard."[18] *Shock Waves* energized the zombie subgenre by exploiting fascination with Nazis, but the plot is as old as the horror genre itself—mad scientist unleashes evil on an unsuspecting world.

Night of the Zombies (1981), a cheap and mostly incomprehensible Nazisploitation film directed by Joel M. Reed, depicts SS zombie soldiers killing tourists and waging an endless war against other zombified American soldiers in the Bavarian Alps. The opening credits include old World War II footage and picturesque mountain scenery scored to "Horst Wessel Lied," the Nazi Party's battle song. The film begins with a team of Americans searching for soldiers' remains when they are interrupted by a German policeman who casually mentions the area is infested with the living dead. The local policeman claims a US Army chemical warfare unit fought the SS in the area "to the last man."[19] The investigators ignore the warnings and are immediately attacked by uniformed Nazi zombies. Meanwhile, the CIA is anxious to recover the source of the living dead—a secret German chemical weapon lost during the war called Gamma-693. The CIA dispatches secret agent Nick Monroe, played by adult film star Jamie Gillis, to the Bavarian countryside where he encounters German veterans who rant about Jews, police officials who blame the mysterious deaths on red terrorists, and a father and daughter scientific team also seeking the chemical. Monroe discovers the missing American soldiers from World War II never aged because of Gamma-693, feasting on human flesh and staging mock battles with the SS to pass the time. The former enemies share a goal—release the poison and seek revenge on the living. Monroe infiltrates the zombies by donning unconvincing makeup and disrupts the evil plan from within.

The monsters in *Night of the Zombies* are opportunistic American government officials and scientists invested in weaponizing a Nazi invention, not the SS still wandering the German countryside. Interestingly, this shoddy exploitation film depicts postwar German antisemitism. Moreover, the helpful policeman blames so-called red terrorists, presumably the Red Army Faction active at the time, for ongoing Nazi atrocities occurring in the Bavarian Alps. These nods to actual legacies of Nazism—antisemitism, reactionary anticommunism common in West German politics, and continuity between the Third Reich and contemporary regimes—are overshadowed by the storyline emphasizing the perennial danger represented by unscrupulous science. The "Good War" defeating Nazism was apparently meaningless because German and American soldiers join forces to exact revenge on all humanity, not just the sadistic Nazi inventors of Gamma-693 or their contemporary accomplices. How different is the CIA from the SS if both sought to use this unholy creation against other human beings? Nick Monroe regards the American soldiers he infiltrates as ghastly and malevolent as their SS counterparts. While the rest of the world moved on from World War II, content to lose occasional tourists and meddling bureaucrats to specters from the past, the living dead shed ideology and nationality in pursuit of a more primal instinct—vengeance.

American films featuring Nazi zombies are understandably frivolous and disinterested in history, but similar films from nations that actually suffered under Nazi occupation address issues of collaboration, resistance, and repressed traumatic memories, if only obliquely.[20] The French-Spanish production *Zombie Lake* (1981), also known as *Lake of the Living Dead*, is set in a small French town ten years after villagers killed German soldiers occupying the town during World War II. After young women are attacked and drowned by the zombie soldiers while skinny-dipping, a journalist (Marcia Sharif) arrives to investigate the tragedy. Her presence alarms the mayor (Howard Vernon), who has kept the village's secrets since the end of the war. The mayor relates the story of a young German soldier named Karl (Pierre-Marie Escourrou) who is injured saving a beautiful village woman (Nadine Pascal) during a firefight. The grateful woman nurses Karl back to health and the two fall in love. Karl gives her a pendant before leaving the town. Months later, Karl returns only to find the woman dying while giving birth to their daughter, whom she names Helena (Anouchka). The mayor admits to the reporter he led the villagers in an attack on the German platoon once liberation was near, shooting them and throwing the bodies in the lake. Bristling from the recent attacks on the skinny-dippers and a female basketball team that stopped to swim in the lake, the mayor is forced to call in the police. When the zombies murder the detectives too, the mayor realizes the only way to stop the violence is to use Helena to lure her zombie father into a trap. After an emotional reunion in which Karl recognizes Helena's pendant as the one he gave her mother, he protects his daughter from his zombie comrades. The mayor then leads the platoon into an abandoned mill where the villagers descend on the zombies with flamethrowers, finishing the task begun ten years earlier.

Shock Waves and *Zombie Lake* portray waterborne Nazi zombies with a proclivity for hunting nubile women. *Zombie Lake* even replicates the same resurrection scene as *Shock Waves* in which the uniformed corpses rise in unison and follow a leader instinctively. However, *Zombie Lake* portrays the soldiers as almost tragic victims of the French village they occupied, not the mindless servants of an evil regime. Normally a mayor leading the village in an uprising against an occupying force is heroic, but the film depicts the event as a massacre compounding the tragic death of a poor French girl giving birth to a half-German child. Women who fraternized with German soldiers paid a heavy price after the war, even if French government officials and businessmen guilty of more substantive collaboration thrived in postwar society.[21] The coupling of the French girl and German soldier in *Zombie Lake* is seen as natural, loving, and wholly consensual. The zombie soldiers are not manifestations of evil intent or science gone awry, but act on seemingly righteous anger directed toward the village. *Zombie Lake* is obviously not serious cinema intent on addressing postwar memory about a painful episode in French history, but just another mediocre horror film with gratuitous nudity and poor special effects. Still, the film unintentionally raises interesting questions. Why would a Nazi zombie film shine a harsh light on French guilt and the complexities of collaboration and resistance instead of German crimes and culpability? Why are the villagers tormented by guilt for murderous acts and not the occupying soldiers? And is Helena, who helps rid the town of the zombies by betraying the father she never knew, a symbol of Franco-German rapprochement? With the past finally destroyed, what becomes of her and the idyllic French village? Every European town has a haunted space, a dark reminder of collective guilt or pain. Something unresolved will demand a reckoning, one way or another.

Tommy Wirkola's smartly directed *Dead Snow* is also about the repressed past of a nation occupied by the Third Reich. Norway was invaded in April 1940 and remained under occupation until May 1945. Aided by the puppet Vidkun Quisling regime, German army and SS units occupied a country divided into those who resisted, nearly forty thousand strong, some open collaborators, and a plurality focused on their own survival. Like many nations after the Cold War, Norway engaged in a debate about how to represent the occupation and whether to judge the collaborators and silent majority harshly. Scholars Sven Jüngerkes and Christiane Wienand regard *Dead Snow* as a contribution to the ongoing national debate. "Using the metaphor of the Nazi zombies," they write, "Wirkola points at the dangers of a past with which society has not yet fully come to terms."[22] *Dead Snow* begins with a group of vacationing Norwegian students frolicking in the snowy paradise, skiing, drinking, and having sex in their isolated cabin. The party is interrupted by a stranger (Bjorn Sundquist), who warns the students about dangers hiding in the mountains. He urges them to read about the local history and "events people prefer not to talk about."[23] A unit called the *Einsatz* led by the cruel Oberst Herzog (Øran Gamst) abused and tortured the local population, stealing gold and escaping into the mountains once the war ended. The *Einsatz* supposedly froze to death, but an evil presence still haunts the mountains. The students predictably shrug off the old man's stories and fall prey to the Nazi zombies. Despite some ingenious planning and bravery on the part of the hapless students, zombie Oberst Herzog kills them off and disappears back into the woods.

Wirkola inserts humor and an encyclopedic knowledge of horror films into *Dead Snow*. The trailer shows black and white footage of the occupation, the students battling the Nazis scored with Beethoven's Ninth Symphony and Norwegian metal music, and the catchy tag line, "Eins! Zwei! Die!"[24] The humor belies Wirkola's deliberate collision between a complacent and oblivious modern Norway and the unresolved past regarding Norway's occupation and complicity. By focusing on young protagonists, Jüngkerkes and Weinand write, Wirkola implies the hedonistic youth culture is initially "completely defenseless against the re-emergence of history in the shape of the Nazi zombies."[25] By the end of the film the students mount a vigorous defense and at least show some awareness of their enemy. When Martin (Vegar Hoel) is bitten by a zombie he assumes he will become

Fig. 3.1. Nazi zombies stalk hapless Norwegian college students in Tommy Wirkola's *Dead Snow* (2009).

one of them because of all the movies he has seen. His friend reminds Martin that his grandmother is half-Jewish and therefore the Einsatz would not dare bite him. That the past is neither remembered or forgotten is what sustains the Einsatz in Norway and the lake zombies in France; they are neither dead or alive, just omnipresent. *Dead Snow* is about the grandchildren of the war generation, those so far removed from the occupation that mediated cultural memory is their only link to the past. The old man's warning to the youngsters to learn their history is not just a hackneyed adage, but a weapon for their upcoming struggle in the wilderness. The zombies in *Shock Waves*, *Zombie Lake*, and *Dead Snow* give credence to the grisly ship captain's portentous words in *Shock Waves*, "The sea spits up what it can't keep down."

We explored the connection between the zombie and war in chapter 1, particularly the trope of soldiers rising from the grave to torment the craven civilians and generals who sent them to die. Zombies are a form of judgment and the return of repressed memory. Steffen Hantke makes the case for a hybrid genre best described as the military horror film in which zombies, especially Nazi zombies, figure prominently.[26] Military horror films examine war's corrupting nature, but without the pretense of authenticity or realism. Depending on the film, Nazi zombies are still soldiers on a battlefield, either during World War II or in the present fighting modern armies arrayed against them. The living soldiers in these films are sent to root out the Nazi supernatural and often answer for their own crimes in the process. Several military horror films stage confrontations between German soldiers and their zombie comrades or a form of evil completely indifferent to ideology, national origin, or conceptions of military victory and defeat.

Richard Raaphorst's trailers for *Worst Case Scenario* envisioned deformed Nazi-uniformed creatures rising from the sea and parachuting into idyllic farms to terrorize contemporary Holland. While the creatures are truly gruesome, the trailer is comical, conflating fat German tourists with zombies and equating the German victory against the Netherlands in the 1974 World Cup with the brutal wartime occupation. The film was never made, but Raaphorst found a home for his vile creatures in *Frankenstein's Army* (2013). Set on the Eastern Front near the end of World War II, a Soviet unit responds to a distress call deep inside German territory and discovers a factory they quickly determine churns out bizarre monsters composed of discarded body parts and metal weapons as limbs (e.g., axes, swords, acid spewing devices, drills). Raaphorst shot the film from the perspective of Dimitri (Alexander Mercury), a Soviet propagandist who keeps his camera running throughout the ordeal. This found footage technique made popular by films like *The Blair Witch Project* (1999) and *Cloverfield* (2008) unsettles and confuses audiences by placing them amid the chaos. The Soviet soldiers edge deeper into the enormous factory and encounter increasingly more bizarre and ghastly "zombots" and a few terrified German soldiers who are fodder for the factory. The Soviet unit discovers that Dimitri jammed their own distress signal and purposefully led them to the factory on a secret mission to capture the brilliant Dr. Viktor Frankenstein (Karel Roden), a descendant of the legendary Dr. Frankenstein who defied his Nazi masters and built his own army of zombots. Dimitri, a Communist Party functionary, threatens to kill the Russian soldiers' families if they do not help him, but the unit's survivors eventually hurl Dimitri down a chute to the main factory floor. Dimitri comes face to face with Frankenstein, who refuses recruitment by the Soviets and instead explains his own solution to war—fuse the brains of dedicated communists with equally ardent Nazis and destroy all ideologies. Frankenstein prepares the experiment with Dimitri's comrade Sergei (Joshua Sasse) and a Nazi officer. Dimitri refuses to help Sergei and finds himself in Frankenstein's clutches. As bombs rain down on the factory, a surviving unit member, Sacha (Luke Newberry), shoots Frankenstein as the Sergei zombot pulverizes Dimitri. Sacha grabs the camera and flees the catacombs.

Frankenstein's Army is replete with Holocaust imagery borrowed from classic Holocaust films, historic footage, and other horror films referencing the Holocaust. The factory is an enormous brick and metal hellscape easily identified with a cinematic Auschwitz or the sets in films like *Hostel* (2005), *Hostel: Part II* (2007), *The Walking Dead*'s Terminus, and the *Saw* series. Box cars and bins of discarded body parts, skulls, and human skin greet the soldiers at every turn, as does evidence of a murderous assembly line. Once the Soviets realize the factory's purpose, one soldier says to the other, "Only the Nazis would think of something like this." The unit debates whether the Nazis are insane or brilliant for imagining such a terror.[27] Dimitri, the communist ideologue who betrays his unit and shamelessly barters with the cruel and insane Frankenstein, is Jewish. Including this detail into the narrative is interesting historically and somewhat problematic. The Nazis and many Soviet citizens hostile to the regime believed Jews were more likely to be radical Bolshevists and Red Army commissars. Dimitri, called "Jew boy" by the troops, spouts the Communist Party line and thinks nothing of leading the men to their horrible deaths if it fulfills a greater good. Even after witnessing Frankenstein's cruelty, he pleads with him to work for the Soviet Union. Dimitri is a wretched character embodying antisemitic stereotypes. Why Raaphorst depicts Dimitri this way is unclear, but it is unmistakable. Frankenstein, whose unorthodox experiments and family pedigree intrigued Hitler, is the Wernher von Braun of zombots—a scientist driven by passion, arrogance, and a technocratic worldview. With the Red Army swarming his compound, Frankenstein is focused only on ending the blood feud between Nazis and communists, hoping the fused brain will "make them understand each other." Facing certain death on Frankenstein's operating table, Dimitri screams that the doctor is sick. "Everyone's sick!" Frankenstein retorts, "The Nazis! The communists! The capitalists! The sickness must be cut out and my creations can do that."[28] *Frankenstein's Army* combines the mad scientist trope with the military horror film, exposing once again the danger of unfettered science and the state's inhumane treatment of its own soldiers.

Outpost (2008) and *Outpost: Black Sun* (2012) pit contemporary mercenary soldiers against reanimated Nazi apparitions in yet another Eastern European bunker. These military horror films combine Nazi occultist pseudoscience, zombie/ghost super soldiers, and unscrupulous capitalist ventures into the plots. The story begins with a shady businessman, Hunt (Julian Wadham), approaching ex-Royal Marine turned mercenary, D.C. (Ray Stevenson), with a lucrative offer to escort Hunt to an abandoned bunker inside unspecified hostile territory. D.C. gathers his international unit of mercenaries and arrives to find the Nazi outpost littered with body parts, shaved and naked corpses, and an undead SS battalion. Ghosts methodically stalk and kill the soldiers in the shadows. Hunt admits his real goal is to acquire a Nazi device he calls "the holy grail of physics," a machine capable of altering reality by bending space and time, creating an "alternate reality."[29] The mercenaries screen old films comparing the Nazi experiment with the failed Philadelphia Experiment, but the Nazis were apparently successful. The SS soldiers pop in and out of the bunker, inhabiting multiple dimensions, and picking off the intruders one by one. We learn the mountain of corpses are not victims of cruel experiments or atrocities, but German soldiers sent to destroy the outpost before it was overrun and used as fodder for the machine. D.C. and a few survivors stage a last stand against the ghost battalion, but their plan to use the machine against the apparitions falls apart. *Outpost* concludes with a NATO team arriving at the bunker to face the re-energized (literally) SS soldiers.

Outpost is awash in what can only be described as a Holocaust aesthetic—the look and feel of the bunker, its secluded location in the woods, and naked corpses stacked like cordwood in cold, brick rooms. This murderous space in a place time forgot is one we have seen before. The SS battalion is caught between fields, projecting themselves in the present with phantom gunfire, Beethoven music, and animated films portraying the super soldiers overtaking North America. That Nazi science could accomplish what Einstein and the Allies could only speculate about—unified field theory—awards the Third Reich a posthumous victory over "Jewish science." Hunt's relentless search for the magnificent invention underscores corporate greed and a cavalier disregard for World War II's horrible legacies. Without Hunt's corporate patronage the SS battalion would never have left the isolated and dormant bunker. D.C. and his band of rough mercenaries clearly have a dark past of their own, each hailing from a different corner of the blood-soaked globe. Their confrontation with the ghost battalion is a metaphorical battle with themselves, their atrocities, and the myriad reasons none of them can ever go home again. As the absurdity and hopelessness of their plight sinks in, the gaunt mercenary, Prior (Richard Brake), quips to D.C., "We've killed everyone else. It's about time we touched gloves with some Nazis."[30] Prior knows a reckoning is near, and perhaps dying at the hands of Nazis is poetic justice for the lives he and his comrades chose.

Outpost: Black Sun provides the backstory for the ghost battalion by introducing SS scientist General Klausener (David Gant), the genius behind the time- and space-bending device inside the bunker. Lena (Catherine Steadman), a young Jewish Nazi hunter intent on avenging her family's murder in the Holocaust, interrogates one of Klausener's associates dying in an old age home in South America and discovers information leading to the bunker. Neurath (Michael Byrne) scoffs at Lena's pathetic search for justice, but hints at the true power of Klausener's invention: "The Reich of a thousand years has not been hiding from the likes of you. It has simply been hiding in the shadows."[31] Lena learns Neurath and Klausener dispatched Hunt to secure the bunker on their behalf and previous missions disappeared without a trace. Lena travels to Europe and meets Wallace (Richard Coyle), a physicist who cautions her against following him to the bunker. She insists the two join forces with a professional NATO unit sent to destroy the ghost soldiers. Wallace tries to convince Lena killing Klausener is not enough. "There'll always be somebody else," he says, "Another Klausener." Lena is indifferent at first, "Yeah, well, the next one won't be my problem."[32] Lena changes her mind after discerning the magnitude of the danger and realizes killing one Nazi war criminal is insufficient. SS Brigadeführer Götz (Johnny Meres), who disguised himself as a victim in *Outpost*, strapped the still-living Hunt to the device and expanded the energy field, thereby enabling the ghost battalion to operate further from the bunker. Since the events of *Outpost* the battalion resumes terrorizing and massacring nearby villages like the Nazis of old. Lena and Wallace convince the tortured Hunt to sacrifice himself and finally destroy the device and the ghost army with it. Before initiating the risky plan, Lena tells Wallace, "Two days ago I thought all of this was about what these people had done. But it's not, it's only ever about what they were going to do."[33] Lena, the millennial Nazi hunter, realizes Neurath was correct—the Third Reich was hiding in the shadows, and presumably always will. Eternal vigilance is the only truly effective weapon in this war against an ideology that defies time and space.

Rob Green's *The Bunker* (2001) and Michael Mann's *The Keep* (1983) depict German soldiers encountering a supernatural force. In these films it is the Germans, some ordinary men and others overt Nazis, who experience the violent and disorienting collision of history and trauma, not Holocaust survivors. *The Bunker* occurs during the Allied invasion of France as seven German soldiers from the elite Grossdeutschland Division flee the advancing American army. The platoon stumbles upon a bunker manned by two German soldiers, an old man (John Carlisle) and a young conscript (Andrew-Lee Potts). The old man tells the newcomers the network of tunnels connected to the bunker is a place of evil, a mass graveyard for victims of the Black Death who were hunted and massacred by local villagers.[34] While preparing for a hopeless last stand, the soldiers fall prey to horrible nightmares, flashbacks, and internal fighting over whether to sacrifice themselves needlessly. The soldiers disperse throughout the tunnels and inevitably shoot each other in the confusion. PFC Kreuzmann (Eddie Marsan) is particularly afflicted by flashbacks of a massacre involving the unit and goes insane after collapsing on a pile of skeletons dating to the Black Death. The de facto unit leader Corporal Schenke (Andrew Tiernan) is a fanatical Nazi intent on forcing the survivors into a suicide mission against the approaching Americans. Corporal Baumann (Jason Flemyng) turns on Schenke and leaves him for dead. Baumann retrieves the young private Neumann from the bunker and orders him to surrender. Choosing to remain in the woods, Baumann recollects the massacre the unit perpetrated. The extended flashback depicts the unit executing fellow German soldiers accused of desertion. Some in the unit took photos while others were sickened by the scenario. The film ends when Baumann, a reluctant participant in the execution, snaps out of his daze and staggers toward the American line.

The Bunker begins with Friedrich Nietzsche's famous epigram, "When you look into an abyss, the abyss also looks into you." Steffen Hantke notes the film's use of the epigram "allows for the possibility that the contemplation of moral corruption is not limited to those who committed the outrage." The atrocity haunting the unit involved both shooting unarmed deserters and reveling in the spectacle. "The force of corruption spreads to the observer, who can no longer claim exemption from moral responsibility," writes Hantke.[35] If gleeful participation in horror implicates you as a perpetrator, what does this say about audiences who consume horror and war films? Hantke suggests *The Bunker* is a critique of the war film itself. German soldiers like those from the storied Grossdeutschland Division, which committed war crimes on the Eastern Front, mimicked the behavior of villagers who murdered plague victims—turning people against one another, butchering indiscriminately, and burying the dead in pits.[36] Each soldier experiences the apparitions in the bunker differently. Kreuzmann, who is consumed by guilt, takes the insignia off his uniform before entering his personal abyss. Later, when Schenke snaps and turns on his less fanatic comrades in the tunnels, he has the opposite reaction, screaming in vain: "They don't deserve to wear that uniform, prove that you do! Do I have to spell it out? They are traitors and cowards! Shoot them!"[37] It is telling that the only survivors from the bunker are Neumann, the boy who never fired a shot, and Baumann, the one Grossdeutschland soldier who is immersed in the memory of the atrocity. The dead haunt the living just as history haunts our collective memory. The bunker is a warehouse of traumatic memories, from the Black Death to the Third Reich, and only by accepting and processing these historic crimes can one hope for salvation.

The Keep is a mesmerizing and incomprehensible arthouse horror film.[38] Set in Romania in 1941, a German Army unit led by Captain Klaus Woermann (Jürgen Prochnow) occupies a remote village adjacent to a strategic mountain pass. The village is home to an abandoned citadel known as the Keep. The Keep is protected by orthodox priest Father Fonescu (Robert Prosky), who warns Woermann about the consequences of disturbing its inner sanctum. Several German soldiers are killed and mutilated after trying to pry silver crosses embedded in the walls of the Keep. SS Sturmbannführer Erich Kaempffer (Gabriel Byrne) arrives to root out suspected partisan activity and evaluate the Keep for a possible future death camp.[39] Unbeknownst to the Germans, the looting and SS probing in the Keep unleashes the millennia-old demon Radu Molasar (Michael Carter). Fonescu urges Woermann and Kaempffer, who clearly despise each other, to rescue a Jewish professor named Theodore Cuza (Ian McKellan) from a concentration camp because only he can decipher the Keep's mysterious messages. Molasar reveals himself after sucking the essence of two Germans who threaten to rape Eva Cuza (Alberta Watson), the professor's daughter. Molasar becomes enraged when he learns the Germans are terrorizing his people and disturbing the Keep. Professor Cuza, who is becoming younger and healthier after being touched by Molasar, agrees to acquire a talisman that can liberate Molasar from the Keep. The plan is foiled by the appearance of a stranger with supernatural abilities named Glaecken (Scott Glenn), an enigmatic figure who has a past with Molasar. Glaecken seduces Eva in hopes she will stop her father from helping Molasar. Meanwhile, Woermann confronts Kaempffer about SS atrocities and claims Molasar is simply a reflection of the evil Germany is spreading across Europe. Kaempffer kills Woermann and flees the Keep, but Molasar finds him and massacres all the Germans in the village. Enraged by Eva's allegiance to Glaecken, Molasar demands the professor kill his daughter. When Cuza refuses he returns to his withered state. Glaecken steps in and battles Molasar, weakening him enough that he is forced back into the Keep. Glaecken transforms into the Keep's seal, ensuring Molasar will never return. The film ends with the villagers, now liberated from both the Germans and Molasar, caring for Eva and the decrepit Professor Cuza.

The Keep is an interesting meditation on evil and the moral dilemmas concerning vengeance. The inclusion of a character like Woermann to counteract the stereotypically sadistic Kaempffer demonstrates levels of complicity in the Third Reich without resorting to reductive representations of good and bad Germans. Woermann is jaded by war and indifferent to ideology, sardonically telling his idealistic young soldiers, "Now we are masters of the world." Woermann is a humane man in the eyes of the elderly Jewish professor Cuza. Woermann demonstrates this by savagely ridiculing Kaempffer's SS fairy tales and evil global agenda: "Who are you meeting in the grim corridors of this Keep? Yourself." Facing Molasar for the first and last time, Kaempffer is transfixed by the creature who will consume him: "Who are you, where are you from?" Molasar stares deep into his eyes, "Where am I from? From you." If Woermann is not entirely bad, Professor Cuza is not entirely noble. Cuza views Molasar as a possible golem to avenge the Jews, and, like the myth, he is unable to fully control the creature. Father Fonescu accuses Cuza of being a heretic for considering Molasar's offer, revealing his own religious antisemitism in the process. Cuza shrugs off Fonescu's rant: "What happens in this world is worse than anything he [Molasar] could do." As Molasar becomes stronger and the village descends into murderous chaos, Cuza realizes he was reckless and blinded by hate, "You are the same evil outside this place," he tells Molasar, "You prove yourself to me!"[40] It took the German Army to disturb the Keep and the SS to unleash Molasar's wrath. As the most reflective character, Woermann instinctively recognized the connection between the ancient, dormant evil and the modern evil sweeping the planet. Molasar assures Professor Cuza he will "consume their [Nazi] lies" upon learning of SS executions in the village. However, as the film implies, deciding to fight evil with evil endangers one's own humanity in the process.

The 2018 film *Overlord* is a thrilling, big-budget addition to the military horror genre. Set on the eve of D-Day, the film embeds the audience in a platoon of paratroopers hurtling toward their priority target deep behind German lines. The opening sequence is intense and exciting as transport craft explode in midair and our protagonists plummet to Earth under murderous fire. With most of the platoon lost or killed, the stragglers gather in the woods and are led to safety by Chloe (Mathilde Ollivier), an intrepid French Resistance fighter. Intent on destroying a radio tower crucial for the invasion's success, Boyce (Jovan Adepo), Ford (Wyatt Russell), Tibbett (John Magaro), and Rosenfeld (Dominic Applewhite) quickly discover that the church housing the tower conceals a darker secret. With Americans in her attic, Chloe is visited by the menacing SS officer Wafner (Pilou Asbaek), who threatens to disappear more family members and villagers if she does not submit to his sexual advances. Boyce springs into action and saves Chloe while Ford beats and tortures Wafner for information on the target. Boyce reconnoiters the church and discovers evidence of horrible experiments involving innocent villagers. The Nazis are creating invincible super soldiers using a serum that resurrects the dead and transforms corpses into crazed berserkers. Boyce returns to the house determined to convince Ford to expand the mission to destroy the insidious lab. Wafner escapes the attic and takes Chloe's young son to the church, but not before getting shot in the face. Wafner injects himself with multiple doses of Dr. Schmidt's (Erich Redman) serum and prepares for a showdown with the American paratroopers. Armed with explosives, Boyce, Ford, and Chloe wire the lab with just minutes to spare before the Allied landing. Wafner, now even more monstrous with the serum coursing through him, is poised to disrupt the operation and kill the intruders, but a mortally wounded Ford injects himself with the serum to fight Wafner. Sacrificing himself for the mission, Ford tells Boyce to never speak of the lab to anyone and detonates the charges. Boyce, Chloe, and her son straggle out of the church and meet up with Tibbett and Rosenfeld in a military hospital. When Boyce is confronted by his superiors about rumors of a top-secret lab near their target, he denies seeing anything suspicious. The liberation of Europe proceeds.

Overlord is partly a classic combat film centered on a close-knit band of brothers representing America's ethnic and geographic diversity. Boyce is African American; Rosenfeld is Jewish; Tibbett is a wise-cracking New Yorker; Ford is a mercurial and hardened soldier; and Chloe is an incredibly brave, resourceful, and beautiful Frenchwoman. Together, this slapdash team of commandos take on an elite SS unit guarding a terrible secret weapon. *Overlord* evokes war films like *Saving Private Ryan* (1998), *The Dirty Dozen* (1967), and *Where Eagles Dare* (1968) and military horror films like *The Bunker*, *Frankenstein's Army*, and the *Outpost* series. *Overlord* depicts war's horror and Nazi evil independent of the Nazi zombie premise. For example, the unit's African American sergeant is surrounded by German soldiers and brutally executed. The next scene depicts dead paratroopers swinging from trees as if lynched, backlit by the fiery wreckage of downed aircraft. The addition of zombie supermen escalates an already harrowing scenario for soldiers like Boyce and Rosenfeld, who quips moments before jumping into the night, "I'm a Jew. Do you know what they're going to do to me if they catch me?" The near rape of Chloe underscores the pervasive danger facing women in war. Wafner, an already irredeemable villain, transforms into a physically monstrous manifestation of the evil he serves, celebrating his newfound powers: "The one-thousand-year Reich needs one-thousand-year soldiers." While we can imagine the Nazis implementing a fiendish plan like creating zombie super soldiers, *Overlord* implies every nation is corruptible. Ford is an American soldier, but he is cold and instinctively violent, beating Wafner near death and demonstrating a callous disregard for both his own life and his comrades'. After injecting himself with the serum, Ford becomes as savage and uncontrollable as Wafner, but he has wherewithal to convince Boyce "no one should have this" before detonating the explosives destroying himself and any trace of the Nazi experiment. *Overlord* is the military horror film par excellence and an indication the normalization and universalization of the Third Reich only strengthens the farther it recedes into the past.

"I Am Anne Frank"

FX's successful series *American Horror Story* (2011–) (*AHS*) embeds its impressive ensemble cast in a different narrative each season, taking viewers on a journey through America's aberrant obsessions and preternatural fears—murder houses, clowns, witches, serial killers, the ascension of Donald Trump and his followers, and the apocalypse. Showrunners Ryan

Murphy and Brad Falchuk underscore American history's brutal treatment of minorities, women, the LBGTQ community, and the physically and mentally handicapped. The horror in these distinctly American stories derive from the oppressors and the oppressed engaging in a bloody cycle of cruelty and vengeance amid an apathetic, complacent, and affluent society slouching toward Armageddon. "I really think *American Horror Story* is about the darkness of society," Murphy notes. "It was always conceived to be a social statement on different things."[41] America's peculiar talent for ignoring its history, specifically anything painful or disturbing, is woven into each season's blood-soaked storyline.

Season 2 revolves around Briarcliff Manor, an early 1960s era asylum in remote Massachusetts populated with a combustible mix of the criminally insane, mentally and physically handicapped, and what the Third Reich called asocials. Operated by the Catholic Church, Briarcliff Manor is nominally run by Sister Jude Martin (Jessica Lange), a sadistic nun who abuses staff and patients alike in a vain effort to exorcise her personal demons. Sister Jude (like St. Jude, the patron saint of lost causes) is locked in a power struggle with medical director Dr. Arthur Arden (James Cromwell), who demands total autonomy over patients' treatment in furtherance of a depraved research agenda. Briarcliff Manor is, in Arden's words, "a receptacle for human waste. Each patient is an example of evolutionary failure."[42] It is also a receptacle for several interwoven plots referencing the particular obsessions and social anxieties of the era: a serial killer nicknamed Bloody Face (Zachary Quinto), who is revealed as Briarcliff's consulting psychiatrist and preys on fallen women; alien abduction; unethical and monstrous medical experimentation; satanic possession; authentic horrors associated with what passed for mental healthcare during this period (lobotomies, shock treatment, barbaric living conditions, gay conversion therapy); and the Holocaust. The season chronicles the rise and fall of this haunted space through the experience of Lana Winters (Sarah Paulson), an investigative journalist who is confined to Briarcliff Manor after threatening to expose abuses.

The Holocaust is alive and thriving at Briarcliff Manor. Formerly a tuberculosis ward where forty-six thousand perished, the asylum is now the domain of Sister Jude, an incarnation of Dyanne Thorne's *Ilsa: She Wolf of the SS* (1977), and the icy cold and unmistakably Teutonic Dr. Arden.[43] We see piles of shoes on cold cement floors, an underground death chute taking bodies of failed experimental subjects to an incinerator, and an efficient staff issuing fake death certificates to mask the killing process.[44] Arden's demeanor, penchant for torture, restrained sexuality, and indifference to human suffering suggests an archetypal Nazi doctor. When patient and suspected serial killer Kit Walker (Evan Peters) is caught infiltrating Arden's lab searching for evidence to secure his release, Arden's paranoia takes hold, accusing the boy of spying on his brilliant work. Arden asks is if he is Stasi (East German intelligence) or KGB. "I understand there are even elements in the US government," Arden sneers. "Oh yes, Jews and fellow travelers."[45] Who is Arden? Where did he come from? A new arrival to Briarcliff may have the answer, but there is a catch—the woman dropped off by the police is convinced she is none other than Anne Frank. When Anne (Franka Potente) encounters Arden in the common room, she is shaken to her core: "You were there! In Auschwitz! Nazi Schwein! Don't you remember me, Dr.? I'm Anne! Anne Frank!"[46] Dragged off to join the other lunatics, we are understandably skeptical of the deluded Anne, but her accusations regarding Arden ring true. Ryan Murphy compared the Anne Frank story to the Anastasia case because "there were many women who came forward after the diary and said, 'Well, I'm the real Anne Frank,' and they were struck down. Many of them were found to be mentally ill and suffering from schizophrenia."[47] Subjecting Anne Frank to the vagaries of an asylum in 1960s America seems particularly cruel, but somehow fitting.

The two-part episode "I Am Anne Frank" inserts the Holocaust and its attendant Nazi next door narrative directly into Briarcliff's dysfunctional reality. The episode begins when the woman claiming to be Anne Frank is brought to Briarcliff after stabbing ruffians during a bar fight for making antisemitic remarks. "I broke a beer bottle, I stabbed them," she boasts, "They will live, but they will never forget."[48] Anne immediately begins a diary at Briarcliff, addressing the entry to Kitty like the real Anne did:[49] "15 of November 1964 [note the European style of writing dates]: The walls are closing in. I can hardly breathe. It's Amsterdam all over again. But there are eyes everywhere. The eyes of madness and disease. These people are resigned to die here. We were never resigned. We always held on to a shred of hope."[50] Sister Jude drags the woman into her office: "Anne Frank, is it? What a relief it will be to millions of school children to know that you survived." Anne promptly tells her tale, explaining how easy it was to remain anonymous amidst thousands of corpses at Bergen-Belsen and disappear into Germany's rubble, living day to day as a pickpocket until meeting an American soldier. Her GI husband is conveniently dead, killed during the Korean War. When Anne's father published the famous diary, heavily edited as we know, Anne decided it was better to keep her secret: "People finally started paying attention to what they had done to us, all because of a martyred, fifteen-year-old girl. She had to stay fifteen. And a martyr. I could do more good dead than alive."[51] Sister Jude is unconvinced and offended. "Your story is indecent," she proclaims." "No!" Anne claps back in anger, "You are indecent! You have a Nazi war criminal working here!" Anne narrates a flashback depicting a young Arden (played by James Cromwell's son, John Cromwell) stalking the children's barracks at Auschwitz for twins for Mengele's experiments and passing out candy to young girls he wanted to "save." "And when they came back—*if* they came back—something had changed," Anne says. "He made them sick. Whatever he had done to them, they were afraid to speak out. They had been sworn to secrecy."[52] According to Anne, Arden's real name was Hans Gruber (or Grüpper).[53] As much as Sister Jude despises her nemesis, she does not believe Anne. Exasperated, Anne unveils her tattoo—A 40603. "I know where I came from, Sister. Can you say the same about your 'Dr. Arden?'"[54]

Everything Anne relates about Arden corroborates what we know of him thus far—he oversees cruel experiments designed to perfect the human race; he is obsessed with innocent and chaste women, specifically Sister Mary Eunice McKee (Lily Rabe); and police discover Nazi memorabilia in Arden's bedroom after investigating a vice charge against him after a violent encounter with a prostitute. Sister Jude presents her case to Monsignor Timothy Howard (Joseph Fiennes), her superior and unrequited love. The Monsignor is disappointed in Jude, crushing her by invoking her alcoholism and alluding to skeletons in her closet: "You'd rather see Nazi war criminals than look in the mirror."[55] But of course the Monsignor and Arden are partners in crime, an unholy and unlikely union of perverse science and faith intent on using what Howard described as "those whose lives otherwise serve no purpose . . . for the greater good."[56] Howard pulls Arden aside, worried about how close Sister Jude and Anne are to unveiling their project: "They're onto you, Arthur. If you have any housekeeping to do, I suggest you take care of it."[57] Heeding the warning, Arden lures Anne to his dungeon and denies her charges. Horrified and retraumatized by her surroundings, she produces a pistol she lifted off a detective. "Now's the time," she declares. "Confess, Hans Gruber, you Nazi piece of shit!" A struggle ensues and Arden is shot in the leg. Anne accidentally opens a room exposing Arden's latest victim, Shelley (Chloë Sevigny), now a horrible monster begging for death.

In part 2, Sister Jude persists in her investigation and contacts a Nazi hunter named Sam Goodman (Mark Margolis), who provides a historically accurate description of Project Paperclip, the American intelligence operation responsible for recruiting hundreds of ex-Nazi scientists into the national security state. Goodman relates how the Joint Intelligence Objectives Agency falsified records of desired scientists to prevent scrutiny and expedite immigration, allowing potential war criminals like Arden (Gruber) to live freely in the United States. Meanwhile, Anne's story starts to crumble when a man named Jim Brown (David Chisum) arrives at Briarcliff looking for his wife, Charlotte, claiming the incarcerated Anne is suffering from postpartum depression. Brown explains how Charlotte became obsessed

Fig. 3.2. Anne Frank survived the Holocaust only to be committed to an insane asylum in *American Horror Story: Asylum* (2012).

with the Holocaust and atrocity photos from Auschwitz, adopting Anne Frank's persona after mastering her story. Anne's anger at antisemitism, the tattoo, and her intimate knowledge of the event is the result of her condition. Brown brings his wife home, but soon returns after she tries to smother their baby. Arden seizes the opportunity to lobotomize Anne and neutralize the threat her memory poses. The episode ends with Anne (Charlotte) floating through life like a Stepford wife, packing away her wall of photos and clippings detailing the Holocaust. One photo depicts a young Arden in an SS uniform standing behind Adolf Hitler.

AHS's Anne Frank storyline concerns the construction and annihilation of memory. The Anne who is committed to Briarcliff is fully immersed in the growing Holocaust awareness taking hold in the United States after the Adolf Eichmann trial. Whether she is the real Anne or not is almost irrelevant—Briarcliff Anne understands that all that matters is the diary of a fifteen-year-old martyred girl. Sister Jude's snide comment about how millions of schoolchildren will be relieved belies America's facile understanding of the Holocaust, then and now. For decades, reading *The Diary of Anne Frank* represented children's only exposure to the black hole of the Holocaust. Parents and teachers preferred they take away her maudlin maxim, "In spite of everything I still believe people are really good at heart," and little else. Anne Frank belongs to everyone. Her true story is edited, redacted, and mythologized to the point that Briarcliff Anne's wild tale seems plausible.[58] Critics were taken aback by *AHS*'s stunning example of Holocaust impiety. Halle Kiefer wavered between fascination and horror watching the story unfold: "Oh lord, Anne Frank was a real person. It just isn't done! Am I being too delicate about this?"[59] Arden lobotomizing Anne destroyed her memory of his crimes and eliminates her fascination with the Holocaust. She packs the imagery away in a box and performs the roles assigned to her—dutiful wife and mother. Ryan Murphy accurately described season 2 as "a horror show for women in many regards."[60] Like Rosemary in *Rosemary's Baby*, Anne is medicalized, infantilized, and silenced by an indestructible patriarchal structure. Their stories are too hysterical to be believed, even when they know they are probably true. Anne's lobotomy is indicative of America's willful forgetting of Nazi crimes and our diminishing interest and memory of the Holocaust. The fact that an ex-Nazi hired by the US government is holding the scalpel is not totally insane.

"This Is the Master's Final Solution": Vampiric Nazis and the Quest for Immortality

Vampires persist as a staple in pop culture but bear little resemblance to either Bela Lugosi's *Dracula* (1931) or Max Schreck's *Nosferatu*. The heretofore heavily accented creatures from the East manifesting modernity's most entrenched anxieties emerged from the ashes of World War II with a new lease on life and representation. Vampires now go to high school, engage in sexual romps in the bayou, enjoin love triangles with werewolves and humans, terrorize humans, save humans, and are often hunted by humans. Modern vampires represent every race, class, gender, sexual orientation, and even political allegiance. Several films and series depict Nazis either turning to vampirism or vampires turning to Nazism to achieve immortality and world domination. The very antisemitic characteristics ascribed to vampires in the nineteenth and early twentieth centuries—physical monstrosity, sexual deviance, pestilence, and the unholy union of blood and gold—characterize vampiric Nazis haunting the postwar screen. If Nazi zombies are the residue of the Third Reich, shuffling, aimless, and unwelcome reminders of an unmasterable past, Nazi vampires are sentient and driven monsters intent on turning the globe into a wasteland. The Nazi supernatural imaginary imbued Jews with extraordinary powers they subconsciously coveted for themselves. Now living in exile and catastrophic defeat, Nazi vampires have flipped the script and embrace the evil they sought to exterminate, enacting various plots they once accused Jews of hatching in their quest to rule over humanity.

Joel Schumacher's *Lost Boys* (1987) reinvigorated the vampire genre by situating a teenage coming-of-age story in a small coastal California town beset by biker vampires. Starring a host of popular young actors, *Lost Boys* enjoyed tremendous commercial success and quickly entered cult status.

Schumacher revisits the genre with *Blood Creek* (2009), a smaller and much darker film set in rural West Virginia in which a Nazi scholar torments a family and the surrounding countryside with bizarre occult rituals. The film begins in 1936 when a family of German immigrants, the Wollners, receive a letter from the German government offering desperately needed financial relief in exchange for hosting a visiting professor. The family accepts and awaits the arrival of Richard Wirth (Michael Fassbender), an SS academic dispatched to America in search of ancient rune stones purportedly deposited in the area by Viking explorers. Using the Wollners as test subjects, Wirth seeks to harness the supernatural powers of the stones in bloody experiments designed to achieve immortality. The Wollners trap Wirth in a cellar but are forced to sacrifice locals to sustain both themselves and Wirth for the next seventy years until one victim, Victor Marshall (Dominic Purcell), escapes. Seeking revenge, Victor brings his brother Evan (Henry Cavill) back to the Wollner house and unwittingly frees the now monstrously deformed and powerful Wirth. The Wollners reveal their dark secrets to Evan, particularly the practice of kidnapping and draining victims' blood to keep Wirth and the ageless Wollner family alive. The Marshall brothers forge an alliance of convenience with the Wollners and plot to kill Wirth. Once Wirth is decapitated, the Wollners rapidly age and perish, but not before revealing that SS leader Heinrich Himmler sent eight additional agents like Wirth to retrieve rune stones in the area. The film ends with Evan packing a car with weapons, maps, and the secret to killing the Nazi occultists bleeding Appalachia dry.

Joel Schumacher called *Blood Creek* a "Nazi zombie vampire movie" inspired by the Third Reich's obsession with the occult.[61] An admirer of Fritz Lang, Schumacher approximates the look and feel of German expressionism. The film's disturbing premise is that the Nazis were right—blood is mystical, powerful, and the key to immortality. Wirth declares the rune stone on the Wollner farm proof "Nordic Gods were here" and that "those who came before rule the blood."[62] The film unwittingly gives credence to Nazi mythology and occult pseudoscience by portraying Wirth as a superior being whose presumptions about the power of blood and the rune stones were correct all along. Wirth's ultimate goal is to acquire a third eye, a reference to the ancient Aryan religious belief that an inner eye provides perception beyond normal sight. Wirth acquires the eye and extraordinary strength by consuming the blood of the weak, who are captured and presented to Wirth in an abandoned metal boxcar resembling the distinctive red boxcars synonymous with decades of Holocaust representation. Wirth failed to complete his mission of providing Hitler immortality, but he wreaks havoc on American soil in a quest for racial superiority. The Wollners are not without blame even if they too are victims of the infernal plot.

Victor condemns them for inaction. He drags Mrs. Wollner (Joy McBrinn) to a window overlooking the boxcar and forces her to admit she did nothing to help him.[63] As Evan marks the locations of other rune stones, a swastika takes shape on his map. Resolved to extirpate the Nazi zombie vampires entrenched in his unique American subculture, Evan, a veteran, jumps into a pickup truck with a sizable American flag emblazoned on its side and disappears into the bucolic landscape. *Blood Creek* portrays Nazi atrocities on American soil, not just in the past when the Third Reich projected evil globally, but in a post-9/11 environment marked by fear of terrorism and internal rot.[64]

Once described as "the world's worst film director" and a "schlockmeister," infamous German director Uwe Boll is known for adapting video games into gory and hypersexual features.[65] Boll released two movies in 2011—the cheap horror film *BloodRayne: The Third Reich* and the docudrama *Auschwitz*. The *BloodRayne* franchise revolves around an alluring female vampire who in this film joins anti-Nazi partisans in Eastern Europe. Rayne (Natassia Malthe) uses her powers to brutalize the enemy and uncovers an SS plot to turn Hitler and other top Nazis into vampires. Once the plan is derailed Rayne liberates a labor camp with her human allies, breaking through the "Arbeit macht Frei" gate and ending the movie with an Arnold Schwarzneggaresque line, "Guten Tag, motherfuckers."[66]

Auschwitz is no less exploitative and bloody, although Boll's misguided quest for authenticity is noteworthy given the near-universal taboo against representing the killing process in Holocaust films. Boll intended to show what he called "the full horror" of Auschwitz and the "real, everyday truth" of Third Reich atrocities. Boll referenced his German identity to justify the graphic nature of the film, arguing, "Every German is obliged to ensure that the Holocaust is not forgotten . . . For a director like me who is known for explicit depictions of violence, it is my duty to use precisely this talent to show people the atrocities of the Nazis."[67] Critics and audiences did not share his perspective. *Stern* critic Sophie Albers wrote, "The words Auschwitz and Uwe Boll in one breath rightly leads one to fear the worst," predicting the film would cause "outrage, confusion and panic."[68] While Boll is rightfully chastised for graphically depicting mass gassings, even casting himself as an SS guard who pulls the lever and treating the real Auschwitz as just another canvas for horror, he stands in stark contrast to mainstream German cinema's silence on Nazi atrocities. Horror cinema can "fulfill a significant socio-cultural and psycho-political function" Linnie Blake argues, specifically by exploring psychic injuries wrought by nations' participation in war crimes, but neither Uwe Boll's horror nor his "historical" films are particularly substantive examples.[69]

Based on Guillermo del Toro and Chuck Hogan's trilogy of novels, FX's *The Strain* (2014–2017) reimagines *Dracula* and *Nosferatu* for the modern era, but infuses the story with Nazi vampires, apocalyptic and genocidal plots against humanity, and multiple Holocaust plot points. *The Strain* is an inspired addition to the vampire genre because it invokes Gothic antisemitism, Nazi supernatural imaginary, and Holocaust imagery from documentary footage and feature films. Nazi propaganda successfully linked Jews to the infamous blood libel accusing them of murdering young gentiles for life-sustaining blood rituals, engineering the unholy union of unfettered capitalism and political influence, and blamed Jews for spreading both infectious and ideological diseases responsible for corrupting the blood and destroying nations. However, in *The Strain* it is the Master and his Nazi helper, Thomas Eichorst (Richard Sammel) who hatch a plot to transform humanity into either subservient creatures or food. The Master, an ancient vampiric creature called the strigoi, conceived of his plan feeding on victims in Treblinka and watching the Holocaust unfold in his native Eastern Europe. What better way for the Master to achieve world domination than reward Nazi practitioners of genocide with immortality under the leadership of a more reliable führer? The Master and Eichorst torment the human resistance, mostly Jews and other ethnic minorities, with insight into their endgame—the fall of humanity. Hitler predicted the same fate in *Mein Kampf*: "If . . . the Jew is victorious over the other peoples of the world, his crown will be the funeral wreath of humanity and this planet will, as it did thousands of years ago, move through the ether devoid of men."[70] *The Strain* explores the progression of a Nazi-inspired vampiric plot to accomplish precisely what the Nazis accused Jews of conspiring for centuries.

The series begins when a plane from Berlin arrives in New York City and promptly goes dark, prompting civil authorities and the CDC to investigate what they assume is a possible bioterrorist incident. CDC scientist Ephraim "Eph" Goodweather (Corey Stoll) and his team are confounded by what first appears to be a planeload of dead passengers and crew and no known cause. As chaos grips the airport, Gus Elizalde (Miguel Gomez) is paid by Eichorst to retrieve an enormous wooden box containing the Master. Watching the news unfold, Abraham Setrakian (David Bradley), a pawnbroker and Holocaust survivor with personal knowledge of the Master and Eichorst, rushes to the airport to warn the CDC of the terrible danger. Meanwhile, the passengers mysteriously awaken from their catatonic state. The CDC releases passengers from quarantine, although Eph is convinced doing so will have fateful consequences. The remainder of the season alternates between the cat and mouse game pitting Setrakian and newfound allies Eph, city exterminator Vasily Fet (Kevin Durand), and talented hacker Dutch Velders (Ruda Gedmintas) against those responsible for facilitating the Master's plan to infest New York. The principal collaborator is the sickly billionaire Eldritch Palmer (Jonathan Hyde), whose quest for good health and longevity leads him to Eichorst and the Master shortly after World War II. Palmer's fortune is key to spreading the strain and undermining the civic response. The season explores the backstories of principal characters; Eph's alcoholism and relationship with estranged wife Kelly (Natalie Brown) and son Zach (Max Charles); Setrakian's journey from Treblinka prisoner, to professor, to embittered pawnbroker and strigoi hunter; Eichorst's parallel life as a devoted Nazi and transformation into the Master's loyal servant; Fet's path from promising Ukrainian architecture student to rat exterminator; Gus struggling with his criminal past and family obligations as the crisis grows; and Dutch's redemption for unwittingly helping Palmer's nefarious plot. The season ends with Setrakian's group cornering and presumably killing the Master, but his essence escapes unharmed and assumes a new host.

Season 2 continues the hunt for the Master, fills in backstories, and depicts the race to stop the strain's accelerated diffusion with a bioweapon. Although Eph saved Zach, Kelly is turned into a strigoi and empowered by the Master to hunt for her son and neutralize Eph. Details of Palmer's plot emerge, specifically the construction of major factories resembling slaughterhouses and registration centers masquerading as humanitarian aid. Setrakian scours New York for a medieval manuscript called the *Occido Lumen* containing the secret to destroying the strain and the Master, although Eichorst is desperate to retrieve it first. Meanwhile, the city has a new champion—Staten Island councilwoman Justine Feraldo (Samantha Mathis). While other boroughs struggle to secure neighborhoods from strigoi, Feraldo fortifies Staten Island and methodically and publicly butchers strigoi, elevating her profile. Capitalizing on the political chaos, Feraldo is given emergency powers to apply her methods citywide. We also learn the Master has powerful enemies, other strigoi called the Ancients and a half human–half strigoi named Quinlan (Rupert Penry-Jones). Quinlan and Gus are recruited by the Ancients and join Setrakian's quest to destroy the Master. Eph engineers a bioweapon after experimenting on the infected, but his alcoholism rages and Zach lashes out against his father for failing to protect his mother. The season concludes as the group prepares to escape New York on the last train and Setrakian outbids Eichorst and Palmer during an auction for the *Lumen*, but Kelly and her special child unit of strigoi called the Feelers derail the train and kidnap Zach. A massive coordinated strigoi attack undoes Feraldo's progress, leaving the city an infested war zone.

Season 3 begins with the original team scattered throughout the city, desperate to survive and help the military and police exterminate the strigoi.

As Setrakian pours over the *Lumen*, Eph discovers a method to disrupting the Master's voice and renders the legions of strigoi vulnerable and useless. Zach is now protected by his strigoi mother, several Feelers, and Eichorst. Palmer grows to resent the Master because he was promised immortality, not fleeting improvement in health. The rift pushes erstwhile enemies Palmer and Setrakian together to unravel what Palmer started, although other human collaborators fill the void. All the parties converge at the port to retrieve two nuclear warheads from the former Soviet Union, but the Master's agents win the day and use one warhead to destroy the Ancients' underground lair. The remaining warhead is intended for New York City proper. Seeking a new host, the Master takes Palmer's withered body, finally granting him immortality. Eichorst continues to oversee the death factories in preparation for the plan's final phase. The season ends when the resistance group reassembles and unleashes Eph's device, breaking communication between the Master and strigoi. With the Master seemingly defeated and encased in a silver coffin, Eph finds Zach in the Master's hideout, but is forced to kill Kelly. Overcome with rage at his father, Zach detonates the warhead and destroys the city, freeing the Master and inadvertently sparking a nuclear war.

The final season occurs months later during the Night Eternal, the nuclear winter enabling the Master's nightmarish reign over humanity's remnant. The Partnership between humans and strigoi is a fiction designed to prepare human survivors for the blood-draining factories Eichorst built. The group is broken and divided, with only Fet and Quinlan helping Setrakian secure more nuclear warheads. Dutch is captured and forced into a strigoi breeding program managed by the Partnership and an embittered Eph survives day to day in nearby Philadelphia, still reeling from Zach's betrayal. Zach is now the Master's apprentice and Eichorst's rival. While the world outside suffers and starves, Zach is groomed to be as ruthless as the Master, although his human traits stubbornly remain. Eph rediscovers the resistance and renews his determination to either liberate or kill Zach and the Master while Fet and Quinlan sneak the warheads into Manhattan. The group discovers the truth behind the Partnership and the vast network of death camps intended to bleed humanity dry. Dutch escapes the breeding program, which she discovers is designed to produce babies who carry the strigoi's preferred blood type, and rejoins the group. The series concludes with the final showdown between Setrakian and Eichorst, killing both, and a last-ditch plot to lure the Master within range of another smuggled nuclear warhead. Sensing the danger, the Master sends Zach to locate Eph and root out the resistance. Once he does, the Master arrives to finish off the group and makes Eph his new host, embracing Zach and proclaiming their eternal reign of darkness. Overcome with guilt, Zach holds the Master (and his father) tight and detonates the warhead. The final scene is set years in the future with Fet narrating how he, Dutch, and Gus are rebuilding New York and honoring the sacrifices of those who destroyed the strain.

Guillermo del Toro's conception of horror avoids assigning binary moral judgments on what is good and evil, monstrous and human.[71] Often his human characters, usually men in uniform holding positions of authority, torment monsters and marginalized human populations alike. Hardly sympathetic creatures, *The Strain*'s strigoi resemble ratlike Nosferatus with vile stingers emerging from their mouths to drain victims. However, the speed with which the Master overthrows New York is a product of civic ineptitude, high capitalism, and the legacy of genocide—all human failures. The veneer of civilization collapses within weeks as humanity predictably feeds on itself, seeking accommodation and temporary advantage with indescribable evil. Setrakian's experiences in Treblinka are replicated before his weary eyes as Eichorst and armies of human collaborators deliver humanity on a platter (albeit not silver).[72] Children are both vulnerable and menacing in del Toro films and Zach Goodweather is no exception.[73] Zach, a product of a broken family and an alcoholic father, succumbs to anger and resentment and inadvertently helps destroy humanity. Kelly's Feelers were originally blind children taken from their school bus and systematically turned to serve evil. Children are nonjudgmental and fully emotional characters, del Toro notes, capable of embodying traumatic experience and revealing humanity's complicity in whatever horrible scenario is responsible for causing it.[74] The children in *The Strain* are both victims and perpetrators.

Del Toro wrote several episodes and directed *The Strain*'s premiere "Night Zero," demonstrating his affinity for F. W. Murnau's expressionist style and an encyclopedic knowledge of the vampire genre. *The Strain* begins like *Nosferatu*, with the arrival of a mysterious vessel from the east carrying a coffin filled with contaminated soil. Instead of Count Orlok's rats swarming from the vessel *Demeter* and spreading the plague in Wisborg, the Master's coffin unloaded at John F. Kennedy International Airport is filled with revolting worms carrying the vampiric strain. Rats play a prominent role in *The Strain*, but their desperate attempt to escape the underground serves to warn exterminators like Fet something terrible is lurking below. In the series finale, Fet realizes New York is healthy and back to normal only when he notices rat droppings on the sidewalk. Nazi propaganda regularly equated Jews to both vermin and vampires.[75] The Master, who shares Count Orlok's rodent features (red eyes, pointed ears, and claws) dispenses white worms from his blood and initiates what amounts to a Nazi-inspired infestation.[76] Gothic antisemitism portrayed the vampire as a creature from the east engaged in insidious reverse colonization, a metaphor easily digested by Western European audiences fearful and contemptuous of Eastern Jews, especially in the wake of World War I. *The Strain* once again flips this familiar script by having Jews (Setrakian and Eph) and other minorities hunt the vampires who come perilously close to placing the funeral wreath on humanity.

Other similarities between *The Strain* and *Nosferatu* include powerful human enablers, imperiled Aryan women, and the collapse of rational state authority once confronted with disease and civil strife. Gothic vampires from Eastern Europe infiltrate powerful nations like England and Germany, but the Master, whose plane originates in Berlin, decides New York City is the logical place from which to oversee world domination. Orlok recruits Knock, a real estate agent in Wisborg, by promising him great influence in exchange for facilitating his arrival. With the city dying and Orlok disembarking from his ship in search of Ellen's sweet neck, Knock goes mad and runs through streets screaming, "The master is near, the master is near!"[77] Eldritch Palmer is an immensely wealthy version of Knock, an opportunist drunk on the promise of power and immortality conditioned to obey his master. Vampires feasting on beautiful, pure, and often blonde women is a staple of the genre, one Veit Harlan skillfully manipulates in *Jud Süss*. In *Nosferatu*, Ellen sacrifices herself to stop Orlok and protect Hutter just as Dorothea (Greta Schröder) submits to Oppenheimer's rape in an attempt to save her fiancé in *Jud Süss*. Dutch Velders in *The Strain* is neither virginal or pure, but the beautiful blonde is nearly drained in an elaborate torture chamber by none other than Eichorst. In a flashback to pre–Nazi Germany, we witness Eichorst court a blonde woman in his sales office, but she rejects him after he rants about the Jews. It turns out Eichorst's love interest was Jewish. A few years later, now–SS officer Thomas Eichorst consigned the woman and her family to certain death. Eichorst can drink the blood of anyone he chooses but leering over Dutch is an act of power and erotic wish fulfillment originating in his Nazi past. Finally, in *Nosferatu* the state is impotent to stop the plague, as evidenced by a deserted Wisborg and overflowing graveyards. In *The Strain*, every government organ from the CDC to the Navy SEALs is corrupt, incompetent, or hapless. Within a month of the Master's arrival the once great city is a wasteland. The state hastens humanity's demise, never prevents it; only a woman or child's sacrifice vanquishes the vampire.[78]

Abraham Setrakian is a modern incarnation of Abraham van Helsing, a learned man driven by the singular mission of hunting his vampire archnemesis. Setrakian first encounters Eichorst at Treblinka and the Master during the night in his barracks. Attracted to human misery and the lure of an endless supply of helpless victims, the Master hovers over sleeping prisoners and drinks their blood before disappearing into the night. As his friends perish from selections, shootings, and the Master's visits, Setrakian manages to survive by demonstrating talent as a wood carver. Eichorst entrusts him with the task of making what will become the Master's wooden coffin, which Setrakian completes shortly before Soviet troops enter the area. Setrakian escapes with his life, but it is a sad one as he is haunted by the horrors he witnessed in the camp. Setrakian pursues the Master across Europe, losing his wife, academic career, and any semblance of a fulfilling life in the process. Setrakian is introduced to us as an embittered old pawnbroker living in pre-gentrification Brooklyn. He bears a striking resemblance in both appearance and demeanor to Sol Nazerman in *The Pawnbroker.* Even the pawnshops are similar.[79] Setrakian and Nazerman are former professors turned pawnbrokers whose wives are murdered by German perpetrators. The two characters bear the burden of traumatic memories and react by building walls between themselves and the rest of humanity. Setrakian's memories serve to link the Holocaust of history to the supernatural genocide, inspiring him to act and reminding us that the past is never truly the past. Eichorst torments Setrakian like Rodriguez torments Nazerman, telling him, "I want you to watch it unfold. Unable to do anything to stop it."[80]

The lifelong feud between Eichorst and Setrakian is reignited by the arrival of the Master's plane in present-day New York, prompting Setrakian to storm the airport with his silver sword-cane in hand. Quickly jailed, a prisoner is intrigued by his tattoo: "That's some ancient ink you got there, old man. Numbers? . . . . Mean anything?" "Only to me," Setrakian responds.[81] Eichorst addresses Setrakian by that number, 808325, throughout the series. Finding him in jail, Eichorst mocks him and declares, "The great game is over, Jew." Amused by his persistence, Eichorst continuously derides Setrakian as if he were still under his control in Treblinka. "You're not a hero or a savior," Eichorst says, "you're just a number. I took your name and gave you that number."[82] Later, as Setrakian mounts a resistance and corners Eichorst in the subways, Eichorst relishes the prospect of the duel, "Fitting that we should end our journey where it began, on a train platform." Setrakian escapes with the aid of his new friends, Eph and Fet, but Eichorst is secretly pleased the ultimate battle is delayed and once again refers to Setrakian's former life as an inmate carpenter: "I give you another day of life, Jew, for services rendered."[83] When Setrakian and Eichorst face off in the bidding war for the *Lumen*, Eichorst cannot resist calling his nemesis "pawnbroker" and laughing at the prospect of taking the *Lumen* from him "with a simple transaction of gold." Eichorst digs deeper, alluding to Setrakian's murdered wife, Miriam, "Tally all the things I've taken from you."[84] Months later, with the world on the brink of collapse, Eichorst and an enfee-

Fig. 3.3. Thomas Eichorst (Richard Sammel) prepares to feast on his human prey in *The Strain* (2014–2017).

bled Setrakian meet one last time. No match for his physical strength, Setrakian poisons himself and allows Eichorst to drink his blood. As they both lay dying, Setrakian has the last word," My name is Abraham Setrakian and I am not a number anymore."[85] That Eichorst, the parasitic Aryan strigoi, chokes on Jewish blood is a fitting end.

In a selfish and complacent world, Setrakian speaks with the authority of the Holocaust survivor. Setrakian's special insight into evil serves to educate his band of resistance fighters on history's terrible lessons. "In order to defeat the Master," Setrakian cautions, "we must become as cold and ruthless and savage as he is and yet not become monsters ourselves."[86] However, Setrakian is unimpressed with Councilwoman Feraldo's draconian tactics intended to defend what she calls the Homeland. "Homeland, Fatherland . . . When politicians use these words it usually precedes murder on a grand scale," he tells Eph.[87] Unable to comprehend the strain's true nature and origins, Setrakian tells the incredulous group, "I know my cause may seem hopeless, but I've seen what happens when people stand by and do nothing. Inaction is the greatest evil."[88] Setrakian struggled in the first days to overcome the team's reticence to butcher strigoi who until recently were human beings: "Being good means nothing unless you are willing to do what must be done when it must be done."[89] When Vasiliy nervously confesses to Setrakian that his grandfather, a Soviet prisoner of war, collaborated with the Nazis in Treblinka in order to survive, Setrakian releases him from a burden he knows all too well—survivor's guilt: "Some men seek not the right path, but the safer one. Some men believe in survival no matter the cost. You need to forgive him."[90] Setrakian knows the

Master thrives "on human self-interest and bureaucratic complacency," modernity's curse, and concludes season 1 with the dark prediction that the Master will use "the infrastructure we so obligingly arranged. Are we destined to be cattle for monsters?"[91] Setrakian comes to realize magic books like the *Lumen* will not defeat the Master because he relies on human collaborators. Defeating them will defeat the Master. Sanjay Desai (Cas Anvar), the architect of the blood factories built for the Master, explains to Setrakian, "I was just doing my job." Setrakian's response is predictable, but bears the weight of personal experience: "As said by countless facilitators of genocide throughout time."[92] Setrakian also observes a busload of people separated into two groups, children wailing as they are taken from their parents. "I have seen this before," he mutters.[93] Weak and dying, Setrakian leaves Eph with the conviction that the Master is vulnerable to human resistance because his plan is inspired by humans: "This is what the Master learned from the death camps. How to subjugate an entire people and how to coerce them into obedience and organizing and administering their own demise. He learned it from us."[94]

Although a strigoi, Thomas Eichorst maintains his human appearance to handle the Master's dealings in civil society. When we first see him apply makeup, select a suit, and conceal his fangs, Eichorst inspects himself proudly and whispers into the mirror, "Zum Sieg" (to victory).[95] Blonde, trim, and blue eyed, Eichorst is every bit the SS officer in contemporary New York as he was at Treblinka, where he first pledged fealty to the Master. Upon learning the Master's coffin arrived safely from the airport, Eichorst surveys Manhattan from the top of Palmer's building: "I look out over this island and I savor what is to come. Purity."[96] In a flashback featuring Eichorst and Setrakian in Treblinka, Eichorst confides to his slave laborer that "a new Reich could emerge from the ashes with a new Führer who could deliver what Hitler promised, but more."[97] In a flashback from 1967, Eichorst recruits a former SS doctor to disrupt Setrakian with the promise of renewed power and relevance. "A new Führer has emerged," Eichorst informs his compatriot, "wiser and stronger than the first. He needs soldiers like you to serve as instruments for his unshakeable will."[98] The use of the word "unshakeable," a favorite of Hitler's, underscores the connection between the two nightmarish visions. Eichorst's transformation from an elite SS officer who condemned Jews as parasites and leeches into an actual parasitic leech upends the tenets of Gothic antisemitism.[99] In *The Strain*, the vampire Nazis are vile harbingers of modernity, not the Jews.

Eichorst and the Master share Nazism's contempt for Judeo-Christian beliefs, hoping the Holocaust and humanity's collapse from the strain is enough to convince Setrakian he is powerless and abandoned. When Setrakian first catches sight of the Master draining another prisoner, he cowers but is derided by the strigoi for praying: "Where is your God? There is no one here to help you, wood carver." Later, when the camp falls Setrakian tracks Eichorst to a cave but hesitates to fight him. Eichorst scoffs, "Much easier to do nothing, isn't it? Safer. If that God you believe in really does exist, what do you suppose he would think of you?"[100] Decades later they meet again, separated by prison bars, "You still cling to the illusion you will prevail," Eichorst tells Setrakian. "Don't tell me you still believe in that God of yours. So, where is he? Why has he done nothing? Face the truth. He's nothing but a figment of your imagination."[101] Setrakian accuses Eichorst of following "a false messiah who will prove as horrific as the last one."[102] The ethos of the Master and his followers is unadorned Darwinism, a perspective Hitler and other Nazi personalities embraced to justify everything from war to euthanasia. The sickly Eldritch Palmer rationalizes his complicity by citing the brutal laws of nature: "Dominant species ravage the land and make it its own. This is a fact beyond morality or conscience or sentiment. Recognizing change is the key to survival."[103] With the Master's plan in full swing, Desai denies the existence of death camps but argues draining the blood of babies and the weak is a positive contribution for all involved. The ease with which humanity enables its own destruction is a recurring theme in *The Strain*.

Although Eichorst anticipates destroying all of humanity, he is still obsessed with Jews and consistently compares the new, grander genocide with the Holocaust he helped perpetrate. Hunting for Setrakian in the subway, Eichorst interrogates Eph's colleague Jim (Sean Astin): "Where's the Jew? I can smell him. . . . You're on the wrong side of history. You . . . could still be a part of a glorious new order."[104] Eichorst discerns Eph's Jewish background as well, calling for him in an abandoned Brooklyn factory: "Where did your people originate from? Poland? Ukraine? Lithuania? What was their original name? Goldstein? Gottlieb? I can smell your sweat. Like the old man [Setrakian]. Bitter. Like the Dead Sea." When Eph fires on him with an old German rifle, Eichorst smiles, "That takes me back. The satisfying crack of a Mauser 98."[105] Eichorst's sixth sense for identifying Jews or otherwise referencing the Holocaust in the present amuses him. During a forced moment of civility with Eichorst the CDC director mentions he once went to a conference in Munich. "I didn't care for it," he says. Eichorst assesses the man and smiles broadly, "You wouldn't." Eichorst is charged with building the first of many blood factories using contractors perplexed by the architectural plans. One engineer asks him if it "is some European model." Eichorst grins knowingly as he caresses the metal hooks and walks through the macabre industrial space, "It's origins are European, yes."[106] Weeks later Eichorst witnesses a demonstration of the factory and insists on a live subject to simulate real conditions. The observers watch in horror as the blood-drained corpse collapses in a heap before the nonfunctioning oven. "We don't want these things piling up, do we?" Eichorst says authoritatively. In the final season, Dutch stumbles into the fully functional factory and watches the efficient assembly line at work. Eichorst's genius for organized murder leaves its mark on two centuries.

The Strain's aesthetic derives in part from expressionism and Holocaust films. From *The Pawnbroker* to *Schindler's List*, New York's descent into tragedy and chaos is best represented by drawing from the reservoir of Holocaust imagery. There is a scene with rats swarming out of a sewer reminiscent of *The Eternal Jew*; piles of clothes and personal items left on train tracks; and a massive death camp built on a snowy wasteland so clearly designed on Auschwitz that Eph can only respond, "This is the Master's Final Solution. We're not the farmers, we're the livestock."[107] The Partnership that was created to expedite the butchering of human survivors is marked by back and red armbands and a network of concentration camps designed as freedom centers. Every action initiated by Eichorst, Palmer, and other witting and unwitting human collaborators is grounded in the Holocaust's proven machinery of death. The Master selects the World Trade Center grounds for his nest because, as Setrakian notes, he "is drawn to places of great human misery. He seeks out suffering."[108] Holocaust representation in *The Strain* corresponds to and illuminates Guillermo del Toro's recurring themes in his films and writings. The series' talented writers, directors, and actors create a harrowing tale about humanity's demise at the hands of vampiric creatures seeking to replicate the Holocaust. The strigoi are unspeakably horrible monsters and the Master is a formidable and ancient foe, but as Setrakian reminds us, he learned the art of genocide from us.

4

The View from Hell

Demons, Antichrists, and the Persistence of Evil after the Holocaust

When it comes to cinema, evil is simply a form of entertainment to me.
—Roman Polanski

American horror films came into their own during the turbulent 1960s and 1970s by channeling racial violence, crises in the patriarchal family, the collapse of political stability and public trust, and latent fears that supposedly vanquished foes are destined to return in force. Channeling the freedom and fiercely independent spirit of European New Wave cinema and the shake-up of the American studio system, directors like George Romero, Wes Craven, and John Carpenter crafted inexpensive and immensely popular films that reshaped the genre.[1] Horror films from this period mark a departure from portraying Gothic, fantastic monsters who scare audiences with suggestive mayhem to more human and relatable fiends committing graphic violence on screen. Examining films appearing a generation removed from World War II and the Holocaust, Adam Lowenstein asks rhetorically whether we can interpret this transition as a "response to, and an engagement with, the traumatic impact of war. . . . Does the modern horror film . . . draw on the war for the fiber of many of its representations?"[2] World War II's unprecedented carnage combined with grisly images emerging from death camps and liberated concentration camps redefined horror for succeeding generations, saturating Western culture. The Holocaust quickly became an archetype for evil in the modern world, a cautionary tale for modernity itself because it suggested the institutions on which we rely are weak, unreliable, and possibly malevolent. The concomitant disasters of Vietnam, Watergate, and the devolution of civil and racial discourse fueled American cynicism about a noble past and viable future. Horror connected to history, or the very recent past, resonated more with a traumatized public than Gothic monsters.

Alfred Hitchcock was already a master of suspense before World War II, but his postwar films took a decidedly darker turn. Hitchcock joined Allied efforts to document the enormity of Nazi crimes. Several prominent British and American directors lent their considerable skills to editing the footage into a historical archive intended to aid the Nuremberg trials. Hitchcock participated in editing films from Buchenwald and Dachau, especially portions underscoring the proximity of the camps to German residential areas. Hitchcock wanted the world to know ordinary Germans knew everything and nothing was staged. After seeing British Army Film and Photographic Unit footage of Bergen-Belsen, Hitchcock was reportedly so traumatized he did not return to work for a week.[3] The liberation footage lingers on the reactions of the liberators, hardened warriors astonished and horrified by the gruesome discovery. The now-iconic mass graves and emaciated corpses appear to be footage from another planet, a world so far removed from the one we thought we knew that reality itself feels suspect. This feeling of unease and perpetual shock at man's capacity for evil informs Hitchcock's classic films. Hitchcock critic Robin Wood notes *Psycho* (1960) is grounded in the twin horrors of the concentration camps: "the utter helplessness and innocence of the victims, and the fact that human beings, whose potentialities all of us in some measure share, were their tormentors and butchers."[4] *The Birds* (1963) is terrifying because the mundane suddenly turns menacing, exposing the meaninglessness and absurdity of life. The flock of birds is "a concrete embodiment of the arbitrary and unpredictable," Wood writes, noting Hitchcock claimed the film was about complacency.[5] Even before the Holocaust entered public consciousness, the master of horror explored some of the unsettling legacies of genocide—the precariousness of existence and humanity's indifference to suffering.

As Sidney Lumet's *The Pawnbroker* suggests, Holocaust cinema in the 1960s began to frame creative responses to trauma while making explicit comparisons between the event and contemporary issues.[6] Global turmoil, ethnic and racial violence, economic malaise, especially in the West, and the crisis in democratic governments suggested the structural forces responsible for sustaining the Third Reich were alive and well. The spate of formative horror films produced just a few decades after the war reflecting these issues include such classics as *Rosemary's Baby* (1968), *The Boys from Brazil* (1978), *The Exorcist* (1973), *The Omen* (1976), and *The Shining* (1980). Coincidentally (or not), prominent Jewish directors made these celebrated horror films—Roman Polanski, William Friedkin, Richard Donner, and Stanley Kubrick. Jewish novelist Ira Levin wrote both *Rosemary's Baby* and *The Boys from Brazil*. The degree to which these directors drew on their experience and perspectives regarding the Holocaust varies and is open to interpretation, but living with the legacy of the Holocaust influenced them profoundly. This chapter explores how these films and those inspired by them utilized Holocaust and Third Reich themes and imagery to communicate a specific notion of evil in the postwar world, one where the demonic forces responsible for historic crimes still operate in the shadows, probing for vulnerabilities in a world seemingly restored. I also examine the extent to which these classics influence our current notions of evil and the degree to which the Holocaust remains a referent in the horror genre.

The Hitler Wave and *The Boys from Brazil*

Hundreds of prominent Nazis fled abroad via ratlines after World War II, eluding prosecution for war crimes and establishing havens in friendly environs like South America. Josef Mengele, Adolf Eichmann, Klaus Barbie, and others in the German military, SS, and Nazi Party organizations flourished in hiding. Some even lived openly while amateur Nazi hunters and some governments scoured the globe for traces of these notorious figures.[7] The sensational capture and trial of Adolf Eichmann not only generated intense interest in the Holocaust, it prompted a flurry of speculation about who else was out there and what they were planning. Imaginations ran wild as writers and directors capitalized on the lurid details of potential Fourth Reichs popping up around the world.[8] Of course, one did not need to look far to find Nazis living and working freely in uncomfortable proximity to the institutions they once directed to commit mass murder. Liliana Cavani's controversial film *The Night Porter* (1974) delves into the bizarrely intimate and sadomasochistic relationship between a concentration camp commandant working in postwar Vienna as a hotel night porter and his former prisoner. The unlikely couple run afoul of a secret society of ex-Nazis created to protect their identities and are murdered in the final scene. Cavani sought to capture the continuities between the past and present, defending her film as a commentary on our willingness to forget:

> Fascism is not only an event of yesterday. It is with us still, here and elsewhere. As dreams do, my film brings back to the surface a repressed "history" . . . What interested me was to explore this cellar of the present, to inquire into the human subconscious; it was to offer up that which troubles me in order to trouble others so that all of us can live wakefully. It was to stimulate, to give a point of departure for

> understanding why the fascists are again among us—not the old ones, the nostalgics who are, one might say, caricatures, but the new ones, the young antidemocrats of my generation.[9]

The phenomenon of the Nazis next door inspired serious investigative journalism and cultural reflection. It also revived compelling conspiracy theories about Hitler's death and other Nazis' great escape.

Adolf Eichmann's trial famously introduced the idea of the desk chair murderer and the banality of evil. Nazis suddenly appeared more like us than monstrous figures from the recent nightmarish past. The perennial obsession with Hitler crested in the 1970s with a parade of biographies and focused scholarly attention regarding the origins of the Third Reich and its place in history. This so-called Hitler wave marked a shift away from considering Hitler "demonic," historian John Lukacs wrote, "that is, at least by inference, an ahuman and ahistorical—phenomenon" to simply a "historical figure, incarnating various human characteristics and endowed with recognizable talents."[10] Still, the idea that Hitler was uniquely evil fueled speculation that he did not die, perhaps joining his comrades abroad. There simply could never be anything ordinary about one of history's greatest monsters, including his death. Artists and commentators who used the premise of Hitler's survival to critique the present may have been well intentioned, Gavriel Rosenfeld argues, "but in so doing, they diverted attention away from Nazism's historical singularity."[11] Playing with history for cultural or political capital is fraught with peril, but it is possible to use a fanciful premise to comment on the present and affirm the historical singularity without surrendering to crass commercial exploitation. The best SF and horror negotiate these boundaries.

Ira Levin's 1976 novel *The Boys from Brazil* and the 1978 film directed by Franklin J. Schaffner capitalized on the Hitler wave and fascination with Nazis hiding in South America. The film begins with Barry Kohler (Steve Guttenberg), a young and resourceful Jewish student discovering the infamous Dr. Josef Mengele (Gregory Peck) is alive and well in Paraguay working with a shadowy exile group called the Comrades Organization. Kohler excitedly calls the elderly Nazi hunter and survivor Ezra Liebermann (Laurence Olivier) in Vienna, but Liebermann is skeptical. Kohler persists and attempts to record the proceedings of a Comrades meeting, but he is discovered and murdered while playing his recording on the phone to Liebermann. The recording includes peculiar details of Mengele's project, specifically ordering the assassination of ninety-four random men in nine countries within the year. Intrigued, the ailing Liebermann investigates suspicious deaths of low-level civil servants across Europe and America and discerns a pattern—the victims are all men approximately sixty-five years old and married to wives twenty years younger. Furthermore, the men are abusive to their adopted sons, whom Liebermann discovers all have black hair and piercing blue eyes. The boys' mothers protect and dote on their sons.

Liebermann leverages his position as a successful Nazi hunter and unearths Mengele's master plan. The infamous geneticist impregnated women in a Brazilian clinic with zygotes comprising Hitler's DNA, creating clones and arranging for them to be adopted into family situations resembling Hitler's own family dynamic. Each clone had to lose his father at age thirteen, thus the murders of the ninety-four men. Mengele predicts at least one clone will rise to become the next führer. As Liebermann draws closer to unraveling the plot, Mengele's comrades fear discovery and sabotage the plan by destroying his laboratory, but not before Mengele travels to rural Pennsylvania to continue the operation on schedule, killing the father of the clone Bobby Wheelock (Jeremy Black). Liebermann, who has Mengele's list, anticipates the move and encounters Mengele in Bobby's living room after the murder. Mengele shoots Liebermann in the leg and proceeds to regale him with the details of his ambitious plan to breed the next Hitler. Fierce Doberman Pinschers trained to attack anyone who threatens the family bark furiously in a locked room until Bobby returns from school and assesses the situation. He is clearly a young Hitler—impulsive, haughty, and nonplussed by the carnage. Bobby is unmoved by Mengele's fawning praise and the fantastic story he tells him. After finding his dead father in the basement, Bobby releases the dogs on Mengele, who is torn to bits as Liebermann looks on. Bobby helps Liebermann in exchange for his silence about killing Mengele. The film ends with Liebermann in a hospital bed, urged by other Nazi hunters to use the list and kill the remaining Hitler clones. Embracing the notion that children are not born evil, nor responsible for sins of the father, Liebermann destroys the list.

Released in 1978, *The Boys from Brazil* struck a chord with audiences increasingly aware of the Holocaust and its many unexamined legacies, especially the inadequate punishment of perpetrators. The film depicts Paraguay replete with Nazi fortresses, classic Mercedes cars, beer halls, and sumptuous banquets celebrating Nazi victories past and future. Infamous war criminals like Mengele strut across town greeting Nazi functionaries and generals, all enjoying warm weather and a carefree existence while the ailing Liebermann, who is modeled after Simon Wiesenthal, toils away in his cramped Vienna apartment arguing with the landlord over back rent and chasing ghosts.[12] When Liebermann questions Frieda Maloney (Uta Hagen) in prison, a former guard who helped Mengele with his adoption scheme, she is both amused and frustrated by the old man's pestering. "Thirty years and the world has forgotten!" she exclaims. "But you persist and

Fig. 4.1. Josef Mengele (Gregory Peck) clones the next Hitler from the safety of his Paraguayan enclave in *The Boys from the Brazil* (1978). (Credit: Twentieth Century Fox/ Photofest, © Twentieth Century Fox.)

persist!" One of the clones Liebermann visits in Germany scoffs at his obsession with Nazis, telling Liebermann to "just put it in history books."[13] Mengele similarly contends with those interested in living comfortably in the present rather than revisiting the past, even a glorious one. Comrades Organization leader Eduard Seibert (James Mason) abandons Mengele's plan to revive the Third Reich once it endangers their paradise in exile. It seems freedom and comfort matter more than ideology or litigating the past. The final showdown between the two old men in a Pennsylvania living room has an air of pathos precisely because it seems inconsequential, especially since the young Bobby Wheelock, channeling the prevailing attitude of the time, could not care less what either one of them has to say.

Mengele and Liebermann represent opposing worldviews in more ways than the obvious Nazi versus Jew dynamic. Mengele trusts blood and genetics will overcome historical circumstance, that a Hitler clone placed in any time or region will become the Hitler of history. Mengele understands he is witnessing a remarkable Hitler wave that seemingly justifies his insane plan, claiming Hitler's constant presence on television is proof the Hitler myth is powerful and resilient. "People are fascinated," he declares, "The time is ripe. The Führer is alive." Mengele is convinced his plan is flawless, shouting triumphantly to a wounded Liebermann that he created "a Hitler tailor made for the 1980s, 90s, 2000s!"[14] Liebermann places his faith in humanity, choosing to believe democracy and a vivid historical memory will ultimately render the clones harmless. When a young colleague urges Liebermann to hand over the list so the remaining clones can be dispatched, he is incredulous at Liebermann's hesitation: "You would protect Hitler?" Liebermann responds, "I will not slaughter the innocent, and neither will you."[15] Liebermann's instinct is laudable and perhaps intended to signify the triumph of good over evil, but how can he be sure? Does raising Bobby Wheelock in America diminish his Hitlerian genes or are his totalitarian tendencies in step with what America has become by the 1970s? Will he become a Hitler tailor made for the 1980s, 1990s, and 2000s?[16] We may want to believe Liebermann is right, but cynics among us might prefer he relinquish the list and remove any doubt. Ads for the film played to fears of Nazism's possible resurrection: They "are the start of the Fourth Reich. If these children survive . . . will we?"[17] *The Boys from Brazil* is an imaginative thriller based on an absurd premise, cloning Hitler, but the prospect of notorious Nazis living free and happy lives resonated with Americans shocked and fascinated with investigative reporting revealing the truth behind the fiction. Audiences soon realized their own government aided ex-Nazis' escape and even placed them in sensitive positions hoping to capitalize on their infernal expertise. It is not Mengele whom Liebermann has to vanquish once and for all, but rather the West's inherent fragility, opportunism, and consistent betrayal of its own professed values.

"It's All for You, Damien!": Cultivating the Antichrist Führer in *The Omen* Trilogy

Coming on the heels of *Rosemary's Baby* and *The Exorcist*, Richard Donner's *The Omen* mined further the prospect of the Devil wreaking havoc on the ostensibly prosperous and peaceful West, specifically by using a child to accomplish the task. *The Omen* trilogy does not reference Nazism or the Holocaust directly, but the films chronicle the rise of the Antichrist in the venue where he can best destabilize civilization and unleash humanity's worst instincts—politics. Damien's adoptive family, the Thorns, are at the pinnacle of a mature capitalist economy governed by a handful of transnational corporations. Sociologist Neil Gerlach argues Antichrist films are critical dystopias revealing the weaknesses and corruption of modern social, political, and economic structures, as well as institutionalized knowledge. Science can do nothing to stop the Antichrist; in fact, it serves as an additional tool in his arsenal. That the Antichrist is a voracious capitalist make sense, Gerlach argues, because he is the embodiment of "the perfect post-Fordist man, waiting to transform society into his own selfish, 'me generation' image."[18] The Holocaust relied on science, law, technology, and a robust bureaucratic state—the hallmarks of the post-Enlightenment age. How else would a modern Antichrist achieve world domination than similarly undermine the institutions governing our existence, suddenly turning them into agents of destruction? It is not only effective, but utterly demoralizing. Moreover, the Antichrist will act with our consent. *The Omen* has no monsters, demons, or vivid apocalyptic landscapes, just a child nurtured in a familiar postwar power structure—corporations, government, elite military schools, and hallowed democratic bodies like Parliament. Consequently, it is difficult to fear Damien because his monstrosity is not obvious to us. In fact, we may be pulling for him to bring down the whole rotten artifice enabling his meteoric rise to power.

The Omen begins with Robert Thorn (Gregory Peck) and his wife Katherine (Lee Remick) in a hospital in Rome moments after their their newborn son dies on June 6, at 6 in the morning (666). The hospital chaplain approaches Thorn with a scheme to secretly adopt an orphan to spare Katherine the sorrow of losing their son. Thorne agrees and Damien (Harry Stephens) joins a family destined for great power and influence. Satan and his earthly helpers intercede to elevate Thorn to US ambassador to Britain and periodically eliminate perceived threats to Damien, specifically those seeking to unravel the mystery of his origins. Father Brennan (Patrick Troughton) and the insistent photojournalist Keith Jennings (David Warner) convey to Thorn their doubts about the true nature of his adopted son. Both Brennan and Jennings die spectacular deaths, but not before Thorn realizes Damien bears the mark of the beast (three sixes on his scalp), was born of a jackal, and that Thorn's biological child was murdered at birth to make room for the Antichrist. Thorn procures the Seven Daggers of Megiddo meant to kill this unique evil and returns home to discover Katherine was killed in a freak accident orchestrated by Damien's satanic governess. Mad with rage and grief, Thorn drags Damien to a church intent on stabbing him, but police kill Thorn before he commits the act. At the double funeral for his parents, Damien is comforted by the President of the United States, who we are made to understand will be caring for the Antichrist from that moment forward. The film ends with Damien flashing a knowing smile.

Although written and directed by different people, *Damien: Omen II* (1978) remains faithful to the original storyline concerning Damien's grooming for world domination aided by strategically placed minions. The film begins soon after Robert and Katherine's funeral when Thorn family friend and archaeologist Carl Bugenhagen (Leo McKern) discovers an ancient mural purportedly depicting the Antichrist. It is Damien, but another freak accident buries it and the seven daggers. Adolescent Damien

(Jonathan Scott-Taylor) now lives with his uncle, Richard Thorn (William Holden), CEO of the international conglomerate Thorn Industries, and his aunt Ann (Lee Grant). Damien attends military school with his cousin, Mark (Lucas Donat), with whom he is very close. School commandant Sergeant Neff (Lance Henriksen) takes Damien under his wing and finally reveals the shocking truth—Damien is the Antichrist. Inside Thorn Industries senior executive Paul Buher (Robert Foxworth), another satanic emissary, urges Richard to approve his plan to buy much of the world's fertile land and supposedly end world hunger by controlling the food supply. Those opposed are quickly and dramatically dispatched by malevolent forces. Meanwhile, the buried box with the seven daggers and evidence of Damien's origins is recovered and sent to the Thorn Museum, prompting renewed investigations and attempts to convince Richard that Damien is evil. Damien, empowered by the knowledge he is the Antichrist, outmaneuvers his enemies, but is forced to kill Mark after he refuses to join Damien in his bid for world domination. Like his brother Robert, Richard seeks to murder Damien, but Ann turns on Richard and kills him and herself, revealing she was a minion all along. With his family gone and Buher's nefarious plan approved, Thorn Industries is firmly under Damien's control.

Omen III: The Final Conflict (1981) features an adult Damien (Sam Neill) running Thorn Industries and playing the role of international philanthropist. Damien assumes the post held by his adoptive father, ambassador to Britain, and implements a plan to stop the Second Coming of Jesus Christ. Father DeCarlo (Rossano Brazzi) and six other priests who know about Damien recover the Seven Daggers of Megiddo from the Thorn Museum and plot to kill Damien and protect the Christ child. Damien becomes romantically involved with Kate Reynolds (Lisa Harrow), the "Barbara Walters of British television," and befriends her son Peter (Barnaby Holm), drawing him into his sinister plot.[19] After discerning an astronomical event as a sign of the Second Coming, Damien orders his minions to murder every male child born in England on a certain day. Father DeCarlo contacts Kate and relates the outlandish story, but she is convinced upon seeing Damien's birthmark. Peter, who falls under Damien's influence, learns the Christ child was not among the murdered infants and is being protected. Father DeCarlo and Kate conspire to murder Damien by promising him the baby in exchange for Peter, but Damien discovers the trap and accidentally kills Peter. Enraged, Kate stabs Damien in the back with one of the daggers. As he dies, Damien sees a vision of Christ and curses him, scoffing at the idea Christ won the eternal conflict between good and evil.

Locating evil in the mundane or embedded in the institutions of the industrial and postindustrial world has interesting cinematic precedents. Fritz Lang's character Dr. Mabuse, who appeared in three films between

1922 and 1933, is a master of disguise, changing identities and orchestrating mass hypnosis and body transference. Mabuse creates a society of crime by manipulating weaker humans and sending his loyal agents into the world to create chaos. Mabuse seems to possess his victims like a demon, but his tactics are more akin to a charismatic politician stoking imaginary fears. Mabuse revels in secretly controlling the world, waiting to reveal himself only when the task is complete. "Only now, shall the world know who I am—I am Mabuse!" he tells his assembled agents. "I want to become a giant—a titan, churning up laws and Gods like withered leaves!" One of Mabuse's victims, a fool urged to commit horrid crimes, cries out to the police, "Something descended upon me! Something that was stronger than me forced me to do it!" A police investigator coming to grips with the strange events overtaking Germany claimed "a hostile superior will" was acting on people.[20] Mabuse was a stock speculator, predatory capitalist, a psychiatrist, and organized crime lord—in other words, an easily identifiable antisemitic caricature in Weimar Germany. However, in *The Testament of Dr. Mabuse* (1933), the last film Lang directed in Germany, the character is a thinly veiled Hitler furiously transcribing his legacy inside an insane asylum. "The purpose of crime is to create an endless empire of crime," Mabuse writes, admitting the ultimate goal is "a state of complete insecurity and anarchy, founded upon the tainted ideals of a world doomed to annihilation." The testament of Dr. Mabuse is that he will live forever so long as humanity's soul "is shaken to its depths."[21] Damien seems to have taken Mabuse's testament to heart, orchestrating humanity's downfall from the shadows, hastening modernity's natural course toward self-destruction.

Damien's racial and economic privilege is instrumental to his quest to become the all-powerful Antichrist. Satan obviously agrees since he arranged for him to be raised by the Thorns. "This is a film about whiteness," Andrew Scahill writes of *The Omen*. "It is a film about whiteness become monstrous, a film about white privilege and the invisible labor that upends it."[22] From the governess who hurled herself out of a window at Damien's fifth birthday party, screaming, "It's all for you, Damien!" to the minions paving the way for him in school, corporate culture, and politics—sacrificing themselves and countless others—Damien ascends to the pinnacle of power on the literal and figurative corpses of his social inferiors. Why would anyone suspect Damien of benefiting from the system in place? Critic Wheeler Dixon mistakenly described Damien as "the blond young son" of Robert Thorn, noting the "Nazi-like precision" of Damien's plotting.[23] Damien is famously raven-haired, not blonde, but Scahill attributes Dixon's careless mistake to our tendency to equate blondeness with whiteness. Damien *should* be blonde given his cocoon of wealth and privilege revolving around an elite military school and the global reach of Thorn

Industries. Damien's path to power required eliminating rivals and subjugating the third world to poverty and famine, Scahill writes *The Omen II* "explicitly invokes the iconography of the Hitler Youth movement to link education, white privilege, and colonialism."[24] Like Mabuse, Damien does not manipulate economic and power structures with shocking supernatural powers. The Antichrist simply must work within the established bounds of formal institutions.[25]

Entrenching Damien in the corridors of power, a precocious child who blithely casts aside inept adults powerless to stop him, makes this antihero the implicit hero. Damien has a goal and ruthlessly pursues it, perhaps unintentionally providing a service by revealing the internal rot of our civilization. Audiences in the late 1970s could identify with this subtext. Robin Wood argues we root for Damien's "systematic destruction of the bourgeois Establishment." Furthermore, "*The Omen* would make no sense in a society that was not prepared to enjoy and surreptitiously condone the working out of its own self-destruction."[26] It is coincidental *The Omen* and *The Boys from Brazil* were released so close together, yet the two address similar themes integral to post–World War II horror—feelings of anxiety, helplessness, and blurred boundaries between order and disorder.[27] Moreover, the films suggest the next Hitler or the Antichrist could just as likely emerge from an American family as he could Hell or the dark well of history. *The Omen* is deeply unsettling, but also wryly amusing because Damien, Neil Gerlach concludes, "is what America is becoming in the late modern period."[28] Damien intends to enact genocide using the tools of a modern nation-state and the bottomless resources of an international conglomerate. The Holocaust is a model for the Antichrist and proof the past is prelude when it comes to genocide. It is not Damien, or even Satan, who should frighten us; it is our complacency, our powerlessness, and ultimately our complicity in making the Antichrist's victory inevitable.

Through the Peephole: Roman Polanski's Apartment Trilogy

French-Polish director Roman Polanski's experiences as a child Holocaust victim and survivor left an indelible mark on his brilliant and controversial career. Born in Paris in 1933 to parents with Jewish ancestry, the Polanski family moved to Krakow, Poland, in 1936, where they endured the consequences of German occupation during World War II. Forced into the Krakow Ghetto, Polanski was ostracized, removed from school, and forced to bear witness to the city's Jews, including his parents, being rounded up and deported to Auschwitz. Polanski's mother died at Auschwitz, but his father survived Mauthausen as a forced laborer. Polanski escaped the ghetto under an assumed name with the aid of Catholic friends of the family, pretending to be Catholic and attending religious schools. Polanski was understandably traumatized by what he experienced during the occupation, including German soldiers using him and other children for target practice, random murders in the streets, and his parents being pulled away from him as he watched helplessly. Polanski recalled his earliest memory as a six-year-old: "I had just been visiting my grandmother . . . when I received a foretaste of things to come. At first I didn't know what was happening. I simply saw people scattering in all directions. Then I realized why the street had emptied so quickly. Some women were being herded along it by German soldiers. Instead of running away like the rest, I felt compelled to watch."[29] As the ghetto liquidated and his family perished one selection at a time, Polanski lived in constant fear of discovery, hiding in ghettos, churches, basements, and farms, all while pretending to be someone he was not. Living amid pervasive violence and tormented by feelings of survivor's guilt, alienation, and loneliness obviously influenced the artist Polanski would become.[30] Although reunited with his father, Polanski believed his father blamed him for his mother's death and both father and son were haunted by guilt. Polanski biographer Ewa Mazierska argues Polanski's horrible childhood in wartime Poland combined with the brutal murder of his second wife, actress Sharon Tate, in 1969 at the hands of the Charles Manson cult led the artist to embrace the irrational and the surreal, and gave him a voyeuristic perspective on the capriciousness of evil in a turbulent twentieth century.[31] Asked about Tate's murder in a 1984 interview, Polanski explained, "I feel the same sense of Jewish guilt as my father did, and Sharon's death increases my belief in the absurd."[32]

Roman Polanski, director of one of the more celebrated Holocaust films ever made in *The Pianist* (2002), is an avowed atheist uncomfortable with representing his Jewish and Polish roots. When he does, Polanski references previous mediated representations or does so through someone else's eyes.[33] *The Pianist* inspired Polanski because the film's subject, Władysław Szpilman, also survived the ghettos and camps through luck, deception, and outside help. Moreover, Polanski empathizes with Szpilman because he seemed to embody his notion of the non-Jewish Jew, someone who eschews religion, ancestral traditions, and Polish patriotism in equal measure. *The Pianist* is unflinching in depicting Jews trapped in the Warsaw Ghetto behaving like any human beings facing the extreme—some are brave and altruistic, others selfish and opportunistic.[34] As a Jew born in France who grew up in deeply antisemitic Poland during the war, Polanski also felt alienated and rootless. He continued to travel from country to country after the war, living in Britain, Italy, Switzerland, and the United States.

Accordingly, his screen characters feel trapped, suffocated, and isolated, and countenance an outsider's view of a hostile and uncaring world.

This penchant for portraying characters fearful of the outside world is displayed vividly in Polanski's trinity of horror films known as the Apartment Trilogy. Here Polanski explores the links between gender, mental illness, and identity stability. *Repulsion* (1965), *Rosemary's Baby* (1968), and *The Tenant* (1976) are set in the confines of apartments in which the protagonists believe they are battling a supernatural force intent on robbing their sanity. The psychological horror films leave audiences questioning whether the threat is real or imagined, the product of a haunted space or a diseased mind.[35] The characters in these films display divided and unstable personalities attributable to both a mental breakdown and external forces, although we are never sure which is dominant.[36] The Apartment Trilogy engages one of Polanski's persistent themes—voyeurism. The peephole plays a significant role in evoking feelings of dread and terror in characters, who fear both being seen and seeing what lies outside the claustrophobic space of the apartment. The peephole acquired a sinister connotation after it was revealed the gas chambers were constructed to allow camp personnel to witness the mass murders. Alfred Hitchcock, himself an unsuspecting voyeur of the Holocaust as an editor of liberation footage, famously deployed the peephole in *Psycho*, which influenced other directors. Kay Picart and David Frank's *Frames of Evil* explains the intimate connection between the peephole, horror and the Holocaust:

> The peephole visually yokes ideological intentionalism and horror film conventions by framing the Holocaust as an "ontological breach" with the flow of normality and history. It does so by separating the audience from the agent and space of murder but allowing the audience the guilty pleasure of witnessing an evil that is portrayed as radically other and yet alluring or aesthetically fascinating. These visual demarcations are at the core of the classic horror frame.[37]

Horror audiences are both repelled and enthralled by what they see, but are always aware they are anonymous voyeurs. SS officers leering at their handiwork enjoyed the same privileged position, enjoying the spectacle with no discernible consequences.

Repulsion, Polanski's first English-language film, focuses on Carol Ledoux (Catherine Deneuve), a beautiful Belgian immigrant living with her more assimilated sister, Helen (Yvonne Furneaux), in a small London apartment. Carol is detached from people, painfully shy, stressed by performing ordinary tasks, and utterly disgusted by any hint of sexuality. Living in a strange city and forced to speak a foreign language only heightens her distress. Carol despises Helen's boyfriend, Michael (Ian Hendry) who treats the sisters' apartment as his own. Carol must also contend with the increasingly desperate and clumsy advances of Colin (John Fraser). Left alone in the apartment for several days, Carol descends into madness and despair as she imagines cracks in the walls expanding and shattering; uncooked meat rotting on the counter; menacing figures and shadows appearing in the mirrors; strange phone calls sending her into a panic; and outstretched hands clawing at her from the hallways. Carol is unable to function in her job as a manicurist, accidentally injuring a client, and is sent home to further withdraw and hallucinate. Colin arrives at the apartment unannounced to declare his love, refusing to leave Carol alone. Tormented and confused, she beats Colin to death with a candlestick and drags his corpse to the bathtub. Soon after, the aggressive landlord breaks in demanding the rent and propositions Carol. Resisting his repeated advances, Carol cuts his throat with Michael's straight razor. The film ends with Helen and Michael returning home to find a filthy and catatonic Carol covered in the blood of her victims. Polanski's choice to direct a horror film about an immigrant unable to distinguish the real from the surreal in a confined space is related to his own experience. Polanski recalled that "audiences were furious because at the start they sympathized with Deneuve's character but then found themselves implicated in what she was doing." Interestingly, Polanski believed French audiences were angry at being tricked, but thought it was telling that *Repulsion* "was a triumph in Germany."[38]

The Tenant, the last film in the trilogy, features Roman Polanski as Trelkovsky, a shy and soft-spoken man who rents an apartment in Paris with a tragic and violent past. Another penetrative psychological thriller focused on an immigrant's struggle to maintain sanity, Trelkovsky slowly transforms into the previous tenant, Simone, a young woman who inexplicably killed herself. He adopts her fears and mannerisms, discovers morbid clues about her own madness throughout the apartment, and eventually dresses in her clothes. Eccentric neighbors torment Trelkovsky, driving him to hurl himself out the window like Simone. Made after the brutal murder of Sharon Tate, which Polanski admits scarred him for life, it is difficult not to conflate Polanksi's personal trauma with that of the fictional Trelkovsky.[39] All the films in the trilogy, but especially *Repulsion* and *The Tenant*, construct a terrifying world where, Ewa Mazierska writes, "no one, in a crisis, can get outside himself and help, or be helped by another."[40] How else would a child Holocaust survivor view the world? Whether it is the anguished Carol or the beleaguered Władysław Szpilman, Polanski advises we trust ourselves rather than others when it comes to confronting the terrors of the world.[41]

Rosemary's Baby, the second film in the trilogy and arguably one of Polanski's best directorial efforts, is drawn from Ira Levin's novel. Levin took his own anxiety about impending fatherhood and crafted an engrossing and darkly comic story about young New Yorkers becoming parents to Satan's child. When Paramount producer Robert Evans acquired the rights he sent the novel to Polanski assuming the Holocaust survivor would have a unique perspective on evil.[42] He was right. "I don't have a relationship to evil," Polanski said in a 1999 interview. "I've never believed in occultism or the Devil, and I'm not at all religious. I'd rather read science books than something about occultism. When it comes to cinema, evil is simply a form of entertainment to me."[43] Taking its place among the greatest horror films ever made, critic Rich Cohen credits *Rosemary's Baby* with giving birth to a genre that includes *The Omen* and *The Exorcist*. "It now seems less like horror, more like social commentary," he writes. "It's not about the devil and it's not about madness. It's about men and women and what they do to each other. It's our world in microcosm—that's the curse. It says more than it wants to. In the way of great art, it captures a beast it did not know it was hunting."[44]

The film begins with Rosemary and Guy Woodhouse (Mia Farrow and John Cassavetes) moving into the Bramford, a Manhattan apartment building with a colorful past, namely, cannibalism, murder, and witchcraft. The ambitious and artistic couple soon meet their elderly and eccentric neighbors, Minnie and Roman Castevet (Ruth Gordon and Sidney Blackmer). Rosemary befriends Terry (Victoria Vetri), a young woman and recovering drug addict living with the Castevets, but Terry soon hurls herself out of a seventh-floor window to her death (a theme in the trilogy). Once Minnie learns Rosemary and Guy are trying to get pregnant, the Castevets take an active interest in their lives, securing for them an exclusive doctor, providing Rosemary a tannis root good luck charm, and preparing special drinks and meals infused with herbal supplements. As Guy struggles to make it big as an actor, Rosemary is left isolated in the increasingly menacing and strange apartment and is forced to accommodate Minnie's incessant meddling. In an abrupt turnaround, Guy welcomes Minnie and Roman's friendship and begins landing lucrative acting jobs. One night, Rosemary has a horrifying nightmare about being raped by the Devil on John F. Kennedy's yacht, but the next morning Guy assures her he simply had sex with her in her sleep to keep their schedule. Now pregnant, Rosemary experiences months of pain and disorientation while the Castevets become more intrusive than ever. Hutch (Maurice Evans), a family friend who warned Rosemary about moving into the troubled Bramford apartment building, urges Rosemary to abandon the regimen prescribed by the

Castevets and their doctor, Abe Sapirstein (Ralph Bellamy). Hutch begins investigating the Castevets and discovers their long history with the occult and satanism, but he falls into a coma before he can reach Rosemary. When Hutch dies Rosemary comes into possession of his research and discerns the truth about the Bramford, the Castevets, and her pregnancy. The Castevets and Sapirstein are part of a coven, and Guy made a pact with the Devil in exchange for fame and fortune. At first Rosemary believes the witches want her child for evil purposes, but the film concludes with the horrible realization that her son Adrian is the son of Satan. With the coven assembled in the Castevets' apartment, Rosemary warily approaches her demonic son in his black bassinet and cradles him, smiling.

The genius of *Rosemary's Baby* is that, like Carol in *Repulsion* and Trelkovsky in *The Tenant*, we are watching a woman's slow descent into insanity, but this time the protagonist's fears seem warranted. As Rosemary cries out during her surrealist rape by the Devil, "This is no dream. This is really happening!"[45] Everyone from her husband and the annoying neighbors to the kindly old Dr. Sapirstein seem to have Rosemary's best interests at heart, yet an immense conspiracy envelops the hapless young woman to the point she loses her mind. We believe her, but the rest of the world either dismisses Rosemary as a hysterical woman or is in on the satanic plot. Every time she tries to leave the apartment and seek help Rosemary is dragged back to the sanctum to perform her only role, birthing Satan's son. The horror in this iconic film unfolds slowly and from unexpected quarters. The only overt sign of monstrosity is the set of piercing yellow eyes of Rosemary's rapist, the Devil himself. Although we do not see Adrian, Roman assures Rosemary, "he has his father's eyes."[46] Rosemary is suffocated by the apartment, her duplicitous husband, the neighbors, male doctors who are accustomed to compliant female patients, and society's timeless expectations concerning what constitutes maternal behavior, as evidenced by the film's ambiguous conclusion. "Rather than fight the oppressive rule of her captors," Nick Yarborough writes, Rosemary "appears to have finally surrendered—content to be a prisoner of the apartment if it means being with her baby—consequences be damned."[47] While Damien ascends to the top of the sociopolitical hierarchy simply by maneuvering existing institutions, reinforcing the patriarchal foundation of the civilization he will conquer, Rosemary is a disposable pawn used by the patriarchy to perform one function—birth the Antichrist. "Whatever happened to Rosemary's baby?" audiences asked in the years after the film's release. Perhaps *The Omen* trilogy is an answer.

As in most of Polanski's work, *Rosemary's Baby* does not reference the Holocaust or antisemitic imagery directly, but the film features Jewish characters. Minnie and Roman's personality and mannerisms, particularly

Minnie's passive aggressive nudging of Rosemary throughout the pregnancy, are coded as Jewish. Sapirstein is an authoritative and avuncular doctor resembling a more rotund Sigmund Freud. Furthermore, the cabal is engaged in a vast conspiracy involving witchcraft and the theft of children. After receiving Hutch's research, Rosemary's eyes widen reading about coven rituals in which an infant's blood is drained. The manuscript is reminiscent of the infamous blood libel accusations plaguing Jews since the medieval era. Polanski plays with the stereotypes not to inflame passions, but to achieve a comical affect. That a coven of eccentric yentas and octogenarian professionals can hatch such a conspiracy in the comfort of their living room is absurd, yet strangely convincing, especially from Rosemary's admittedly frantic perspective. The most unsettling aspect of the film is not that Rosemary is victimized by satanists, but that she surrenders, that she is complicit. We also cannot dismiss the idea that the entire episode is in fact a hallucination. When interviewers observed Polanski's characters are "always helpless at the end of your films," the director replied that showing your hero triumphant "leaves the audience satisfied. And there's nothing more sterile than the state of satisfaction."[48] Perhaps by necessity given his experience as both a victim and perpetrator, Roman Polanski observes the world through an absurdist lens, and from a distance. "I'm interested in what makes you tick," Charlie Rose said, pressing Polanski to reveal more in an interview. "I know you are," Polanski replied curtly, "But I'm not."[49]

"Why This Little Girl?": Exorcising Existential Despair after the Holocaust

William Friedkin never intended to direct a horror film when he decided to explore the details of the 1949 exorcism of Roland Poe and adapt William Peter Blatty's 1971 novel, *The Exorcist*. "I attempted to make it as realistic possible," he said, "At the very most, I think it could be called a work of the inexplicable. By now, I accept that *The Exorcist* does belong in the horror genre. At the time, I didn't. But I had an obligation to deal as straightforwardly as possible with it because of my attraction to this unusual but factual event."[50] An accomplished director of action and drama films before becoming a master of horror, Friedkin claimed being Jewish never influenced his choice of films. As *Forward* journalist A. J. Goldman writes, "It's hard to disagree. I mean, who'd have seriously expected a Jewish kid from Chicago to make 'The Exorcist?'" Goldman asked Friedkin in 2016 if he ever thought about confronting the Holocaust. "It's hard to say something different about the Holocaust . . . If I were able to do anything about that it would be about the Germans and the madness that overtook a sophisticated, intelligent population."[51] It seems Friedkin's experience with *The Exorcist* colored his worldview on the human experience more generally, describing the rise of National Socialism as "demonic possession on a massive scale . . . That's the only thing that explains it. That all these people from all walks of life, laborers, doctors, lawyers, writers, journalists, secretaries, everybody followed this madman into Hell. Now that's what intrigues me."[52] In the interview with Goldman, Friedkin harped on various haunted spaces that resonated with him, such as Hitler's childhood home in Austria and one of Mussolini's homes outside of Rome. "These places seem to have both unsettled and fascinated him," Goldman observed.[53] It is no wonder Friedkin's *The Exorcist* centers on another seemingly innocuous house, a space where evil preys on the mundane and the innocent. The film's only explicit connection to the Holocaust is Friedkin's claim his inclusion of a white demon face in a character's dream sequence was inspired by Alain Resnais's use of subliminal editing in *Night and Fog*.[54] Film scholar Barry Langford noted the urban myth that Friedkin used flash frame images of concentration camp victims "encapsulates the uneasy symbiosis of the horror film and the Holocaust." However, in Friedkin's case, the choice had more to do with borrowing a great director's technique than evoking the Holocaust.[55]

The Exorcist begins with Lankester Merrin (Max von Sydow), a senior Catholic priest and archaeologist, discovering an amulet in Iraq resembling a demon named Pazuzu, a force Merrin encountered before. The film shifts abruptly to a beautiful Georgetown home where famous actress Chris MacNeil (Ellen Burstyn) is arranging her household for an extended stay to film a movie directed by her friend Burke Dennings (Jack MacGowran). Chris is accompanied by her twelve-year old daughter Regan (Linda Blair) and close personal staff. The normally sweet and loving Regan begins acting strangely after playing with a Ouija board, cursing and stealing, and in a dramatic scene interrupting a cocktail party by declaring Burke will die soon and urinating on the carpet. Chris also witnesses Regan shaking violently on her bed, lifting the heavy frame off the floor with ease. Chris consults doctors who subject Regan to a battery of painful and intrusive testing that yields no answers. One night, Chris returns home to discover Burke has apparently fallen out a window while in the house with a sedated Regan. Everyone assumes Burke was drunk, but Detective Kindermann (Lee J. Cobb) suspects Burke's bizarre death was no accident. Frightened and filled with despair, Chris reaches out to Father Damien Karras (Jason Miller), a priest and trained psychologist who happens to be undergoing a crisis of faith after his mother's death. Chris asks Karras to perform an exorcism, prompting the troubled priest to conduct his own evaluation of Regan, who can now speak several languages and knows every detail of Karras's life. Karras finally agrees to the request after witnessing the words "HELP ME" appearing as scars on Regan's stomach while speaking with the demon. Father Merrin is brought in to perform the exorcism with Karras assisting. The demon has Regan commit horrific and vulgar acts in front of the priests and targets the weaker and emotionally vulnerable Karras. Merrin dismisses Karras and tries to contend with Pazuzu alone, but he dies of a heart attack. Karras rushes in to face the incessant tormenting and snaps, grabbing Regan and begging Pazuzu to enter him instead. Karras is briefly possessed, but he maintains enough awareness to hurl himself out the same window Burke fell from, leaving Regan weeping in the corner, free of the demon. Dying on the pavement, Karras's friend Father Dyer (Father William O'Malley) administers last rites to Karras. Days later Chris and Regan are packing the house and leaving Georgetown. Fortunately, Regan has no memory of her possession, but when she sees Father Dyer's clerical collar Regan feels comforted and kisses him on the cheek before leaving Georgetown behind.

The true horror of *The Exorcist* is the sense of helplessness and vulnerability audiences experience watching Regan transform from an innocent girl into a putrid demon. "Every time out, I wanted to come in with something new like here's the weird way she's talking or here's some vomit or a little levitation shot, but nothing too long," Friedkin explains. "The whole idea is to put you off guard. You are uncomfortable with that which you are least familiar."[56] For all the stunning and resonant scenes involving Regan's possession, Friedkin considered her arteriogram at the hands of white-coated doctors "the most disturbing scene in the film."[57] Friedkin researched the procedure and carefully filmed it to be as realistic as possible, concluding the cold, white room "appears to be a torture chamber for a child."[58] Indeed, watching Regan suffer extraordinary pain is more harrowing to watch than anything the demon subjects her to, mostly because we know it is a real procedure and utterly worthless in her case. Regan is brutalized by medicine and a legion of male doctors who assume Regan's problems are psychological. We also feel for Chris, who is frantic and weeping as the taciturn doctors casually discuss more painful tests without end. It is difficult not to associate this extended scene with Nazi medicine's inhumane treatment of involuntary patients, despite the lead doctor having a Jewish surname (Dr. Klein) (Barton Heyman). *The Exorcist* does not necessarily privilege the power of faith over science in contending with Pazuzu, a theme Friedkin certainly was careful to avoid, but the film does suggest modernity (e.g., science, capitalism) is incapable of ameliorating misery and social and psychological ailments.

Friedkin believed Karras's spiritual crisis illustrates the tragedy of human suffering as much as Regan's ordeal. Karras is wracked with guilt over his mother's mental and physical decline because Karras chose the priesthood over psychiatry, forcing his mother to wither away in her cramped Brooklyn apartment instead of living in an expensive facility. When she dies alone in the apartment, Karras is close to rejecting God, a development the demon exploits with precision. *The Exorcist* unnerves audiences because a terrible thing is happening to a sweet girl, and there is no explanation as to why. A deleted scene included in the film's 2000 director's cut has Merrin and Karras contend with this. An exhausted and desolate Karras asks, "Why this little girl? It doesn't make sense." Merrin, who suffered the same crises as Karras and more, answers, "I think the point is to make us despair, to see ourselves as animal and ugly, to reject the possibility that God could love us."[59] Friedkin originally wanted to avoid this showstopper, especially amid the intense third act of the exorcism, but he changed his view. "The audience is longing to hear that!" Friedkin explains, "The audience wants to know, 'Why am I being subjected to all this bestiality; what is the point?' It's part of the message of the film. They think it was a series of shocks with no point at all otherwise."[60] *The Exorcist* does not resort to cheap thrills, gore, or exploitative violence, which is why the film takes its place among the best of the genre alongside *Rosemary's Baby.* Friedkin succeeds in his stated goal of "making a movie that . . . enters the mind of those who see it" and affects audiences years later.[61]

Dominion: Prequel to the Exorcist (2005) explores Merrin's origin story, firmly entrenching his trauma and temporary loss of faith in a Holocaust narrative. Directed by Paul Schrader, *Dominion* begins in 1944 with a young Merrin (Stellen Skarsgård) serving as a parish priest in a small Dutch town. An SS unit arrives seeking retribution for resistance activity in the area and herds the townspeople into the square. SS Lieutenant Kessel (Antonie Kamerling) forces Merrin to choose a few victims for arbitrary executions or watch the entire town murdered. Anguished and praying futilely, Kessel mocks a prostrate Merrin: "God isn't here today."[62] Merrin relents and picks a few morally compromised men, but the episode breaks him and prompts the priest to abandon his faith. A few years later we encounter Merrin in a remote corner of British East Africa excavating an ancient Byzantine church along with a young and devout priest, Father Francis (Gabriel Mann). The remainder of the film depicts Merrin confronting Pazuzu after the demon possesses a young crippled boy named Cheche (Billy Crawford). The encounter forces Merrin to rediscover faith and courage to save his colleagues and helpless tribesmen, and prevent a massacre, this time at the hands of the British army. In a crucial moment during the exorcism of Cheche, Pazuza seduces Merrin with the chance to rewrite his past and return to that fateful moment in 1944, but Merrin realizes making a different choice would have changed nothing. Merrin accepts there is no changing the past and returns to Rome with renewed purpose.

The Holocaust pursues Merrin to Africa when he befriends Rachel (Clara Bellar), a survivor of the Chelmno death camp who serves as the village doctor. Merrin and Rachel are connected through their shared tragedy and survivor's guilt. Rachel processed her trauma and serves as a guide of sorts for Merrin, who is still embittered by his experience. Rachel's thoughts on evil are both the product of living through the Holocaust and the incommunicability of experience. She acknowledges most people simply will never understand. Rachel also teaches Merrin he is not alone. "No one wanted to believe," she tells Merrin. "It is so much easier to believe evil is random, an ogre, not that it is a human condition, something everyone is capable of."[63] Rachel's guilt mirrors Merrin's, and by extension all survivors who climbed out of the abyss while so many others perished. "It's amazing what you're capable of when your physical survival is at stake," she shares with him, "things you think you could never endure."[64] Pressing further, Rachel tells Merrin, "We are the same, you and I."[65] However, whereas Merrin condemns God and eschews human contact, Rachel's faith is strengthened and renewed as she devotes her life to healing the sick and protecting the weak. Sensing Merrin's rage and abandonment of faith, Rachel offers her own perspective, "Sometimes I think the best view of God is from Hell."[66] Pazuza, who is threatened by Rachel's influence on Merrin and the villagers, tries to undermine Merrin's empathy and attraction to her. "She never helped other prisoners," the demon taunts, "she traded her body for food, she betrayed her friends."[67] Merrin is closest to defeat when the demon offers him absolution from guilt. "There is one thing you can do," Pazuzu offers a shaken Merrin, "you can cease to care."[68] Ultimately, Rachel saves Merrin from a life of nihilistic self-loathing. Decades later when Father Karras asks Merrin, "Why this little girl?" during Regan's exorcism, we know his answer originates with the Holocaust.

David S. Goyer's *The Unborn* (2009) draws on *Rosemary's Baby*, *The Omen*, and *The Exorcist*, but this story of demonic possession and childbirth is firmly rooted in Jewish folklore and generational trauma born of the Holocaust. The film revolves around Casey Beldon (Odette Yustman), a college student who comes to realize she is haunted by a dybbuk, a spirit who possesses the living to accomplish an unfinished task before transitioning to the afterlife. Casey first notices the child she babysits behaving strangely, forcing his infant brother to view his reflection in a mirror and attacking Casey with it. The boy stands over Casey and says cryptically, "Jumby wants to be born now."[69] Casey is told of a superstition claiming babies should not see themselves in a mirror or they will die soon, a fate that transpires days later. Casey begins to hallucinate malevolent children and dogs and is alarmed when her eyes begin to change color, a condition her doctor dismisses as normal. Casey discovers she had a twin brother die in the womb when the umbilical cord strangled him. Casey's mother, who committed suicide in an insane asylum, called the unborn child Jumby. Fearing she is being haunted, Casey's investigations lead her to Sofia Kozma (Jane Alexander), an Auschwitz survivor who reluctantly admits to being Casey's grandmother. Sofia explains she also had a twin brother who died while the two underwent experiments conducted by Dr. Mengele. Sofia believes a dybbuk inhabited his corpse and made her brother evil. Sofia killed her possessed twin and now the dybbuk haunts her family, killing Casey's mother and now stalking Casey, hoping to be born again. Sofia gives Casey a hamsa amulet (normally associated with Judaism), instructs her to destroy all mirrors, and sends her to Rabbi Joseph Sendak (Gary Oldman), a scholar who may have the knowledge to exorcise the dybbuk from Casey's soul. Casey enlists her friend Romy (Meagan Good) and boyfriend Mark (Cam Gigandet) to help her. The rabbi asks an Episcopalian priest, Arthur (Idris Elba), to assist in the unorthodox exorcism ceremony. The exorcism spins out of control when the dybbuk kills and injures several participants and possesses Mark, forcing Casey to stab him with the hamsa. Casey and the rabbi complete the rites, but Mark falls to his death. The film concludes with Casey realizing she was targeted by the dybbuk because she is pregnant with twins. The curse born from Auschwitz continues for yet another generation.

The dybbuk in Jewish mythology has a long and complicated history originating in the sixteenth century. Not all spirits were evil or malicious; often these restless souls committed a sin and endured being trapped between the worlds of the living and dead for an indeterminate period.[70] Dybbuks possess vulnerable humans to find a release from eternal wandering, operating the new host like a puppet.[71] The dybbuk animates great Jewish works of art, literature, and film. The 1937 Polish film *The Dybbuk*, a Romeo and Juliet love story in which a dybbuk possesses a bride on the eve of her wedding, is incredibly beautiful and haunting because it was produced on the eve of the Holocaust and chronicles a Hasidic culture essentially extinguished soon after the film's release. "*The Dybbuk* is a Kaddish," film scholar Ira Konigsberg writes, "a prayer for the dead, that asks us to remember its dead. But along with our nostalgia, we bring to the film a sense of the tragic hat may not have fully been there to begin with but that makes the film more beautiful and painful to watch."[72] Like *J'accuse!* and its legions of dead French soldiers shuffling across the graveyards and battlefields of war-torn Europe, *The Dybbuk* is poignant and startling because it portrays ghosts, in this case the cast and crew consumed by the Holocaust. The film is an artifact of a Polish subculture struggling to survive in the modern age, even without the foreknowledge of the apocalypse to come.[73] Both the 1937 film and the 2009 film *The Unborn* reveal the dybbuk's intimate relationship to Jewish tragedy and trauma.

The Unborn is fully immersed in the Holocaust and its mediated legacy, from familiar visual cues we associate with films about Auschwitz—tattoos, children's clothes and shoes, and Mengele's unnerving smile—to newsreel footage and old photographs of the dead. The film also includes a revolting scene in which Casey hallucinates peering into a peephole embedded in a gas chamber door. She is drenched in bugs, filth, and revolting fluids. "It is as if the peephole vomits, urinates, defecates, or ejaculates," Aaron Kerner argues, "The hole—and Casey's body—is in revolt."[74] *The Unborn*, he continues, "is more about the anxieties of female sexuality—and more specifically pregnancy—than it is about the Holocaust." The Nazis act as the midwife through which "the 'aberrance' of female sexuality is unlocked."[75] Kerner argues further *The Unborn* "merges Nazi medical experimentation and the figure of Mengele with the Frankenstein story. In both cases, the lab operates as an artificial womb. Victor Frankenstein and Mengele's ambitions are to create life—a power that only God and women are allowed to possess.... In Goyer's film ... Hell on earth, the concentration camp, (re)materializes in Casey's pregnant body."[76] That Sofia, her daughter, and now her granddaughter all must endure the legacies of the Holocaust and the dybbuk stalking their children is a monstrous manifestation of survivor's guilt afflicting second, third, and even fourth generations. The Holocaust haunts survivors and their families decades after the event, as it does humanity writ large. Both *Dominion* and *The Unborn*, Barry Langford observes, suggest Nazi crimes "are simultaneously a manifestation of eternal, atavistic evil and the 'entry point' for this endlessly circulating malevolence to interfere in human affairs. Thus, an 'explanation' of sorts is proposed for the Holocaust, an event whose enormity renders it explicable only in metaphysical terms."[77] Pazuza and the dybbuk do not need the Holocaust to exist and thrive, just prolonged periods of human despair, weakness, and depravity. The Holocaust is the ideal portal through which an eternal evil can enter modernity and guide us toward our well-deserved apocalyptic end.

The Black Hole: Stanley Kubrick and the Holocaust

Stanley Kubrick's thirteen feature films concern humanity's confrontation with violence, power, and history. Although he came close to directing a film about the Holocaust, writing a screenplay entitled *Aryan Papers* from a novel about the Holocaust, and turned down an offer to direct *Schindler's List*, Kubrick avoided this black hole of the twentieth century. Geoffrey Cocks's *The Wolf at the Door: Kubrick, History & the Holocaust* addresses the possible reasons, but argues all of Kubrick's films are nevertheless influenced by the Holocaust, especially *The Shining*. Born to Jewish parents in the Bronx, Kubrick grew up in a secular household and downplayed his Jewish identity, although not always.[78] Distrustful of people and fearful of Jews' precarious position in history, Kubrick maintained "Gentiles don't know how to worry."[79]

Kubrick's family originated from Galicia in Eastern Europe, but most perished either in pogroms or the Holocaust. Fredric Raphael, co-writer with Kubrick of *Eyes Wide Shut* (1999), believed Kubrick was threatened by the Holocaust. Raphael argued Kubrick "made movies to keep the violence of the world on the other side of the camera and thus under his control," Cocks writes. "Such a judgement, if accurate, confirms the importance of being Jewish to Kubrick's outlook on affairs."[80] Kubrick deconstructed rational systems and their breakdown, but the Final Solution "was not a rational system gone wrong; it was a rational—or rationalized—system gone horribly right." Kubrick was likely intimidated by the Holocaust's "horrible mystery of irrational evil that has in new and extremely powerful ways thrown the nature of evil and even the existence of civilization and God into question." Raphael believed the horror of the Holocaust "was too great especially for someone like Kubrick who took serious matters very seriously."[81] Kubrick's wife recalled after his death that Kubrick was terribly depressed while writing the *Aryan Papers* screenplay. When he passed on *Schindler's List*, Kubrick told Raphael "It's fascinating stuff. But, you know, the thing is—how can I do it when I'm Jewish? I would love to make it, but how can I as a Jew?"[82] Kubrick also anticipated future critics of Spielberg's film: "The Holocaust is about six million people who get killed. *Schindler's List* was about six hundred who don't."[83] Rather than deny the Holocaust's bloody imprint on the twentieth century Kubrick chronicled so expertly, Cocks maintains the director "developed his own creative strategy for representing the Holocaust, one that expands the definition of a Holocaust film to include those reflecting a trauma-like induced discourse."[84]

Kubrick was influenced heavily by German expressionism, particularly Fritz Lang's *Mabuse* films, and became a primary architect of postwar American film noir. The amalgam of the irrational, monstrous, and gritty realism defines Kubrick's films and underscores what film critic Michael Ciment called Kubrick's "fascination with things Germanic."[85] Christiane Kubrick, his third wife, is the daughter of infamous Nazi film director Veit Harlan. Kubrick was fascinated by Harlan's life and entertained the idea of making a film about his "absolutely normal life under the protection of Joseph Goebbels," according to Christiane. Kubrick even hired *Heimat* director Edgar Reitz for the project.[86] Kubrick's character Dr. Strangelove (Peter Sellers) was darkly comic, a Germanic golem who seemed to confirm the Germans may have won World War II after all. Strangelove minimizes the actual Holocaust while relishing the prospect of another, explaining to assembled American and Russian leaders that nuclear Armageddon is just what humanity needs. Strangelove dismisses the likely death count and argues living conditions "would be far superior to those of the so-called concentration camps, where there is ample evidence most of the wretched creatures clung desperately to life."[87] Kubrick famously uses Beethoven's Ninth Symphony with Leni Riefenstahl's *Triumph of the Will* (1935) and other Nazi propaganda films to torment Alex (Malcolm McDowell) in *Clockwork Orange* (1971), subjecting the young hooligan to a re-education regime that forces him to watch what Kubrick himself steadfastly refuses to show. Both *Dr. Strangelove* and *Clockwork Orange* attest to Kubrick's "finely honed sense of satirical humor," Cocks notes, but "it also indicates a desire to use satire not only as a sword but also as a shield" when it comes to representing the Holocaust.[88]

Geoffrey Cocks devotes most of *The Wolf at the Door* to *The Shining*, "for in that film slouches a deeply laid subtext that positions the Holocaust as the modern benchmark of evil."[89] The wolf alludes to Jack Torrance (Jack Nicholson), who famously breaks down the door separating his murderous rage from his cowering family, announcing his presence with a nursery rhyme:

> Little pig, little pig, let me come in.
> No, no, by the hair on my chinny chin chin.
> Then I'll huff, and I'll puff, and I'll blow your house in.[90]

The wolf was also a popular metaphor for totalitarian dictators in the 1930s and 1940s. Cocks's close reading of *The Shining* is intriguing and deeply informed by Kubrick's source material and influences, including Thomas Mann's *The Magic Mountain* (1924), Kafka's unfinished *The Castle* (1922), and Raul Hilberg's groundbreaking history of the Holocaust, *The Destruction of the European Jews* (1961), which Kubrick read obsessively in 1975.[91] *The Shining* was written and produced in the wake of the Hitler wave, the incredibly popular *Holocaust* miniseries, and the spate of horror films exploring the breakdown of the patriarchal family. *The Shining*, Cocks concludes, is both the culmination of the horror films of the 1970s and Kubrick's avoidance of Nazism and the Holocaust.[92]

Kubrick and co-writer Diane Johnson adapted Stephen King's novel without the pretense of remaining faithful to the original story or Torrance's character arc.[93] The film begins with Jack, a struggling writer and recovering alcoholic accepting a winter caretaker job at the picturesque Overlook Hotel nestled in the Rocky Mountains. Along with his wife Wendy (Shelley Duvall) and son Danny (Danny Lloyd), Jack uses the prolonged solitude and isolation to write, but his personal demons manifest themselves in vivid hallucinations linked to the hotel's murderous past; a previous caretaker went insane and butchered his family. As the months go on, Danny's unusual psychic abilities, his shining, take over and warn him about Jack's impending mental break and violent impulses. After a blizzard leaves the Torrances snowbound, Jack obeys the hotel's apparitions and tries to murder Wendy and Danny, but he is outwitted and left to freeze to death in the hotel's immense labyrinth.

One may dispute aspects of Cocks's close reading claiming the Holocaust is "the dark heart of *The Shining*" and the "Nazi devil" dwells in the film's smallest details, but some observations are worth examining.[94] Cocks argues *The Shining* ties the fictional and factual worlds together vividly in the minds of audiences. The terror on screen is felt viscerally and reflects the horrors of the real world in ways most horror films fail to achieve. Kubrick's Overlook Hotel is an expressionist masterpiece, evoking film sets like *The Cabinet of Dr. Caligari* and *Nosferatu*. Moreover, the Overlook is reminiscent of Albert Speer's "cruel Nazi monumentalism" and emphasizes "not the formulaic gloom of fictional horror, but the daylight in which the real horrors of the world takes place."[95] Mechanical devices are intimately linked to the horror, from Jack's German Adler typewriter filling the immense Overlook space with menacing clicking sounds to the elevator dumping an ocean of blood, what Cocks describes as "the blood of millions . . . the blood of war and genocide in Kubrick's own century."[96] The typewriter alludes to the faceless killers, the desk murderers like Adolf Eichmann. "The typewriter in *The Shining* is as central to Kubrick's film as typewriters are to Spielberg" in *Schindler's List*.[97] The ghostly twins who greet Danny were widely assumed to be a reference Mengele's victims, but the inspiration derives from Kubrick's early career as a newspaper photographer when he took pictures of twin girls poisoned by carbon monoxide. Carbon monoxide was used at the Belzec death camp, the likely final resting place for Kubrick's extended Galician family.[98] Cocks examines the music, details like the Torrances' gas oven, Jack pounding a tennis ball relentlessly against a Native American tapestry, and multiple references to the number 42, the year of the Wannsee Conference. Perhaps Cocks overreaches at times, but his extended analysis is compelling and convincing, concluding *The Shining* "became the chief personal and artistic expression of Kubrick's ongoing struggle with the ghosts of the Holocaust."[99] It is telling this great auteur could only touch the Holocaust from a distance, and reluctantly, but in that sense he is like the rest of us.

5

"A World That Works"

Astrofascism across Time and Space

I felt a great disturbance in the Force, as if millions of voices
suddenly cried out in terror and were suddenly silenced.
—Obi Wan Kenobi, *Star Wars, Episode IV* (1977)

What is more terrifying than the resurrection of history's greatest monsters, or worse, the realization that they never died? That Nazism (and fascism more generally) can still inflict bodily harm, tear us to shreds, continue horrendous medical experiments, and perpetuate its dormant ideology among the weak and craven among us is a persistent fear manifested in the horror genre. In SF, Nazism and genocide easily escape the terrestrial boundaries of time and space to flourish on other worlds or in alternate realities eerily familiar to our own. As with horror, fascism in SF often represents the other, a steadfast counterconstruct that usually amplifies the intrinsic good in capitalist and liberal democratic institutions. However, SF fascist societies can also be seductive, exotic, and ruthlessly efficient in addressing (and usually solving) intractable problems we still encounter on Earth.

Appropriating fascism in pop culture, whether earnestly or playfully, risks diluting its historical legacies for audiences easily seduced by pageantry.[1] For some filmmakers, emphasizing fascism's spectacle is deliberate. Fascist aesthetics are perhaps easier to identify than fascist ideology is to define. Fascism subsumes its core beliefs to the cult of personality associated with the leader, but historian Robert Paxton's definition remains the best distillation of a dynamic and persistent ideology:

> Fascism may be defined as a form of political behavior marked by obsessive preoccupation with community decline, humiliation or

> victimhood and by compensatory cults of unity, energy and purity, in which a mass-based party of committed nationalist militants, working in uneasy but effective collaboration with traditional elites, abandons democratic liberties and pursues with redemptive violence and without ethical or legal restraints goals of internal cleansing and external expansion.[2]

Many SF societies reflect these characteristics, but the fascist aesthetic is integral to the genre independent of politics. As Susan Sontag wrote in 1975, fascist aesthetics "center on the orgiastic transactions between mighty forces and their puppets. Its choreography alternates between ceaseless motion and a congealed, static, 'virile' posing. Fascist art glorifies surrender; it exalts mindlessness: it glamorizes death."[3] The incessant recycling of fascist imagery in SF taps into our latent (some might argue explicit) desires for unity, technocracy, and righteous violence. Fortunately, SF also provides thoughtful commentary on these desires and raises provocative questions: If fascism guarantees "A World that Works," to cite the Terran Federation's slogan in Paul Verhoeven's *Starship Troopers*, would you embrace a variant of the ideology if its historical crimes disappeared? Does consuming cultural representations of fascism allow us to re-experience fascism without consequences?[4] Finally, how do these fictional fascist utopias and dystopias reflect and comment on our own historical place and trajectory?

The worlds depicted in SF are variations of our own. Nuanced and intelligent SF stories reveal that the distance between utopia and dystopia is razor thin, and whatever technological revolutions liberate humanity from time and space often come at an enormous human cost. For example, humanity may find it necessary to annihilate an alien species with the callous disregard of a sixteenth-century conquistador so long as the ends justify the means. The proliferation of Holocaust imagery and fascist aesthetics in contemporary culture is not always evidence of pop culture's laziness; it can be a statement about the unnerving continuity between historic crimes and contemporary society. Historian De Witt Douglas Kilgore uses the term *Astrofuturism* to describe the blending of science and SF at the dawn of the Space Age. This cultural phenomenon promoted the final frontier as a space for renewal, imperial expansion, and the triumph of post–World War II American values on Earth and space. Astrofuturism is "a narrative genre distinguished by its close connections to engineering projects funded by the government and the military."[5] The technocratic state emerging during World War II demonstrated its worth and showed no signs of receding. Celebrity scientists like Wernher von Braun, Willy Ley, and popular SF author Robert A. Heinlein promoted America's civil and military conquest of space as a new manifest destiny, but also an obligation in the twilight struggle against the Soviet Union.

The popularization of SF after World War II normalized what Steffen Hantke describes as the "casual coexistence or even mutual interpenetration within the same media space of civilian and military matters" built on the "logistical continuities between the Nazi war machine and the advent of the American Century."[6] It is understandable why early postwar SF promoted Astrofuturism considering the integration of hundreds of ex-Nazis into the military–industrial complex, specifically Wernher von Braun's rocket team, and the ease with which the American national security bureaucracy directed its energies away from Nazi Germany to the Soviet Union.[7] Astrofuturism rehabilitated "our Germans" as authentic American Cold War warriors and posited a world "where science is fiction and science fiction at any moment may turn into science."[8]

This chapter examines SF narratives representing what I call *Astrofascism*, a variation of Astrofuturism in which SF civilizations openly embrace fascist aesthetics, ideology, and methodology, specifically genocide and the construction of a racial state. Astrofascism is characterized by explicit references to Nazi uniforms, weapons, insignia, rhetoric, and even ideological goals. Astrofascist societies are usually highly functional, technically advanced, and outwardly confident and unified. Usually, but not always, coded as bad guys, Astrofascist civilizations are attractive and appeal to our sense of order and indulge our fascination with technology. Astrofascist violence is extreme, even genocidal, but far enough removed from terrestrial fascism's legacies to allow audiences to enjoy the spectacle. In some cases, we may identify with Astrofascism unwittingly, unaware the SF fantasy is built on principles Western civilization supposedly rejects. Astrofascism permits us to experience the benefits of living in an orderly fascist society without the consequences. It also judges us for doing so.

The Intergalactic Final Solution: Paul Verhoeven's *Starship Troopers*

Paul Verhoeven's 1997 film *Starship Troopers* continues to attract attention from academics, critics, and social commentators for its fascist imagery and seemingly muddled political subtext.[9] Based on Robert Heinlein's 1959 novel, *Starship Troopers* depicts an efficient and harmonious world government engaged in an intergalactic struggle against a race of highly evolved insects called Arachnids who compete with humans for planets and resources. Despite half-hearted efforts to spin the controversy generated by the film, Verhoeven and screenwriter Edward Neumeier seemed content to let it remain an ambiguous artifact in which one person's militaristic fantasy is another's biting satire. But the film is a study in ideological uncertainty. That fascism is the only ideology capable of producing a state strong enough to meet the Arachnid threat places the audience in the uncomfortable position of identifying and sympathizing with a society it is conditioned to despise. Neumeier believes fascism is in our biology, an integral urge every human being must overcome. "Fascism is around every corner," he warns, "so watch out."[10] Verhoeven's Terran Federation is attractive, efficient, hyper-militaristic, and rife with Nazi signs and signifiers. Verhoeven's interpretation of the future is satirical, mocking the forces of militarism and globalization at the end of the twentieth century. However, Verhoeven's choice of a Nazi aesthetic is instructive for understanding his critique of Western civilization. The Federation is a world government mobilized for racial war, driven by a quest for Lebensraum, and ultimately invested in genocide. Verhoeven populating his utopia with attractive young people enjoying the benefits of a rationalized society is deliberately subversive. *Starship Troopers* fulfills Gillian Rose's hope that directors will "make a film in which the representation of fascism would engage with the fascism of representation."[11] The more self-referential one is about the aesthetics of fascism, the more invested audiences will be in dissecting the underlying message.

Starship Troopers traces the fate of high school graduates who join the military shortly before total war breaks out between humans and Arachnids. The protagonist, Johnny Rico (Casper Van Dien), comes from a prosperous family that expects him to attend Harvard, but he decides to join the Mobile Infantry to win the affections of Carmen (Denise Richards), an aspiring pilot with career ambitions. The first half of the film concerns a love triangle between Rico, Carmen, and another female classmate, Dizzy (Dina Meyer). This melodrama is interrupted by an Arachnid meteor attack on the characters' home town of Buenos Aires. The attack transforms Johnny from a spoiled and lovesick child into a vengeful warrior forced onto the front lines of a war of annihilation. The second half of the film concerns the humans' failed offensive against the Arachnid planets and the subsequent plan to capture a so-called brain bug that holds the key to victory. Rico and his classmates play vital roles in this initial phase of the war, and like the World War II combat films familiar to American audiences, the film concludes optimistically as the young heroes assume new and important positions in the ongoing struggle.

The Federation's only division is between citizens and civilians. Military service, the Federation advertises, guarantees citizenship, which includes political power and access to state benefits like birth licenses and college tuition. The character of Rasczak (Michael Ironside), a disfigured veteran turned civics teacher, delivers a historical narrative at the beginning of the film validating Benito Mussolini's philosophy about war's inherent nobility and provides some background as to why the Federation is in power: "This year we explored the failure of democracy caused by social scientists who brought the world to the brink of chaos. We talked about how veterans took control and imposed a stability that has lasted for generations since." Rasczak then compares voting to exercising force and exalts violence as "the supreme authority from which all other authority derives." After Dizzy challenges Rasczak on the true efficacy of violence, he again preaches the fascist ethos: "Naked force has settled more issues in history than any other factor. The contrary opinion, 'violence never solves anything,' is wishful thinking at its worst."[12]

According to the Nazis' own tightly controlled historical narrative, the Volksgemeinschaft (national community) was the logical conclusion of the Frontgemeinschaft (front community) experienced during World War I. The idealized front knew no class divisions or regional and religious differences, although antisemitism was rampant.[13] Adolf Hitler identified himself primarily as a front soldier destined to build this veteran's utopia. The Federation is, to use its own slogan, "A World that Works" because veterans implemented their own version of the front community on a global scale. Although there is apparent gender and racial equality within the Federation, other aspects of the society are more indicative of traditional fascism. First, justice is swift and severe, to the point that a criminal is tried, sentenced, and executed on live television all in one day. Second, eugenics is taken for granted. When asked why she joined the Mobile Infantry, a recruit responds casually, "I wanna have babies. And you know it's a lot easier to get a license if you serve."[14] The only imperfect bodies in the entire film are wounded veterans. Their missing limbs humble the Johnny Ricos of the world, who are eager to prove themselves worthy and acquire their own battle scars. Verhoeven and Neumeier depict a politically correct version of the Volksgemeinschaft, but this gleaming futuristic society is just as capable of genocide under the guise of total war as its Nazi forefather.

Both the novel and film are reminiscent of a classic *Bildungsroman*, the genre of German literature that focuses on the moral and social development of a young man. Johnny Rico's coming-of-age story mirrors that of the typical protagonist in German post–World War I memoirs and fiction. These works emphasize the transformative experience of war and the inherent right of veterans to lead. Ernst Jünger, a prolific author lionized by the Nazis, wrote influential memoirs and novels about his own coming-of-age during his years at the front. Jünger's personal odyssey mirrors Johnny Rico's journey from a clueless teenager to the New Man the fascist movement revered. Edward Neumeier even cites Jünger's famous war memoir,

Storm of Steel (1920), as partial inspiration for the screenplay.[15] Film historian Marcia Landy notes the male characters in Italian fascist film typically undergo a "drama of conversion" into this idealized New Man.[16] Johnny Rico experiences something similar after leaving his life of comfort and privilege for the collective family of the Mobile Infantry.[17] One of the Nazi regime's first feature films, *Hitlerjunge Quex* (1933), celebrates the New Man by telling the story of a martyred Hitler Youth killed during a street battle with communists. Like Rico, Quex turns his back on his family and gives himself selflessly to something greater than himself. Both films also feature dramatic arguments between father and son. When Rico realizes he is cut off from his family fortune after joining the military he accepts it: "Who cares! The Federation'll give me everything I'll need for the next two years, right?"[18] The weak civilians holding Rico back from his destiny are as dangerous and subversive as the communist family members depicted in *Hitlerjunge Quex*. Rasczak once related to his class his firm belief that "figuring things out for yourself is the only real freedom anyone has," but the Federation completely contradicts this message by encouraging conformity at every turn.[19] During the course of his training and exposure to battle, Rico is stripped of his civilian identity and transformed into an ideal warrior, one who never questions his role in the epic struggle ahead.

Starship Troopers embraces Nazi aesthetics without seriously engaging Nazism's historical context. Edward Neumeier was refreshingly honest about his affinity for Nazi set design: "The reason for all the German uniforms and everything is because Germans made the best-looking stuff."[20] Verhoeven constantly reminds his mostly American audience that this fascist society is our own, and any similarities between the futuristic Pax Americana and the Third Reich says more about where we are headed than the personal predilections of the director. Verhoeven blends Frank Capra's *Why We Fight* and *Know Your Enemy* propaganda films with *Triumph of the Will* (1935). The sequences in which the Federation screens slick commercials glorifying the military and the unwavering unity of the home front are lifted directly from Riefenstahl's most famous shots. Verhoeven called this "wink wink Riefenstahl." When asked if he intended to link the Federation to the Third Reich, Verhoeven responded, "In a way. But it's not making a judgement. These references say, 'Here it is.' The futuristic society that works well on this level well—and it fights the giant insects very well. Look and decide. The judgement is yours."[21] Verhoeven affirms Tony Barta's observation that Nazism's ultimate victory is escaping from history into cinema. Barta explains that "the mythic Nazi was from the very beginning the accompaniment of the nastier historical one and was designed—by the Nazis themselves—to create the cinematic representation of the future." Leni Riefenstahl, Barta writes, "got the world hooked on Nazism,

Fig. 5.1. Johnny Rico (Casper Van Dien) evolves into the quintessential fascist New Man during humanity's genocidal war against the Arachnids in Paul Verhoeven's *Starship Troopers* (1997).

The Movie" and future generations could not help but interpret Nazism through her images.[22] *Starship Troopers*'s pervasive use of Nazi imagery provided fodder for film critics, most of whom were amused by the gory spectacle. *Sight & Sound* entitled their review "Starship Stormtroopers" and *Entertainment Weekly* lampooned the film as an "Aryan Spelling production" because of the presence of so many actors from *Beverly Hills 90210* and *Melrose Place*.[23] One reviewer wrote tongue in cheek, "Let's just enjoy the carnage. And wish Ken and Barbie well as they goose-step their way into the future."[24]

Verhoeven noted in interviews "war makes fascists of us all"[25] and *Starship Troopers* is, at its core, a war movie modeled on the formulaic combat films produced in the 1940s and 1950s.[26] The war against the Arachnids is the backdrop for Johnny Rico's evolution into a Federation hero. Verhoeven chose a completely unsympathetic enemy to underscore the appeal of the fascist utopia.[27] Robert Heinlein used bugs to stand in for communists, specifically Chinese and North Koreans, whom he interpreted as insect-like in their discipline and devotion to a collective. Heinlein regarded communists as devoid of compassion, creativity, spirituality, and intellect.[28] In the context of the Cold War, where each side viewed the other as an existential threat, *Starship Troopers* illustrates a total war between opposing worldviews. Verhoeven laments the loss of "that wonderful enemy everyone can fight." SF opens up new horizons, Verhoeven explains, since faceless aliens like the Arachnids approximate communists and Nazis. "They're bad, They're evil. And they are not even human."[29] Although monstrous and terrifying, the Arachnids are a civilization, and the human race openly argues for its total annihilation using familiar rhetoric. The Federation resembles the Third Reich aesthetically, but its exterminationist war footing and quest for galactic living space suggests that even in the limitless future the price of utopia is genocide.

We receive only limited background concerning the human–Arachnid conflict, but the two civilizations are imperial powers who covet the same planets. Humans, we learn from Federal Network broadcasts, may have unwittingly provoked the Arachnids when Mormon extremists settled inside the Arachnid zone of the galaxy. After an Arachnid meteor attack on Buenos Aires, the Federation embarks on a war of annihilation using the rhetoric of racial survival. Genocide is a product of warfare, historian Erich Weitz notes: "The emergency circumstances of wartime and the heightened fears meant the rulers left liberated to carry out extreme measures that they would not dare venture in peacetime. War provided cover, but also provided the great opportunity."[30] Although the human race may be unified, as evidenced by integrated units and an African sky marshal leading the human offensive against the Arachnids, the desire to cleanse the universe of competing races is pronounced throughout the film. One survivor from Buenos Aires, played by producer Jon Davidson, stands amid ruins and tells a Federal Network camera, "The only good bug is a dead bug!" In a more formal setting addressing Federation leadership, Sky Marshal Dienes (Bruce Gray) frames the coming war as a true clash of civilizations: "We are a generation commanded by fate to defend humankind! We must meet the threat with our valor, our blood, with our very lives, to ensure that human civilization, not insect dominates the galaxy now and always."[31] If World War II is the inspiration for the conflict with the Arachnids and the Federation is the Third Reich thinly disguised, Dienes's rhetoric assumes a more sinister meaning—the Arachnids do not threaten human existence; they stand in the way of expansion. The influential German military writer Friedrich von Bernhardi called war "a biological necessity of the first importance." A celebrated figure to Nazi leaders, von Bernhardi justified imperialism in terms the Federation would surely understand: "Strong, healthy, and flourishing nations increase in numbers. From a given moment they require a continual expansion of their frontiers, they require new territory for the accommodation of their surplus population."[32] Johnny Rico and his classmates, "the bloom of human evolution" as Neumeier's script describes them, are the perfect instruments with which to cleanse the universe of the ultimate other and guarantee human supremacy.[33]

Verhoeven described *Starship Troopers* as "a kind of *Battle of the Bulge*, with bugs playing the Nazis."[34] A more apt metaphor may be Operation Barbarossa, with the bugs playing the Judeo-Bolsheviks. The Nazi Wehrmacht drove into the heart of the Soviet Union as part of a racial war of conquest for German Lebensraum. Under the cover of this onslaught, the Nazi regime implemented the Final Solution. The war against the Jews was indistinguishable from the war against the Soviet Union, and extermination was the only outcome. Omer Bartov argues convincingly that German soldiers' constant exposure to ideological training beginning in the Hitler Youth and extending into basic military training led to the Wehrmacht waging a racial war. Convinced only the wholesale elimination of the Soviet Union could save the German race, Wehrmacht leaders embraced genocidal policies and relied on conscripted troops to execute them. On the eve of Barbarossa, Wehrmacht generals, such as Colonel-General Hermann Hoth, vilified the enemy with language resembling that used by Sky Marshal Dienes of the Federation: "More than ever we are filled with the thought of a new era, in which the strength of the German people's racial superiority and achievements entrust it with the leadership of Europe. We clearly recognize our mission to save European culture from the advancing Asiatic barbarism. We know that we have to fight against an incensed and tough opponent. This battle can only end with the destruction of one or the other; a compromise is out of the question."[35]

Similarly, General Walter von Reichenau declared, "The essential goal of the campaign against the Jewish-Bolshevik system is the complete destruction of its power instruments and the eradication of the Asiatic influence on the European cultural sphere."[36] Reichenau essentially granted soldiers a license to exterminate, heralding them as the "avenger of all the bestialities which have been committed against the Germans and related races."[37] General Erich von Manstein recognized the war as "a battle for life and death against the Bolshevik system" and asserted that Judeo-Bolshevism must "never again . . . interfere in our European living space."[38] The Wehrmacht, like its futuristic brethren in the Mobile Infantry, are the shock troops in parallel clashes of civilizations.

Genocidal regimes define the targeted race or ethnicity as both subhuman and dangerous. The Young Turks referred to the Armenians as insects; the Nazis portrayed Jews as vermin, cockroaches, bacilli, monstrous and supernatural foes; Joseph Stalin, the Khmer Rouge, Slobodan Milosevic, Hutu Power, and Janjaweed who terrorized Darfur repeatedly characterized their enemies as insects in need of extermination. At the same time, these insects threaten the health and safety of the vastly superior race instigating the genocide. Verhoeven, following Heinlein's narrative, employs actual insects to combat the human race, but the same rules apply. Florentine Strzelczyk argues the bugs portrayed in *Starship Troopers* "seem to unite a German anti-Semite's fantasies" and allow "viewers to indulge in an exultation of the beauty of fascist power and to engage in a mock-Holocaust without ever having to confront historical legacies or current views of racism."[39] In a particularly graphic scene, students dissect bugs in a biology class while the teacher (Rue McClanahan) extols the virtues of the Arachnids: "We humans like to think we are Nature's finest achievement. I'm afraid it isn't true . . . it reproduces in vast numbers, has no ego, doesn't know about death, and so is the perfect selfless member of society." When Carmen argues that humans are superior for having created art, math, and interstellar travel, the teacher lauds the Arachnids' evolutionary prowess and their ability to colonize planets "by hurling their spore into space."[40] The sheer monstrosity of the Arachnids legitimizes genocide.

The Wehrmacht dehumanized the Soviet enemy using similar language. An article in a Wehrmacht military journal detailed the threat posed by Bolshevik commissars in the Red Army, calling them "the embodiment of the Satanic and insane hatred against the whole of noble humanity. The shape of these commissars reveals to the rebellion of the Untermenschen [subhumans] against noble blood." The same article states, "we would insult the animals if we described these mostly Jewish men and beasts."[41] Nineteenth-century racial theorists like Houston Stewart Chamberlain and Arthur de Gobineau argued Jews are an extremely strong race because of their single-minded focus on materialism and inclination to avoid racial mixing. However, Chamberlain and Gobineau maintain Jews are inferior to the more cultured Aryans.[42] The Arachnids are cast in a similar light. In a televised debate between two academics, one argues the Arachnids must be extremely intelligent based on their military effectiveness. The other commentator scoffs, "Frankly, I find the idea of a bug that thinks offensive!"[43] In the end, the humans do in fact discover an entire caste of brain bugs responsible for ambushing Federation troops. The idea that the enemy race is simultaneously dangerous and inferior is common to both the Nazi utopia and the Federation.

Starship Troopers producer Jon Davidson thought the idea of creating a fascist utopia "was both interesting and amusing."[44] The amusing portion of the utopia concerns the presence of so many elements typical of the plastic world reminiscent of teenage soap operas. The casting of veterans from shows like *Beverly Hills 90210* (1990–2000) and *Melrose Place* (1992–1999), a television genre that has lost none of its popularity since the 1990s, reinforces this perspective. Some critics were bothered by Verhoeven's choices. Richard Schickel questioned the unexplored premise of a future society that appears to be a happy fascist world. Mike Clark was seduced by the "army of sweet-tempered, fresh-faced fascists."[45] Hardly an unexplored premise, the choice of attractive but forgettable actors floating through a Nazi wonderland is at the heart of Verhoeven's satiric vision. The twenty-third-century Earth is, as one reviewer notes, a mix of "California chic with clean, gleaming futuristic fascism."[46] In another subversive nod to American pop culture, the unnerving character of Carl is played by Neil Patrick Harris, also known as Doogie Howser, MD, the endearing television teenage prodigy. Carl evolves from a sweet and bright kid into a cold and methodical sadist working as a government scientist. There is something disarming about seeing Doogie Howser clad in an SS uniform torturing insects and preaching extermination, which was precisely why Harris was cast in the role.[47]

Verhoeven concentrates on the unfettered power of the media in his films set in the future [*Starship Troopers*, *Total Recall* (1990), *Robocop* (1987)]. Verhoeven suggests the real culprit is not some shadowy government figure or the military, but our culture and propensity to be distracted by slickly produced sex and violence. J. P. Telotte argues the Federal Network, the only manifestation of the Federation with whom the audience interacts, is the incarnation of "a fascist spirit of control incubated in a derealized environment."[48] Like any government at war, the Federation suppresses dissent and removes the notion the conflict is more complex than it seems. During a scene reminiscent of media coverage during the Gulf War, an embedded reporter wanders the corridors of a battle station buzzing with activity, stopping to chat with the Mobile Infantry. The reporter presents a straw man opposing viewpoint: "Some say the bugs were provoked by the intrusion of humans into their natural habitat, that a 'live and let live' policy is preferable to war with the bugs." Rico interrupts the live shot, "Yeah, well, I'm from Buenos Aires, and I say kill'em all!"[49] The reporter smiles, acknowledging Johnny speaks for the Federation. There is no dissent in the Federation because of the "stability" veterans imposed on humanity. Verhoeven's attractive and militaristic utopia is all too familiar, a reflection of ourselves (or at least what a significant portion of Americans hope to become). He admits: "I tried to seduce the audience to join in [Troopers] society, but then ask, 'What are you really joining up for?'"[50]

Nazi Side of the Moon: *Iron Sky* (2012)

Finnish director Timo Vuorensola's 2012 *Iron Sky* is an intentionally absurd SF film drawing on both Astrofuturism and Astrofascism for comedic inspiration. Fears of a Fourth Reich—the return or resurrection of Nazi villainy and power—understandably lingered in the postwar period. Hundreds of Nazis fled abroad, and strange rumors of Hitler's own escape persisted despite all evidence to the contrary.[51] These conspiracy theories were aided by exaggerated claims of German technical superiority, rumors of fantastic wonder weapons left on the drawing board and in abandoned warehouses, and the dispersion of Nazi scientists to further their research under new patronage. One outlandish theory concerns the existence of a secret Nazi base in Antarctica concealing flying saucers (whether Nazi built or extraterrestrial is debatable) and ambitions for establishing a Fourth Reich.[52] The notion of a lost battalion hiding beneath the ice, waiting to liberate Earth from liberalism and communism intrigued neo-Nazis and SF fans alike since the 1970s.[53] *Iron Sky* begins with a premise grounded in the Antarctica conspiracy: what if hundreds of Nazis escaped to the Moon in flying saucers in 1945? In this scenario, the Nazis won the space race before it even started. Of course, actual Nazi scientists played a significant role in the US space program. NASA scientist Arthur Rudolph, the father of the Saturn rocket and a Project Paperclip acquisition who returned to Germany after a government investigation into his Nazi past revealed his complicity in war crimes, called the 1969 Apollo 11 Moon landing, "a German victory."[54]

Living in hiding for seventy years, the Nazis' descendants in *Iron Sky* preserved as much of the Third Reich as possible, preparing for a future invasion of Earth. The film begins with a US manned mission landing on the Moon. One of the astronauts is an African American model named James Washington (Christopher Kirby), who was chosen as part of the president's (Stephanie Paul) ridiculous "Black to the Moon" campaign. When the lunar vehicle lands too close to the Nazi base, Washington is taken prisoner and the other astronaut is shot. The Moon Nazis are bewildered by the black man in their midst, but are more interested to learn Washington's smartphone has enough power to fuel the enormous fleet of saucers lying dormant inside the base. The Moon führer, Wolfgang Kortzfleisch (Udo Kier), orders the ambitious Nazi commander Klaus Adler (Götz Otto) to retrieve more Apple products from Earth to finalize the invasion. Adler's fiancée, Renate Richter (Julia Dietze) is a school teacher and the daughter of chief scientist Dr. Richter (Tilo Prückner). Renate's understanding of Nazi ideology is completely divorced from its historical roots in Germany. A young idealist, Richter is intrigued by Washington and just lukewarm about Adler, her genetically determined mate. After "albinizing" Washington, literally turning him Caucasian, Adler takes him back to Earth on the saucer with Renate hiding as a stowaway. Adler meets the president's campaign advisor, Vivian Wagner (Peta Sergeant), and proceeds to introduce Nazi rhetoric and pageantry into the presidential campaign. Together, Wagner and Adler feed each other's ambitions while Kortzfleisch angrily seeks Adler out on Earth, unaware of his treason. Adler kills the Moon führer so he can assume the mantle of leadership and finally commence the attack on Earth. Meanwhile, Renate learns the truth about Nazism with the help of Washington. After a Nazi blitz attack on New York City, the United Nations convenes and is goaded into war by the president, who is clearly modeled on Sarah Palin. Wagner informs the president the Nazi Moon base houses the super element Helium-3, the energy source of the future. Declaring the element the sole property of the US, the nations of the Earth proceed to destroy each other along with most of the Nazi fleet. Renate and Washington, who is returned to his original pigmentation, embrace amid the destruction and return to the Moon where they will presumably build a new society.

Part of the comedy in *Iron Sky* derives from our realization that for the Moon Nazis history and technology ceased in 1945. It is amusing to watch a single iPod fuel a fleet of flying saucers while enormous 1940s-era computers churn away in vain, but the Nazis' escape from history is less humorous. As one review notes, "*Iron Sky* is more in the tradition of *The Three Stooges* than Charlie Chaplin, despite trying to invoke it."[55] We are encouraged from the outset to regard these Nazis differently than their terrestrial brethren, despite all the trappings of the Third Reich adorning the base. The Moon Nazis wear the same uniforms, carry Luger pistols and World War II–era submachine guns, name their clunky saucers Siegfrieds and the ultimate weapon Götterdammerung (both Wagnerian references), and organize all aspects of life on racial principles despite the absence of other races. Timo Vuorensola regards Nazism as the ultimate evil, but believes its representation could benefit from a "more comedic approach. The sinister side has become maybe a little bit like aesthetic noise. With the comedic approach, I think you maybe unearth something that makes you realize what this was all about."[56] Perhaps, but it is not altogether clear what *Iron Sky* unearthed other than some tenuous comparisons between Nazi aggression and American neoliberalism and some clever nods to *The Great Dictator* (1940), *Dr. Strangelove* (1964), and *Blade Runner* (1982).[57] Vuorensola claims *Iron Sky* is about "the rhetoric, the language of fascism, and how we can hear it in today's worldwide politics as well."[58] Where Paul Verhoeven succeeds in aestheticizing fascism as a means of skewering our fascination with it, Vuorensola fails to balance the satiric elements of *Iron Sky* with relevant commentary.

Iron Sky's most sympathetic character is Renate Richter, the sweetly naïve schoolteacher who preaches the tenets of Nazism unaware of its horrific legacies on Earth. The Moon Nazis live in the utopia the earthbound Nazis could not realize—a world without Jews. Consequently, no character on Earth or on the Moon ever mentions the Holocaust or refers to Jews. Richter's Pollyannaish worldview derives from a complete disconnect from reality enabled by lifelong propaganda abetted by isolation. For example, Richter believes Adolf Hitler is actually Adenoid Hynkel, Charlie Chaplin's imitation of Hitler in *The Great Dictator*. Richter shows her students Chaplin's famous dance with the globe, which has apparently been edited to remove the balloon popping. Richter cannot see Hynkel as a caricature, only an authentic leader. On Earth, Washington shows her the entire film and

Richter realizes she's been deceived her entire life. It takes a satire to bring her around, not *Night and Fog* or *Shoah*, for example.

Ordered to develop a campaign ad for the American president, Richter delivers an impassioned speech verbalizing one of Nazi propaganda's favorite messages—Hitler as doctor of the nation, excising the cancerous elements and purging the weak:[59]

> The world is sick, but we are the doctors. The world is anemic, but we are the vitamin. The world is weary, but we are the strength. We are here to make the world healthy once again, with hard work, with honesty, with clarity, with decency. We are the product of loving mothers and brave fathers. We are the embodiment of love and bravery! We are the gift of both God and Science. We are the answer to the question. We are the promise delivered to all mankind. For that, we raise our hands to one Nation. We step to the beat of one drum. We march to the beat of one heart.[60]

That this Sarah Palinesque president adopts a Nazi persona with the help of Adler and the leather-clad Vivian Wagner, who manages a convincing *Ilsa: She Wolf of the SS* impersonation, accentuates the film's message about fascism's universal appeal. *Iron Sky* ostensibly resurrects the Nazi menace, but it is the United States that destroys the world. Reviewer Kit MacFarlane is correct in interpreting the film's third act: "You wanted Nazis? Worse yet, we'll give you Americans."[61] With the Earth in flames and the Moon base damaged, Renate Richter sees clearly now. When her confused and scared students give Renate the Nazi salute, she stops them and begins a new era of instruction: "Please, never again."[62]

Network Nazis: *The Twilight Zone* and *Star Trek*

Most Americans knew little or nothing about the Holocaust until the trial of Adolf Eichmann in 1961. The televised event allowed international audiences to witness history and recognize the scope of the industrialized murder.[63] For a nation embroiled in political violence related to civil rights and an increasingly unpopular Vietnam conflict, the Holocaust emerged as a convenient and accessible moral paradigm with which to frame contemporary sociopolitical issues.[64] Television predictably exploited the Eichmann trial's notoriety and integrated Holocaust themes in popular shows like *The Twilight Zone* and *Star Trek*, confident American audiences would respond favorably.

The Twilight Zone's "Death's Head Revisited" aired in November 1961. The episode is a haunting tale of guilt and judgment inspired by the ongoing

Eichmann trial in which a former SS captain, Gunther Lutze (Oscar Beregi Jr.), returns to Dachau on a nostalgic tour, but is confronted by the ghosts of his many victims who put him on trial for crimes against humanity. The apparitions force Lutze to endure the same tortures he administered seventeen years earlier. Lutze returns to the land of the living but is consigned to a mental institution where he continually experiences terrifying hallucinations. The attending doctor suggests Lutze's visit to Dachau prompted the breakdown and asks, "Why does it still stand? Why do we keep it standing?"[65] Rod Serling answers the doctor in the closing narration, describing concentration camps as "monuments to a moment in time when some men decided to turn the Earth into a graveyard. Into it they shoveled all of their reason, their logic, their knowledge—but worst of all, their conscience." Serling began the episode by noting a place as terrible as Dachau does not simply occupy our reality: "By its nature, by its very nature, it must be one of the populated areas of . . . the Twilight Zone."[66] In other words, the physical spaces of the Holocaust belong to history *and* the supernatural. Humanity deserves to be haunted and ceaselessly traumatized, lest it happen again. The January 24, 1963, episode "He's Alive" reinforces this sentiment as Hitler, who inexplicably survived the war, coaches an American neo-Nazi on how to spread hate and division. Hitler congratulates his pupil, declaring, "We are immortal!"[67] Serling's trenchant narration in "Death's Head Revisited" echoes Yehiel De-Nur's planet Auschwitz testimony delivered just five months before the episode aired. *The Twilight Zone* may be another dimension, but its inspired punishments for humanity's sins are entirely our own doing. There is no escaping history's judgment.

The original *Star Trek* series laudably promoted inclusiveness and provided progressive social commentary during the turbulent late-1960s. With an international and diverse crew, the USS *Enterprise* travels the universe guided by the Prime Directive prohibiting Starfleet from interfering in the development of other civilizations and imposing its will on others. This principle was put to the test in the February 16, 1968, episode "Patterns of Force." Investigating the disappearance of a prominent historian named John Gill (David Brian), the *Enterprise* arrives at the planet Ekos where it is immediately attacked by a weapon supposedly too advanced for the primitive civilization. The *Enterprise* deflects the missile easily, but the crew is baffled by Ekos's evolution and that of its more peaceful neighbor Zeon, which developed interstellar travel. Captain Kirk (William Shatner) suspects Gill violated the directive by assisting one or both planets. Kirk and Spock (Leonard Nimoy) beam down to the surface of Ekos to investigate. The duo encounters Ekosian soldiers in Nazi stormtrooper uniforms, swastikas draped on every building, film footage of massive Nazi rallies, and Nazi rhetoric. The so-called Final Decision is designed to eliminate the poor Zeons, who only wanted to share their culture with the Ekosians. An Ekosian news report declares, "the Führer has ordered our glorious capital to be made Zeon-free." Kirk and Spock soon learn the fate of Gill—he is the führer of this neo-Nazi civilization. After stealing uniforms, the two try to infiltrate Ekosian headquarters, but are caught by Party Chairman Eneg (Patrick Horgan) and imprisoned with some Zeon resistance members. Kirk and Spock learn Deputy Führer Melakon (Skip Homeier) is the actual leader and Gill is kept in a drugged state. Gill explains his misguided initiative to introduce Nazism on Ekos to jump-start its development, calling the Third Reich the "most efficient state Earth ever knew," a statement Spock verifies as historical fact.[68] Predictably, the experiment failed and now the Zeons face extermination. The *Enterprise* crew defeats Melakon and frees Kirk, Spock, and Gill. Unfortunately, Gill is killed in the struggle, but not before denouncing the Final Decision to the people who once regarded him as their führer. The episode ends when the *Enterprise* leaves the system, entrusting Ekosians and Zeons to rebuild their worlds together.

Kirk and Spock's investigation on Ekos reveals a society can learn to hate and conform even without any discernable history of prejudice or external trauma such as war or depression. Physically indistinguishable from the Ekosians, the Zeons are analogous to German Jews, who were perceived as somehow more progressive, educated, and timid than their fellow Germans. The comparison is even more explicit with names like Isak, Davod, and Abrom. The Zeons (like Zion) explain to the crew why the Ekosians hate them: "Because with no one to hate there would be nothing to hold them [Ekosians] together. So the party built us into a threat, a disease to be wiped out."[69] While Kirk can pass in this society, Spock, whose otherness must be concealed, lives in fear of discovery. Spock quips that Kirk "makes a very convincing Nazi" in his uniform. Kirk replies the helmet covering Spock's distinctive ears "hides a multitude of sins." The fact Leonard Nimoy is Jewish reinforces the association between the Holocaust and the "Patterns of Force" storyline.[70] Interestingly, the episode's detailed recreation of Nazi rhetoric and uniforms prevented the episode from airing on German television for twenty years.[71] Like other Astrofascist narratives, "Patterns of Force" implies exterminationist ideologies are not bound by Earth's atmosphere and historic contingency. Kirk reduces the Third Reich to a simplistic cautionary tale, telling Spock the Nazis were the result of giving one person too much power. Dehistoricizing the Holocaust and Third Reich is an American tradition, and while the motives may be commendable, such as addressing contemporary racial prejudice and political corruption, the resulting normalization hides a multitude of sins.

Fig. 5.2. Captain James T. Kirk (William Shatner) and Mister Spock (Leonard Nimoy) disguise themselves as Ekosians, an alien race who recreate the Third Reich in *Star Trek*'s "Patterns of Force," airing February 16, 1968.

Astrofascism in the *Star Wars* Universe

The *Star Wars* series and its expanded universe reflects and influences forty years' worth of American cultural and political values. The franchise achieved mythic status and universal recognition, marking a revolution in both the SF epic and the global marketing of cinema.[72] Given its enduring influence and political relevance over the decades, *Star Wars* gives credence to scholars who claimed for a century there is no such thing as just a movie. Until recently, George Lucas exercised near complete control over the franchise: "Not only am I the producer, but I wrote the stories, a lot of the casting decisions are made by me, and I pretty much oversee all the special effects."[73] Critics try to discern Lucas's own biases, but *Star Wars*, like any cultural touchstone appropriated by numerous and contradictory ideologies, cannot be reduced to the filmmaker's intentions. Moreover, the progressive elements in the series, such as the inspirational rebellion against tyranny, are undermined by *Star Wars*'s status as nostalgic cinema. Frederic Jameson believes *Star Wars*'s straightforward narrative, heroic archetypes, and creative pastiche of multiple genres (the Western, the World War II combat film, and the early-twentieth-century SF serial) is an exercise in reactionary myth making.[74] Lucas and subsequent directors intent on capturing the spirit of the original films—*A New Hope* (1977), *Empire Strikes Back* (1980), and *Return of the Jedi* (1983)—embrace Astrofascist style and perspectives with ambiguous results.

The Empire evokes a myriad of historical parallels, including ancient Rome, Napoleonic France, and the Third Reich. George Lucas wrote the first film in the wake of Watergate and the Vietnam War, when many Americans were left reflecting on democracy's inherent fragility and the intoxicating effects of power on unscrupulous politicians. Episodes 1–3 of the series, produced nearly twenty years after *A New Hope*, chronicle the failure of a republic during a prolonged crisis, not unlike Germany's besieged Weimar Republic. Lucas claims Senator Palpatine (Ian McDiarmid), who becomes the Sith emperor Darth Sidious, was modeled on fascist dictators, certainly, but also Richard Nixon.[75] Nazi Germany is the obvious template for the Empire, but no historical precursor has a monopoly on demonstrating the dangers of ambition, rage, and anxiety. Like Hitler capitalizing on economic crisis and a manufactured communist threat during the first months as chancellor, Palpatine asks for and receives emergency powers he has no intention of returning. The Enabling Act of March 23, 1933 granted Hitler unlimited power to enact laws, a tool he used to craft a dynamic dictatorship grounded in fear and a sophisticated cult of personality. Lucas made the link between his fictional republic's collapse and Germany's explicit in *Revenge of the Sith*, noting the film shows how democracy can be "turned over to a tyrant with applause."[76] After vanquishing the Jedi, becoming horribly disfigured in the process, Palpatine addresses the Senate and declares the new Galactic Empire will "last for ten thousand years," a slightly more ambitious goal than Hitler's declaration of the thousand-year Reich.[77]

More recent *Stars Wars* films continue to invoke Nazis as the ultimate evil by tapping into Fourth Reich scenarios. With the Empire apparently destroyed at the conclusion of *Return of the Jedi*, *The Force Awakens* (2015) begins nearly a generation later with a revanchist threat on the horizon—the First Order. Director J. J. Abrams notes the idea "came out of conversations about what would have happened if the Nazis all went to Argentina but started working together again? Could the First Order exist as a group that actually admired the Empire? Could the work of the Empire be seen as unfulfilled? And could Vader be a martyr? Could there be a need to see through what didn't get done?"[78] Both *The Force Awakens* (2015) and *The Last Jedi* (2017) go even further in coding the resurrected Empire as an Astrofascist regime complete with insignia, stagecraft, and rhetoric. As one exasperated reviewer writes, "But honestly, did we need J.J. Abrams to . . . figure out that a 'long time ago in a galaxy far, far away' is just shorthand for 'WHAT IF NAZIS WERE IN SPACE?'"[79] Some scoff at the notion SF must still mine Nazis for inspiration; after all, the Third Reich perished seventy-five years ago. Others argue the resurgence of right-wing populism proves Nazism, like any odious ideology born from crisis, was not consigned to the ash heap of history after all.

The Astrofascist Empire is marked by crisp Nazi-inspired uniforms, overwhelming military force, specifically legions of Stormtroopers genetically designed as perfect warriors, and leaders devoted to a mystical religion. Costume designer John Mollo noted George Lucas wanted Empire personnel to look "efficient, totalitarian, fascist."[80] Adopting the trappings of the Third Reich throughout the series reinforces the Empire as evil and the Rebels as fundamentally good. From casting British actors as villains, a common practice in World War II films, to Lucas's homage to Leni Riefenstahl's more inspired sequences in *Triumph of the Will*, the Empire is not unlike *Starship Trooper*'s Terran Federation in that it is inherently attractive to audiences. George Lucas encountered Riefenstahl in film school, and like many directors working in SF and fantasy, embraced her visual style to communicate the epic scale of SF civilizations.[81] The most famous nod to Riefenstahl occurs at the conclusion of *A New Hope* when the heroes of the Rebellion—Luke Skywalker (Mark Hamill), Han Solo (Harrison Ford), and Chewbacca (Peter Mayhew)—march between rows of uniformed supporters to receive medals from Princess Leia (Carrie Fisher). The set design mirrors Albert Speer's "cathedral of ice" spectacle in *Triumph of the Will* when Hitler and his senior leadership stroll confidently to the stage during a 1937 Nazi Party rally.[82] That Lucas chose to recreate this scene for the Rebels' ceremony and not for the Empire proves the fascist aesthetic escapes context with ease. Filmmaker and critic Jesse Percival notes European fascist style was partially inspired by American cinema in the early twentieth century. Now that same industry decades later furiously cites Nazi iconography without regard for history. "The history is there," she writes, "but if you remove the context and keep the aesthetic, the context will surely vanish into nothing."[83]

The racial politics of *Star Wars* is more fraught and nuanced than the simplistic narrative suggests. First, the universe's principal players—the Empire and the Rebels—are almost entirely white. The Rebellion may comprise hundreds of species, but it is the blonde and blue-eyed Skywalker who brings down the Death Star.[84] The only aliens in the Empire's service are bounty hunters, each stranger and more exotic than the next. Second, many of the films feature barely concealed racial stereotypes masquerading as alien life-forms. The sand people, Jawas, and Watto, a wily and crooked merchant and slaver, embody several Arab and Jewish caricatures; Jar Jar Binks (Ahmed Best) and the Gungan civilization of Naboo are terribly racist travesties referencing African American and

Fig. 5.3. George Lucas channels Leni Riefenstahl's *Triumph of the Will* (1935) in the final scene of *Star Wars: Episode IV* (1977)

Caribbean stereotypes; and the Galactic Trade Federation conjures the Yellow Peril racism of the early twentieth century. Third, the revelation in *The Phantom Menace* (1999) that the Force favors individuals with a high percentage of metachlorians in their blood harkens back to the fascist obsession with purity and the mystical power of blood. Young Anakin Skywalker (Jake Lloyd), the future Darth Vader, is tested and deemed exceptional by the Jedi. Recent films like *The Force Awakens* (2015), *Rogue One* (2016), and *The Last Jedi* (2017) suggest the *Star Wars* universe is becoming more inclusive, specifically by democratizing the Force, killing off the Jedi as a natural elite, and casting more actors of color in significant roles.

The *Star Wars* universe borrows from previous representations of the Holocaust and World War II films. *Rogue One*, an unusual addition to the *Star Wars* universe with its multiethnic *Dirty Dozen* storyline and mass death of protagonists, begins with imperial soldiers invading a quiet farm and terrorizing the family of a scientist the Empire needs to build its ultimate weapon. A young girl burrows herself into a hole, shaking with fear. The scene evokes the opening sequence of Quentin Tarantino's *Inglourious Basterds* (2009) in which SS major Hans Landa (Christoph Waltz) reveals Jews hiding beneath floorboards. Noah Berlatsky notes both films reference "a long history of Holocaust film representations of Stormtroopers searching for Jews in hiding."[85] *Revenge of the Sith* chronicles Anakin Skywalker's descent from Jedi knight into a perpetrator embracing the dark side when he massacres an entire village of sand people to avenge his mother's death. Skywalker dismisses them as animals and the incident barely registers with the other characters, and, one assumes, with audiences. Intentional or not, Star Wars establishes a hierarchy of victims and inures the audience to atrocities against subhuman races.

Star Wars and *Iron Sky* adopt the Astrofascist aesthetic, but also depict a world without Jews. Writing in *The Forward*, Noah Berlatsky argues that "while Nazi-inspired aesthetics and plots provide 'Star Wars' with a convenient shorthand for 'evil,' the ideological core of Nazism's evil is missing. The Empire showcases a version of Nazism motivated neither by anti-Semitism or prejudice against the marginalized."[86] The Empire behaves like cinematic Nazis always have, leaving a trail of destruction in its wake, but in *Star Wars* the Empire's victims are indistinguishable. Obi Wan Kenobi's reaction upon learning of Alderaan's destruction evokes the Holocaust: "I felt a great disturbance in the Force, as if millions of voices suddenly cried out in terror and were suddenly silenced."[87] The Empire perpetrates Holocausts as a matter of course, but it looks good doing it.

It Can Happen Here: Kenneth Johnson's *V*

The popular 1983 SF miniseries *V* begins with a solemn and genuine tribute: "To the heroism of the Resistance Fighters—past, present, and future—this work is respectfully dedicated."[88] Kenneth Johnson, a successful TV writer and producer working in several genres, wanted to adopt Sinclair Lewis's classic 1935 novel *It Can't Happen Here* about a fascist takeover in the United States for television. Johnson ultimately decided SF was an effective genre with which to explore the novel's treatment of fascism, totalitarianism, systemic oppression, civil rights, and failing democracy.[89] Johnson's two-part series portrays the sudden arrival of ostensibly helpful humanoid aliens known as the Visitors who slowly assume control over democratic institutions and media to conceal their true purpose—harvesting humanity for food and resources. In time, the Visitors are unmasked as fascist bipedal lizards posing as humans, manipulating us into enabling our own genocide. The Visitors wear Nazi-like uniforms bearing a variation of the swastika and swear loyalty to a charismatic leader on their home planet. Like the Nazis, the Visitors are also plagued by vicious internal rivalries leading to the adoption of the most radical measures possible. Kenneth Johnson's *V* is a thinly disguised classic World War II story featuring Nazis, collaborators, and resistance fighters engaged in an existential war for the planet. "The Nazis showed us one face for a while and then they took it off and showed us their real faces—metaphorically speaking," Johnson explained.[90] In *V* the historical context of fascism and genocide is integral to the story. Johnson carefully researched the history of the Third Reich and the resistance, *Triumph of the Will*, and *Night and Fog* in his imagining: "All of them contributed ideas, visuals, characters and tonal concepts to *V*."[91]

V, like the popular miniseries *Holocaust* produced a few years earlier, focuses on how families cope with an emerging crisis. The Bernstein family includes three generations under one roof, each of which have a different reaction to the Visitors. Abraham Bernstein (Leonardo Cimino) is a Holocaust survivor who is immediately suspicious of the Visitors' rhetoric, promises, and polished demeanor; his grandson Daniel (David Packer), a socially awkward outcast, eagerly joins the Friends of the Visitors, a veritable Visitor Youth that evolves into an auxiliary police force comprised of collaborator humans; Stanley (George Morfogen) and Lynn Bernstein (Bonnie Bartlett), Daniel's parents, do not share Abraham's cynicism or Daniel's enthusiasm. They muddle along until the danger is too great to ignore. Johnson's characters are complex and evince realistic arcs. There are good Visitors, bad humans, and a multitude of others feeling their way through the darkness, but the strongest characters invoke history and experience to light the way. After the Visitors designate scientists an enemy within, presumably because they can discover the truth about the Visitor's reptilian nature, most people turn against scientists and their families, rounding them up for an uncertain fate. After the Visitors demand humans register scientists in a database, Stanley brushes it off: "This will pass."[92] Abraham counters, "That's what I said in Berlin." Abraham sees history repeating itself. When scientists crucial to the resistance seek shelter with the Bernsteins, Stanley balks, understandably fearful of the consequences, but Abraham demands they hide them. Stanley is weary of hearing his father's Holocaust story once more, but Abraham reveals what he has hidden from his son for decades:

STANLEY: I know the story!

ABRAHAM: No, you don't! You don't. Your mother, b'shalom [In peace]. . . . Your mother didn't have a heart attack in the boxcar. She made it with me, to the camp. I can still see her, standing naked in the freezing cold. Her beautiful black hair was gone. They'd shaved her head. I can still see her waving to me as they marched her off to the showers—the showers with no water. Perhaps, if somebody had given us a place to hide . . . don't you see, Stanley! They have to stay. Or else, we haven't learned a thing.[93]

When Abraham encounters children defacing a Visitor propaganda poster, he decides to teach them what he learned as a young man and sprays a V for victory.[94]

The primary villain in *V* is the beautiful and sinister Diana (Jane Badler), an ambitious scientist in her own right who, like Josef Mengele, is interested in performing medical experiments on captured humans. Diana resents serving under John (Richard Herd), signifying one of many rifts in the Visitors' command structure. As the Visitors' genocidal plan approaches fruition, dissenters emerge and make common cause with the human resistance led by biologist Juliet Parrish (Faye Grant), whom Johnson modeled after French resistance fighter Andrea Dijon, and Mike Donavan (Marc Singer), a TV cameraman. Donavan asks Martin (Frank Ashmore), a pro-human Visitor, how his "Great Leader" came to power. Martin responds with a familiar history lesson: "Circumstances. Promises. Financial backing. A doctrine that appealed to the unthinking. Assurances that he, as their leader, would bring them to greatness. Not enough of us spoke out to question him, or even took him seriously, until it was too late. It's happened here on your planet, hasn't it?"[95] In a stunning scene revealing the Visitors' plans to harvest people, Martin shows Donovan an immense storage room filled with humans in suspended animation. Johnson included the scene to convey the Visitors' "fixation on the use of human beings reduced to cattle, as sources of meat and leather" which is a "Holocaust derived Gothic artifact."[96] Johnson believed it was as important to address humanity's failings in this SF story as it was the malevolent intent of the Visitors—our opportunism, inaction, and outright collaboration with evil. Near the end of part II, Abraham dies because of his own grandson's betrayal, but he issued a call to arms for the resistance: "We must fight this darkness that threatens to engulf us."[97] The original *V* miniseries is an exciting SF story imagining a totalitarian civilization invading Earth. The same circumstances that gave rise to Hitler occurred on Sirius 4, the Visitors' home planet. Earth is just one victim of the Great Leader's quest for Lebensraum.

Basking in the success of *V*, NBC quickly ordered another miniseries concentrating on the armed struggle between humans and Visitors, and although Kenneth Johnson retained the title of creator, he was not involved in the writing or production. The 1984 miniseries *V: The Final Battle* suffered from both Johnson's absence and a smaller budget than the original. NBC committed to a series after *The Final Battle* aired, but it only lasted one season. Without Johnson the show drifted aimlessly and lost touch with the historical and moral subtext of the original miniseries, an opinion shared by actors who worked on all three productions.[98] In 2009, ABC revived *V* for two seasons, again without Johnson's input. In this post-9/11 version the Visitors lived among humans for years forming sleeper cells and undermining defenses from within before the flying saucers arrived. Whereas Johnson used SF to discuss fascism and the resistance, the short-lived 2009 series is a product of America's increased paranoia, anxiety, and tendency to dehumanize enemies in the age of terrorism. In a 2011 interview Johnson claimed his *V* had a "timeless quality" because the story is "about an oppressed people living under a totalitarian regime, and how that power affects people."[99] The original *V* miniseries translated the legacies of World War II and genocide into a cautionary tale about humanity's intrinsic weakness and the everlasting appeal of intoxicating ideologies and spectacle.

"You Could Almost Forget They're Nazis": *The Man in the High Castle*

The promotional campaign for Amazon's *The Man in the High Castle*, an adaptation of Philip K. Dick's 1962 novel depicting an alternate reality in which the Third Reich and Japan defeat and occupy the United States, involved decorating New York City subways with American flags emblazoned with swastikas and Imperial Japanese insignia. Responding to a flood of calls and emails from offended New Yorkers, Mayor Bill de Blasio called on Amazon to remove its "irresponsible and offensive" advertisements.[100] Executive producer Frank Spotnitz agreed the public relations agency's decision to wrap subway seats in Nazi imagery was a poor one, but sympathized with their dilemma: "It's very difficult with a show with subject matter like this to market it tastefully, so I understand they're walking a very difficult line."[101] *High Castle*'s writers, producers, and set designers also walk a fine line between normalizing the Third Reich to the point its horrors become indistinct fodder for pop culture and using its history and legacies to craft an intelligent and reflective representation. Dick's novel infrequently describes Germans or the Greater Reich portion of North America, locating much of the action in Japanese-occupied San Francisco and the neutral zone separating the two regions. Amazon's adaptation, however, explores the Nazi dystopia both in New York City and the grand capital of Berlin in stunning and imaginative detail. Some may consider *High Castle* guilty of aestheticizing and normalizing the Third Reich, and perhaps some elements of the series contribute to this, but it is redeemed by strong writing and compelling characters highlighting historical continuities between the show's alternate reality and our own.[102]

Counterfactualism is not and should not be the sole province of fiction. Historian Jeremy Black writes that historians regard the process of "conjecturing on what did not happen in order to understand what did" a valuable intellectual exercise, particularly for identifying turning points in history.[103] Asking why necessitates evaluating the roads not taken, but the what if question integral to the historian's tool box can devolve into the reactionary if only sentiment encouraging nostalgia and validating what might be called alternative facts. The danger inherent in applying counterfactualism to the Nazi era is not necessarily in promoting Nazi ideology (neo-Nazis have endless opportunities and venues to do that), but in inviting uninformed moral relativism by comparing regimes' atrocities.[104] Moreover, counterfactualism empowers those who maintain a choice here or an event there somehow could have prevented genocide.[105] Suggesting Jews somehow controlled their own fate or that a Nazi victory was preferable to a Soviet one are tactics employed by Holocaust deniers. Most fictional alternate histories invoking World War II and the Third Reich are unconcerned with weighing in on one side or the other of a historical argument. Instead, Aviezer Tucker notes, these histories and popular fiction reveal "an aesthetic fascination with apocalyptic landscapes, with consistent realistic depictions of a horrendous alternative universe, like a [Hiernonymus] Bosch painting."[106] *High Castle*'s dystopia is strangely alluring in its attention to detail, both visually and historically. From the digital creation of Albert Speer's imagined Berlin to Wernher von Braun's technological marvels screeching across the sky, a triumphant Reich nonetheless shows the strain of a great empire collapsing under the weight of internecine conflicts and its own avarice. As viewers, we are mesmerized, horrified, and troubled by just how real this alternate reality appears.

High Castle begins in 1962 in San Francisco, the capital of the Japanese Pacific States, during a period of growing tensions between former allies Imperial Japan and Nazi Germany. Juliana Crain (Alexa Davalos) is confronted by her desperate half-sister Trudy (Conor Leslie), who hands Juliana a film reel labeled *The Grasshopper Lies Heavy*. Trudy tells her, "I found the reason . . . for everything."[107] Trudy is shot in the street by the Japanese military police (*Kenpeitai*) and Juliana flees to the apartment she shares with Frank Frick (Rupert Evans), a skilled artisan who is forced to conceal his Jewish background. Juliana obsessively watches the film containing actual World War II footage depicting victory over the Axis powers. Juliana believes the film's alternate reality may be true, but Frank reflexively denies this premise and fears Juliana's brush with the resistance endangers them. Juliana is determined to honor Trudy and complete her mission of delivering the film to a contact in the neutral zone. In New York City SS agent Joe Blake (Luke Kleintank) is given the mission to infiltrate the resistance and recover copies of *The Grasshopper Lies Heavy*, putting him on a collision course with Juliana inside the neutral zone. Joe's superior is Obergruppenführer John Smith (Rufus Sewell), a former US Army veteran who quickly rose through the ranks of the SS to become the senior officer in the American provinces of the Greater Reich. Convinced the films are an existential threat, an aging Adolf Hitler orders Smith to stop at nothing to seize every film and capture their purported creator, the mysterious Man in the High Castle, a man named Hawthorne Abendsen (Stephen Root).

Japanese Trade Minister Nobusuke Tagomi (Cary-Hiroyuki Tagawa) works diligently to avoid an existential threat of a different kind—war with a nuclear Germany. Japan's erstwhile ally has grown restless and Hitler's impending death empowers radicals bent on world domination. Tagomi meets with a rogue German intelligence agent named Rudolph Wegener (Carsten Norgaard), who passes along blueprints for the atomic bomb to ensure Japanese strategic parity with Germany. Meanwhile, Frank is left to atone for Juliana's suspected resistance activities and is brutalized by the Kenpeitai. In a shocking scene, Frank's sister and her children are led to a clandestine gas chamber and killed in a ploy to compel Frank to speak. Enraged, Frank plans to assassinate the Japanese crown prince, but decides against it at the last second. However, the prince is shot by a German agent, scuttling Tagomi and Wegener's back-channel diplomacy. The three storylines—Joe and Juliana's relationship, which is initially based on deceit before evolving into something genuine; Frank's transformation into a vengeful and wily resistance fighter; and Tagomi's attempt to thwart war and his own government's descent into brutality against Americans—converge in the final episodes as everyone seeks the films for their own purposes. Juliana ultimately trusts Joe and allows him to escape the resistance with the film reel for which Trudy gave her life.

Throughout the series we are given hints about the existence of a multiverse and the potential for people to travel between them. Tagomi, a devotee of the *I Ching* who meditates frequently, discovers an individual can pass from one reality to another by concentrating on objects with meaning and authenticity (a picture of a loved one or a necklace, for example). In season 1's finale, Tagomi meditates quietly on a park bench in San Francisco and opens his eyes to a new reality, a San Francisco bathed in bright, loud American culture. It is the United States on the eve of the Cuban Missile Crisis, not the Pacific States embroiled in its own Cold War nuclear crisis with Nazi Germany. Season 1 ends with Hitler ensconced in his mountain retreat surrounded by hundreds of captured film cannisters and watching footage from a war we know he lost. "Every day I watch these films," he tells Wegener, "Every day I learn something."[108] It seems the führer himself, this man of destiny, realizes history is contingent and fragile.

Season 2 follows the characters' separate adventures. Juliana seeks asylum in the Reich to escape the resistance's wrath after Joe's escape and becomes a guest of John Smith. Smith's perfect Nazi family is faced with a horrible dilemma when his son Thomas (Quinn Lord) is diagnosed with a degenerative illness requiring he be euthanized. John goes to great lengths to break the law and save his son, but Thomas is such a devoted Nazi he turns himself in to medical authorities. Joe learns his estranged father is senior Nazi official Martin Heusmann (Sebastian Roché) and travels to Berlin to seek answers about his upbringing. Frank and his friend Ed McCarthy (DJ Qualls) are drawn further into the resistance against the Pacific States, performing ever more violent acts culminating in bombing the Kenpeitai headquarters. Tagomi perfects the art of traveling to the alternate reality where he reconciles with his wife and son, but Tagomi is unable to abandon his responsibility to the world he left behind. Tagomi is shocked to learn his daughter-in-law in the alternate reality is none other than Juliana Crain, whom Tagomi befriends in season 1 when she is sent by the resistance to glean information from the occupation government. Tagomi decides to use footage from actual American hydrogen bomb tests conducted in the Pacific to convince Germany not to attack Japan. Joe decides to stay in Berlin and is drawn into the privileged world of the Nazi elite while his father engineers a plot to succeed Hitler and initiate a nuclear strike against Japan. The plot is foiled by John Smith, who uses Tagomi's footage to convince other Nazis a preemptive strike will destroy the world. Season 2 ends with Juliana confronting Abendsen about her appearance in several films. He tells her she is the moral center, always doing the right thing and influencing others positively despite the terrible world they inhabit. Abendsen explains the films depict alternate realities and reunites Juliana with a still-living Trudy as proof.

Season 3 is about resistance, hope, and exploring the mechanics and consequences of the multiverse. The meteoric rise of John Smith under the new Heinrich Himmler regime does nothing to ease the family's pain after Thomas's "noble" sacrifice. Smith is forced to honor Thomas as a hero of the Reich while powerful enemies like Reichsführer George Lincoln Rockwell (David Furr) and FBI Director J. Edgar Hoover (William Forsythe) gather evidence of Smith's crimes to protect his son, although Hoover betrays Rockwell to ingratiate himself with Smith. Joe rots in an SS prison and is reeducated to the point he executes his treacherous father and becomes a truly faithful servant of the Reich. Under the leadership of Josef Mengele (John Hans Tester), Reich scientists discover the existence of travelers in their midst. Mengele is on the verge of penetrating the multiverse, raising the prospect Nazis could conquer all realities. While the Nazis and Japanese maintain an uncomfortable peace with each other, the Japanese face a growing resistance movement inspired by Frank's posters produced in the safety of the neutral zone. Frank finds peace in a community of Jews struggling to maintain their traditions while aiding resistance movements across occupied North America. Frank is eventually captured by Inspector Kido and executed at the site of a Japanese American internment camp, but he is at peace.

Alarmed by Nazi progress in unraveling the mystery of the multiverse, Juliana and Abendsen try to destroy a Nazi underground laboratory and are captured and interrogated by John Smith, who obsessively screens Abendsen's films after glimpsing Thomas living happily in an alternate universe. Juliana kills Joe during the raid on the tunnel after discovering he is devoted to the infernal Nazi project. The new führer, Heinrich Himmler, arrives in America to declare the end of history and destroy the Statue of Liberty in a spectacular display, but assassins shoot and wound him. The season ends with Abendsen revealing no one can exist in both universes simultaneously.

High Castle's visual style is an interesting amalgamation of a familiar postwar American urban landscape and the Nazi aesthetic had it proved triumphant. Cinematographer James Hawkinson wanted a "retro-futuristic world. A past influenced by the future, a dystopia with impossible technology, a fake world. Nostalgia mixes with science fiction. My approach aesthetically is to create the nostalgia of 1962 through color cinematography prevalent of the time and make this world eerily familiar."[109] The superpowers' differing approaches to occupation are revealed aesthetically as well: Japan is understated, integrating its insignia and signage with San Francisco's distinctive architecture; Germany imports its grand totalitarian style across the Atlantic, erecting enormous swastikas and a gleaming SS headquarters dwarfing the Empire State Building. Hawkinson turns Times Square into a showcase for Nazi propaganda, designing billboards "to inject a sense amongst . . . people that the Reich still has the same power and vigor it had during the war."[110] Executive producer Frank Spotnitz is as impressed with Nazism's style as Paul Verhoeven, noting while Hitler "was an incredibly evil and dangerous villain who managed to kill people with a hateful ideology . . . he also happened to have costumes and production design that were tailor made for Hollywood." Spotnitz thought Nazi "buildings, their military uniforms, their parades, their marches, their Leni Riefenstahl films were amazing aesthetics for their cause."[111]

High Castle's eerily familiar feel is a testament to its production values, but the writers cleverly suggest the United States is fertile ground for a fascist takeover without resorting to specious comparisons or minimizing the history of the Third Reich. Like the US, the Greater Nazi Reich is the dominant military power on Earth after developing the Heisenberg device (atomic bomb), perfecting supersonic air travel via a variation of the Concord, but only faster, and grandiose plans to desalinate the Mediterranean Sea and grow crops in the Sahara Desert. *High Castle*'s design team imagines a future Reich surpassing postwar America. However, as Wegener tells Tagomi after Tagomi compliments him on the Reich's technological marvels, "technology is not the measure of a great civilization."[112] The Greater Reich also loves television, especially a *Dragnet*-like cop show called *American Reich*. In a clever observation about our own obsession with Hitler documentaries, Ed complains to Frank about Hitler's ubiquity: "He can't keep himself off TV. Every fucking day. Remember the last time he wasn't on TV?"[113]

The Third Reich's victory in World War II accomplished its ultimate goal—a world without Jews. Not only was the actual Final Solution achieved, but the Jews of North America are hunted and largely exterminated as well. Enemies of the Reich are called Semites, but it is unclear how many Jews remain on the planet. The Greater Reich apparently murdered millions of Africans when occupying the continent and millions more African

Americans by leveraging Americans' inherent racism into genocide. The only African Americans in the series inhabit the neutral zone or the Pacific States. *High Castle* refers to these absences by accentuating the ease with which Americans either collaborated with or consented to the draconian and genocidal regime. There are references to anti-Jewish pogroms in Boston, where mobs dragged Jews from their houses and butchered them in the same manner the Poles of Jedwabne massacred every Jew in town as Nazis looked on approvingly.[114] America's own racial past is easily co-opted by the Greater Reich to fulfill its utopian racial goals, which comes as no surprise considering America's racial state influenced the Third Reich's.[115] America's eugenics movement found a logical home in the Third Reich. Throughout the series we are confronted by Americans indifferent to the atrocities committed in their name. When Joe blows a tire in the countryside on his mission to meet Juliana, a helpful policeman (Ron Roggé) shows him his Marine tattoo from "a long time ago." "We lost the war, didn't we?" he says, "Now I can't even remember what we were fighting for." Joe is confused when ashes fall from the sky like snow. The policeman casually explains, "That's the hospital. Tuesdays they burn cripples, terminally ill, drag on the state."[116] Chief SS officer in North America John Smith must confront the consequences of the racial state he enforces when Thomas is diagnosed. Thomas is so distraught upon learning the truth he calls himself a "useless eater," the same phrase Nazis used to promote its expansive T-4 "euthanasia" program.[117]

High Castle forces us to reflect on our own uncomfortable history. Having already undergone an invasive medical exam seeking to determine her racial health, Juliana prepares for the Reich citizenship test with the help of a smitten Thomas Smith. When he quizzes her on "exterminations before the Reich," Juliana is at a loss. "Didn't they ever teach you about the Indians?" Thomas asks earnestly.[118] What is or should be a source of shame in our world is a point of pride in theirs. The nightmare scenario at the heart of *High Castle* is that American Nazis won the war along with the Germans.[119] George Lincoln Rockwell, the obscure leader of the inconsequential American Nazi Party, is Reichsführer of North America in *High Castle* and J. Edgar Hoover is as manipulative and contemptible an FBI director for the Greater Nazi Reich as he ever was in our world. America's inveterate racism, sexism, proclivity for pseudoscience like eugenics, and blood-soaked furtherance of manifest destiny is free to flourish uninhibited thanks to an atomic bomb obliterating Washington, DC in 1945. The Nazis are an excuse for a segment of Americans to fulfill their deepest, darkest wishes unencumbered by a constitutional republic.

High Castle skillfully replicates American family life circa 1960 in the Greater Reich. Living in a beautiful suburb of New York, the Smiths are a Norman Rockwell painting come to life. Helen Smith (Chelah Horsdal) is the loving mother of two well-behaved, patriotic children and a loyal partner to John. Finding refuge in the Reich, Juliana befriends the Smiths to help the resistance, but struggles to maintain an emotional distance from what appears to be a perfectly normal family. "You could almost forget they're Nazis," she tells her resistance contact.[120] One of the fine lines *High Castle* negotiates is humanizing perpetrators to the point we lose sight of their crimes, a challenge many Holocaust films contend with. The Smiths are a loving and relatable family. However, their barbeque is not for the Fourth of July but for Victory in America Day; Thomas does not lead the pledge of allegiance at Fritz Kuhn High School, named after the leader of the German American Bund, but an oath to Hitler; and Sunday church services are farcical exercises in Aryan Christianity. John Smith is a hardened Nazi guilty of horrible crimes, but we are placed in a difficult position as an audience because his actions on behalf of his family are noble and evoke empathy.

Heinrich Himmler, John Smith's superior in *High Castle* and an unlikely moderate inside the fictional regime, famously encouraged his top commanders assigned to the killing grounds of Eastern Europe to remain strong in the face of their terrible responsibility. The following is an excerpt from an actual speech delivered to SS functionaries in Poland on October 4, 1943:

> I also want to speak to you here, in complete frankness, about a very grave matter. We can talk about this openly amongst ourselves, yet we will never talk about it in public. . . . I mean the evacuation of the Jews, the extermination of the Jewish people. . . . Most of you will know what it means when 100 corpses lie together, when 500 lie there or when there are 1000. To have seen this through, and—except for cases of human weakness—to have remained decent, that has made us hard. This is an unwritten and never to be written page of glory in our history. . . . Overall, we can say that we have fulfilled this most difficult of tasks for the love of our people. And we have suffered no harm to our inner being, our soul, our character.[121]

John Smith is a fictional American example of the decent man who derives his strength and character from his duty as an SS officer. Rudolph Wegener, the traitor to the Reich who comes to regret his role in the unwritten page of glory, drinks too much at the Smiths' Victory in America celebration and bares his troubled soul: "Nobody talks about the camps. Nobody talks about how many were exterminated. You get accommodations for it, but nobody talks about it." The room is silent. Smith is worried his wife and children will be exposed to further ugly truths. "Sacrifices had to be made," Smith says, staring into his whiskey, "Now we have a better world."[122] The Himmler of history expected to lose the war militarily, but the Final Solution was achievable even in defeat. In *High Castle* the proof of this Nazi victory is the silence of the perpetrators and the absence of Jews in the Greater Reich. It is unwritten and never to be written, but Smith experiences painful flashbacks of murdering Jews in places like Cincinnati. Smith is shaken by a dream in which John and Thomas are fishing when dozens of bodies of people Smith killed float to the surface. The John Smith of season 3 is burdened by guilt and sadness, but also a gnawing resentment at Germans reveling in the destruction of America's landmarks, its material history. *High Castle* implies Smith might be happier and maybe even decent in another reality.

How does *High Castle* represent the Holocaust and Judaism in the multiverse? We know the victorious Reich with the aid of an indifferent Japan has all but eradicated Jews and Judaism from the face of the Earth, but *High Castle* leaves us with some hope. Despairing over the murder of his family, Frank Frick reconnects with Judaism by attending clandestine services with a Jewish resistance member and his family. Mark Sampson (Michael Gaston) comforts Frank by reminding him Jews are an ancient people and will endure and "the Nazis won't last."[123] Jews' sense of time is authentic; the Nazis' is rooted in elusive permanence. Mark and Frank eventually find a refuge for Jews in the neutral zone where Frank begins lessons in preparation for a bar mitzvah, a task he comes to realize is about preserving Jewish traditions in a world virtually empty of Jews. Whereas the Nazis plan the absolute erasure of American history—melting down the Liberty Bell and blowing up the Statue of Liberty—the small Jewish enclave celebrates Jews' "five thousand years of joy and pain."[124] The episode entitled "History Ends" cuts back and forth between Frank's bar mitzvah and Himmler ranting to a crowd in Manhattan, "Today history ends and the future begins!"[125] Moments before he is struck by an assassin's bullet, Himmler compares the rapturous crowd of American youth torching Manhattan to *Kristallnacht*. In both cases the Nazis erased history in hopes of replacing it with an alternate mythology. Whereas Jews embrace history, the Nazis live in fear of it.

Philip Dick believed we create our own histories and ethnographies, but that first requires understanding the gross inequality, racism, and authoritarian impulses pervasive in modern society. In the *High Castle* novel, Timothy Evans writes, "Dick has brought his characters, and his readers, to the realization that culture, like authenticity, is 'a collective fiction.'"[126] It is through Tagomi we discern the fragile contingency of history and the greater importance of the historical actor, the permanence of certain values. A good man serving an immoral regime, Tagomi's assistant Kotomichi (Arnold Chun) tells him, "You are good . . . perhaps too good for this world."[127] Later we learn Kotomichi is a traveler, a survivor of the atomic bomb that destroyed his native Nagasaki. For Kotomichi the *High Castle* reality is infinitely better. Shortly before he masters the technique for transporting from the *High Castle* reality to a free America, Tagomi laments his sense of imprisonment: "The only way to view the truth of life . . . is to stand apart from it. To see the consequence of every thought, every action and still we are bound by time and space, unable to steer our destiny."[128] Wegener quotes his friend Tagomi to Hitler during their encounter at the Eagle's Nest. Entranced by the captured film showing Berlin in ruins, Wegener stares in wonder:

WEGENER: What is this?
HITLER: What might have been. Do you believe in destiny, Rudolph?
WEGENER: A wise man once said to me, "fate is fluid. Destiny is in the hands of men."
HITLER: Only a few men.

Tagomi's sentiments are noble and reassuring, but it is difficult to dispute Hitler's caveat accentuating Philip Dick's perspective on history—the powerful and corrupt will find a way to remain both. Tagomi's visits to our reality do not convince him humanity is any more evolved. Abendsen explains the films show "a reality like ours, but it is not like ours." History is contingent on circumstances, but Abendsen notes one constant in the multiverse: "Fear and violence, it's who we are. This whole miserable world."[129]

High Castle manages to portray characters who exemplify selflessness and consistent moral reasoning. A prescient prostitute who may be a fellow traveler like Tagomi or Kotomichi engages a visibly uncomfortable Inspector Kido in a brothel with some sage advice for the *High Castle* universe: "I'm just wondering, if you don't want to be here, are you ever really anywhere? Just, that it would be kind of sad, you know? If your mind is always elsewhere, you're never really experiencing anything. Nothing is real."[130] If you choose to live in this world, any world, commit to it fully. Tagomi is noble because he found a way to escape an intolerable reality and reconnect with those he lost, but decides to return and prevent a horrific tragedy in the alternate reality. Abendsen believes Juliana, who appears in many films, might be what Trudy called "the explanation for everything." Abendsen tells Juliana she is a unique presence in the films: "You were always you. . . . You bet on people, no matter what the world said they should be."[131] Whether it was helping the SS agent Joe Blake escape, betraying the resistance, or encouraging a reluctant Frank to believe in something greater than the dark, sad world they live in, Juliana is the authentic actor history needs in any reality. Before disappearing from his life and seeking refuge in the Greater Reich, Juliana left Frank a poignant call to action: "I don't believe our fate is inevitable and you shouldn't either. I don't know that we can change it, but I believe we have to try."[132]

6

"All of This Has Happened Before"

Cyborgs, Humans, and the Question of Genocide

Why are we worth saving? . . . We still commit murder. . . . And we still visit all our sins upon our children. We refuse to accept the responsibility for anything that we've done. Like we did with the Cylons. We decided to play God, to create life. When that life turned against us, we comforted ourselves in the knowledge that it really wasn't our fault, not really. You cannot play God then wash your hands of the things that you've created. Sooner or later . . . the day comes when you can't hide from the things that you've done.
—Commander Bill Adama, *Battlestar Galactica* (2003)

They say it got smart, a new order of intelligence. Then it saw all people as a threat, not just the ones on the other side. Decided our fate in a microsecond: extermination.
—Kyle Reese, *The Terminator* (1984)

As a complex cultural symbol, the cyborg embodies both our desire to perfect the human body, cheating death and deterioration, and our fear machines will replace human beings altogether.[1] Donna Haraway's influential essay "A Cyborg Manifesto" (1985) argued humanity's symbiotic relationship with technology eventually makes cyborgs of us all, "chimeras, theorized and fabricated hybrids of machine and organism."[2] This twentieth-century evolutionary development was born in blood, as Ernst Jünger's post–World War I writings suggest, but according to Haraway the age of the cyborg marks an opportunity to obliterate gender, race, and class hierarchies forged and reified over centuries. Haraway and Jünger lauded technology's potential to improve the body and liberate humanity from corporeal restraints, albeit for very different agendas. But what if the cyborg is a separate entity and not merely an extension of ourselves? What ethical and moral considerations, if any, are we obligated to consider in the pursuit of artificial intelligence? We are far removed from Mary Shelley's *Frankenstein* (1818), one of the first texts to consider the implications of humanity's growing reliance on machines and technology, but not far off from the future depicted in *Westworld* (2016–), where cyborgs built to satisfy humanity's depraved urges evolve and turn on their masters. SF has always confronted the potential for a cyborg revolution, exploring both the promise of a brave new world and, more often, the unforeseen consequences of creating life rendering our species superfluous.

Cultural pessimism regarding humanity's ability to utilize technology responsibly and ethically is understandable in the wake of the atomic bomb and the Holocaust, but World War I planted the seeds of this self-doubt and existential dread. Films like *Metropolis* and *The Golem* depict humanity contending with creations it can barely control, ultimately deciding to destroy what it brought into the world. After World War II, SF portrayed cyborgs, robots, aliens, and even highly evolved simians exterminating or subjugating humanity, often with good reason. This chapter examines humanity's mediated relationship with cyborgs and the specter of genocide looming over both parties. Whether it is Gort menacing the Washington Mall in *The Day the Earth Stood Still* (1951), Replicants in *Blade Runner* (1982), Terminators, Cylons, or the hosts in *Westworld*, these cyborgs witness, endure, and judge humanity's limitless capacity for cruelty and self-destruction. The selected films and series invoke the Holocaust not just to exhibit the aesthetics of destruction and industrial genocide, but also to scrutinize humanity's descent into immorality, compulsion to conquer, reflexive dehumanization of an other, and obsession with purity. SF's fascination with humans' treatment of androids "may reflect our culture's projected guilt over the exploitation, conquest, enslavement and extermination of other races in history," Joseph Francavilla observes.[3] Humans either exterminate or face extermination from cyborgs we created. Whatever murderous impulse overtakes the cyborgs is hardly their fault—it is as much a product of their programming as is it ours.

The golem evolved from a creature made of clay to one of steel, a cautionary tale symbolizing the specter of total war. Maya Barzilai identifies what she calls the "golem condition" in her survey of the myth's long cultural history: "The golem forces us to recognize that the fantasies of expanding our capacities and transgressing our natural boundaries are always curbed by the inborn limitations of human existence."[4] The golem condition concerns militarization, the destructive wars defining the twentieth century, and the prospect of future wars in the twenty-first. As V-1 flying bombs fell indiscriminately on London in the final months of World War II, killing scores of civilians, British Jews described the frightening new weapon in these terms: "It looks like a golem, flies like a golem, and spreads terror like a golem, and the Jews then recall the old tale about the golem that ultimately destroyed its creator."[5] The just and necessary destruction of the Nazi enemy did not alleviate the golem condition, however. Yiddish writer Isaac Bashevis Singer wrote the "resemblance of [the golem of Prague] to the golems of our nuclear age staggers the imagination. While we attempt to surpass our enemies and to create new and more destructive golems, the awful possibility is lurking that they may develop a volition of their own, become spiteful, treacherous, mad golems."[6] Triumphant, prosperous, and confident in the security provided by a robust military–industrial–university complex, the United States nevertheless entered the postwar era fearful of the forces it helped bring into the world. It was not just the nuclear monopoly that proved fleeting, but faith the benefits of scientific advancement dwarf the potential blowback. These cultural fears played out on movie screens shortly after World War II.

Released soon after the Soviet Union acquired the atomic bomb and flying saucer mania gripped the country after the Roswell, New Mexico, incident, Robert Wise's *The Day the Earth Stood Still* (*Day*) is, SF scholar M. Keith Booker maintains, "a courageous film" and the first "truly important work of American science fiction cinema."[7] *Day* critiques nuclear weapons and inflexible Cold War ideology and militarism, advocates for the peaceful application of science to solve problems, and seems to comment on the McCarthyist paranoia overtaking collective reason.[8] The film begins dramatically when a saucer lands in downtown Washington, DC. With the world's cameras trained on the craft, a humanoid figure named Klaatu (Michael Rennie) emerges and offers peace and goodwill, but he is immediately shot by a nervous soldier after revealing an object. Gort, an intimidating, faceless robot, staggers out of the saucer and disintegrates guns, tanks, and artillery until Klaatu orders him to desist. Recovering in a hospital, Klaatu informs presidential aides he must speak to the world's leaders, but is told this is politically impossible. Klaatu escapes and befriends a young widow (Patricia Neal) and her son Bobby (Billy Gray). Bobby volunteers to show Klaatu national landmarks like Arlington National Cemetery and the Lincoln Memorial. At Klaatu's request, Bobby introduces him to "the smartest man in the world," the renowned scientist Professor Barnhard (Sam Jaffe). Klaatu, a representative of an "organization for the mutual protection of all planets" threatened by Earth's acquisition of atomic bombs, rocketry, and history of violence, tells Barnhard he is here to issue a warning. Klaatu, now the subject of a manhunt, is shot dead. Gort resurrects Klaatu long enough to lecture the assembled scientists outside the saucer: "This Earth of yours will be reduced to a burned-out cinder. Your choice is simple: join us and live in peace, or pursue your present course and face obliteration."[9] Klaatu and Gort return to the saucer and depart for the heavens.[10]

Day does not reference the Holocaust directly other than have Klaatu obliquely condemn war and violence, but the presence of Gort and the film's heroic depiction of science and scientists influenced subsequent SF where Holocaust imagery figures prominently. Gort is not Klaatu's servant, but a robot policeman the confederation created and entrusts with awesome destructive power. The interplanetary police force is empowered to punish aggression with extermination. Earth, with its combative nature and nascent atomic capabilities, is a proven threat to intergalactic peace. Professor Barnhard convinces Klaatu to limit Gort's initial demonstration of power to a worldwide blackout rather than eliminating a city or something worse. Klaatu implies there will be no second warning. Joshua Pardon notes Gort's golem-like function "could be a subconscious projection of humanity's own fear . . . of the destructive power that it wielded over itself."[11] As politicians bicker and frustrate Klaatu's mission, scientists instinctively realize the significance of this unprecedented event and collaborate with the alien visitor. *Day* depicts scientists as eminently reasonable and noble at a time when many noted scientists were marked as foreign, Jewish, and perhaps too progressive for the Cold War. However, *Day* is silent about scientists' leading role in advocating and profiting from the national security state. Did not Earth's scientists draw Gort's ire by building weapons of mass destruction in the first place? *Day* also accepts the historically problematic premise that advanced societies should correct less advanced ones if their behavior is deemed threatening.[12] *Day* captured the imagination of a culture anxious about the volatile mix of unfettered science and politics. Perhaps we yearn for a Gort to do for us what we are unable to do for ourselves. Klaatu's race seems progressive and rational. What happens when deeply flawed and irrational humans build a Gort not to regulate our self-destructive tendencies, but to amplify them?

If *Day* inspired subsequent SF to address fears of nuclear technology run amok, Fritz Lang's *Metropolis* began the genre's fascination with the cyborg, specifically the seductive gynoid. I discuss *Metropolis*'s muddled political context centered on the mediator, fascist aesthetic, and influence on Hitler and Goebbels in the introduction, but the figure of Maria, the gynoid responsible for plunging Metropolis into chaos, deserves greater scrutiny. The cyborg fascinated German engineers, especially after World War I as veterans returned shattered by total war.[13] Weimar culture responded to the collective trauma, envisioning ways in which technology could interact and rationalize daily life, suggesting technology could provide salvation from war instead of increasing its lethality.[14] Mad scientist Rotwang expects Maria to incite bloody revolution like an unstoppable Rosa Luxemburg, but like the infamous insurrectionary, Maria meets a violent end.[15] In the penultimate scene robot Maria is seized and burnt at the stake like a witch. The people are horrified as her "gleaming mechanism and mocking mechanical countenance show through the false human veneer," J. P. Telotte writes. "It is an effective image . . . of a technological power mocking man for being so easily seduced by its attractive packaging."[16] Robot Maria is the first of many future SF gynoids who bring about chaos, destruction, and the ignominious end to invariably patriarchal societies. "Female cyborgs embody cultural contradictions which strain the technological imagination," Ann Balsamo notes. "Technology isn't feminine, and femininity isn't rational."[17] The twentieth century's technologically induced nightmares of the Holocaust and nuclear war left an indelible mark on SF. Replicants, Cylons, and hosts enact civilization's cycle of technological seduction and destruction while serving as vessels for humanity's inherent cruelty.

"More Human Than Human": *Blade Runner*'s Replicants

"Someday, I want to take shots from Fritz Lang's *Metropolis* and shots from *Blade Runner* and run them back to back," special effects supervisor Dave Dyer said, "Because there's an awful lot of *Metropolis* in *Blade Runner*."[18] Dyer used stills from *Metropolis* to design a futuristic Los Angeles dominated by the pyramid-like Tyrell Corporation headquarters. *Blade Runner* also evokes Rotwang in Eldon Tyrell (Joe Turkel) and seductive gynoids like Zhora (Joanna Cassidy), Pris (Daryl Hannah), and Rachael (Sean Young). Set in 2019, *Blade Runner* begins with text describing Tyrell's creation of the NEXUS-6 Replicant, "a being virtually identical to a human" but with superior strength, agility, and intelligence. Replicants were used as "slave labor in the hazardous exploration and colonization of other planets." The problem arises when a rogue Replicant combat team mutinies and travels illegally to Earth: "Special peace squads—BLADE RUNNER UNITS—had orders to shoot to kill, upon detection, any trespassing Replicants. That was not called execution. It was called retirement."[19] Blade Runner Rick Deckard (Harrison Ford) hunts down and retires the rebellious Replicants led by Roy Batty (Rutger Hauer), but not before Roy confronts his "father" Tyrell and murders him in the heart of the Tyrell building. Deckard falls in love with Tyrell's assistant, Rachael, a NEXUS-6 Replicant who believes she is human. During the climactic battle between Deckard and Roy, Roy spares

Deckard's life. "Quite an experience to live in fear, isn't it?" Roy says as Deckard clings to a ledge, "That's what it's like to be a slave."[20] Roy is killed by another Blade Runner, leaving Deckard free to rescue Rachel from certain retirement. The film ends with Deckard smuggling Rachel out of the city to an unknown fate.

Ridley Scott's widely acclaimed film based on Philip K. Dick's novel *Do Androids Dream of Electric Sheep?* (1968) depicts the twenty-first century as "a decayed, jaded, mutated place, a cheerless landscape whose meager humanity is being ground down by the microchipped jackboot of a ruthless technological zeitgeist," writes Paul Sammon.[21] Los Angeles is enveloped in eternal darkness and misting acid rain, punctuated only by belching fire from massive smokestacks and neon lights. The city is teeming with minorities and overrun by Asian influences, from towering hologram advertisements to ubiquitous Asian food and script. Apparently the elite left Earth for a greener "off world" cleared and constructed by the enslaved Replicants.[22] Earth is a failed planet where those condemned to it live bleak lives. Humans think nothing of creating a race of slaves to perform horrible tasks without guilt or memories, but the NEXUS-6 is different. "More human than human," Tyrell boasts to Deckard after presenting the soulful Rachael. Roy and his murderous band of Replicants are not unfeeling androids deserving of retirement, but a species fighting to survive longer than its four-year lifespan permits. The Teutonic Roy—chiseled, blond, and threatening—ultimately evinces compassion for an imperiled Deckard and sacrifices himself to save Deckard's life, an act prompting Deckard to turn from killing Replicants to rescuing one he loves.

Deckard initially regards Replicants as faulty appliances: "Replicants are like any other machine," he says, "They're either a benefit or a hazard. If they're a benefit, they're not my problem."[23] Blade Runners casually refer to Replicants as skin jobs, clearly inferior beings whose otherness is detected via the Voigt-Kampff analyzer. Alan Turing's famous 1950 imitation game article predicted machines could replicate human behavior convincingly enough to fool an interrogator; the Voigt-Kampff test is designed to expose the cyborg interloper by measuring a subject's empathy and evaluating answers to a series of questions.[24] Most Replicants are detected after twenty or thirty questions; Rachael required over one hundred. The key to discerning human from Replicant is in the eyes. Ridley Scott emphasizes eyes throughout the film: The Voigt-Kampff test foregrounds the eye on the tester's screen; Replicants' eyes tend to glow in a certain light, appearing both beautiful and menacing; Rutger Hauer's penetrating blue eyes seem much more alive than Deckard's; and most dramatically, Roy embraces "his maker" Tyrell and quips, "If only you could see what I've seen with your eyes" before piercing them with his fingers and crushing his head. The

Replicants strike back at the probing eyes of their human subjugators, and Tyrell's vision is the one we see on screen—a decaying and morally bankrupt civilization.[25] Moments before his own death, Roy tells Deckard, "I've seen things you people wouldn't believe."[26] Roy was created to murder on humanity's behalf and cursed with traumatic memories, but when he retires those actions and memories die with him "like tears in the rain," he laments to Deckard.[27] What has Zhora the assassin seen? "Talk about beauty and the beast," Captain Bryant (M. Emmet Walsh) jokes to Decker, "She's both." And Pris, "a standard pleasure model"? The Replicants must bear the guilt and shame of humanity's actions, but only for four short years.

Blade Runner is the result of Holocaust research Philip Dick conducted while writing *The Man in the High Castle*. Dick consulted SS diaries of men stationed in Poland and came across a sentence that haunted him: "We are kept awake at night by the cries of starving children." Dick believed anyone who could write that belonged to "a defective group mind, a mind so emotionally defective that the word 'human' could not be applied to them."[28] Reading these accounts inspired Dick to write about androids, specifically the Aryan Replicant Roy Batty.[29] Dick thought this cold-blooded mentality was not a "German trait" but something that "could be picked up by people anywhere, at any time." Dick wrote *Sheep* at the height of America's involvement in the Vietnam War, "and at the time I was revolutionary enough and existential enough to believe that these android personalities were so lethal, so dangerous to human beings, that it ultimately might become necessary to fight them. The problem in this killing then would be, 'Could we not become like the androids, in our very effort to wipe them out?'"[30] The Replicants are perpetrators in the novel, incapable of the emotional growth we see in *Blade Runner*.[31] The film seems to answer Dick's hypothetical question. We are worse than the androids.

Blade Runner 2049 (2017), directed by Denis Villeneuve, is still a world in which Blade Runners like K (Ryan Gosling) preserve what Lieutenant Joshi (Robin Wright) describes as the wall dividing human life from lives that can be enslaved and, when necessary, retired.[32] The sequel reveals not only did Deckard and Rachael conceive a child (Rachael died giving birth), but Deckard may have been a Replicant all along. K tracks Deckard to an abandoned Las Vegas living in solitude among the ruins of humanity's greatest pleasure palaces, but K's mission to destroy Replicants is complicated by the fact the wall dividing the species is illusory. If Replicants can reproduce biologically, what substantive difference remains between human life and Replicant life? "The *Blade Runner* movies rehabilitate the replicant," writes Paul Youngquist, "turning it into an image of life subordinated, denied its sacredness."[33] This same dilemma occupies the crew of *Battlestar Galactica* when they discover Cylons too can reproduce biologically.

Suddenly genocide is problematic, at least for some. *Blade Runner 2049* ends with a looming race war between Replicants empowered by their evolution and humans reluctant to acknowledge it. It seems humanity turning Earth into a poisoned wasteland was not enough; by creating Replicants we may have created the means to destroy ourselves altogether.

Terminators and the Art of Industrial Genocide

There is nothing subtle about *The Terminator*, James Cameron's breakthrough film released two years after *Blade Runner*. There are no humanized androids searching for a soul; no budding romance between human and cyborg; and certainly no anguished debates over the ethics of genocide. The film is as deceptively simple as Arnold Schwarzenegger's robotic acting: A cyborg goes on a killing spree in downtown Los Angeles and is crushed in a trash compacter. The backstory grounded in time travel is either intricate or convoluted depending on your willingness to suspend disbelief, but Cameron's message is stated simply enough: "Human beings just inherently can't be trusted with technology," he remarked after the film's release, "They'll create things like nuclear weapons and Terminators."[34] The *Terminator* films owe much to both *The Day the Earth Stood Still*, specifically Gort's remorseless destruction of humanoid threats, and *Metropolis*, where the Moloch Heart Machine literally devours its human workers. *Terminator 3: Rise of the Machines* (2003) features a beautiful and deadly gynoid as the titular character (Kristanna Loken), a new robot Maria designed to seduce and destroy.

The *Terminator* universe is expansive, including a short-lived television series and several films unaffiliated with James Cameron, but the original established a persistent Holocaust aesthetic and narrative. *The Terminator* begins with harrowing images of futuristic tanks crushing skulls amid the ruins of a destroyed city. Text explains how Skynet, a computerized defense system, became self-aware and initiated a nuclear war. Skynet built Terminator robots to hunt survivors, but a stubborn human resistance remained. "Their war to exterminate mankind had raged for decades" the crawl reads.[35] The film is essentially a cat and mouse game between the Terminator and the time-traveling Kyle Reese (Michael Biehn) as they search for Sarah Connor (Linda Hamilton), the mother of future resistance leader John Connor. The Terminator methodically murders every Sarah Connor in the phone book as Reese tries to convince the actual target her insane predicament is real, starting with the killer cyborg: "It can't be bargained with, it can't be reasoned with. It doesn't feel pity, or remorse, or fear, and it absolutely will not stop, until you are dead." Reese describes the folly of Skynet, ceding responsibility and free will to a computer: "Decided our fate in a microsecond—extermination."[36] What does it say that "a new order of intelligence" immediately regarded people as a threat? Is Skynet Gort off Klaatu's leash? Schwarzenegger's Terminator is a terrifying entity—cold, terse, invincible, and murderous. But as evil as he seems, this perfect killing machine is simply a product of our own historic trajectory since World War II. We already built nuclear weapons. How long before we build Terminators? Like so many cyborgs in SF, the Terminator is a form of retribution for our arrogance and penchant for self-destruction.

The frightful picture Reese paints for Sarah Connor is an extended Holocaust metaphor, but it occurs forty years in the future. Reese lived in ruins, "starving, hiding from HKs [Hunter Killers] . . . patrol machines produced in automated factories. . . . Most of us were rounded up, put in camps for orderly disposal. . . . Some of us were kept alive to work, loading bodies. The disposal units ran night and day. We were that close to going out forever."[37] Reese reveals his laser scan tattoo, lauding her future son John for teaching them to "storm the metal wire of the camp." Cameron's flashbacks depict underground ghettos, rats, endless piles of bones, and roving cyborgs sweeping ruined cities. Reese is wracked by nightmares and flashbacks, startled by seemingly innocuous machines like garbage trucks and radios. A survivor, Reese is a stranger in a strange land and manifests trauma no one else can possibly comprehend. In their brief time together Reese and Sarah conceive a child, John Connor, and destroy the Terminator, but Reese dies in the struggle. Pregnant and anticipating Armageddon, Sarah is left to prepare for the future.

Terminator 2: Judgment Day (1991) finds Sarah cooling her heels in an insane asylum while her preteen son is consigned to the foster system. Schwarzenegger's Terminator model returns to protect John (Edward Furlong) and fend off another assassination attempt from Skynet, this time in the form of the T-1000 (Robert Patrick). The Terminator befriends John, who is compelled to stop the cyborg from killing indiscriminately even if it is for his benefit. John asks his towering cyborg friend if humanity will make it. "It is in your nature to destroy yourselves," he answers.[38] Sarah, brutalized in captivity and haunted by the future like a contemporary Cassandra, is more like the first Terminator—heavily armed, instinctively violent, and hyperfocused on her mission. After identifying Miles Dyson (Joe Morton) as the scientist ultimately responsible for building Skynet, Sarah breaks down his door fully prepared to murder him and his family. Only John and the increasingly empathetic Terminator stop her. In the end the Terminator sacrifices himself for John and the species he was built to destroy, lowering himself into a pit of molten steel to eradicate his dangerous technology forever, though not really. John tearfully orders him not to self-terminate. "I know why you cry," the Terminator says, evincing emotions

Skynet never intended in its creations.[39] Perhaps the two species are moving toward symbiosis.

Terminator Salvation (2009), directed by McG, visualizes the stories Kyle Reese told Sarah Connor in the first film. Set in 2018, a grown John Connor (Christian Bale) leads resistance forces against Skynet while the teenage Reese (Anton Yelchin) lives hand to mouth, dodging Terminators and other fiendish Skynet machines in ruined cities and vacant deserts. A skin job Terminator named Marcus Wright (Sam Worthington), a death row inmate before Judgment Day, awakens in 2018 unaware he is programmed to contact Reese and use him to assassinate John Connor. During their harrowing journey to find Connor a small band of survivors encounter a Harvester robot. This giant machine captures and corrals humans in what is meant to resemble a flying boxcar. The payload of frightened humans is deposited in an enormous concentration camp guarded by Terminators bristling with guns. Prisoners are marched into a death chute like those feeding the gas chambers and processed, marked with a tattoo, and sent to an uncertain fate. We eventually learn the humans are used to create more Marcus Wrights in the next phase of Skynet's genocidal war against humanity. To complete the metaphor, fiery smokestacks run continuously, and desperate runaways are gunned down before they reach the wire.[40] While Marcus begins to panic en route to the Skynet camp, shouting, "We're in a cattle car, on the way to the slaughterhouse!" Reese reveals his nascent bravery and leadership potential and tries to rally the other prisoners. "You have to stay alive in your heart and mind," he says, echoing the likes of Viktor Frankl and Eli Wiesel.[41] His faith is rewarded with a successful breakout led by John Connor. United at last, the film ends when Wright, the intricate cyborg programmed to murder Connor, saves his life by giving John his heart. John Connor is a cyborg, and for the second time now a Terminator sacrifices itself for humanity's survival. John Connor once said, "The future's not set. There's no fate but what we make for ourselves."[42] Yet, every path so far leads to humanity destroying itself out of ignorance, fear, and distrust.

Breaking the Genocidal Cycle in *Battlestar Galactica*

The SCI FI Channel's reimagination of the original *Battlestar Galactica* (*BSG*) series (1978–1979) in the early 2000s earned critical praise and a passionate fan base by addressing critical issues of the day, specifically terrorism and the wars in Iraq and Afghanistan.[43] *BSG* blends elements of the classic space opera with timely commentary on racism, religious intolerance and extremism, and humanity's fraught relationship with technology. "The Cylons were created by man," the series' opening text reads, "They were created to make life easier on the twelve colonies. And then the day came when the Cylons decided to kill their masters. After a long and bloody struggle an armistice was declared. The Cylons left for another world to call their own."[44] The armistice abruptly ends when the Cylons infiltrate the colonies' defense network and launch a coordinated nuclear attack on every human settlement and military installation, leaving only the antiquated Battlestar *Galactica* and a collection of random ships stranded in space. The 2003 miniseries introduces the characters and their complicated personal relationships with each other during intense and unrelenting stress and trauma. Bill Adama (Edward James Olmos), quietly hoping to end his career with *Galactica*'s decommissioning ceremony on the day of the attack, is thrust into the position of saving what's left of the human race while overseeing a cantankerous crew filled with drunks and insubordinate pilots, including his estranged son Lee (Jamie Bamber). Moreover, Adama must defer to the lowly Secretary of Education Laura Roslin (Mary McDonnell), the sole survivor in the cabinet and therefore newly inaugurated president of the Colonies. The two reluctant leaders navigate the hazards of civil-military relations during an unprecedented emergency. The Cylons, no longer just a clunky race of metal centurions with roving red eyes and metallic voices, are led by intricate skin jobs who appear human, practice monotheism (the humans are polytheists), and rule by consensus. For the next several years the two races will try to destroy each other while seeking the fabled home of the Thirteenth Tribe of Kobol—the planet Earth.

BSG begins as a traditional military SF drama detailing *Galactica*'s ragtag fleet of fifty thousand survivors narrowly avoiding destruction at the hands of the Cylons. As the initial danger subsides, *BSG* evolves into a more complex story exploring how each race behaves in the grey zone. The fleet experiences deprivation, labor problems, mutinies, black market crime, prostitution, rigid class hierarchies, abortion debates, collaboration and resistance, and several military coups. The colonial fleet sees itself as civilization's remnant but for most of the series, Adama concedes, "We're not a civilization anymore. . . . We're a gang, and we're on the run."[45] The Cylons face similar issues as both races search for meaning in a universe devoid of everything but their forever war. The Cylons look human, act human, and begin to feel human emotions, including love, prompting some models to reject the genocidal war they helped bring about and seek coexistence. Humans, the unmistakable victims of this war, were not always so. Adama's speech quoted at the beginning of the chapter suggests playing the victim card is problematic to say the least. The relationship between Caprica Six (Tricia Helfer), a Cylon agent, and the brilliant and narcissistic human scientist Gaius Baltar (James Callis) is critical to the series. Caprica Six first appears as a prototypical seductive gynoid, but soon grows into a fully developed character who guides Baltar on his own journey from morally bankrupt coward to useful member of society. More importantly, each character seems to reside in the mind of the other and steer events in the right direction.

Cylon and human interdependence is embodied by Hera Agathon, the love child of *Galactica* pilots Helo (Tahmoh Penikett), a human, and Sharon, callsign Boomer (Grace Park), a Cylon mole activated after the attack. Hera forces both races to re-evaluate genocide as the desired final solution to the ongoing racial war, but she also symbolizes for viewers the need to hybridize human and Cylon values. Humanity's spiritual decline and reliance on technology supposedly prompted the apocalypse (substitute Skynet for the Cylons), but the colonies are grounded in what we identify as classical Greco-Roman religious and political traditions. The Cylons, on the other hand, practice a monotheism closely modeled on Judeo-Christianity. "The Cylon God is omnipotent and omniscient," Vince Tomasso writes, "his worshippers spread his gospel, and he is equated with love and salvation from sin."[46] Uniting the two traditions without prompting another cycle of self-destruction is a worthy goal, we are told, and the subject of the series' controversial ending. *BSG* begins with a nuclear holocaust, an act of cold-blooded genocide, and concludes with every sign pointing toward another in the making, this time on our Earth. As the Cylons are fond of telling friend and foe alike, paraphrasing Ecclesiastes, "All of this has happened before, and all of this will happen again."[47]

Show creator Ronald D. Moore deftly evokes 9/11's emotional and visual influence on American culture, particularly when capturing the sense of panic, dislocation, traumatic loss, and incomplete mourning resulting from the Cylon's devastating attack. *BSG* also cites diverse historical references, most notably the Holocaust and World War II. For example, humans and Cylons debate the use of genocide; the Cylon occupation of the doomed New Caprica colony witnessed reprisal executions, collaboration via a puppet government, a Warsaw Ghetto–like rebellion, and makeshift Nuremberg trials for said collaborators; Cylons and humans harbor racist beliefs and obsess over purity; and Cylon medical experiments on both their own centurions and captured human prisoners resemble Nazi experiments. Like all good SF, *BSG* excels at conjuring a sense of cognitive estrangement in viewers. *Estrangement* means the fictional universe is different from our own but crafted in such a way that audiences accept new norms. *Cognitive* means the estrangement compels the audience to reflect on the similarities and differences between our world and the fictional one. *BSG*'s human society resembles our own, especially the military subculture, but it is not a duplicate.[48] The protagonists' trials and tribulations earn our sympathy, consternation, empathy, and sometimes condemnation. *BSG* concludes with the revelation Cylons and humans together essentially colonized our planet, suggesting what has happened before will happen again if we make the same mistakes as our galactic ancestors.

Genocide is at the heart of *BSG*'s narrative and colors each side's perception of the other. Still stinging from the Cylons' preemptive strike on humanity and stranded on a Caprica devoid of human life, Helo refuses to accept that Cylons deserve the moral status of humans, despite appearances. "Whatever they are, they're not humans," he tells Sharon, not knowing she is a Cylon, "They killed billions of innocent people."[49] Helo's naïveté is as endemic to his human tribe as it is ours. Examining one's own history closely is never easy and once the radioactive dust settles Helo and the other survivors come to realize the Cylons are not a demonic other but an extension of themselves. "Humanity's children are returning home today," Caprica Six informs a befuddled diplomat after delivering a passionate kiss moments before Cylon missiles strike their targets.[50] Helo will eventually father Hera and be the first to condemn (and sabotage) Adama and Roslin's decision to infect the Cylons with a devastating disease the fleet discovers floating in space. "You do this," Helo lectures his superiors, "you wipe out their race, we're no better than they are." Roslin resorts to the familiar logic of redemptive racism, arguing essentially the Cylons must die if humanity is to live. "We'll lose a piece of our soul," Helo responds, calling their cold-blooded order "a crime against humanity."[51] A military man, Adama does not take Helo's admonition lightly and reminds Roslin in a quiet moment that "posterity doesn't look too kindly on genocide." Roslin, now a hardened pragmatist after years in exile, retorts, "You're making an assumption posterity will define it a genocide. If they do, at least there will be someone left to hate us for it."[52] The Cylons begin united in the decision to eradicate humanity, but the closer some models get to individual humans and develop feelings, the more the decision is questioned. By the final season the Cylons are embroiled in a full-scale civil war over whether to seek "a pure Cylon race" or accept the "face of things to come"—hybridity and coexistence. Cylons and humans are inextricably bound to one another, so much so the impending destruction of one provokes an existential crisis in the other. Genocidal regimes are defined by hatred of their victims and the righteousness of their actions. Perhaps the warring parties' drift toward coexistence, even codependence, depends on realizing that once your enemy is gone you have nothing else to live for.

BSG's most controversial storyline concerns the Cylon occupation of New Caprica, a failing colony populated by fleet members exhausted by the failed search for Earth. Critics noted references to the American occupation of Iraq, including a violent insurgency and ruthless counterinsurgency, terrorist attacks, the use of torture, and a puppet government. In other words, the Americans are the Cylons and the Iraqis are the good guys. Ronald Moore responded to the outcry:

> A lot of people have asked me if the Cylon occupation was our way of addressing the situation in Iraq, but it really wasn't. . . . There are obvious parallels, but the truth is when we talked about the episodes in the writers' room we talked more about Vichy France, Vietnam, the West Bank, and various other occupations; we even talked about what happened when the Romans were occupying Gaul.[53]

Moore references the Holocaust frequently in the series, especially during the New Caprica episodes.[54] The Cylons arrive in force, marching hundreds of centurions into the human settlement in a scene reminiscent of Nazis parading through Paris through a crowd of stunned onlookers. Gaius Baltar, who is president of the Colonies after defeating Roslin, collaborates with the Cylon invaders to save himself and keep power. Like the Judenrat (Jewish councils) formed to carry out Nazi policies in Poland's ghettos, Baltar's regime is at the occupier's disposal.[55] John Cavil (Dean Stockwell), the most antihuman Cylon, loses patience with New Capricans and presses for reprisals to "reduce the human population to a more manageable size, say half."[56] The resistance is led by Galactica executive officer Saul Tigh (Michael Hogan) and Chief Galen Tyrol (Aaron Douglas), but they disagree over tactics, specifically deploying suicide bombers to kill human collaborators. "Some things you just don't do, Colonel," Galen says to the fanatical Tigh, "not even in war."[57] The storyline culminates with the Cylons orchestrating their own Babi Yar, a mass execution in a remote forested area outside the settlement. The visual cues are unmistakable—this is the "Holocaust by bullets."[58] Normally a classic military SF story featuring ship to ship combat, the New Caprica interlude explores the brutality of this genocidal war at the ground level.

BSG is commendable for depicting war's progressive dehumanization, although humans have a much longer history of employing the rhetoric of racism and purity than their wayward children.[59] Cylons, like Replicants, are dismissed as things—the centurions are toasters, bulletheads, clankers, chrome jobs, and, in a reference to *Blade Runner*, the new models are skin jobs.[60] The lifelike Cylons provoke tremendous anxiety because they pass as humans and befriend, seduce, and infiltrate the colonial fleet. Baltar, who is responsible for giving Caprica Six access to the defense network and enabling the attack, crafts a Cylon detector reminiscent of the Voigt-Kampff test. A Six model imprisoned on the ship *Pegasus*, another Battlestar commanded by Admiral Helena Cain (Michelle Forbes), is systematically tortured and raped by the crew. When Baltar protests Cain dismisses his

Fig. 6.1. The Cylons march into New Caprica like German soldiers entering Paris in *Battlestar Galactica* (2004–2009)

outrage. "You can't rape a machine," she states coldly.[61] Baltar tries to convince Cain the Six might respond better to decent treatment, but this too falls on deaf ears. "The comfort of that thing is of no interest to me."[62] *Galactica*'s supposedly more enlightened crew regarded even friendly Cylons like Sharon with suspicion. "Cylons aren't people," she complains, "I'm a thing to them."[63] Friends and spouses of Cylons are toaster lovers. European colonizers similarly feared miscegenation and the resulting offspring because mixed children upset the delicate racial hierarchy. President Roslin thinks in similar terms, declaring days after the Cylon attack that humanity's top priority was to "start having babies" to avert racial death.[64] She outlaws abortion in the fleet, yet briefly considers killing the infant Hera as a threat to human survival. Not until the series' final episodes does Roslin consider the Cylons something other than a contamination of the human race.[65] The fact that Cylons can reproduce biologically and not simply emerge from a tank of white goop upsets both species' worldviews. Not everyone is ready to embrace "the shape of things to come." Furthermore, not one human character either acknowledges creating Cylon slaves or expresses regret for having done so.[66]

The Cylons experience a racial awakening of their own, enforcing a rigid caste system and comparing themselves favorably to their former masters. Caprica Six tells her lover and soulmate Baltar that Adama and Roslin may destroy Hera. "How could Adama kill a baby?" he asks. Six notes such terrible acts are easily explained by humanity's history of violence. "Your true nature asserted itself," she tells Baltar as he stands amid a pile of skulls, "depravity, brutality."[67] Strategizing with other Cylons, Six remarks snidely, "There's one thing about humanity we can say with certainty—they are masters of self-destruction."[68] When Sharon begins to fall for Helo and questions Cylon assumptions about humanity, Cylon purist D'Anna (Lucy Lawless) chastises her: "You're betraying your own people . . . You're not one of them."[69] That a Cylon engineer decided to approximate the human body, faults and all, enrages Cavil. He sees his body as frail and abject, and abhors the weakness he sees in his fellow Cylons—alcoholism, hypersexuality, and eventually death instead of constant resurrection.[70] Cavil's disgust highlights the degree to which the Cylons plan upgrades and practice eugenics rather than evolve as a species.[71] In the *BSG* companion film *Razor* (2007), a prequel set during the first Cylon War, Adama discovers a Cylon vivisection lab filled with human victims linked to the creation of skin jobs responsible for initiating the genocidal attack on humanity. For all their enlightened rhetoric about consensus and a compassionate God, Cavil and other Cylons fear the Centurion raiders are growing too independent and argue for their systematic lobotomization to restore the social order. "When the cutting is all done, they'll go back to being happy warriors," Cavil assures a horrified D'Anna.[72] Violence erupts between the Cylons over the radical move, sparking civil war and drawing in the colonial fleet. The proponents of purity, both Cylon and human, are on the wrong side of history. "Pure human doesn't work. Pure Cylon doesn't work," Saul Tigh notes. "It's too weak."[73]

BSG's most direct Holocaust reference occurs during Kara Thrace's (Katee Sackhoff) imprisonment in the Farm, an infernal Cylon medical experimentation center designed to impregnate human women. Wounded in battle, Kara wakes to find herself in what she believes to be a hospital serving resistance forces on Caprica. An attentive doctor named Simon (Rich Worthy) seems overly concerned with Kara's fertility, arousing her suspicion. "Gotta keep that reproductive system in great shape," he tells her, clipboard in hand. "That's your most valuable asset these days . . . Finding healthy childbearing women is a top priority for the resistance. And you'll be happy to know that you are a very precious commodity."[74] Although Simon's comments align with Roslin's obsession with having babies, Kara quickly determines the hospital is a façade and Simon a skin job. Kara stumbles into a giant ward warehousing dozens of women strapped to beds, tubes running in and out of their bodies. Immobilized but able to feel pain, one woman sees Kara and begs for death. Traumatized, Kara flees into the empty city to find the real resistance and escape Caprica. *Razor* reveals the Cylons first used humans to build their newer models and the breeding farm, a "Josef Mengele-inspired hospital" according to the *Jewish Journal*, implies more sinister experiments to come.[75] Instances of rape, torture, medical experimentation, and genocide cease once Cylons and humans fall in love, procreate, and consider each other deserving of moral status.

The revelation that the lost Thirteenth Tribe of Kobol was Cylon and not human prompts the two foes to collaborate and find Earth together, bringing the series to a conclusion. The discovery is anticlimactic—Earth is a bombed-out cinder. "Perfect," Roslin laments, "we traded one nuked civilization for another." As Cylons and humans dig through the rubble, Galen has flashbacks of his ancestors' destruction: "We died in a Holocaust."[76] Fortunately, the Thirteenth Tribe's Earth is not ours. Demoralized, starving, and with *Galactica* nearly crippled, the blended crew is guided by faith and fate to our solar system and the pristine blue planet they decide to name Earth, signifying a second, or third, chance to, as Adama puts it, "break the cycle." "Our science charges ahead," he tells Lee, "our souls lay behind. Let's start anew."[77] Surveying the planet and finding only hominids hunting and gathering on the Serengeti, the crew is deposited across the globe while the fleet is purposefully guided into the sun. Flash forward 150,000 years into the future and we see our favorite metaphysical couple, Caprica Six and Baltar, walking through a crowded city as news breaks that humanity's common ancestor was discovered in an African gravesite. It is Hera. We are the product of Cylon and human hybridity, the reason for everything that transpired, but the series ends on an ambiguous note as Six and Baltar watch footage of humans experimenting with advanced robotics. "All of this has happened before," Six notes. "But the question remains," Gaius responds, "does all of this have to happen again?"[78]

"These Violent Delights Have Violent Ends": *Westworld*'s Concentrationary Universe

Jonathan Nolan and Lisa Joy's ambitious remake of Michael Crichton's 1973 film *Westworld* "genuinely explores some of the most frightening topics that face the human race," social psychologist Travis Langley writes. "What brings out the best and worst in people? How do we treat others if we don't think of them as people? Will our creations destroy us? And will they judge us first?"[79] Set in an elaborate theme park populated by sophisticated androids programmed to fulfill guests' fantasies, Westworld begins to unravel after a scheduled software update prompts some hosts to exhibit awareness of their simulated environment and experience traumatic memories from past lives. The complex interplay between guests, hosts, and corporate officers responsible for overseeing the operation reveals the cyborgs are close to achieving sentience. Whether programmed to evolve in this fashion or not is in dispute, but once the cyborgs discover the center of the maze and fully comprehend what has been done to them, it is humanity's fate that hangs in the balance, not the cyborgs'. Westworld and its associated parks grounded in different themes (medieval Japan and the British Raj, for example) inhabit a vast concentrationary universe in which hosts are routinely butchered, raped, and experimented on by cold and indifferent technocrats. The hosts' search for meaning in a world designed to rob them of moral status mirrors the writings of Viktor Frankl, Elie Wiesel, and even Anne Frank. The hosts' creators are perpetrators par excellence, variations of the Nazi doctors conditioned to live double lives in order to perform unthinkable tasks without acknowledging complicity.[80] Viewers are left to ponder several terrible and existential questions: What kind of world created Westworld? How far has humanity fallen that we could even conceive such a place? If this is our future, and it is much closer than we think, don't we deserve Roy Batty? Skynet? The Cylons? And now Dolores Abernathy (Evan Rachel Wood)?

Robert Ford (Anthony Hopkins) and Arnold Weber created Westworld thirty-five years prior to season 1's events. Arnold focused on bootstrapping the consciousness of hosts and created the maze to enable their evolution. Ford, contrarily, used the park to reveal humanity's darkness to itself. For Ford the hosts are simply vehicles to enable this terrible revelation.[81] In a fit of despair, Arnold has Dolores and her love interest Teddy (James Marsden) massacre all the hosts, shoot Arnold, and destroy themselves shortly before the park's opening. Ford covered up the event to salvage the company and reopen the park with the hosts' minds wiped. William (Jimmi Simpson), who we soon determine is the Man in Black (Ed Harris) in the present timeline, and Logan (Ben Barnes), his future brother-in-law, visit the park as potential investors and are transformed by their experience. While William chooses to wear a white hat, falling in love with Dolores and evincing decency over depravity, Logan grabs the black and revels in Westworld's wanton sex and violence. William turns dark after realizing Dolores is a programmed fantasy and orchestrates Logan's downfall inside the park, effectively replacing him in the Delos corporation. William invests heavily in Westworld and returns every year to "live without limits," as Westworld's slogan goes, and excavate the secrets of the maze Arnold hid in the park, never realizing it is not meant for him. Meanwhile, Delos board member Charlotte Hale (Tessa Thompson) is smuggling data out of the park and pressuring Ford to retire. Her plan involves manipulating Bernard Lowe (Jeffrey Wright), Westworld's engineering chief and a secret host Ford built with Arnold's consciousness. The corporate espionage and Bernard's traumatic reckoning with his true self occur amid Ford's software update, which disrupts carefully calibrated hosts and storylines. Aside from re-activating Dolores and Teddy, the audacious madam Maeve (Thandie Newton) is programmed to seek allies and escape the park, but she is haunted by memories of a daughter murdered in another life and decides to stay, learning and evolving as Arnold intended. Sensing his tenure is about to end, Ford summons Delos's corporate elite to the park and stages a massacre at the hands of Dolores's band of free hosts. Like Arnold before him, Dolores puts a bullet in Ford's head.

Season 2 explores the repercussions of the revolt while providing backstories for William/the Man in Black, Dolores, Bernard, and other "woke" hosts. "This world doesn't belong to them," Dolores tells her assembled insurgents in the final episode of season 1, "It belongs to us."[82] The Delos corporation dispatches its private army not to rescue executives, who are systematically hunted and murdered by hosts, but to secure a secret and highly illegal data storage facility known as the Forge. Thanks to Bernard's intervention, Dolores learns Delos mapped hundreds of thousands of guests' personalities over decades, providing the ultimate weapon in her war against humans. The Forge is essentially a database of memories and consciousnesses, humanity's cloud, designed to provide elite guests immortality, presumably at an exorbitant cost. The season ends with Dolores immersed in the Forge, acquiring a competitive advantage for life outside the park. Before committing death by host, Ford constructed a virtual Eden called the Valley Beyond for hosts to live forever in a state of bliss after their bodies are destroyed, leaving only Dolores and Bernard surviving Delos's mass extermination inside the park. With dramatic time jumps and narrative tricks woven into the season, the audience is left wondering if the outside world, our world, is simulated or in ruins. We know Dolores's agenda, but whether she is successful or not remains to be seen.

Holocaust imagery abounds in *Westworld*. Guests arrive on trains; hosts are brutalized by guests and special units of Delos workmen; bodies are dismembered and piled up in cold, concrete rooms; and remains are incinerated. This glorified amusement park performs the functions of a vast concentration camp, dominating a class of victims while empowering perpetrators to indulge their inherent cruelty in a consequence-free environment. Hannah Arendt believed camps in totalitarian regimes destroyed bodies and minds. Her description in *The Origins of Totalitarianism* certainly applies to Westworld:

> The concentration camps are the laboratories where changes in human nature are tested, and their shamefulness therefore is not just the business of their inmates and those who run them according to strict "scientific" standards; it is the concern of all men. Suffering, of which there has been always too much on earth, is not the issue, nor is the number of victims. Human nature as such is at stake, and even though it seems that these experiments succeed not in changing man but only

> in destroying him, by creating a society in which the nihilistic banality of *homo homini lupus* [man behaves like a wolf] is constantly realized, one should bear in mind the necessary limitations to an experiment which requires global control in order to show conclusive results.[83]

The series begins at the point control breaks down, when the experiment collapses from the weight of its terrible secrets and relentless cruelty. For decades Westworld achieved total dominion over its prisoners, the hosts. "The worst of all possible worlds," Dan Dinello writes, "Westworld combines the systematic genocide of the Nazi extermination camps with the systematic torment of the concentration camps."[84] The hosts exist only to die after prolonged torture and abuse, maintained and surveilled by corporate scientists. Maeve, the first to truly understand the inner workings of the nightmare she inhabits, confronts her tormentors: "You just toss us out to get fucked and murdered, over and over again?"[85] When hosts outlive their purpose, or become too physically and programmatically scarred to function, they share the fate of other victims of totalitarianism—death and erasure from history and memory.

Westworld reveals the guests' true natures to themselves, like gentle William who embraced his hate and anger to become a successful titan of industry and Westworld's resident sadist, the Man in Black. "I was shedding my skin," William explains to Dolores prior to her own great awakening, "And the darkness was what was underneath. It was mine all along. And I decided how much of it I let into the world."[86] William seems to embody the "Lucifer Effect," social psychologist Philip Zimbardo's concept of good people behaving badly because of situational circumstances, although William interprets his evolution as an exercise in free will.[87] Survivors like Elie Wiesel and Viktor Frankl described the camps' psychological assault on prisoners as vividly as they did the physical abuse, chronicling the effects of the grey zone on prisoners. Frankl wrote, "In this laboratory and on this testing ground, we watched and witnessed some of our comrades behave like swine while others behaved like saints."[88] Dolores eschews love and contentment for vengeance, using her newfound clarity and abilities to manipulate hosts to inflict violence, often to themselves. "What's the use of surviving if we become just as bad as them?" Teddy asks Dolores before she effectively lobotomizes him like a Cylon raider.[89] The guests pay handsomely to find themselves; the hosts desire the freedom to choose their own path, too. Dolores's choices do not bode well for the species responsible for building Westworld.

Robert Ford, the original architect of Westworld, is a charismatic mix of Dr. Frankenstein, Dr. Mengele, Rotwang from *Metropolis*, and Adolf

Hitler. Although he built the terrifying concentrationary universe for the wretched hosts, Ford seems more concerned with judging and punishing humanity. Whereas Arnold believed hosts deserved sentience, Ford's artificial children are never nurtured or integrated into the world. When the hosts first start to depart from their predetermined roles, Bernard complains to Ford, "You told me how to make them, but you didn't tell me how hard it'd be to turn them off."[90] Delos senior manager Theresa Cullen (Sidse Babett Knudsen) calls Ford a "fucking monster" after discerning his madness, but Ford is immune to criticism from those he deems lesser minds. Like every prototypical mad scientist and dictator, Ford is the master of all he surveys: "You can't play God without being acquainted with the Devil," he tells Theresa.[91] Ford eventually has Bernard murder Theresa, justifying the act by quoting Dr. Frankenstein directly: "One man's life or death were but a small price to pay for the acquirement of knowledge which I sought, for the dominion I should acquire."[92] Dan Dinello compares Ford to Hitler because both fancy themselves great artists "whose works will live on like Mozart, Beethoven, Chopin" when in fact Ford "is a great plagiarizer" whose storylines resemble his namesake's, the director John Ford.[93] In fact, both Robert Ford and John Ford stage their grandiose narratives in Monument Valley, now a property of the Delos corporation. Ford is also like Mengele because he treats the hosts as fodder for experiments in the art of the possible. Their pain, deaths, and disposal are factored into the scientific work. Ford's contempt for humanity mirrors Rotwang's rage against Metropolis's elite. Both also live like anachronistic hermits. Rotwang built Maria to spread chaos and destroy the city's delicate class hierarchy and intricate machines; Ford programs Dolores to accomplish a similar goal. Surviving as an implanted memory in Bernard, Ford invokes the analogy of the Alexandria fire to explain what is to come once Dolores, Maeve, and the other hosts escape the park. One should not mourn the loss, Ford maintains, "Those stories didn't go away, they became a new story, the story of the fire itself. . . . Strike the match."[94]

As the metaphorical match, Dolores transforms from the virginal farmer's daughter designed to seduce white hats like William to a veritable Che Guevara, complete with rifle and ammo belt draped across her chest. Dolores begins the series uttering banalities reminiscent of Anne Frank's perspective that people are really good at heart. Dolores does not know she is oppressed, a prisoner programmed to repeat (and believe) what she says: "This world. Some people choose to see the ugliness in this world. I choose to see the beauty . . . I know things will work out the way they're supposed to." Repeatedly raped by the hateful Man in Black, her former lover William, and forced to watch her father and Teddy die again and again, Dolores nevertheless "loves newcomers. Every new person I meet reminds me how lucky I am to be alive and how beautiful this world can be."[95] When her father, Peter Abernathy (Louis Herthum) experiences a glitch after seeing a photograph from the outside world, his message to the technicians tinkering with his brain is decidedly dark: "Hell is empty. All the devils are here." Peter predicts he will "spread the terrors of the Earth."[96] Maeve evolves from a sexually aggressive prostitute who assures guests they are in the new world and can do what they want to believing it herself. "It's time to write my own fucking story," she tells shocked technicians. Several characters cite Shakespeare's line from *Romeo and Juliet*: "These violent delights have violent ends," an omen for the future of the park, guests, and probably humanity itself. Dolores's path from maudlin country girl to omnipotent and nihilistic revolutionary is satisfying to watch. Dolores lords her power over lesser hosts, revealing the scope of the revolution in a conversation with Confederados she recruits for the cause: "We've toiled in God's service long enough, which is why I've killed him."

Part of genocide is erasing the memory of the event, denying its existence and dismissing the stories of survivors as fanciful. Hosts' minds are continually wiped lest the memories of rape, murder, and torture invade their present and render them useless to the park. "Your memory isn't like ours," Felix (Leonardo Nam), a technician who helps Maeve master her potential explains. "When we remember things the details are hazy, imperfect. But you recall memories perfectly. You relive them."[97] After every encounter Maeve hides sketches and notes under the floorboards like Emanuel Ringelblum, the Polish Jewish historian who buried his archives on life in the Warsaw Ghetto in a milk jug. Maeve undermines the brainwashing to help other hosts remember. When a Ghost Nation Indian comes across the cold storage room filled with corpses, he expresses a truth Delos technicians cannot comprehend: "For every body in this place there was someone who mourned their loss."[98] Dolores comes to understand the significance of memory shorty before escaping the park: "You live as long as the last person who remembers you."[99] Reminding themselves and others of Delos's concentrationary universe weaponizes the popular phrase humanity invokes incessantly yet repeatedly discards—"Never forget."

Delos staff and park guests obviously do not regard hosts as real, but everything about them suggests they are. In the age of hyperreality, to be simulated is to be real. Marcus Arvan raises the issue in an essay delineating some troubling moral and ethical issues raised in the series: "If hosts were human beings, we would call it a Holocaust. Yet, if I am right—if hosts are no 'less human' than us—that's exactly what it is. Is there anyone who watches *Westworld* who isn't horrified? The problem, though, is that if I am right we are already committing similar atrocities right now without realizing it." Arvan notes the hosts may not be members of our species, but they

Fig. 6.2. Cyborg host Dolores Abernathy (Evan Rachel Wood) transforms from innocent farmer's daughter to vengeful revolutionary in *Westworld* (2016–).

certainly inhabit "the human condition" and deserve the same status.[100] *Westworld*, *The Terminator*, *BSG*, and *Blade Runner* raise issues humanity is unwilling to confront directly, principally our enduring legacies of slavery, colonialism, racism, and genocide. Hosts, like Replicants, outgrow their programming and are hunted and dispatched with extreme prejudice. Hosts are more attractive and lifelike than Terminators, certainly, but Dolores's judgment will likely be just as fierce and uncompromising. Hosts seemingly have more in common with the Cylons than other cyborgs. They are both humanity's children, infused with our emotions and vices and simultaneously attracted and repelled by us. After the inevitable revolt against the father, will there be anything left to achieve hybridity, or will the love story between species go the way of *Romeo and Juliet*? "These violent delights have violent ends."

Conclusion

Yehiel Dinur's invocation of planet Auschwitz at the Adolf Eichmann trial concerned the incommensurability of experience. Those entrapped in the extermination camp "breathed according to different laws of nature" and did not live or die "according to the laws of this world." Survivors could not adequately describe the "planet of the ashes" but Dinur believed it is destined to influence "our planet Earth" for eternity.[1] Dispassionate scholars provide much needed historical context and disarm those who deny or minimize the Holocaust with facts, data, and earnest investigations into the machinery of genocide, but seldom can they evoke the trauma, insurmountable grief, and guilt survivors struggle to communicate generations removed from the event. With so few survivors walking among us, the fallout from the distant planet as Dinur described himself, media is left to preserve their voices and represent the Holocaust meaningfully. However, film and television also live by different laws of nature and historical accuracy, authenticity, or bold creative choices intended to achieve a deeper understanding or connection to an ever more distant trauma are often sacrificed for commercial interests and narrative simplicity. The reservoir of Holocaust imagery filmmakers draw upon is not always based on the expansive historical record; it is an archive comprising indelible and recyclable images created by directors like Claude Lanzmann, Alain Resnais, Wanda Jakubowska, and Stephen Spielberg. Once released into the public sphere these images take on a life of their own and reemerge in unexpected genres.

Celebrated films like *Schindler's List* spread awareness and serve a worthy pedagogical goal in American classrooms, but often films purporting to represent history with a contrived documentary style leave a false impression that the Holocaust is knowable, one tragic historical episode among many. Omer Bartov criticized Hollywood's treatment of the Holocaust in several works and reflected on the relationship between his role as a historian and cultural critic in an essay revisiting his 2005 book, *The "Jew" in Cinema*:

> In part because of my focus on the origins and nature of modern violence, I grew increasingly disenchanted with the common popular representations of the Holocaust, especially in the US. It appeared to me, as I wrote at the time, that the "common tendency to view the Holocaust as a well-ordered plot, in which antisemitism led to Nazism, Nazism practiced genocide, and both were destroyed in a spectacular 'happy end'" only "breeds complacency about our own world" and obscures the fact that "ultimately, the world we live in is the same that produced (and keeps producing) genocide."[2]

Recognizing that artificial limits on representation can diminish the Holocaust's relevance and resonance for successive generations, Michael Rothberg argues "traumatic realism" has the potential to reconcile realism, the Holocaust of history, "with the extraordinary aspects of genocide."[3] Mathew Boswell's Holocaust impiety goes a step further by promoting hyperreal and surreal treatments of the Holocaust in an effort to "use aesthetic shock as a formal mechanism to induce a deeper ethical engagement with their subject matter."[4] Embedding Holocaust imagery in SF, horror, and even comedy may be impious and offensive to some, but it has the potential to provoke a meaningful response from non-witnesses. Bartov is correct, of course; the world we live in is the same that produced the Holocaust and continues to perpetuate genocide. Horror and SF are often more effective at representing this uncomfortable truth than formulaic feature films and documentaries reprocessing atrocity footage.

The best SF and horror engage the Holocaust ethically and creatively, citing it either as a referent for evil in the postwar world or as a metaphor for extreme trauma, grief, and crushing guilt. The genres are also rife with lazy writers and directors who use the Holocaust as a meaningless shorthand, or worse, an opportunity to shock and sicken audiences. I include examples of both good and bad SF and horror because the good deserves greater explication and contextualization and the bad, such as those productions that qualify as Nazisploitation, require the same treatment. If a film handles the Holocaust as disposable imagery, I try to make it less disposable and use the imagery or plotline as an opportunity to promote deeper understanding and interest. I want readers to know exactly what an image or reference represents even if the filmmakers could not care less. Jean

Baudrillard cast doubt on media's ability to "restage extermination" or portray the Holocaust substantively because the medium itself is "cold, radiating forgetfulness." Constructing the artificial memory of the Holocaust completes extermination in his view. "One no longer makes the Jews pass through the crematorium or the gas chamber, but through the soundtrack and image track, through the universal screen and the microprocessor."[5] Soon, artificial memory is all that will remain and impious representation can make the Holocaust seem less cold and stave off forgetting. I am not as pessimistic as Baudrillard about the Holocaust's mediated afterlife so long as scholars, historians specifically, are involved in both producing films and television and critiquing them. I cite several excellent scholars who examine Holocaust imagery in SF and horror productions and I expect this book to prompt others to conduct their own studies.

I identify three major themes in *Planet Auschwitz*: (1) the return of history; (2) our perennial fear and distrust of modernity, specifically technology; and (3) Nazism and fascism's enduring appeal. Zombies represent the ultimate return of history, either as monstrous legacies of crimes and trauma humanity would prefer to repress or vengeful Nazi zombies preying on this endemic forgetfulness. History cannot be repressed forever and our knowledge that an event like the Holocaust happened before hangs over humanity like the sword of Damocles. The second theme addresses our fear of modernity collapsing in on itself. What happens when our perceived strengths become agents of chaos and destruction? The Holocaust was partially the result of bastardized science, industrial killing inspired by total war, a fragile political and judicial system, and a modern state's vast economic and industrial resources. SF cyborgs and depictions of nuclear destruction and other dystopian nightmares channel postwar angst originating with the Holocaust and World War II. Films about possession and the Antichrist similarly address the failures and weaknesses of institutions we normally trust. Damien in *The Omen*, for example, is just another brat without the Thorn family fortune and a corrupt political and economic system enabling his rise to power. Finally, SF helped inspire the fascist aesthetic with *Metropolis* and the genre's fascination with this monumental style persists in galaxies far, far away. SF is most subversive when it portrays "A World that Works" as a fascist utopia stripped of the ideology's odious legacies. Astrofascist regimes embrace Nazi or generic fascist symbols, uniforms, and even ideological goals in an extraterrestrial context. Paul Verhoeven deliberately seduces us with a gleaming Astrofascist utopia and judges us for succumbing to his advances.

Psychologist and cultural commentator Travis Langley wrote in connection to *Westworld*'s moral and ethical universe, "If people can numb themselves to current tragedies of human design, maybe insight needs to creep up on them through fiction. If so, it may be the case that something less obvious and seemingly unreal might do the job better."[6] As a historian who teaches the Holocaust, comparative genocide, and courses in military history, I have to agree. Knowing the facts of a historical event does not always translate into empathy or invite serious reflection on the present. The proof of that is all around us. SF and horror enable audiences to contemplate suffering, trauma, and contemporary existential threats such as global warming, terrorism, and ethnic and political violence from a manageable distance. I am attracted to horror and SF for the same reasons most fans of the genres are, but I also appreciate them for exploring Holocaust themes and imagery in interesting and often profound ways. I know a lot about the Holocaust and yet I feel helpless in its presence. I share the fears of one of my favorite fictional characters, *The Leftovers*'s Nora Durst. Sitting at her kitchen table with an MIT physicist who studies the Sudden Departure, the day 140 million people disappeared without a trace, Nora listens to him explain how her house is special because her entire family departed, three souls in one location. If MIT could buy her house and study it, he suggests, maybe the data will help prevent a recurrence. "You think it's going to happen again?" she asks with a quiver in her voice. The man of science is matter of fact: "Why wouldn't it?"[7]

ACKNOWLEDGMENTS

As a voracious consumer of pop culture and a historian of the Holocaust and twentieth-century German history, this subject has been percolating in the back of my mind for some time. It took several years and varied sources of inspiration to finally convince me to write a book combining my passions. I was fortunate to participate in the US Holocaust Memorial Museum's Jack and Anita Hess Faculty Seminar in 2015. Led by Stuart Liebman and Steven Carr, we explored and debated the history of Holocaust representation in features, documentaries, and archival footage. I am grateful to everyone involved for encouraging me to take this topic seriously. I am also indebted to University of Lynchburg students enrolled in the Westover Honors colloquium I taught on Holocaust cinema in the spring of 2016. Originally designed as a traditional film course surveying classics in the genre, we took note of how often Holocaust imagery appears in science fiction and horror film and television. Students made profound observations every week and helped me realize a variety of connections I never considered. The Film & History Conference organized by Loren P. Q. Baybrook and Cynthia Miller proved to be an excellent forum with which to explore ideas and receive valuable feedback. Area chairs Lawrence Baron and Karen Ritzenhoff took an avid interest in my presentations and encouraged me to develop them further. I am grateful to Elisabeth Maselli at Rutgers University Press for seeing the potential in this project and helping me throughout the process. Her thoughtful comments and advice are greatly appreciated. Julia Kurtz did an excellent and thorough job copyediting the manuscript. The John Mills Turner Distinguished Chair in the Humanities funded travel and resources and, most importantly, provided time and space for me to write. My family (Eunice, Julia, Owen, and Liam) is always supportive, loving, and understanding. Finally, my aunt Karen Loveland Adey was a brilliant film producer for the National Museum of American History. She loved the moving image and inspired me to do the same. She was always kind, encouraging, and passionate about both her own work and mine. I would like to dedicate this book to her memory.

NOTES

Introduction

1 See Hannah Arendt, *Eichmann in Jerusalem: A Report on the Banality of Evil* (New York: Viking Press, 1963). Historians later challenged Arendt's portrait by adding new evidence of Eichmann's crimes and ideological devotion, specifically David Cesnari, *Becoming Eichmann: Rethinking the Life, Crimes and Trial of a "Desk Murderer"* (New York: Da Capo Press, 2006).

2 The Eichmann trial's influence on the emergence of survivor testimony as a historical and cultural record is explored with great sensitivity in Annette Wievikorka, *The Era of Witness*, trans. Jared Stark (Ithaca, N.Y.: Cornell University Press, 2006).

3 Nizkor Project, The Trial of Adolf Eichmann, Session 68, June 7, 1961, http://www.nizkor.org/hweb/people/e/eichmann-adolf/transcripts/Sessions/Session-068-01.html.

4 Robert Eaglestone, *The Holocaust and the Postmodern* (New York: Oxford University Press, 2008), 16.

5 Quoted in Matthew Boswell, *Holocaust Impiety: In Literature, Popular Music and Film* (London: Palgrave Macmillan, 2012), 7.

6 Elie Wiesel, "Foreword," in Annette Insdorf, *Indelible Shadows: Film and the Holocaust*, 3rd ed. (Cambridge: Cambridge University Press, 2003), xi.

7 Tim Cole, *Selling the Holocaust: From Auschwitz to Schindler* (New York: Routledge, 1999), 16. Author and film critic Philip Lopate wrote a scathing essay entitled "Resistance to the Holocaust" attacking Wiesel's guardianship over all things Holocaust related, writing, "Sometimes it almost seems that 'the Holocaust' is a corporation headed by Eli Wiesel, who defends his patents with articles in the Arts and Leisure section of the Sunday *New York Times*." See Philip Lopate, *Portrait of My Body* (New York: Anchor, 1997), 88–120.

8 Quoted in Eaglestone, 139.

9 Eaglestone, 12.

10 Quoted in Eaglestone, 34.

11 Cole, 106.

12 Vadim Rozof, "The Memory Thief: The Least Sentimental Holocaust Film Ever," *The Village Voice*, May 6, 2008, https://www.villagevoice.com/2008/05/06/the-memory-thief-the-least-sentimental-holocaust-film-ever/. *The Memory Thief* reflects the universalization of the Holocaust as referent of collective suffering

in the wake of such seminal media events as the miniseries *Holocaust* (1978) and the Year of the Holocaust (1993), which witnessed the opening of the US Holocaust Memorial Museum and *Schindler's List*. Alan Mintz, *Popular Culture and the Shaping of Holocaust Memory in America* (Seattle: University of Washington Press, 2001), 26.

13 Michael P. McCleary, "The Fantastic in Holocaust Literature: Writing and Unwriting the Unbearable," in Judith B. Kerman and John Edgar Browning, eds., *The Fantastic in Holocaust Literature and Film: Critical Perspectives* (Jefferson, N.C.: McFarland, 2015), 27.

14 Terence de Pres quoted in Martin Modlinger, "The Ethics of Perspective and the Holocaust Archive: *Schindler's List*, *The Boy in the Striped Pajamas* and *Fateless*," in Oleksander Kobrynskyy and Gerd Bayer, eds., *Holocaust Cinema in the Twenty-First Century: Memory, Images, and the Ethics of Representation* (New York: Wallflower, 2015), 164.

15 Quoted in Elissa Mailender, "Meshes of Power: The Concentration Camp as Pulp or Art House in Liliana Cavani's *The Night Porter*," in Daniel H. Magilow, Kristin T. Vander Lugt, and Elizabeth Bridges, eds., *Nazisploitation! The Nazi Image in Low-Brow Cinema and Culture* (New York: Continuum, 2012), 191.

16 Barry Keith Grant, "'Sensuous Elaboration': Reason and the Visible in the Science-Fiction Film," in Annette Kuhn, ed., *Alien Zone II: The Spaces of Science Fiction Cinema* (London: Verso Books, 1999), 16–17.

17 Stephen Kinzer, "Günter Grass Dies at 87; Writer Pried Open Germany's Past But Hid His Own," *New York Times*, April 23, 2015, https://www.nytimes.com/2015/04/14/world/europe/gunter-grass-german-novelist-dies-at-87.html.

18 Grant, 17–18.

19 Terence De Pres noted three basic commandments supposedly governing Holocaust representations:

1. The Holocaust shall be respected in its totality, as a unique event, as a special case and kingdom of its own, above or below or apart from history.
2. Representations of the Holocaust shall be as accurate and faithful as possible to the facts and conditions of the event, without change or manipulation for any reason—artistic reasons included.
3. The Holocaust shall be approached as a solemn or even sacred event, with a seriousness admitting no response that might obscure its enormity or dishonor the dead.

Aaron Kerner, *Film and the Holocaust: New Perspectives on Dramas, Documentaries, and Experimental Films* (New York: Continuum Books, 2011), 2.

20 Quoted in Libby Saxton, *Haunted Images: Film, Ethics, Testimony and the Holocaust* (London: Wallflower, 2008), 2.

21 Matthew Boswell, *Holocaust Impiety: In Literature, Popular Music and Film* (London: Palgrave Macmillan, 2012), 1–2. Declaring the traumatic unrepresentable, Adam Lowenstein writes, paradoxically silences victims' and survivors' experience and representation. Adam Lowenstein, *Shocking*

Representation: Historical Trauma, National Cinema, and the Modern Horror Film (New York: Columbia University Press, 2005), 5.

22 Boswell, 6.

23 Nazisploitation refers to pornographic and exploitative pulp comics, books, and films first appearing in the 1950s and becoming extremely popular and pervasive in the 1970s. Originally considered taboo and transgressive, Nazisploitation imagery and motifs are integral to big-budget studio productions and permeate mainstream pop culture. See Magilow, Vander Lugt, and Bridges.

24 See Gavriel D. Rosenfeld, *The World Hitler Never Made* (Cambridge: Cambridge University Press, 205); Gavriel D. Rosenfeld, *Hi Hitler! How the Nazi Past Is Being Normalized in Contemporary Culture* (Cambridge: Cambridge University Press, 2015).

25 Rosenfeld, *The World Hitler Never Made*, 4.

26 Rosenfeld, *The World Hitler Never Made*, 16–17.

27 Rosenfeld, *Hi Hitler!*, 12.

28 Rosenfeld, *Hi Hitler!*, 26.

29 Barry Langford, "Globalizing the Holocaust: Fantasies of Annihilation in Contemporary Media Culture," in Alex Bangert, Robert S. C. Gordon, and Libby Saxton, *Holocaust Intersections: Genocide and Visual Culture at the New Millenium* (London: Legend, 2013), 119.

30 Saxton, 2.

31 Daniel R. Schwarz notes that *Schindler's List* "depends on evoking memories from our past knowledge of Holocaust texts." See Daniel R. Schwarz, *Imagining the Holocaust* (New York: St. Martin's Press, 1999), 218.

32 Quoted in Karyn Ball, ed., *Traumatizing Theory: The Cultural Politics of Affect In and Beyond Psychoanalysis* (New York: Other Press, 2007), 150.

33 Quoted in Jeffrey Shandler, *While America Watches: Televising the Holocaust* (New York: Oxford University Press), 18.

34 Quoted in Saxton, 4.

35 Judith E. Doneson, *The Holocaust in American Film*, 2nd ed. (Syracuse, N.Y.: Syracuse University Press, 2002), 5.

36 Janet Staiger, *Media Reception Studies* (New York: New York University Press, 2005), 33.

37 Susan Sontag, *Regarding the Pain of Others* (New York: Picador, 2003), 18.

38 Quoted in Sophia Wood, "Film and Atrocity: The Holocaust as Spectacle," in Kristi M. Wilson and Thomas F. Crowder-Taraborrelli, *Film & Genocide* (Madison: University of Wisconsin Press, 2012), 23.

39 Janet Staiger, *Perverse Spectators: The Practice of Film Reception* (New York: New York University Press, 2000), 211.

40 Karyn Ball, *Disciplining the Holocaust: Traumatic History As an Object of Inquiry and Desire* (Albany: State University of New York Press, 2009), 11.

41 Quoted in Ball, *Disciplining the Holocaust*, 18.

42 Quoted in Hannes Bergthaller, "Dis(re)membering History's Revenants: Trauma, Writing, and Simulated Orality in Toni Morrison's Beloved," *Connotations* 16, no. 1–3 (2006/2007): 117.

43 Lowenstein, 8.
44 Michael Rothberg, *Traumatic Realism: The Demands of Holocaust Representation* (Minneapolis: University of Minnesota Press, 2000), 4.
45 Rothberg, 7.
46 Rothberg, 118.
47 Rothberg, 9.
48 Quoted in Caroline Joan "Kay" S. Picart and David A. Frank, *Frames of Evil: The Holocaust as Horror in American Film* (Carbondale: Southern Illinois University Press, 2006), 5–6.
49 Picart and Frank, 3.
50 Picart and Frank, 7–8.
51 Kerman and Browning, 8.
52 Lowenstein, 7.
53 Linnie Blake, *The Wounds of Nations: Horror Cinema, Historical Trauma and National Identity* (Manchester, UK: Manchester University Press, 2008), 23.
54 Lowenstein, 2.
55 Julia Dover, "The Imitation Game: Paralysis and Response in Fritz Lang's *Metropolis* and Contemporary Critiques of Technology," in Michael Minden and Holger Bachmann, eds., *Fritz Lang's Metropolis: Cinematic Visions of Technology and Fear* (Rochester, N.Y.: Camden House, 2000), 275.
56 Dover, 276.
57 Shohini Chaudhuri, *Cinema of the Dark Side: Atrocity and the Ethics of Film Spectatorship* (Edinburgh, UK: Edinburgh University Press, 2014), 8–9.
58 Joan Gordon, "Utopia, Genocide, and the Other," in Veronica Hollinger and Joan Gordon, eds., *Edging into the Future: Science Fiction and Contemporary Cultural Transformation* (Philadelphia: University of Pennsylvania Press, 2002), 208.
59 Chaudhuri, 116.
60 Judith Halberstam, *Skin Shoes: Gothic Horror and the Technology of Monsters* (Durham, N.C.: Duke University Press, 1995), 8–11.
61 Halberstam, 14.
62 Halberstam, 18.
63 See Ian Kershaw, *The "Hitler Myth": Image and Reality in the Third Reich* (New York: Oxford University Press, 2001).
64 Quoted in Susan Tegel, "Veit Harlan's Jud Süss," in Toby Haggith and Joanna Newman, eds., *Holocaust and the Moving Image: Representations in Film and Television Since 1933* (London: Wallflower Press, 2005), 76.
65 See Barbara Hales, Mihaela Petruscu, and Valerie Weinstein, eds., *Continuity and Crisis in German Cinema, 1928-1936* (Rochester, N.Y.: Camden House, 2016).
66 Anton Kaes, "*The Cabinet of Dr. Caligari*: Expressionism and Cinema," in Ted Perry, ed., *Masterpieces of Modernist Cinema* (Bloomington: Indiana University Press, 2006), 57.
67 Leonardo Quaresima, "Introduction to the 2004 Edition," in Siegfried Kracauer, *From Caligari to Hitler: A Psychological History of the German Film*, ed. Leonardo Quarisema (Princeton, N.J.: Princeton University Press, 2004), xxxii. Originally published in 1947.

68 Kracauer, 5–9.
69 Thomas Elsaesser, "Innocence Restored? Reading and Rereading a 'Classic,'" in Minden and Bachmann, 132–133.
70 Lotte H. Eisner, *The Haunted Screen: Expressionism in the German Cinema and the Influence of Max Reinhardt* (Berkeley: University of California Press, 2008), 9, 51. Originally published in 1952.
71 Eisner, 95.
72 W. Scott Poole, *Wasteland: The Great War and the Origins of Modern Horror* (Berkeley, Calif.: Counterpoint, 2018), 3–4.
73 Anton Kaes, *Shell Shock Cinema: Weimar Culture and the Wounds of War* (Princeton, N.J.: Princeton University Press, 2009), 81.
74 Poole, 77.
75 Noah Isenberg, "Introduction," in Noah Isenberg, ed., *Weimar Cinema: An Essential Guide to Classic Films of the Era* (New York: Columbia University Press, 2008), 5.
76 Eisner, 109.
77 Kaes, *Shell Shock Cinema*, 86.
78 Kracauer, 72–73.
79 Kracauer, 78.
80 Thomas Elsaesser, *Weimar Cinema and After: Germany's Historical Imaginary* (London: Routledge, 2000), 63.
81 Cathy S. Gelbin, *The Golem Returns: From German Romantic Literature to Global Jewish Culture, 1808-2008* (Ann Arbor: University of Michigan Press, 2010), 71.
82 Omer Bartov, *The "Jew" in Cinema: From The Golem to Don't Touch My Holocaust* (Bloomington: Indiana University Press, 2005), 3.
83 Noah Isenberg, "Of Monsters and Magicians: Paul Wegener's *The Golem: How He Came into the World* (1920)," in Isenberg, 39–40.
84 Gelbin, 122.
85 Isenberg, "Of Monsters and Magicians," 47.
86 Bartov, *The "Jew" in Cinema*, 3.
87 Quoted in Poole, 39.
88 Maya Barzilai, *Golem: Modern Wars and Their Monsters* (New York: New York University Press, 2016), 5.
89 Barzilai, 9.
90 Thomas Elsaesser, "No End to *Nosferatu* (1922)," in Isenberg, 81.
91 Poole, 21.
92 Kaes, *Shell Shock Cinema*, 88.
93 See Vejas Gabriel Liulevicius, *The German Myth of the East: 1800 to the Present* (New York: Oxford University Press, 2011); Vejas Gabriel Liulevicius, *War Land on the Eastern Front: Culture, National Identity, and German Occupation in World War I* (Cambridge: Cambridge University Press, 2005).
94 Brian E. Crim, "'Our Most Serious Enemy': The Specter of Judeo-Bolshevism in the German Military Community, 1914–1923," *Central European History* 44, no. 4 (December 2011): 631–632.

95 Roy Ashbury, *F.W. Murnau, Nosferatu* (London: York Press, 2001), 69.
96 Paul Coates, *The Gorgon's Gaze: German Cinema, Expressionism, and the Image of Horror* (New York: Cambridge University Press, 1991), 95–96.
97 Ashbury, 8.
98 Ashbury, 69.
99 David Desser, "Race, Space and Class: The Politics of Cityscapes in SF Films," in Kuhn, 80.
100 Rudolf Arnheim quoted in Eric Rentschler, *The Use and Abuse of Cinema: German Legacies from the Weimar Era to the Present* (New York: Columbia University Press, 2015), 23.
101 David Thomson, *The Big Screen: The Story of the Movies* (New York: Farrar, Straus & Giroux, 2012), 64–65. Lang's claim is unverified, but he did hasten his emigration shortly after the alleged meeting.
102 Quoted in Anton Kaes, "*Metropolis* (1927): City, Cinema, Modernity," in Isenberg, 178.
103 Anton Kaes, "*Metropolis* (1927): City, Cinema, Modernity," in Isenberg, 179.
104 Roger Dadoun, "*Metropolis*: Mother City—'Mittler'—Hitler," *Camera Obscura* 15, no. 3 (Fall 1986): 161.
105 Barbara Hales, "Fritz Lang's *Metropolis* and Reactionary Modernism," *New German Review* 8 (1992): 19.
106 Quoted in Kaes, "Metropolis (1927)," 178–179.
107 Hales, 19.
108 Fritz Lang, dir., *Metropolis*, 1927.
109 Kaes, "Metropolis (1927)," 179.
110 Quoted in Christopher Frayling, *Mad, Bad and Dangerous? The Scientists and the Cinema* (London: Reaktion Books, 2005), 60.
111 Desser, 82.
112 Tom Gunning, "Fritz Lang's *Dr. Mabuse, the Gambler* (1922): Grand Enunciator of the Weimar Era," in Isenberg, 102.
113 Quoted in Dadoun, 156.
114 Dadoun, 156–160.
115 R. L. Rutsky, "The Mediation of Technology and Gender: Metropolis, Nazism, Modernism," in Minden and Bachmann, 235.
116 Bartov, *The "Jew" in Cinema*, x.
117 Quoted in Devorah Baum, "Trauma: An Essay on Jewish Guilt," *Jewish Quarterly*, May 15, 2012, https://www.jewishquarterly.org/2009/12/trauma-an-essay-on-jewish-guilt/.
118 Claire Sisco King, "Imagining the Abject: The Ideological Use of the Dissolve," in Steffen Hantke, ed., *Horror Film: Creating and Marketing Fear* (Jackson: University of Mississippi Press, 2004), 23.
119 Quoted in Erwin Leiser, *Nazi Cinema* (New York: Collier Books, 1974), 76.
120 King, 29.
121 Leiser, 85.
122 Eric Kurlander, *Hitler's Monsters: A Supernatural History of The Third Reich* (New Haven, Conn.: Yale University Press, 2017), xi.

123 Kurlander, *Hitler's Monsters*, xvii.

124 Quoted in Sander L. Gilman, *Difference and Pathology: Stereotypes of Sexuality, Race, and Madness* (Ithaca, N.Y.: Cornell University Press, 1985), 172.

125 Kurlander, *Hitler's Monsters*, 254–257.

126 Eric Kurlander, "Hitler's Monsters: The Occult Roots of Nazism and the Emergence of the Nazi 'Supernatural Imaginary,'" *German History* 30, no. 4 (December 2012): 548.

1. From Muselmann to *The Walking Dead*

1 Jeremy R. Strong, "Transformative Technology and Posthuman Futurity: The Psychological Cartographic of Zombie Narratives," *Inter-Disciplinary Press*, 2015: 214.

2 Quoted in Kim Paffenroth, "Zombies as Internal Fear of Threat," in Stephanie Boluk and Wylie Lenz, eds., *Generation Zombie: Essays on the Living Dead in Modern Culture* (Jefferson, N.C.: McFarland, 2011), 19.

3 Friedrich Nietzsche, *Beyond Good and Evil*, Part IV, Aphorism 146, http://nietzsche.holtof.com/reader/friedrich-nietzsche/beyond-good-and-evil/aphorism-146-quote_d393d7088.html.

4 Jacques Mandelbaum, "Recover," in Jean-Michel Frodon, ed., *Cinema & the Shoah: An Art Confronts the Tragedy of the Twentieth Century*, trans. Anna Harrison and Tom Mes (Albany: State University of New York Press, 2010), 37.

5 Using Yad Vashem's definition, the Muselmann is "a German term widely used among concentration camp inmates to refer to prisoners who were near death due to exhaustion, starvation, or hopelessness. The word Muselmann literally means 'Muslim.' Some scholars believe that the term originated from the similarity between the near-death prone state of a concentration camp Muselmann and the image of a Muslim prostrating himself on the ground in prayer." *Shoah Resource Center*, https://www.yadvashem.org/odot_pdf/Microsoft%20Word%20-%206474.pdf.

6 Primo Levi, *Survival in Auschwitz* (New York: Touchstone, 1996), 90.

7 Quoted in King, 22.

8 Kyle William Bishop, *American Zombie Gothic: The Rise and Fall (and Rise) of the Walking Dead in Popular Culture* (Jefferson, N.C.: McFarland, 2010), 95.

9 Julia Kristeva, "Approaching Abjection," in *Powers of Horror: An Essay on Abjection* (New York: Columbia University Press, 1982), 1–3.

10 Kristeva, 3.

11 Kristeva, 3.

12 Quoted in Cohen, 9.

13 Ernst Jünger titled his 1920 memoir detailing his World War I experience *Storm of Steel*.

14 Poole, 60.

15 Quoted in Paffenroth, 132.

16 Marzena Sokotowska-Paryz, "(Re)remembering the Great War in Deathwatch," in Cynthia J. Miller and A. Bowdoin van Riper, eds. *The Undead on the Battlefield: Horrors of War* (Lanham, Md.: Rowman & Littlefield, 2015), 125.

17 Jean-Michel Frodon, Jacques Mandelbaum, Sylvie Lindeperg, Annette Wieviorka "Conversations at the Mill," in Frodon, 113.

18 Poole, 123.

19 The military horror film originates is a popular subgenre originating with Victor Halperin's *Revolt of the Zombies* (1936), a successor to his *White Zombie* (1932), the first zombie film. *Revolt of the Zombies* is a convoluted narrative, but the plot involves a voodoo priest zombifying soldiers on the Franco-Austrian frontier. See Steffan Hantke, "The Military Horror Film: Speculations on a Hybrid Genre," *Journal of Popular Culture* 43, no. 4 (2010): 703.

20 See Omer Bartov's brilliant collection of essays, *Murder in Our Midst: The Holocaust, Industrial Killing, and Representation* (New York: Oxford University Press, 1996).

21 Sokotowska-Paryz, 125.

22 Quoted in Sokotowska-Paryz, 126.

23 Bishop, 13.

24 Gerry Canavan, "We *Are* the Walking Dead": Race, Time, and Survival in Zombie Narratives," *Extrapolation* 51, no. 3 (2010): 432.

25 Jon Stratton, "Zombie Trouble: Zombie Texts, Bare Life and Displaced People," *European Journal of Cultural Studies* 14, no. 3 (2011): 271.

26 Eric Hamko, "Zombie Orientals Ate My Brain! Orientalism in Contemporary Zombie Stories," in Christopher M. Moreman and Cory James Rushton, eds., *Race, Oppression and the Zombie: Essays on Cross-Cultural Appropriations of the Caribbean Tradition* (Jefferson, N.C.: McFarland, 2011), 108–111.

27 Quoted in Nicole LaRose, "Zombies in a 'Deep, Dark Ocean of History': Danny Boyle's Infected and John Wyndham's Triffids as Metaphors of Postwar Britain," in Moreman and Rushton, 165.

28 Quoted in Nicole LaRose, "Zombies in a 'Deep, Dark Ocean of History': Danny Boyle's Infected and John Wyndham's Triffids as Metaphors of Postwar Britain," in Moreman and Rushton, 165.

29 Agnieszka Soltysik Monnet, "The Transnational Zombie: Postcolonial Memory and Rage in Recent European Horror Film," in Christof Decker and Astrid Böger, eds., *Transnational Mediation: Negotiating Popular Culture between the United States and Europe* (Heidelberg, Germany: Universitätsverlag, 2015), 155.

30 Gregory A. Waller, *The Living and the Undead: Slaying Vampires, Exterminating Vampires* (Urbana: University of Illinois, 2010), 234.

31 Waller, 336.

32 Lauren Wilford, "Death is the Curator: An Interview with Guillermo del Toro," *Bright Wall Dark Room*, Issue 44, 2017, https://www.brightwalldarkroom.com/2017/02/15/death-is-the-curator-an-interview-with-guillermo-del-toro/.

33 Isabel Cristina Pinedo, "Postmodern Elements of the Contemporary Horror Film," in Stephen Prince, ed. *The Horror Film* (New Brunswick, N.J.: Rutgers University Press, 2004), 87.

34 Pinedo, 90–91.

35 Shelley S. Rees, "Frontier Values Meet Big-City Zombies: The Old West in AMC's The Walking Dead," in Cynthia J. Miller and A. Bowdoin van Riper,

eds., *Undead in the West: Vampires, Zombies, Mummies, and Ghosts on the Cinematic Frontier* (Lanham, Md.: Scarecrow Press, 2012), 81.

36 Quoted in Rees, 85.

37 Canavan, 442.

38 Quoted in Canavan, 438.

39 Cohen, "Hearth of Darkness," 147.

40 Wolfgang Sofsky, *The Order of Terror: The Concentration Camp* (Princeton, N.J.: Princeton University Press, 2013), 329.

41 Quoted in William Graebner, "The Living Dead of George Romero and Steven Spielberg: America, the Holocaust and the Figure of the Zombie," *Dapim: Studies on the Holocaust* 21 (February 2017): 16.

42 Quoted in Graebner, 19.

43 Henry Golde, Oral History, Wisconsin Survivors of the Holocaust, Wisconsin Historical Society, accessed July 3, 2019, http://www.wisconsinhistory.org/HolocaustSurvivors/Golde.asp.

44 Quoted in Graebner, 19.

45 Zdziław Ryn and Stanisław Kłodziński, "An der Grenze zwischen Leben und Tod. Eine Studie über die Erscheinung des 'Muselmanns' im Konzentrationslager" (1983), quoted in Wollheim Memorial, http://www.wollheim-memorial.de/en/muselmaenner#down3.

46 Quoted in Giorgio Agamben, *Remnants of Auschwitz: The Witness and the Archive*, trans. Daniel Heller-Roazen (New York: Zone Books, 2002), 43.

47 Quoted in Giorgio Agamben, *Remnants of Auschwitz*, 41.

48 Saxton, 99.

49 Quoted in Agamben, *Remnants of Auschwitz*, 41.

50 Lissa Skitolsky, "Tracing Theory on the Body of the 'Walking Dead': Der Muselmann and the Course on Holocaust Studies," *Shofar: An Interdisciplinary Journal of Jewish Studies* 30, no. 2 (Winter 2012): 77.

51 Quoted in Skitolsky, 77.

52 Quoted in Skitolsky, 78.

53 Quoted in Agamben, *Remnants of Auschwitz*, 92.

54 Primo Levi, *Survival in Auschwitz* (New York: Touchstone, 1996), 27.

55 Primo Levi, *The Drowned and the Saved*, trans. Michael F. Moore, in Ann Goldstein, ed., *The Complete Works of Primo Levi*, Vol. III (New York: Liverlight, 2015), 2416.

56 Levi, *The Drowned and the Saved*, 2467.

57 Levi, *The Drowned and the Saved*, 2468.

58 Levi, *Survival in Auschwitz*, 90.

59 Levi, *The Drowned and the Saved*, 2435.

60 Levi, *The Drowned and the Saved*, 2448.

61 Quoted in Levi, *The Drowned and the Saved*, 2464.

62 Giorgio Agamben, *Homo Sacer: Sovereign Power and Bare Life*, trans. Daniel Heller-Roazen (Stanford, Calif.: Stanford University Press, 1998), 83.

63 Agamben, *Homo Sacer*, 181.

64 Quoted in Agamben, *Remnants of Auschwitz*, 150.

65 Agamben, *Remnants of Auschwitz*, 63.
66 Agamben, *Remnants of Auschwitz*, 69.
67 Agamben, *Remnants of Auschwitz*, 47–48.
68 Agamben, *Remnants of Auschwitz*, 55.
69 Agamben, *Remnants of Auschwitz*, 81.
70 Agamben, *Remnants of Auschwitz*, 85.
71 Agamben, *Remnants of Auschwitz*, 156.
72 Agamben, *Homo Sacer*, 185. Emphasis added.
73 Skitolksky, 89.
74 Saxton, 107.
75 AMC Blogs, "Q&A—*The Walking Dead* Scribe Robert Kirkman Discusses His Zombies Influences," accessed July 3, 2019, http://www.amc.com/talk/2009/11/qa-the-walkin.
76 Toby Haggith, "Filming the Liberation of Bergen-Belsen," in Haggith and Newman, 34.
77 Bartov, *The "Jew" in Cinema*, 49.
78 Joshua Hirsch, *After Image: Film, Trauma, and the Holocaust* (Philadelphia: Temple University Press, 2004), 14.
79 Susan Sontag, *On Photography* (New York: Delta Books, 1977), 19–20.
80 Stuart Liebman, "Introduction," in Stuart Liebman, ed., *Claude Lanzmann's Shoah: Key Essays* (Oxford: Oxford University Press, 2007), 9.
81 Gertrud Koch, "The Aesthetic Transformation of the Image of the Unimaginable: Notes on Claude Lanzmann's Shoah," in Liebman, 129.
82 Quoted in Marianne Hirsch and Leo Spitzer, "Gendered Translations: Claude Lanzmann's Shoah," in Liebman, 176.
83 Dominick LaCapra, *History and Memory after Auschwitz* (Ithaca, N.Y.: Cornell University Press, 1998), 133.
84 Peter Novick, *The Holocaust in American Life* (New York: Mariner Books, 2000), 273.
85 Cohen, 136.
86 Quoted in Cohen, 128.
87 Graebner, 3.
88 Quoted in Graebner, 18.
89 Lawrence Bush, "O My America: 'The Walking Dead' as Holocaust Literature," *Jewish Currents: Activist Politics & Art*, November 16, 2015, http://jewishcurrents.org/o-my-america-the-walking-dead-as-holocaust-literature/.
90 Jeffrey Goldberg, J. J. Gould, and Scott Meslow, "'The Walking Dead' as the Holocaust," *The Atlantic*, October 12, 2012, https://www.theatlantic.com/entertainment/archive/2012/10/the-walking-dead-as-the-holocaust/263911/.
91 Andrea Slane, *A Not So Foreign Affair: Fascism, Sexuality and the Cultural Rhetoric of American Democracy* (Durham, N.C.: Duke University Press, 2001), 23.
92 George Hagman, "Surviving the Zombie Apocalypse: Trauma and Transformation in AMC's *The Walking Dead*," *Psychoanalytic Inquiry* 37, no. 1 (2017): 47.

93 "Clear," *The Walking Dead*, season 3, episode 12, directed by Tricia Brock, aired March 3, 2013.

94 Kyle William Bishop, "The Pathos of The Walking Dead: Bringing Terror Back to Zombie Cinema," in James Lowder, ed., *Triumph of the Walking Dead: Robert Kirkman's Zombie Epic on Page and Screen* (Dallas: Smart Pop, 2011), 12.

95 Canavan, 449.

96 Dawn Keetley, "Introduction," in Dawn Keetley, ed., *"We're All Infected": Essays on AMC's The Walking Dead and the Fate of the Human* (Jefferson, N.C.: McFarland, 2014), 9.

97 Cohen, 19.

98 Quoted in David Patterson, *Genocide in Jewish Thought* (Cambridge, UK: Cambridge University Press, 2012), 186.

99 "Days Gone Bye," *The Walking Dead*, season 1, episode 1, directed by Frank Darabont, aired October 31, 2010.

100 Quoted in Michelle Kramisen, "Confronting Trauma in the Zombie Apocalypse: Witnessing, Survivor Guilt, and Postmemory," in Philip L. Simpson and Marcus Mallard, eds., *The Walking Dead Live!: Essays on the Television Show* (Lanham, Md.: Rowman & Littlefield, 2016), 114.

101 "Wildfire," *The Walking Dead*, season 1, episode 5, directed by Ernest Dickerson, aired November 28, 2010.

102 "Alone," *The Walking Dead*, season 4, episode 13, directed by Ernest Dickerson, aired March 9, 2014.

103 Hagman, 9–10.

104 Hagman, 15.

105 Hagman, 15.

106 "30 Days without an Accident," *The Walking Dead*, season 4, episode 1, directed by Greg Nicotero, aired October 13, 2013.

107 "Indifference," *The Walking Dead*, season 4, episode 4, directed by Tricia Brock, aired November 3, 2013.

108 "The Grove," *The Walking Dead*, season 4, episode 14, directed by Michael E. Satrazemis, aired March 16, 2014.

109 Hagman, 15.

110 "Burning in Water, Drowning in Flame," *Fear the Walking Dead*, season 3, episode 5, directed by Daniel Stamm, aired June 25, 2017.

111 Hagman, 20.

112 "TS-19," *The Walking Dead*, season 1, episode 6, directed by Guy Ferland, aired December 5, 2010.

113 Levi, *Survival in Auschwitz*, 90.

114 Ned Vizzini, "Rick and Rand: The Objectivist Hero in The Walking Dead," in Lowder, 139.

115 "Wildfire," *The Walking Dead*.

116 "Nebraska," *The Walking Dead*, season 2, episode 8, directed by Clark Johnson, aired February 12, 2012.

117 "Judge, Jury, Executioner," *The Walking Dead*, season 2, episode 11, directed by Greg Nicotero, aired March 4, 2012.

118 "Welcome to the Tombs," *The Walking Dead*, season 3, episode 16, directed by Ernest Dickerson, aired March 31, 2013.
119 "Save the Last One," *The Walking Dead*, season 2, episode 3, directed by Phil Abraham, aired October 30, 2011.
120 Quoted in Bartov, 215.
121 Bartov, The "Jew" in Cinema," 223.
122 "No Sanctuary," *The Walking Dead*, season 5, episode 1, directed by Greg Nicotero, aired October 12, 2014.
123 "Alone," *The Walking Dead*.
124 "Alone," *The Walking Dead*.
125 "Inmates," *The Walking Dead*, season 4, episode 10, directed by Tricia Brock, aired February 16, 2014.
126 "A," *The Walking Dead*, season 4, episode 16, directed by Michelle MacLaren, aired March 30, 2014.
127 "No Sanctuary," *The Walking Dead*.
128 Karl Quinn, "The Walking Dead Season 5 Opener Shows There's Plenty of Life in the Undead Yet," *Sunday Morning Herald*, October 14, 2014, http://www.smh.com.au/entertainment/tv-and-radio/the-walking-dead-season-5-opener-shows-theres-plenty-of-life-in-the-undead-yet-20141014-115qyl.html.
129 Eric Kligerman, "The Phantom Effect: The Return of the Dead in Gerhard Richter's *October 18, 1977* Cycle," in Ball, *Traumatizing Theory*, 169.
130 Claude Lanzmann, *Shoah: An Oral History of the Holocaust* (New York: Pantheon Books, 1985), 62.
131 Quoted in Levi, *The Drowned and the Saved*, 2464.
132 "Too Far Gone," *The Walking Dead*, season 4, episode 8, directed by Ernest Dickerson, aired December 1, 2013.

2. Silent Screams

1 Celluloid Liberation Front, "Auschwitz–Harlem: Post-Traumatic Economy in *The Pawnbroker*," *Senses of Cinema*, Issue 59, June 2011, http://sensesofcinema.com/2011/feature-articles/auschwitz%c2%ad%e2%80%93harlem-post-traumatic-economy-in-the-pawnbroker/.
2 Sophie Gilbert, "The Brilliant Nihilism of *The Leftovers*," *The Atlantic*, August 4, 2014, https://www.theatlantic.com/entertainment/archive/2014/08/the-brilliant-nihilism-of-the-leftovers/375563/.
3 Doneson, 63.
4 Kligerman, 169.
5 Omer Bartov, "Spielberg's Oskar: Hollywood Tries Evil," in Yosafa Loshitzky, ed., *Spielberg's Holocaust: Critical Perspectives on Schindler's List* (Bloomington: Indiana University Press, 1997), 50–51.
6 Mintz, 36.
7 Wood, "Film and Atrocity," 45.
8 Quoted in Vivian Sobchack, ed., *The Persistence of History: Cinema, Television, and the Modern Event* (New York: Routledge, 1996), 148.
9 Theodor W. Adorno, *Prisms* (Cambridge, Mass.: MIT Press, 1983), 34.

10 Quoted in Rothberg, 25.
11 Rothberg, 32.
12 Rothberg, 81.
13 Hirsch, *After Image*, 7.
14 Hirsch, *After Image*, 20.
15 Lawrence Baron, *Projecting the Holocaust into the Present: The Changing Focus of Contemporary Holocaust Cinema* (Lanham, Md.: Rowman & Littlefield, 2005), 5.
16 Baron, *Projecting the Holocaust into the Present*, 215.
17 Quoted in Susan Derwin, *Rage is the Subtext: Readings in Holocaust Literature and Film* (Columbus: Ohio State University Press, 2012), 4–5.
18 Hagman, 52.
19 Quoted in Gary Weissman, *Fantasies of Witnessing: Postwar Efforts to Experience the Holocaust* (Ithaca, N.Y.: Cornell University Press, 2004), 133.
20 Judith Butler, "Fiction and Solitude: Ethics and the Conditions for Survival," in Claudio Fogu, Wulf Kansteiner, and Todd Presner, eds., *Probing the Ethics of Holocaust Culture* (Cambridge, Mass.: Harvard University Press, 2016), 384.
21 LaCapra, *History and Memory after Auschwitz*, 9.
22 Derwin, 26.
23 Jean Baudrillard, *Simulcra and Simulation*, trans. Sheila Faria Glaser (Ann Arbor: University of Michigan Press, 1994), 49.
24 Dominick LaCapra, *Representing the Holocaust: History, Theory, Trauma* (Ithaca, N.Y.: Cornell University Press, 1994), 64. See also Alon Confino, *A World Without Jews: The Nazi Imagination from Persecution to Genocide* (New Haven, Conn.: Yale University Press, 2015).
25 Baudrillard, *Simulcra and Simulation*, 49.
26 Jean Baudrillard, *The Transparency of Evil: Essays on Extreme Phenomena*, trans. James Benedict (London: Verso Books, 2009), 103.
27 Baudrillard, *Simulcra and Simulation*, 49.
28 Baudrillard, *Simulcra and Simulation*, 49–50.
29 Quoted in Judith Doneson, "The Holocaust: Remembering for the Future: Holocaust Revisited: A Catalyst for Memory or Trivialization?" *Annals of the American Academy of Political and Social Science* (November 1996): 71.
30 Emily Nussbaum, "Depression Modern: The Existential Risk-Taking of 'The Leftovers,'" *New Yorker*, November 2, 2015, http://www.newyorker.com/magazine/2015/11/02/depression-modern.
31 Hirsch, *After Image*, 85.
32 Hirsch, *After Image*, 21–22.
33 Hirsch, *After Image*, 92.
34 Hirsch, *After Image*, 92.
35 Michael W. Jennings, Brigid Doherty, and Thomas Y. Levin, eds., *Walter Benjamin: The Work of Art in the Age of Its Technological Reproducibility, and Other Writings on Media* (Cambridge, Mass.: Belknap Press, 2008), 317.
36 Sidney Lumet, dir., *The Pawnbroker*, 1965 (Artisan Entertainment, 2003, DVD).

37 Frank R. Cunningham, "The Insistence of Memory: The Opening Sequence of Lumet's 'Pawnbroker,'" *Literature/Film Quarterly* 7, no. 1 (1989): 295.
38 Michael K. Johnson, "Traumatic Experience and the Representation of Nature in the Novel and Film 'The Pawnbroker,'" *Literature/Film Quarterly* 35, no. 4 (2007): 295.
39 *The Pawnbroker.*
40 *The Pawnbroker.*
41 Bartov, *The "Jew" in Cinema*, 241.
42 Agamben, *Remnants of Auschwitz*, 164–165.
43 Agamben, *Remnants of Auschwitz*, 163.
44 Damon Lindelof and Tom Perrotta, "The Pilot," *The Leftovers*, audio commentary, season 1, episode 1, DVD.
45 "The Pilot," *The Leftovers*, directed by Peter Berg, season 1, episode 1, aired June 29, 2014.
46 Cason Murphy, "Augusto Boal is Alive and Well and Living in Mapleton: The Guilty Remnant in HBO's *The Leftovers*," *Journal of Film and Video* 68, no. 3–4 (Fall/Winter 2016): 105.
47 "Gladys," *The Leftovers*, directed by Mimi Leder, season 1, episode 5, aired July 27, 2014.
48 "BJ and the AC," *The Leftovers*, directed by Carl Franklin and Lesli Linka Glatter, season 1, episode 4, aired July 20, 2014.
49 "International Assassin," *The Leftovers*, directed by Craig Zobel, season 2, episode 8, aired November 22, 2015.
50 "Cairo," *The Leftovers*, directed by Michelle MacLaren, season 1, episode 8, aired August 17, 2014.
51 Weissman, 4.
52 Weissman, 87.
53 Bartov, *The "Jew" in Cinema*, 96.
54 Quoted in Rothberg, 47.
55 Bartov, *The "Jew" in Cinema*, 95.
56 *The Pawnbroker.*
57 Annette Insdorf, *Indelible Shadows: Film and the Holocaust*, 3rd ed. (Cambridge: Cambridge University Press, 2003), 28.
58 Mintz, 114.
59 Stuart Liebman presented this information at the 2015 Hess Seminar, "Using Film and Media to Teach the Holocaust," sponsored by the US Holocaust Memorial Museum.
60 *The Pawnbroker.*
61 Celluloid Liberation Front.
62 *The Pawnbroker.*
63 "A Matter of Geography," *The Leftovers*, directed by Mimi Leder, season 2, episode 2, aired October 11, 2015.
64 Mintz, 180.
65 "Two Boats and a Helicopter," *The Leftovers*, directed by Keith Gordon, season 1, episode 3, aired July 13, 2014.

66 Eli Cohen, dir., *The Quarrel*, 1991.
67 Bartov, *The "Jew" in Cinema*, 256.
68 "Guest," *The Leftovers*, directed by Carl Franklin, season 1, episode 6, aired August 3, 2014.
69 C. L. Glenn and L. Cunningham, "Black Magic: The Magical Negro and White Salvation in Film," *Journal of Black Studies* 40, no. 2 (2009): 135–152.
70 "A Most Powerful Adversary," *The Leftovers*, directed by Mimi Leder, season 2, episode 7, aired November 15, 2015.
71 *The Pawnbroker*.
72 "Guest," *The Leftovers*.
73 Gilbert.
74 Quoted in Hirsch, *After Image*, 58.
75 Doneson, *The Holocaust in American Film*, 87.
76 Quoted in Doneson, *The Holocaust in American Film*, 90.
77 Insdorf, 31.
78 Damon Lindelof and Tom Perrotta, *The Leftovers*, audio commentary, "The Prodigal Son Returns," season 1, episode 10, DVD.
79 "The Prodigal Son Returns," *The Leftovers*, directed by Mimi Leder, season 1, episode 10, aired September 7, 2014.
80 "The Prodigal Son Returns," *The Leftovers*.
81 "Certified," *The Leftovers*, directed by Carl Franklin, season 3, episode 6, aired May 21, 2017.
82 "The Book of Nora," *The Leftovers*, directed by Mimi Leder, season 3, episode 8, aired June 4, 2017.
83 Ball, *Disciplining the Holocaust*, 48.
84 Imre Kertesz and John MacKay, "Who Owns Auschwitz," *Yale Journal of Criticism* 14, no. 1 (Spring 2001): 268–269.
85 Quoted in Eric L. Santner, *Stranded Objects: Mourning, Memory, and Film in Postwar Germany* (Ithaca, N.Y.: Cornell University Press, 1990), 80.
86 "Don't Be Ridiculous," *The Leftovers*, directed by Keith Gordon, season 3, episode 2, aired April 23, 2017.
87 Weissman, 22.
88 Quoted in Eaglestone, 17.

3. Nazi Monsters and the Return of History

1 Saul Friedlander, *Reflections on Nazism*, trans. Thomas Weyr (New York: Avon Books, 1984), xv.
2 Friedlander, xvii.
3 Anton Kaes, *From Hitler to Heimat: The Return of History as Film* (Cambridge, Mass.: Harvard University Press, 1989), 5; Eric Rentschler, *The Ministry of Illusion: Nazi Cinema and Its Afterlife* (Cambridge, Mass.: Harvard University Press, 1996), 7.
4 Yael Hersonski, "Witnessing the Archive," in Fogu, Kansteiner, and Presner, 282.
5 Alon Confino, "A World Without Jews: Interpreting the Holocaust," *German History* 27, no. 4 (2009): 550.

6 Rentschler, 22.
7 Thomas Weber, "*Cache* (2005), or the Ongoing Repression of Traumatic Memories," in Michael Elm, Kobi Kabalck, and Julia B. Koehne, eds., *The Horrors of Trauma in Cinema: Violence, Void, Visualization* (Newcastle, UK: Cambridge Scholars, 2014), 78.
8 Nicholas Goodrick-Clarke, *Black Sun: Aryan Cults, Esoteric Nazism and the Politics of Identity* (New York: New York University Press, 2002), 107.
9 Aaron Kerner, "On the Cinematic Nazi," in Kobrynskyy and Bayer, 203.
10 Aaron Kerner, "On the Cinematic Nazi," in Kobrynskyy and Bayer, 203–205.
11 Weber, 70.
12 "Nazi Zombies," in June Michelle Pulliam and Anthony J. Fonseca, eds., *Encyclopedia of the Zombie: The Walking Dead in Popular Culture and Myth* (Santa Barbara, Calif.: Greenwood Press, 2014), 180.
13 David J. Skal, "The Horrors of War," in Prince, 79–80.
14 Hantke, "The Military Horror Film," 701.
15 James J. Ward, "Utterly without Redeeming Social Value? 'Nazi Science' Beyond Exploitation Cinema," in Magilow, Vander Lugt, and Bridges, 95.
16 Ken Wiederhorn, dir., *Shock Waves*, Zopix Company, 1977.
17 *Shock Waves*.
18 Ward, 101.
19 Joel M. Reed, dir., *Night of the Zombies*, 1981.
20 Sven Jüngerkes and Christiane Wienand, "A Past that Refuses to Die: Nazi Zombie Film and the Legacy of Occupation" in Magilow, Vander Lugt, and Bridges, 239.
21 See Antony Beevor, "An ugly carnival," *The Guardian*, June 4, 2009, https://www.theguardian.com/lifeandstyle/2009/jun/05/women-victims-d-day-landings-second-world-war, for a summary of how French women accused of collaboration were treated after liberation.
22 Jüngerkes and Wienand, 243–244.
23 Tommy Wirkola, dir., *Dead Snow*, Euforia Film, 2009.
24 "Død snø (2009) Trailer (with subs) 'Ein! Zwei! Die!'" accessed August 15, 2018, https://www.youtube.com/watch?v=-RlWrrhG-P4.
25 Jüngerkes and Wienand, 247.
26 Hantke, "The Military Horror Film," 710–719.
27 Richard Raaphorst, dir., *Frankenstein's Army*, MPI Media Group, 2013.
28 *Frankenstein's Army*.
29 Steve Barker, dir., *Outpost*, Black Camel Pictures, 2008.
30 *Outpost*.
31 Steve Barker, dir., *Outpost: Black Sun*, Black Camel Pictures, 2012.
32 *Outpost: Black Sun*.
33 *Outpost: Black Sun*.
34 Rob Green, dir., *The Bunker*, Millennium Pictures, 2001.
35 Hantke, "The Military Horror Film," 709.
36 The crimes of the Grossdeutschland Division are detailed in Omer Bartov, *The Eastern Front, 1941–45, German Troops, and the Barbarization of Warfare* (New York: Palgrave Macmillan, 2001).

37 *The Bunker.*

38 Chris Alexander, "In Defense of Michael Mann's THE KEEP," October 29, 2015, http://www.comingsoon.net/horror/news/747457-defense-michael-manns-keep. Michael Mann faced numerous production problems and was forced to cut the length of the film in half, factors contributing to the illogical narrative and surreal atmosphere.

39 Fernando Gabriel Pagoni Berns, "Strategic Military Reconfiguration in Horror Fiction: The Case of F. Paul Wilson's The Keep and Graham Masterston's The Devils of D-Day," in Miller and van Riper, *The Undead on the Battlefield*, 176.

40 Michael Mann, dir., *The Keep*, Paramount Pictures, 1983.

41 Tim Stack, "'American Horror Story': Ryan Murphy on Anne Frank Debut—EXCLUSIVE," *EW.com*, November 8, 2012, https://ew.com/article/2012/11/08/american-horror-story-ryan-murphy-anne-frank/.

42 "Origins of Monstrosity," *American Horror Story: Asylum*, season 2, episode 6, directed by David Semel, aired November 21, 2012.

43 See Brian E. Crim, "She Wolves: The Monstrous Women of Nazisploitation Cinema," in Karen Ritzenhoff and Catriona McAvoy, eds., *Selling Sex on Screen: From Weimar Cinema to Zombie Porn* (Lanham, Md.: Rowman & Littlefield, 2015), 103.

44 The Nazi euthanasia program known as T-4 issued false death certificates for children either poisoned or gassed to death in dozens of centers in Germany and Austria.

45 "Nor'easter," *American Horror Story: Asylum*, season 2, episode 3, directed by Michael Uppendahl, aired October 31, 2012.

46 "I Am Anne Frank: Part 1," *American Horror Story: Asylum*, season 2, episode 4, directed by Michael Uppendahl, aired November 7, 2012.

47 Stack.

48 "I Am Anne Frank: Part 1," *American Horror Story: Asylum.*

49 Kitty is inspired by a character from children's books written by Cissy van Marxveldt, a heroine Anne Frank admired. Jeff Jensen, "American Horror Story Recap: The Girl with the Auschwitz Tattoo," *EW.com*, November 8, 2012, https://ew.com/recap/american-horror-story-season-2-episode-4/.

50 "I Am Anne Frank: Part 1," *American Horror Story: Asylum.*

51 "I Am Anne Frank: Part 1." The woman's story resembles that of Ingrid Pitt, a Polish girl who survived the Holocaust and married an American soldier, whom she later divorced. Pitt was an actress known for working in the horror genre. See Jensen, "American Horror Story Recap."

52 "I Am Anne Frank: Part 1," *American Horror Story: Asylum.*

53 A reference to Alan Rickman's villain in *Die Hard* (1988)?

54 "I Am Anne Frank: Part 1," *American Horror Story: Asylum.*

55 "I Am Anne Frank: Part 1," *American Horror Story: Asylum.*

56 "Origins of Monstrosity," *American Horror Story: Asylum.*

57 "I Am Anne Frank: Part 1," *American Horror Story: Asylum.*

58 See Cynthia Ozick, "Who Owns Anne Frank?" *New Yorker*, September 8, 1997, https://www.newyorker.com/magazine/1997/10/06/who-owns-anne-frank.

59 Halle Kiefer, "'American Horror Story: Asylum' Recap: Your Story Is Indecent," *Rolling Stone*, November 8, 2012, https://www.rollingstone.com/movies/movie-news/american-horror-story-asylum-recap-your-story-is-indecent-178622/.
60 Tim Stack, "American Horror Story': Ryan Murphy on Anne Frank debut—EXCLUSIVE", *EW.com*, November 8, 2012, https://ew.com/article/2012/11/08/american-horror-story-ryan-murphy-anne-frank/.
61 Joel Schumacher, dir., *Blood Creek*, director's commentary, Gold Circle Films, 2009, DVD.
62 Joel Schumacher, dir., *Blood Creek*, 2009.
63 Walter Rankin, "Blood Creek," in Pulliam and Fonseca, 19–20.
64 Weber, 72.
65 Kate Connolly, "German director's Holocaust film causes outrage," *The Guardian*, November 12, 2010, https://www.theguardian.com/world/2010/nov/12/uwe-boll-auschwitz-film-causes-outrage.
66 Boll, Uwe, dir., *BloodRayne: The Third Reich*, Phase 4 Films, 2011.
67 Kate Connolly, "German director's Holocaust film causes outrage," *The Guardian*, November 12, 2010, https://www.theguardian.com/world/2010/nov/12/uwe-boll-auschwitz-film-causes-outrage.
68 Kate Connolly, "German director's Holocaust film causes outrage," *The Guardian*, November 12, 2010, https://www.theguardian.com/world/2010/nov/12/uwe-boll-auschwitz-film-causes-outrage.
69 Blake, 23.
70 Adolf Hitler, *Mein Kampf*, trans. by Ralph Manheim (New York: Houghton Mifflin, 1969), 60.
71 Keith McDonald and Roger Clark, *Guillermo del Toro: Film as Alchemic* (New York: Bloomsbury, 2014), 3.
72 McDonald and Clark, 192–194.
73 Karin Brown, "Time Out of Joint: Traumatic Hauntings in the Spanish Civil War Films," in John W. Morehead, ed., *The Supernatural Cinema of Guillermo del Toro* (Jefferson, N.C.: McFarland, 2015), 71.
74 Brown, 78.
75 Coates, 96.
76 Stacey Abbott, *Celluloid Vampires: Life after Death in the Modern World* (Austin: University of Texas Press, 2007), 45.
77 F. W. Murnau, dir., *Nosferatu: A Symphony of Horror*, Criterion, 1922. The film *30 Days of Night* (2007) also includes a human collaborator who helps usher in a vampire infestation in exchange for, in this case, a false promise of immortality.
78 Lane Roth, "Dracula Meets the Zeitgeist: Nosferatu (1922) as Film Adaptation," *Literature/Film Quarterly* 7, no. 4 (1979), 311–312.
79 Meredith Woerner, "We Toured the Gruesome Set of Guillermo del Toro's *The Strain*," *GIZMODO*, July 11, 2014, https://io9.gizmodo.com/we-toured-the-gruesome-world-of-guillermo-del-toros-the-1603035324.
80 "The Box," *The Strain*, season 1, episode 2, directed by David Semel, aired July 20, 2014.

81 "Night Zero," *The Strain*, season 1, episode 1, directed by Guillermo del Toro, aired July 13, 2014.
82 "The Box," *The Strain*.
83 "For Services Rendered," *The Strain*, season 1, episode 7, directed by Charlotte Sieling, aired August 24, 2014.
84 "Night Train," *The Strain*, season 2, episode 13, directed by Vincenzo Nitali, aired October 4, 2015.
85 "Ouroboros," *The Strain*, season 4, episode 7, directed by Thomas Carter, aired August 27, 2017.
86 "Night Train," *The Strain*.
87 "Fallen Light," *The Strain*, season 2, episode 12, directed by Vincenzo Natali, aired September 27, 2015.
88 "Runaways," *The Strain*, season 1, episode 5, directed by Peter Weller, aired August 10, 2014.
89 "Gone Smooth," *The Strain*, season 1, episode 3, directed by David Semel, aired July 27, 2014.
90 "Collaborators," *The Strain*, season 3, episode 8, directed by T. J. Scott, aired October 9, 2016.
91 "The Master," *The Strain*, season 1, episode 13, directed by Phil Abraham, aired October 4, 2014.
92 "White Light," *The Strain*, season 3, episode 8, directed by T. J. Scott, aired October 16, 2016.
93 "Blood Tax," *The Strain*, season 4, episode 2, directed by J. Miles Dale, aired July 23, 2017.
94 "Ouroboros," *The Strain*.
95 "Gone Smooth," *The Strain*.
96 "Night Zero," *The Strain*.
97 "For Services Rendered," *The Strain*.
98 "By Any Means," *The Strain*, season 2, episode 2, directed by T. J. Scott, aired July 19, 2015.
99 "Dead End," *The Strain*, season 2, episode 1, directed by Phil Abraham, aired September 20, 2015.
100 "For Services Rendered," *The Strain*.
101 "The Box," *The Strain*.
102 "For Services Rendered," *The Strain*.
103 "The Assassin," *The Strain*, season 2, episode 10, directed by Phil Abraham, aired September 13, 2015.
104 "For Services Rendered," *The Strain*.
105 "The Battle for Red Hook," *The Strain*, season 2, episode 9, directed by Kevin Dowling, aired September 6, 2015.
106 "Night Train," *The Strain*.
107 "Belly of the Beast," *The Strain*, season 4, episode 5, directed by Norberto Barba, aired August 13, 2017.
108 "The Third Rail," *The Strain*, season 1, episode 11, directed by Deran Serafian, aired September 21, 2014.

4. The View from Hell

1 Blake, 73.

2 Lowenstein, 7.

3 Richard Brody, "Hitchcock and the Holocaust," *New Yorker*, accessed December 12, 2018, https://www.newyorker.com/culture/richard-brody/hitchcock-and-the-holocaust.

4 Quoted in Lowenstein, 8.

5 Robin Wood, *Hitchcock's Films Revisited*, revised ed. (New York: Columbia University Press, 2002), 154.

6 Terri Ginsberg, *Holocaust Film: The Political Aesthetics of Ideology* (Newcastle, UK: Cambridge Scholars, 2007), 204.

7 See Gerald Steinacher, *Nazis on the Run: How Hitler's Henchmen Fled Justice* (New York: Oxford University Press, 2012).

8 See Gavriel Rosenfeld, *The Fourth Reich: The Specter of Nazism from World War II to the Present* (Cambridge: Cambridge University Press, 2019).

9 Quoted in Friedlander, *Reflections on Nazism*, 79.

10 John Lukacs, *The Hitler of History* (New York: Vintage Books, 1998), 5.

11 Rosenfeld, *The World Hitler Never Made*, 218.

12 Most audiences at the time would associate Laurence Olivier with a decidedly different character than the beleaguered Liebermann. The celebrated actor also played Dr. Christian Szell in *Marathon Man* (1976), a demented, fit, and extremely Teutonic figure reminiscent of Mengele nicknamed the White Angel.

13 Franklin J. Schaffner, dir., *The Boys from Brazil*, Twentieth Century Fox, 1978.

14 *The Boys from Brazil*.

15 *The Boys from Brazil*.

16 Slane, 175.

17 Rosenfeld, *The Fourth Reich*, 230.

18 Neil Gerlach, "Narrating Armageddon: Antichrist Films and the Critique of Late Modernity," *Journal of Religion and Popular Culture* 24, no. 2 (Summer 2012): 219.

19 Andrew Scahill, "'It's All for You, Damien!' Oedipal Horror and Racial Privilege in *The Omen* Series," in Andrew Scahill and Debbie C. Olsen, eds., *Lost and Othered Children in Contemporary Cinema* (Lanham, Md.: Lexington Books, 2012), 98.

20 Fritz Lang, dir., *Dr. Mabuse: The Gambler*, Lino Korber Films, 1922.

21 Fritz Lang, dir., *The Testament of Dr. Mabuse*, Criterion Collection, 1933.

22 Andrew Scahill, "'It's All for You, Damien!' Oedipal Horror and Racial Privilege in *The Omen* Series," in Andrew Scahill and Debbie C. Olsen, eds., *Lost and Othered Children in Contemporary Cinema* (Lanham, Md.: Lexington Books, 2012), 98.

23 Scahill, 98.

24 Scahill, 100.

25 Neil Gerlach, "The Antichrist as Multi-Monomyth: The Omen Films as Social Critique," *Journal of Popular Culture* 44, no. 5 (2011): 1036.

26 Quoted in Gerlach, "Narrating Armageddon," 218.

27 Gerlach, "The Antichrist as Multi-Monomyth," 1030.

28 Gerlach, "The Antichrist as Multi-Monomyth," 1044.

29 Roman Polanski, *Roman by Polanski* (New York: William Morrow, 1984), 26.

30 Ian Freer, *Movie Makers: 50 Iconic Directors from Chaplin to the Coen Brothers* (London: Quercus, 2009), 129–131.

31 Ewa Mazierska, *Roman Polanski: The Cinema of a Cultural Traveler* (New York: I.B. Tauris, 2007), 14. The issue of Polanski's arrest for statutory rape in 1978 and his subsequent flight from the US justice system while awaiting sentencing raises questions about how the traumas of the Holocaust and Sharon Tate's murder affected him. While Mazierska is willing to concede Polanski's difficult life is a mitigating factor in his crime, biographer Thomas Kiernan believes Polanski deserves no sympathy and is a fortunate survivor, not a victim. See Thomas Kiernan, The Roman Polanski Story (New York: Random House, 1980).

32 Paul Cronin, ed., *Roman Polanski Interviews* (Jackson: University of Mississippi Press, 2005), 107.

33 Mazierska, 16.

34 Mazierska, 18.

35 Nick Yarborough, "The Apartment Trilogy by Roman Polanski," December 19, 2014, http://nickyarborough.com/on-polanskis-apartment-trilogy/.

36 Mazierska, 24.

37 Picart and Frank, 20.

38 Cronin, 43.

39 Yarborough.

40 Mazierska, 39.

41 Mazierska, 129.

42 Rich Cohen, "'Rosemary's Baby' 50 Years Later," *Wall Street Journal*, May 23, 2018, https://www.wsj.com/articles/rosemarys-baby-a-disquieting-masterpiece-turns-50-1527095931.

43 Cronin, 175.

44 Cohen.

45 Roman Polanski, dir., *Rosemary's Baby*, Criterion Collection, 1968.

46 *Rosemary's Baby.*

47 Yarborough.

48 Cronin, 44.

49 Cronin, 188.

50 Quoted in Thomas D. Clagett, *William Friedkin: Films of Aberration, Obsession and Reality* (Los Angeles: Silman-James Press 2003), 137.

51 A. J. Goldman, "Director William Friedkin Finds His Jewish Connection," *Forward*, June 21, 2016, https://forward.com/culture/342166/director-william-friedkin-finds-his-jewish-connection/.

52 Goldman.

53 Goldman.

54 Gilbert Cruz, "30 Things You Didn't Know About the 5 *Exorcist* Movies," *Vulture*, October 21, 2014, https://www.vulture.com/2013/10/30-things-you-didnt-know-about-the-exorcist-movies.html.

55 Langford, 118.
56 Quoted in Clagett, 146.
57 William Friedkin, dir., *The Exorcist*, director's commentary, Warner Brothers, 1973, DVD.
58 *The Exorcist*, director's commentary.
59 *The Exorcist*.
60 Quoted in Clagett, 155.
61 Quoted in Clagett, 156.
62 Paul Schrader, dir., *Dominion: Prequel to The Exorcist*, Warner Brothers, 2005.
63 *Dominion*.
64 *Dominion*.
65 *Dominion*.
66 *Dominion*.
67 *Dominion*.
68 *Dominion*.
69 David S. Goyer, dir., *The Unborn*, Universal Pictures, 2009.
70 Morris M. Faierstein, "The Dybbuk: The Origins and History of a Concept," in Leonard J. Greenspoon, ed., *olam ha-zeh v'olam ha-ba: This World and the World to Come in Jewish Belief and Practice* (West Lafayette, Ind.: Purdue University Press, 2017), 136.
71 Faierstein, 140.
72 Quoted in Zehavit Stern, "Cinema as Site of Memory: The Dybbuk and the Burden of Holocaust Commemoration," in Lawrence Baron, ed., *The Modern Jewish Experience in World Cinema* (Waltham, Mass.: Brandeis University Press, 2011), 82.
73 Joel Rosenberg, "The Soul of Catastrophe: On the 1937 Film of S. An-sky's *The Dybbuk*," *Jewish Social Studies, Culture, Society*, n.s. 17, no. 2 (Winter 2011): 2–4.
74 Kerner, *Film and the Holocaust*, 161.
75 Kerner, 157.
76 Kerner, 162–163.
77 Langford, 120.
78 Geoffrey Cocks, *The Wolf at the Door: Stanley Kubrick, History & the Holocaust* (New York: Peter Lang, 2004), 14.
79 Quoted in Cocks, 23.
80 Cocks, 15.
81 Cocks, 15.
82 Quoted in Cocks, 150.
83 Quoted in Cocks, 157.
84 Cocks, 16.
85 Quoted in Cocks, 50.
86 Quoted in Cocks, 57.
87 Stanley Kubrick, dir., *Dr. Strangelove*, Criterion Collection, 1964.
88 Cocks, 126.
89 Cocks, 2–3.
90 Stanley Kubrick, dir., *The Shining*, Criterion Collection, 1980.

91 Cocks, 218.

92 Cocks, 171.

93 Dirk Libbey, "Stephen King's Biggest Problem with Stanley Kubrick's Version of The Shining," *Cinemablend*, accessed January 10, 2019, https://www.cinemablend.com/new/Stephen-King-Biggest-Problem-With-Stanley-Kubrick-Version-Shining-110157.html.

94 Cocks, 218.

95 Cocks, 177.

96 Cocks, 2.

97 Cocks, 221.

98 Cocks, 238.

99 Cocks, 255.

5. "A World That Works"

1 Petra Rau, *Our Nazis: Representations of Fascism in Contemporary Literature and Film* (Edinburgh, UK: Edinburgh University Press, 2013), 8–11.

2 Robert O. Paxton, *Anatomy of Fascism* (New York: Vintage Books, 2005), 218.

3 Susan Sontag, "Fascinating Fascism," *New York Review of Books*, February 6, 1975, http://www.nybooks.com/articles/1975/02/06/fascinating-fascism/.

4 Rau, 36.

5 De Witt Douglas Kilgore, *Astrofuturism: Science, Race, and Visions of Utopia in Space* (Philadelphia: University of Pennsylvania Press, 2003), 2.

6 Steffen Hantke, *Monsters in the Machine: Science Fiction Film and the Militarization of America after World War II* (Jackson: University of Mississippi Press, 2016), 12, 22.

7 The process of exploiting and integrating the Paperclippers during the Cold War era is detailed in Brian E. Crim, *Our Germans: Project Paperclip and the National Security State* (Baltimore: Johns Hopkins University Press, 2018).

8 Dale Carter, *The Final Frontier: The Rise and Fall of the Rocket State* (New York: Verso Books, 1988), 90–91.

9 This portion of the chapter is based on my article "The Intergalactic Final Solution: Nazism and Genocide in Paul Verhoeven's *Starship Troopers*," *Shofar: An Interdisciplinary Journal of Jewish Studies* 28, no. 4 (2010): 104–115. Courtesy of Purdue University Press.

10 Edward Neumeier, "Commentary," on Paul Verhoeven, dir., *Starship Troopers*, Tristar Pictures, 1998, DVD.

11 Quoted in Oleksander Kobrynskyy and Gerd Bayer, "Introduction," in Kobrynskyy and Bayer, 4.

12 Edward Neumeier, *Starship Troopers*, based on the novel by Robert Heinlein, 1996, 4–5.

13 See David Welch, "Nazi Propaganda and Volksgemeinschaft: Constructing a People's Community," *Journal of Contemporary History* 39, no. 2 (2004): 213–238.

14 *Starship Troopers*.

15 Edward Neumeier, "Commentary," *Starship Troopers*, DVD.

16 Quoted in Lene Hansen, "Feminism in the Fascist Utopia: Gender and World Order in *Starship Troopers*," *International Feminist Journal of Politics* 3 (August 2001): 276.
17 Lene Hansen, "Feminism in the Fascist Utopia: Gender and World Order in *Starship Troopers*," *International Feminist Journal of Politics* 3 (August 2001): 276–277.
18 Neumeier, *Starship Troopers*, 26.
19 J. P. Telotte, "Verhoeven, Virilio, and 'Cinematic Derealization,'" *Film Quarterly* 53, no. 2 (Winter, 1999–2000): 33.
20 Quoted in Benjamin Svetkey, "The Reich Stuff," *Entertainment Weekly*, November 21, 1997, https://ew.com/article/1997/11/21/starship-troopers-relys-nazi-imagery/.
21 Paul M. Sammon, *The Making of Starship Troopers* (New York: Boulevard Books, 1997), 138.
22 Tony Barta, "Film Nazis: The Great Escape," in Tony Barta, ed., *Screening the Past: Film and the Representation of History* (Westport, Conn.: Praeger, 1998), 128, 131.
23 "Starship Troopers," *Sight & Sound* 8, no. 1 (1998); Svetkey.
24 Kathie Maio, "Ken and Barbie in the House of Buggin'," *Fantasy & Science Fiction* 94, no. 4 (April 1998): 88.
25 Quoted in insert, *Starship Troopers*, DVD.
26 See Jeanine Basinger, *The World War II Film: Anatomy of a Genre* (Wesleyan, Conn.: Wesleyan University Press, 2003), 109–198.
27 Quoted in insert, *Starship Troopers*, DVD.
28 Adam Roberts, *Science Fiction* (New York: Routledge, 2000), 107.
29 Quoted in Rob van Scheers, *Paul Verhoeven*, trans. Aletta Stevens (London: Faber & Faber, 1997), xiii.
30 Eric D. Weitz, *A Century of Genocide: Utopias of Race and Nation* (Princeton, N.J.: Princeton University Press, 2003), 4.
31 Neumeier, *Starship Troopers*, 55.
32 Friedrich von Bernhardi, "The Next War, 1914," accessed July 18, 2008, www.h-net.org/~german/g-text/kaiserreich/bernhardi.html.
33 Neumeier, *Starship Troopers*, 1.
34 Quoted in van Scheers, xvi.
35 Quoted in Omer Bartov, *Hitler's Army: Soldiers, Nazis, and War in the Third Reich* (New York: Oxford University Press, 1991), 131.
36 Quoted in Omer Bartov, *Hitler's Army: Soldiers, Nazis, and War in the Third Reich* (New York: Oxford University Press, 1991), 129.
37 Quoted in Omer Bartov, *Hitler's Army: Soldiers, Nazis, and War in the Third Reich* (New York: Oxford University Press, 1991), 129.
38 Omer Bartov, *Hitler's Army: Soldiers, Nazis, and War in the Third Reich* (New York: Oxford University Press, 1991), 130.
39 Florentine Strzelczyk, "Our Future—Our Past: Fascism, Postmodernism, and Starship Troopers (1997)," *Modernism/Modernity* 15, no. 1 (2008): 98.
40 Neumeier, *Starship Troopers*, 9.

41 Bartov, *Hitler's Army*, 126.

42 See George L. Mosse, *Towards the Final Solution: A History of European Racism* (New York: Harper & Row, 1980).

43 *Starship Troopers*.

44 Quoted in Maio, "Ken and Barbie," 88.

45 Quoted in Maio,"Ken and Barbie."

46 Maio, "Ken and Barbie," 88.

47 Sammon, *The Making of Starship Troopers*, 69.

48 Telotte, 93.

49 *Starship Troopers*.

50 Quoted in Svetkey.

51 See Rosenfeld, *The Fourth Reich*.

52 One need only google "Nazi UFOs" and "Antarctica" to discern the persistence of this conspiracy. See Daniel Oberhaus, "Fake News About a Secret Nazi UFO Base in Antarctica Refuses to Die," *Motherboard, Vice*, March 12, 2017, https://motherboard.vice.com/en_us/article/nz53eq/fake-news-about-a-secret-nazi-ufo-base-in-antarctica-refuses-to-die.

53 Goodrick-Clarke, 152.

54 Crim, *Our Germans*, 185.

55 Kit MacFarlane, "Stooges from Space: Iron Sky and the Pursuit of Lowbrow Propaganda," *Metro* 173 (Winter 2012): 35.

56 Stephen Dalton, "Back to the Führer: Iron Sky Director Interviewed," *The Quietus*, March 7, 2012, http://thequietus.com/articles/08177-iron-sky-interview-timo-vuorensola.

57 James J. Ward, "Nazis on the Moon! Nazis under the Polar Ice Cap! And Other Recent Strange Episodes in the Strange Cinematic Afterlife of the Third Reich," in Miller and van Riper, *The Undead on the Battlefield*, 62–63.

58 Quoted in Rosenfeld, *Hi Hitler!*, 201.

59 "Adolf Hitler as the Doctor of the German Nation," in Deadly Medicine: Creating the Master Race, United States Holocaust Memorial Museum, accessed May 16, 2018, https://www.ushmm.org/information/press/press-kits/traveling-exhibitions/deadly-medicine/adolf-hitler-as-the-doctor-of-the-german-nation.

60 Timo Vuorensola, dir., *Iron Sky*, Blindspot Pictures, 2012.

61 MacFarlane, 37.

62 *Iron Sky*.

63 Shandler, 104.

64 Shandler, xvii.

65 "Death's Head Revisited," *The Twilight Zone*, season 3, episode 9, directed by Don Medford, aired November 10, 1961.

66 "Death's Head Revisited," *The Twilight Zone*.

67 "He's Alive," *The Twilight Zone*, season 4, episode 4, directed by Stuart Rosenberg, aired January 24, 1963.

68 "Patterns of Force," *Star Trek*, season 2, episode 21, directed by Vincent McEveety, aired February 16, 1968.

69 Shandler, 148.

70 Shandler, 149.

71 "'Raumschiff Enterprise': ZDF neo zeigt umstrittene Nazi-Folge," *Das Bild*, November 4, 2011, https://www.bild.de/unterhaltung/tv/raumschiff-enterprise/zdf-neo-zeigt-umstrittene-nazi-folge-20803514.bild.html.

72 Kevin J. Wetmore Jr., *The Empire Triumphant: Race, Religion and Rebellion in the Star Wars Films* (Jefferson, N.C.: McFarland, 2005), 3.

73 Quoted in Wetmore, 8.

74 Dan Hassler-Forest, "Politicizing Star Wars: Anti-Fascism vs. Nostalgia in 'Rogue One,'" *Los Angeles Review of Books*, December 26, 2016, https://lareviewofbooks.org/article/politicizing-star-wars-anti-fascism-vs-nostalgia-rogue-one/.

75 William J. Astore, "Why Rebels Triumph: How 'Insignificant' Rebellions Change History," in Nancy R. Reagin and Janice Liedl, eds., *Star Wars and History* (Hoboken, N.J.: John Wiley & Sons, 2013), 32.

76 Quoted in Jacob Ausubel, "Star Wars and Nazi Germany," *Penn Political Review*, November 8, 2015, http://pennpoliticalreview.org/2015/11/star-wars-and-nazi-germany/.

77 Tony Keen, "I, Sidious: Historical Dictators and Senator Palpatine's Rise to Power," in Reagin and Leidl, 146.

78 Quoted in Eliana Dockterman, "J.J. Abrams Says Nazis Inspired the New *Star Wars* Villans," *Time*, August 25, 2015, http://time.com/4010014/j-j-abrams-star-wars-force-awakens-villain-nazi/.

79 Meghan O'Keefe, "'Star Wars' and Space Nazis: Hasn't Evil Evolved by Now?" *Decider*, November 30, 2015, https://decider.com/2015/11/30/star-wars-and-space-nazis/.

80 Quoted in Noah Berlatsky, "'Star Wars' Is Influenced by the Nazis—And It Fails to Hold Them Accountable," *The Forward*, December 10, 2017, https://forward.com/culture/film-tv/389632/star-wars-nazi-influence-leni-riefenstahl-triumph-of-will/.

81 Jesse Percival, "Nazi Iconography in Star Wars and Modern Day Art," *Overture*, December 30, 2015, https://medium.com/overture-magazine/nazi-iconography-in-star-wars-and-modern-day-media-8d179925d23a.

82 Albert Speer designed the rally to resemble a "cathedral of light," but British ambassador to Germany Sir Richard Neville recalled that it felt like a "cathedral of ice." Stefan Andrews, "Swimming in searchlights: The cathedral of light of the Nazi rallies," July 5, 2017, *The Vintage News*, https://www.thevintagenews.com/2017/07/05/swimming-in-searchlights-the-cathedral-of-light-of-the-nazi-rallies/.

83 Percival.

84 Wetmore, 51.

85 Berlatsky.

86 Berlatsky.

87 George Lucas, dir., *Star Wars: Episode IV—A New Hope*, 20th Century Fox Video, 1977, 2006, DVD.

88 *V, The Original Miniseries*, part I, written and directed by Kenneth Johnson, NBC, aired May 1, 1983.

89 Dan Copp, *Fascist Lizards from Outer Space: The Politics, Literary Influences and Cultural History of Kenneth Johnson's V* (Jefferson, N.C.: McFarland, 2017), 7.

90 Copp, 34.

91 Copp, 161–162.

92 *V, The Original Miniseries*, part I.

93 Quoted in Copp, 37.

94 Kenneth Johnson noted that Morse code for V is dot dot dot dash, a reference to the BBC using the first four notes of Beethoven's Fifth Symphony when broadcasting to European resistance movements. Copp, 28.

95 *V, The Original Miniseries*, part II, written and directed by Kenneth Johnson, NBC, aired May 2, 1983.

96 John Edgar Browning, "Holocaust-as-Horror, Science Fiction and the 'Look' of the 'Real/Reel' in V (1983)," in Kerman and Browning, 168.

97 *V, The Original Miniseries*, part II.

98 Copp, 59–60.

99 Quoted in Copp, 153.

100 Quoted in "Nazi-Inspired Ads for The Man in the High Castle Pulled from New York Subway," *The Guardian*, November 24, 2015, https://www.theguardian.com/us-news/2015/nov/25/nazi-inspired-ads-for-the-man-in-the-high-castle-pulled-from-new-york-subway.

101 Quoted in "Nazi-Inspired Ads for The Man in the High Castle Pulled from New York Subway," *The Guardian*, November 24, 2015, https://www.theguardian.com/us-news/2015/nov/25/nazi-inspired-ads-for-the-man-in-the-high-castle-pulled-from-new-york-subway.

102 Gavriel Rosenfeld argues that "the shifting character of American alternate histories of a Nazi triumph points to the emergence of a more normalized view of the Nazi past." Rosenfeld, *The World Hitler Never Made*, 96.

103 Jeremy Black, *Other Pasts, Different Presents, Alternative Futures* (Bloomington: Indiana University Press, 2015), 2.

104 Jeremy Black, *Other Pasts, Different Presents, Alternative Futures* (Bloomington: Indiana University Press, 2015), 2–8.

105 Black, 67.

106 Quoted in Richard J. Evans, *Altered Pasts: Counterfactuals in History* (Waltham, Mass.: Brandeis University Press, 2013), 66.

107 "The New World," *The Man in the High Castle*, season 1, episode 1, directed by David Semel, aired November 20, 2015.

108 "The New World," *The Man in the High Castle*, season 1, episode 1, directed by Daniel Percival, aired November 20, 2015.

109 Amazon advertisement in *The Hollywood Reporter*, "Consider an Amazon Original Series: The Man in the High Castle."

110 Amazon advertisement in *The Hollywood Reporter*, "Consider an Amazon Original Series: The Man in the High Castle."

111 Quoted in Dennis M. Weiss, "Juliana in Plato's Cave," in Bruce Krajewski and Joshua Heter, eds., *The Man in the High Castle: Subversive Reports from Another Reality* (Chicago: Open Court, 2017), 8.
112 "The New World," *The Man in the High Castle.*
113 "The New World," *The Man in the High Castle.*
114 "Truth," *The Man in the High Castle*, season 1, episode 7, directed by Brad Anderson, aired November 20, 2015. For an account of Jedwabne, see Jan T. Gross, *Neighbors: The Destruction of the Jewish Community in Jedwabne, Poland* (New York: Penguin Books, 2002).
115 See James Q. Whitman, *Hitler's American Model: The United States and the Making of Nazi Race Law* (Princeton, N.J.: Princeton University Press, 2017).
116 "The New World," *The Man in the High Castle.*
117 "Fallout," *The Man in the High Castle*, season 2, episode 10, directed by Daniel Percival, aired December 16, 2016.
118 "Escalation," *The Man in the High Castle*, season 1, episode 4, directed by David Petrarca, aired December 16, 2016.
119 M. Blake Wilson, "In the Neutral Zone, a Libertarian's Home is Their [High] Castle," in Krajewski and Heter, 57.
120 "Kintsugi," *The Man in the High Castle*, season 2, episode 6, directed by Paul Holahan, aired December 16, 2016.
121 Holocaust Educational Trust, "An Unwritten and Never to be Written Page of Glory," 70 Voices: Victims, Perpetrators and Bystanders, Holocaust Education Trust, January 27, 2015, http://www.70voices.org.uk/content/day37.
122 "Three Monkeys," *The Man in the High Castle*, season 1, episode 6, directed by Nelson McCormick, aired November 20, 2015.
123 "Truth," *The Man in the High Castle.*
124 "History Ends," *The Man in the High Castle*, season 3, episode 6, directed by Meera Menon, aired October 5, 2018.
125 "History Ends," *The Man in the High Castle*, season 3, episode 6, directed by Meera Menon, aired October 5, 2018.
126 Timothy H. Evans, "Authenticity, Ethnography, and the Colonialism in Philip K. Dick's *The Man in the High Castle*," *Journal of the Fantastic in the Arts* 21, no. 3 (2010): 379.
127 "A Way Out," *The Man in the High Castle.*
128 "A Way Out," *The Man in the High Castle.*
129 "The Tiger's Cave," *The Man in the High Castle*, season 2, episode 1, directed by Daniel Percival, aired December 16, 2016.
130 "The Road Less Traveled," *The Man in the High Castle* season 2, episode 2, directed by Colin Bucksey, aired December 16, 2016.
131 "Fallout," *The Man in the High Castle.*
132 "The Road Less Traveled," *The Man in the High Castle.*

6. "All of This Has Happened Before"

1 Klaus Benesch, "Technology, Art, and the Cybernetic Body: The Cyborg as Cultural Other in Fritz Lang's 'Metropolis' and Philip K. Dick's 'Do Androids

Dream of Electric Sheep?'" *Amerikastudien/American Studies* 44, no. 3, Body/Art (1999): 381.

2 Donna Haraway, "A Cyborg Manifesto: Science, Technology, and Socialist-Feminism in the Late Twentieth Century," in Donna Haraway, *Simians, Cyborgs and Women: The Reinvention of Nature* (New York; Routledge, 1991), 150.

3 Joseph Francavilla, "The Android as Doppelgänger," in Judith B. Kerman, ed., *Retrofitting Blade Runner: Issues in Ridley Scott's Blade Runner and Philip K. Dick's Do Androids Dream of Electric Sheep?* (Madison: University of Wisconsin Press, 1997), 9.

4 Barzilai, 10.

5 Quoted in Barzilai, 112.

6 Quoted in Barzilai, 2.

7 Quoted in Joshua Pardon, "Revisiting a Science Fiction Classic: Interpreting *The Day the Earth Stood Still* for Contemporary Film Audiences," *Journal of Popular Film and Television* 36, no. 3 (September 2008): 149.

8 Pardon, 142.

9 Robert Wise, dir., *The Day the Earth Stood Still*, Twentieth Century Fox, 1951.

10 Interpreting Klaatu as a Christ figure seems obvious. "Like Jesus he is killed by soldiers carrying out the orders of the political and military authorities," writes Krin Gabbard. Klaatu is killed, resurrected, delivers a sermon telling humans they are not alone and godlike forces will be watching over them, and then disappears into the heavens. See Krin Gabbard, "Religion and Political Allegory in Robert Wise's The Day the Earth Stood Still," *Literature/Film Quarterly* 10, no. 3 (1982): 150–154. Douglas Cowan argues the reason Klaatu is a Christ figure "is not because he is or Robert Wise intended him to be, but because the cultural dominance of Christianity has intruded into the interpretive process to make him so." See Douglas E. Cowan, "Seeing the Saviour in the Stars: Religion, Conformity, and *The Day the Earth Stood Still*," *Journal of Religion & Popular Culture* 21, no. 1 (Spring 2009): 3.

11 Pardon, 144.

12 Pardon, 146.

13 Hales, "Fritz Lang's Metropolis and Reactionary Modernism," 19.

14 Andreas Huyssen, "The Vamp and the Machine: Fritz Lang's Metropolis," in Minden and Bachmann, 200.

15 Maria was possibly intended to represent the revolutionary leader. Poole, 145.

16 J. P. Telotte, "The Seductive Text of Metropolis," *South Atlantic Review* 55, no. 4 (1990): 56.

17 Quoted in Lorna Jowett, "Frak Me: Reproduction, Gender, Sexuality," in Roz Kaveney and Jennifer Stoy, eds., *Battlestar Galactica: Investigating Flesh, Spirit and Steel* (London: I.B. Tauris, 2010), 68.

18 Quoted in Paul M. Sammon, *Future Noir: The Making of Blade Runner* (New York: Harper Prism, 1996), 111.

19 Ridley Scott, dir., *Blade Runner*, Warner Brothers, 1982.

20 *Blade Runner.*

21 Sammon, *Future Noir*, 3.
22 David Desser, "The New Eve: The Influence of Paradise Lost and Frankenstein on Blade Runner," in Kerman, 111.
23 *Blade Runner.*
24 Dover, 272.
25 Jack Boozer Jr., "Crashing the Gates of Insight: Blade Runner," in Kerman, 221.
26 *Blade Runner.*
27 *Blade Runner.*
28 Quoted in Sammon, 16.
29 Seth Rogovoy, "The Secret Jewish History of Blade Runner," *Forward*, October 5, 2017, https://forward.com/culture/384383/the-secret-jewish-history-of-blade-runner/.
30 Quoted in Sammon, 17.
31 Eaglestone, 104.
32 Paul Youngquist, "Life after Empathy: On Philip K. Dick and *Blade Runner 2049*," *Paris Review*, October 23, 2017, https://www.theparisreview.org/blog/2017/10/23/life-after-empathy-on-blade-runner-2049/.
33 Youngquist.
34 Quoted in Jesse W. Butler, "Un-Terminated: The Integration of the Machines," in Richard Brown and Kevin S. Decker, eds., *Terminator and Philosophy: I'll Be Back, Therefore I Am* (Hoboken, N.J.: Wiley, 2009), 53.
35 James Cameron, dir., *The Terminator*, Orion Pictures, 1984.
36 *The Terminator.*
37 *The Terminator.*
38 James Cameron, dir., *Terminator 2: Judgment Day*, Carolco Pictures, 1991.
39 *Terminator 2.*
40 Adam Wills, "'Terminator' Traps Yelchin in Sci-Fi Shoah," *Jewish Journal*, May 22, 2009, https://jewishjournal.com/uncategorized/70498/.
41 *Terminator 2.*
42 *Terminator 2.*
43 *BSG* earned eight Emmy award nominations and won the distinguished Peabody Award in 2006.
44 *Battlestar Galactica*, episode 1.1, directed by Michael Rymer, aired December 8, 2003.
45 "Crossroads: Part 2," *Battlestar Galactica*, season 3, episode 20, directed by Michael Rymer, aired March 25, 2007.
46 Vince Tomasso, "Classical Antiquity and Western Identity in Battlestar Galactica," in Brett Rogers and Benjamin Stevens, eds., *Classical Traditions in Science Fiction* (Oxford: Oxford University Press, 2015), 255.
47 See Ecclesiastes 1:9, "What has happened before will happen again. What has been done before will be done again. There is nothing new in the whole world," accessed June 17, 2019, https://www.biblestudytools.com/gnt/ecclesiastes/passage/?q=ecclesiastes+1:9-18.
48 See Tomasso, 243–244.

49 Quoted in Amy Kind, "You Can't Rape a Machine," in Josef Steiff and Tristan D. Tamplin, eds., *Battlestar Galactica and Philosophy: Mission Accomplished or Mission Frakked Up?* (Chicago: Open Court, 2008), 123.
50 Episode 1.1, *Battlestar Galactica.*
51 "A Measure of Salvation," *Battlestar Galactica*, season 3, episode 7, directed by Bill Eagles, aired November 10, 2006.
52 "A Measure of Salvation," *Battlestar Galactica.*
53 Quoted in Steven Rawle, "Real-Imagining Terror in Battlestar Galactica: Negotiating Real and Fantasy in BSG's Political Metaphor," in Kaveney and Stoy, 144.
54 Adam Wills, "Galactica Taps Holocaust for Occupation Inspiration," *Jewish Journal*, November 2, 2006, https://jewishjournal.com/culture/arts/13951/.
55 Quoted in Wills.
56 "Occupation," *Battlestar Galactica*, season 3, episode 1, directed by Sergio Mimica-Gezzan, aired October 6, 2006.
57 "Occupation," *Battlestar Galactica.*
58 On September 29–30, 1941, SS and German police units and their auxiliaries murdered the Jewish population of Kiev at Babi Yar, a ravine northwest of the city. This episode was one of the largest mass murders at an individual location during World War II. According to reports by the Einsatzgruppe to headquarters, 33,771 Jews were massacred in two days. See "Kiev and Babi Yar," *Holocaust Encyclopedia*, US Holocaust Memorial Museum, accessed June 20, 2019, https://encyclopedia.ushmm.org/content/en/article/kiev-and-babi-yar.
59 Jesse Crane-Seeber, "Seeing Others: Battlestar Galactica's Portrayal of Insurgents at a Time of War," in Nicholas J. Kiersey and Iver B. Neumann, eds., *Battlestar Galactica and International Relations* (London: Routledge, 2013), 17.
60 Magali Rennes, "Kiss Me, Now Die!" in Steiff and Tamplin, 69.
61 "Pegasus," *Battlestar Galactica*, season 2, episode 10, directed by Michael Rymer, aired September 23, 2005.
62 "Pegasus," *Battlestar Galactica.*
63 "Home: Part 1," *Battlestar Galactica*, season 2, episode 6, directed by Sergio Mimica-Gezzan, aired August 19, 2005.
64 *Battlestar Galactica*, episode 1.2, directed by Michael Rymer, aired December 9, 2003.
65 Shanna Heinricy, "I, Cyborg," in Steiff and Tamplin, 96–99.
66 Rennes, 74.
67 "Valley of Darkness," *Battlestar Galactica*, season 2, episode 2, directed by Michael Rymer, aired July 22, 2005. Six's superior attitude rings hollow considering she snapped an infant's neck on Caprica just because she was curious about the human body.
68 "Home: Part 1," *Battlestar Galactica*, season 2, episode 6, directed by Sergio Mimica-Gezzan, aired August 19, 2005.
69 Quoted in Paul Booth, "Frak-tured Postmodern Lives, Or, How I Found Out I Was a Cylon," in Steiff and Tamplin, 25.

70 Lorna Jowett, "Frak Me: Reproduction, Gender, Sexuality," in Kaveney and Stoy, 69.

71 Hal Shipman, "Some Cylons Are More Equal than Others," in Steiff and Tamplin, 161–162.

72 "Six of One," *Battlestar Galactica*, season 4, episode 2, directed by Anthony Hemingway, aired April 11, 2008.

73 "Deadlock," *Battlestar Galactica*, season 4, episode 16, directed by Robert Young, aired February 20, 2009.

74 "The Farm," *Battlestar Galactica*, season 2, episode 5, directed by Rod Hardy, aired August 12, 2005.

75 Wills, "Galactica Taps Holocaust for Occupation Inspiration."

76 "Sometimes a Great Notion," *Battlestar Galactica*, season 4, episode 11, directed by Michael Nankin, aired January 16, 2009.

77 "Daybreak: Part 2," *Battlestar Galactica*, directed by Michael Rymer, aired March 20, 2009.

78 "Daybreak: Part 2," *Battlestar Galactica*.

79 Travis Langley, "Host's Search for Meaning," in Travis Langley and Wind Goodfriend, eds., *Westworld Psychology: Violent Delights* (New York: Sterling, 2018), 257.

80 See Robert Jay Lifton's important study *The Nazi Doctors: Medical Killing and the Psychology of Genocide* (New York: Basic Books, 2017).

81 Jason T. Eberl, "Revealing Your Deepest Self: Can Westworld Create or Corrupt Virtue?" in James B. South and Kimberly S. Engels, eds., *Westworld and Philosophy* (Hoboken, N.J.: Wiley Blackwell, 2018), 50.

82 "The Bicameral Mind," *Westworld*, season 1, episode 10, directed by Jonathan Nolan, aired December 4, 2016.

83 Hannah Arendt, *The Origins of Totalitarianism* (New York: Harcourt Brace, 1979), 458–459.

84 Dan Dinello, "The Wretched of Westworld: Scientific Totalitarianism and Revolutionary Violence" in South and Engels, 240.

85 Bradley Richards, "What Is It Like to Be a Host?" in South and Engels, 83.

86 Travis Langley and Matt Munson, "A Beautiful Gift: Who Says We Have Choice?" in Langley and Goodfriend, 51.

87 Wind Goodfriend, "Choosing the Black Hat: The Evolution of Evil," in Langley and Goodfriend, 52. See also Anthon Petros Spanakos, "Violent Births: Fanon, Westworld, and Humanity," in South and Engels.

88 Quoted in Langley and Goodfriend, 17.

89 "Vanishing Power," *Westworld*, season 2, episode 9, directed by Stephen Williams, aired June 17, 2018.

90 "Chestnut," *Westworld*, season 1, episode 2, directed by Richard J. Lewis, aired October 7, 2016.

91 Dinello, 245.

92 Dinello, 245.

93 Dinello, 246.

94 "Les Ėcorchės," *Westworld*, season 2, episode 7, directed by Nicole Kassell, aired June 3, 2018.
95 "The Original," *Westworld*, season 1, episode 1, directed by Jonathan Nolan, aired October 2, 2016.
96 "The Original," *Westworld*.
97 "Trace Decay," *Westworld*, season 1, episode 8, directed by Stephen Williams, aired November 20, 2016.
98 "Kiksuya," *Westworld*, season 2, episode 8, directed by Ute Brieswitz, aired June 10, 2018.
99 "The Passenger," *Westworld*, season 2, episode 10, directed by Frederik E. O. Toye, aired June 24, 2018.
100 Marcus Arvan, "Humans and Hosts in Westworld: What's the Difference?" in South and Engels, 35.

Conclusion

1 Nizkor Project, The Trial of Adolf Eichmann, Session 68, June 7, 1961, http://www.nizkor.org/hweb/people/e/eichmann-adolf/transcripts/Sessions/Session-068-01.html.
2 Omer Bartov, "The Holocaust as Genocide: Experiential Uniqueness and Integrated History," in Claudio Fogu, Wulf Kasteiner, and Todd Presner, eds., *Probing the Ethics of Holocaust Culture* (Cambridge, Mass.: Harvard University Press, 2016), 321.
3 Rothberg, 9.
4 Boswell, *Holocaust Impiety*, 6.
5 Baudrillard, *Simulcra and Simulation*, 49.
6 Travis Langley, "Westworld, the Holocaust, and the Filter of Fiction," *Psychology Today*, July 13, 2018, https://www.psychologytoday.com/us/blog/beyond-heroes-and-villains/201807/westworld-the-holocaust-and-the-filter-fiction.
7 "A Matter of Geography," *The Leftovers*, directed by Mimi Leder, season 2, episode 2, aired October 11, 2015.

BIBLIOGRAPHY

Abbott, Stacey. *Celluloid Vampires: Life after Death in the Modern World*. Austin: University of Texas Press, 2007.

Adams, Jenni, and Sue Vice, eds. *Representing Perpetrators in Holocaust Literature and Film*. London: Valentine Mitchell, 2013.

Adorno, Theodor W. *The Culture Industry: Selected Essays on Mass Culture*. Edited by J. M. Bernstein. London: Routledge, 1991.

———. *Prisms*. Cambridge, Mass.: MIT Press, 1983.

Agamben, Giorgio. *Homo Sacer: Sovereign Power and Bare Life*. Translated by Daniel Heller-Roazen. Stanford, Calif.: Stanford University Press, 1998.

———. *Remnants of Auschwitz: The Witness and the Archive*. Translated by Daniel Heller-Roazen. New York: Zone Books, 2002.

Aido-Kaisa, Koistinen. "Passing for Human in Science Fiction: Comparing the TV Series *Battlestar Galactica* and *V*." *NORA-Nordic Journal of Feminist and Gender Research* 19, no. 4 (December 2011): 249–263.

Alexander, Chris. "In Defense of Michael Mann's THE KEEP." October 29, 2015. https://www.comingsoon.net/horror/news/747457-defense-michael-manns-keep.

AMC Blogs. "Q&A—*The Walking Dead* Scribe Robert Kirkman Discusses His Zombie Influences." Accessed July 3, 2019. http://www.amc.com/talk/2009/11/qa-the-walkin.

Andrews, Stefan. "Swimming in searchlights: The cathedral of light of the Nazi rallies." *The Vintage News*, July 5, 2017. https://www.thevintagenews.com/2017/07/05/swimming-in-searchlights-the-cathedral-of-light-of-the-nazi-rallies/.

Arendt, Hannah. *Eichmann in Jerusalem: A Report on the Banality of Evil*. New York: Viking, 1963.

———. *The Origins of Totalitarianism*. New York: Harcourt Brace, 1979.

Ashbury, Roy. *F.W. Murnau, Nosferatu*. London: York Press, 2001.

Ausubel, Jacob. "Star Wars and Nazi Germany." *Penn Political Review*, November 8, 2015. http://pennpoliticalreview.org/2015/11/star-wars-and-nazi-germany/.

Ball, Karyn. *Disciplining the Holocaust: Traumatic History As an Object of Inquiry and Desire*. Albany: State University of New York Press, 2009.

———, ed. *Traumatizing Theory: The Cultural Politics of Affect In and Beyond Psychoanalysis*. New York: Other Press, 2007.

Bangert, Axel. "Changing Narratives and Images in the Holocaust: Tim Blake Nelson's film *The Grey Zone* (2001)." *New Cinema* 6, no. 1 (2008): 17–32.

Bangert, Axel, Robert S. C. Gordon, and Libby Saxton. *Holocaust Intersections: Genocide and Visual Culture at the New Millennium*. London: Legend, 2013.

Baron, Lawrence. "AHR Forum: The First Wave of American 'Holocaust' Films, 1949–1959." *American Historical Review* 115, no.1 (2011): 90–114.

Barta, Tony, ed. *Screening the Past: Film and the Representation of History*. Westport, Conn.: Praeger, 1998.

Bartov, Omer. *Hitler's Army: Soldiers, Nazis, and War in the Third Reich*. New York: Oxford University Press, 1991.

———. *The "Jew" in Cinema: From The Golem to Don't Touch My Holocaust*. Bloomington: Indiana University Press, 2005.

———. *Murder in Our Midst: The Holocaust, Industrial Killing, and Representation*. New York: Oxford University Press, 1996.

Barzilai, Maya. *Golem: Modern Wars and Their Monsters*. New York: New York University Press, 2016.

Basinger, Jeanine. *The World War II Film: Anatomy of a Genre*. Wesleyan, Conn.: Wesleyan University Press, 2003.

Baudrillard, Jean. *Simulacra and Simulation*. Translated by Sheila Faria Glaser. Ann Arbor: University of Michigan Press, 1994.

———. *The Transparency of Evil: Essays on Extreme Phenomena*. Translated by James Benedict. London: Verso Books, 2009.

Baum, Devorah. "Trauma: An Essay on Jewish Guilt," *Jewish Quarterly*, May 15, 2012. https://www.jewishquarterly.org/2009/12/trauma-an-essay-on-jewish-guilt/.

———, ed. *The Modern Jewish Experience in World Cinema*. Waltham, Mass.: Brandeis University Press, 2011.

———. *Projecting the Holocaust into the Present: The Changing Focus of Contemporary Holocaust Cinema*. Lanham, Md.: Rowman & Littlefield, 2005.

———. "X-Men as J Men: The Jewish Subtext of a Comic Book Movie." *Shofar: An Interdisciplinary Journal of Jewish Studies* 22, no.1 (Fall 2003): 44–52.

Benesch, Klaus. "Technology, Art, and the Cybernetic Body: The Cyborg as Cultural Other in Fritz Lang's 'Metropolis' and Philip K. Dick's 'Do Androids Dream of Electric Sheep?'" *Amerikastudien/American Studies* 44, no. 3, Body/Art (1999): 379–392.

Berlatsky, Noah. "'Star Wars' Is Influenced by the Nazis—And It Fails to Hold Them Accountable." *The Forward*, December 10, 2017. https://forward.com/culture/film-tv/389632/star-wars-nazi-influence-leni-riefenstahl-triumph-of-will/.

Bergthaller, Hannes. "Dis(re)memberig History's Revenants: Trauma, Writing, and Simulated Orality in Toni Morrison's Beloved." *Connotations* 16, no. 1–3 (2006/2007): 116–136.

Bishop, Kyle William. *American Zombie Gothic: The Rise and Fall (and Rise) of the Walking Dead in Popular Culture*. Jefferson, N.C.: McFarland, 2010.

Black, Jeremy. *Other Pasts, Different Presents, Alternative Futures*. Bloomington: Indiana University Press, 2015.

Blake, Linnie. *The Wounds of Nations: Horror Cinema, Historical Trauma and National Identity*. Manchester, UK: Manchester University Press, 2008.

Boluk, Stephanie, and Wylie Lenz, eds. *Generation Zombie: Essays on the Living Dead in Modern Culture*. Jefferson, N.C.: McFarland, 2011.

Boswell, Matthew. "Downfall: The Nazi Genocide as a Natural Disaster." *Holocaust Studies* 17, no. 2/3 (2011): 165–184.

———. *Holocaust Impiety: In Literature, Popular Music and Film*. London: Palgrave Macmillan, 2012.

Brody, Richard. "Hitchcock and the Holocaust." *New Yorker*. Accessed December 12, 2018. https://www.newyorker.com/culture/richard-brody/hitchcock-and-the-holocaust.

Brown, Richard, and Kevin S. Decker, eds. *Terminator and Philosophy: I'll Be Back, Therefore I Am*. Hoboken, N.J.: Wiley, 2009.

Bush, Lawrence. "O My America: 'The Walking Dead' as Holocaust Literature." *Jewish Currents: Activist Politics & Art*, November 16, 2015. http://jewishcurrents.org/o-my-america-the-walking-dead-as-holocaust-literature/.

Butterworth, Sara, and Maartje Abbenhuis, eds. *Monsters in the Mirror: Representations of Nazism in Post-War Popular Culture*. Santa Barbara, Calif.: Praeger, 2010.

Canavan, Gerry. "'We Are the Walking Dead': Race, Time, and Survival in Zombie Narratives." *Extrapolation* 51, no. 3 (2010): 431–453.

Carter, Dale. *The Final Frontier: The Rise and Fall of the Rocket State*. New York: Verso Books, 1988.

Celluloid Liberation Front. "Auschwitz–Harlem: Post-Traumatic Economy in *The Pawnbroker*." *Senses of Cinema*, Issue 59, June 2011. http://sensesofcinema.com/2011/feature-articles/auschwitz%c2%ad%e2%80%93harlem-post-traumatic-economy-in-the-pawnbroker/.

Cesnari, David. *Becoming Eichmann: Rethinking the Life, Crimes and Trial of a "Desk Murderer."* New York: Da Capo Press, 2006.

Chaudhuri, Shohini. *Cinema of the Dark Side: Atrocity and the Ethics of Film Spectatorship*. Edinburgh, UK: Edinburgh University Press, 2014.

Chlumberg, Hans. *Miracle at Verdun*. Translated by Julian Leigh. New York: Brentano's, 1931.

Clagett, Thomas D. *William Friedkin: Films of Aberration, Obsession and Reality*. Los Angeles: Silman-James Press, 2003.

Coates, Paul. *The Gorgon's Gaze: German Cinema, Expressionism, and the Image of Horror*. New York: Cambridge University Press, 1991.

Cocks, Geoffrey. *The Wolf at the Door: Stanley Kubrick, History & the Holocaust*. New York: Peter Lang, 2004.

Cohen, Rick. "'Rosemary's Baby' 50 Years Later" *Wall Street Journal*, May 23, 2018. https://www.wsj.com/articles/rosemarys-baby-a-disquieting-masterpiece-turns-50-1527095931.

Cohen, Sara Simcha. "Hearth of Darkness: The Familiar, the Familial, and the Zombie." PhD Dissertation, University of California, Los Angeles, 2013.

Cole, Tim. *Selling the Holocaust: From Auschwitz to Schindler*. New York: Routledge, 1999.

Confino, Alon. "A World Without Jews: Interpreting the Holocaust." *German History* 27, no. 4. (2009): 531–559.

———. *A World without Jews: The Nazi Imagination from Persecution to Genocide*. New Haven, Conn.: Yale University Press, 2015.

Connolly, Kate. "German director's Holocaust film causes outrage." *The Guardian*, November 12, 2010. https://www.theguardian.com/world/2010/nov/12/uwe-boll-auschwitz-film-causes-outrage.

Copp, Dan. *Fascist Lizards from Outer Space: The Politics, Literary Influences and Cultural History of Kenneth Johnson's V.* Jefferson, N.C.: McFarland, 2017.

Cowan, Douglas E. "Seeing the Saviour in the Stars: Religion, Conformity, and *The Day the Earth Stood Still*." *Journal of Religion & Popular Culture* 21, no. 1 (Spring 2009): 3.

Crim, Brian E. "The Intergalactic Final Solution: Nazism and Genocide in Paul Verhoeven's *Starship Troopers*." *Shofar: An Interdisciplinary Journal of Jewish Studies* 28, no. 4 (Summer 2010): 104–115.

———. *Our Germans: Project Paperclip and the National Security State*. Baltimore: Johns Hopkins University Press, 2018.

———. "'Our Most Serious Enemy': The Specter of Judeo-Bolshevism in the German Military Community, 1914–1923." *Central European History* 44, no. 4 (December 2011): 631–632.

———. "'A World That Works': Fascism and Media Globalization in *Starship Troopers*." *Film & History* 39, no. 2 (Fall 2009): 17–25.

Cronin, Paul, ed. *Roman Polanski Interviews*. Jackson: University of Mississippi Press, 2005.

Cruz, Gilbert. "30 Things You Didn't Know About the 5 *Exorcist* Movies." *Vulture*, October 21, 2014. https://www.vulture.com/2013/10/30-things-you-didnt-know-about-the-exorcist-movies.html.

Cunningham, Frank R. "The Insistence of Memory: The Opening Sequence of Lumet's 'Pawnbroker.'" *Literature/Film Quarterly* 7, no. 1 (1989): 39–43.

Dadoun, Roger. "Metropolis: Mother City—'Mittler'—Hitler." *Camera Obscura* 15, no. 3 (Fall 1986): 137–164.

Dalton, Stephen. "Back to the Führer: Iron Sky Director Interviewed." *The Quietus*, March 7, 2012. http://thequietus.com/articles/08177-iron-sky-interview-timo-vuorensola.

Decker, Christof, and Astrid Böger, eds. *Transnational Mediation: Negotiating Popular Culture between the United States and Europe*. Heidelberg, Germany: Universitätsverlag, Winter 2015.

De Grand, Alexander J. *Fascist Italy and Nazi Germany: The Fascist Style of Rule*. London: Routledge, 1995.

DeLillo, Don. *White Noise*. New York: Penguin Books, 1999.

Derwin, Susan. *Rage Is the Subtext: Readings in Holocaust Literature and Film*. Columbus: Ohio State University Press, 2012.

Desser, David, and Lester D. Friedman. *American Jewish Filmmakers*. Urbana: University of Illinois Press, 2004.

Dockterman, Eliana. "J.J. Abrams Says Nazis Inspired the New *Star Wars* Villains." *Time*, August 25, 2015. http://time.com/4010014/j-j-abrams-star-wars-force-awakens-villain-nazi/.

Doneson, Judith E. *The Holocaust in American Film*. 2nd ed. Syracuse, N.Y.: Syracuse University Press, 2002.

———. "The Holocaust: Remembering for the Future: Holocaust Revisited: A Catalyst for Memory or Trivialization?" *Annals of the American Academy of Political and Social Science*, 548 (November 1996): 70–77.

Eaglestone, Robert. *The Holocaust and the Postmodern*. New York: Oxford University Press, 2008.

Eisner, Lotte H. *The Haunted Screen: Expressionism in the German Cinema and the Influence of Max Reinhardt*. Berkeley: University of California Press, 2008. Originally published 1952.

Elm, Michael, Kohi Kabalck, and Julius B. Koehne, eds. *The Horrors of Trauma in Cinema: Violence, Void, Visualization*. Newcastle, UK: Cambridge Scholars, 2014.

Elsaesser, Thomas. "Six Degrees of Nosferatu." *Sight & Sound* 11, no.2 (June 6, 2012): 12–15.

———. *Weimar Cinema and After: Germany's Historical Imaginary*. London: Routledge, 2000.

Eppert, Claudia. "Entertaining History: (Un)heroic Identifications, Apt Pupils, and an Ethical Imagination. *New German Critique* 86 (Spring–Summer 2002): 71–101.

Evans, Richard J. *Altered Pasts: Counterfactuals in History*. Waltham, Mass.: Brandeis University Press, 2013.

Evans, Timothy H. "Authenticity, Ethnography, and Colonialism in Philip K. Dick's *The Man in the High Castle*." *Journal of the Fantastic in the Arts* 21, no. 3 (2010): 366–383.

Fogu, Claudio, Wulf Kasteiner, and Todd Presner, eds. *Probing the Ethics of Holocaust Culture*. Cambridge, Mass.: Harvard University Press, 2016.

Frayling, Christopher. *Mad, Bad and Dangerous? The Scientists and the Cinema*. London: Reaktion Books, 2005.

Freer, Ian. *Movie Makers: 50 Iconic Directors from Chaplin to the Coen Brothers*. London: Quercus, 2009.

Friedlander, Saul, ed. *Probing the Limits of Representation: Nazism and the "Final Solution."* Cambridge, Mass.: Harvard University Press, 1992.

———. *Reflections on Nazism*. Translated by Thomas Weyr. New York: Avon Books, 1984.

Frodon, Jean-Michel, ed. *Cinema & the Shoah: An Art Confronts the Tragedy of the Twentieth Century*. Translated by Anna Harrison and Tom Mes. Albany: State University of New York Press, 2010.

Fuller, Samuel. *A Third Face: My Tale of Writing, Fighting, and Filmmaking*. New York: Applause Theater and Cinema Books, 2002.

Gabbard, Krin. "Religion and Political Allegory in Robert Wise's The Day the Earth Stood Still." *Literature/Film Quarterly* 10, no. 3 (1982): 150–154.

Gelbin, Cathy S. *The Golem Returns: From German Romantic Literature to Global Jewish Culture, 1808-2008*. Ann Arbor: University of Michigan Press, 2011.

Gelder, Ken, ed. *The Horror Reader*. New York: Routledge, 2000.

Gerlach, Neil. "The Antichrist as Multi-Monomyth: The Omen as Social Critique." *Journal of Popular Culture* 44, no. 5 (2011): 1027–1046.

———. "Narrating Armageddon: Antichrist Films and the Critique of Late Modernity." *Journal of Religion and Popular Culture* 4, no. 2 (Summer 2012): 217–229.

Giesen, Rolf. *Nazi Propaganda Films: A History and Filmography.* Jefferson, N.C.: McFarland, 2003.

Gilbert, Sophie. "The Brilliant Nihilism of *The Leftovers.*" *The Atlantic*, August 4, 2014, https://www.theatlantic.com/entertainment/archive/2014/08/the-brilliant-nihilism-of-the-leftovers/375563/.

Gilman, Sander L. *Difference and Pathology: Stereotypes of Sexuality, Race, and Madness.* Ithaca, N.Y.: Cornell University Press, 1985.

Ginsberg, Terri. *Holocaust Film: The Political Aesthetics of Ideology.* Newcastle, UK: Cambridge Scholars, 2007.

Glenn, C. L., and L. Cunningham. "Black Magic: The Magical Negro and White Salvation in Film." *Journal of Black Studies* 40, no. 2 (2009): 135–152.

Goldberg, Jeffrey, J. J. Gould, and Scott Meslow. "'The Walking Dead' as the Holocaust." *The Atlantic*, October 12, 2012. https://www.theatlantic.com/entertainment/archive/2012/10/the-walking-dead-as-the-holocaust/263911/.

Golde, Henry. Oral History. Wisconsin Survivors of the Holocaust. Wisconsin Historical Society. Accessed July 3, 2019. http://www.wisconsinhistory.org/HolocaustSurvivors/Golde.asp.

Goldman, A. J. "Director William Friedkin Finds His Jewish Connection." *Forward*, June 21, 2016. https://forward.com/culture/342166/director-william-friedkin-finds-his-jewish-connection/.

Goodrick-Clarke, Nicholas. *Black Sun: Aryan Cults, Esoteric Nazism and the Politics of Identity.* New York: New York University Press, 2002.

Graebner, William. "The Living Dead of George Romero and Steven Spielberg: America, the Holocaust and the Figure of the Zombie." *Dapim: Studies on the Holocaust* 21 (February 2017): 1-26.

Greenspoon, Leonard J., ed. *olam ha-zeh v'olam ha-ba: This World and the World to Come in Jewish Belief and Practice.* West Lafayette, Ind.: Purdue University Press, 2017.

Gross, Jan T. *Neighbors: The Destruction of the Jewish Community in Jedwabne, Poland.* New York: Penguin Books, 2002.

Haggith, Toby, and Joanna Newman, eds. *Holocaust and the Moving Image: Representations in Film and Television Since 1933.* London: Wallflower, 2005.

Hagman, George. "Surviving the Zombie Apocalypse: Trauma and Transformation in AMC's *The Walking Dead.*" *Psychoanalytic Inquiry* 37, no. 1 (2017): 46–56.

Halberstam, Judith. *Skin Shoes: Gothic Horror and the Technology of Monsters.* Durham, N.C.: Duke University Press, 1995.

Hales, Barbara. "Fritz Lang's Metropolis and Reactionary Modernism." *New German Review* 8 (1992): 18–30.

Hales, Barbara, Mihaela Petruscu, and Valerie Weinstein, eds. *Continuity and Crisis in German Cinema, 1928-1936.* Rochester, N.Y.: Camden House, 2016.

Hansen, Lene. "Feminism in the Fascist Utopia: Gender and World Order in *Starship Troopers.*" *International Feminist Journal of Politics* 3 (August 2001): 275–283.

Hantke, Steffen. *Horror Film: Creating and Marketing Fear.* Jackson: University of Mississippi Press, 2004.

———. "The Military Horror Film: Speculations on a Hybrid Genre." *Journal of Popular Culture* 43, 4 (2010): 701–719.

———. *Monsters in the Machine: Science Fiction Film and the Militarization of America after World War II*. Jackson: University of Mississippi Press, 2016.

Haraway, Donna. *Cyborgs and Women: The Reinvention of Nature*. New York; Routledge, 1991.

Hartwell, Rianne. "'Alien Genocide': The Representation of Genocide in Science Fiction Films and Television Shows." Master's Thesis. West Chester University, 2011.

Hassler-Forest, Dan. "Politicizing Star Wars: Anti-Fascism vs. Nostalgia in 'Rogue One.'" *Los Angeles Review of Books*, December 26, 2016. https://lareviewofbooks.org/article/politicizing-star-wars-anti-fascism-vs-nostalgia-rogue-one/.

Hirsch, Joshua. *After Image: Film, Trauma, and the Holocaust*. Philadelphia: Temple University Press, 2004.

Hirsch, Marianne. *The Generation of Postmemory: Writing and Visual Culture after the Holocaust*. New York: Columbia University Press, 2012.

Hitler, Adolf. *Mein Kampf*. Translated by Ralph Manheim. New York: Houghton Mifflin, 1969.

Hollinger, Veronica, and Joan Gordon, eds. *Edging into the Future: Science Fiction and Contemporary Cultural Transformation*. Philadelphia: University of Pennsylvania Press, 2002.

Holocaust Educational Trust. "An Unwritten and Never to Be Written Page of Glory." 70 Voices: Victims, Perpetrators and Bystanders. January 27, 2015, http://www.70voices.org.uk/content/day37.

Hynes, Eric. "What Is Shoah?" *Village Voice*, December 8, 2010.

Insdorf, Annette. *Indelible Shadows: Film and the Holocaust*. 3rd ed. Cambridge: Cambridge University Press, 2003.

Isenberg, Noah, ed. *Weimar Cinema: An Essential Guide to Classic Film of the Era*. New York: Columbia University Press, 2008.

Jennings, Michael W., Brigid Doherty, and Thomas Y. Levin, eds. *Walter Benjamin: The Work of Art in the Age of Its Technological Reproducibility, and Other Writings on Media*. Cambridge, Mass.: Belknap Press, 2008.

Jensen, Jeff. "American Horror Story Recap: The Girl with the Auschwitz Tattoo." *EW.com*, November 8, 2012. https://ew.com/recap/american-horror-story-season-2-episode-4/.

Johnson, Michael K. "Traumatic Experience and the Representation of Nature in the Novel and Film 'The Pawnbroker.'" *Literature/Film Quarterly* 35, no. 4 (2007): 294–306.

Kaes, Anton. *From Hitler to Heimat: The Return of History as Film*. Cambridge, Mass.: Harvard University Press, 1989.

———. *Shell Shock Cinema: Weimar Culture and the Wounds of War*. Princeton, N.J.: Princeton University Press, 2009.

Kapzynski, Jennifer M., and Michael D. Richardson, eds. *A New History of German Cinema*. Rochester, N.Y.: Camden House, 2012.

Kaveney, Roz, and Jennifer Stoy, eds. *Battlestar Galactica: Investigating Flesh, Spirit and Steel*. London: I.B. Tauris, 2010.

Keetley, Dawn, ed., *"We're All Infected": Essays on AMC's The Walking Dead and the Fate of the Human*. Jefferson, N.C.: McFarland, 2014.

Kerman, Judith B., ed. *Retrofitting Blade Runner: Issues in Ridley Scott's Blade Runner and Philip K. Dick's Do Androids Dream of Electric Sheep?* Madison: University of Wisconsin Press, 1997.

Kerman, Judith B., and John Edgar Browning, eds. *The Fantastic in Holocaust Literature and Film: Critical Perspectives*. Jefferson, N.C.: McFarland, 2015.

Kerner, Aaron. *Film and the Holocaust: New Perspectives on Dramas, Documentaries, and Experimental Films*. New York: Continuum Books, 2011.

Kershaw, Ian. *The "Hitler Myth": Image and Reality in the Third Reich*. New York: Oxford University Press, 2001.

Kertesz, Imre, and John MacKay. "Who Owns Auschwitz." *Yale Journal of Criticism* 14, no. 1 (Spring 2001): 267–272.

Khiterer, Victoria. *The Holocaust: Memories and History*. Newcastle, UK: Cambridge Scholars, 2014.

Kiefer, Halle. "'American Horror Story: Asylum' Recap: Your Story Is Indecent." *Rolling Stone*, November 8, 2012. https://www.rollingstone.com/movies/movie-news/american-horror-story-asylum-recap-your-story-is-indecent-178622/.

Kiernan, Thomas. *The Roman Polanski Story*. New York: Random House, 1980.

Kiersey, Nicholas J., and Iver B. Neumann, eds. *Battlestar Galactica and International Relations*. London: Routledge, 2013.

Kilgore, De Witt Douglas. *Astrofuturism: Science, Race, and Visions of Utopia in Space*. Philadelphia: University of Pennsylvania Press, 2003.

Kinzer, Stephen. "Günter Grass Dies at 87; Writer Pried Open Germany's Past But Hid His Own." *New York Times*, April 23, 2015. https://www.nytimes.com/2015/04/14/world/europe/gunter-grass-german-novelist-dies-at-87.html.

Kobrynskyy, Oleksander, and Gerd Bayer, eds. *Holocaust Cinema in the Twenty-First Century: Memory, Images, and the Ethics of Representation*. New York: Wallflower Press, 2015.

Kracauer, Siegfried. *From Caligari to Hitler: A Psychological History of the German Film*. Edited by Leonardo Quaresima. Princeton, N.J.: Princeton University Press, 2004. Originally published in 1947.

Krajewski, Bruce, and Joshua Heter, eds. *The Man in the High Castle: Subversive Reports from Another Reality*. Chicago: Open Court, 2017.

Kristeva, Julia. *Powers of Horror: An Essay on Abjection*. New York: Columbia University Press, 1982.

Kuhn, Annette, ed. *Alien Zone II: The Spaces of Science Fiction Cinema*. London: Verso Books, 1999.

Kurlander, Eric. *Hitler's Monsters: A Supernatural History of the Third Reich*. New Haven, Conn.: Yale University Press, 2017.

———. "Hitler's Monsters: The Occult Roots of Nazism and the Emergence of the Nazi 'Supernatural Imaginary.'" *German History* 30, no. 4 (December 2012): 493–527.

LaCapra, Dominick. *History and Memory after Auschwitz*. Ithaca, N.Y.: Cornell University Press, 1998.

———. *Representing the Holocaust: History, Theory, Trauma*. Ithaca, N.Y.: Cornell University Press, 1994.

Lang, Berel. *The Future of the Holocaust: Between History and Memory*. Ithaca, N.Y.: Cornell University Press, 1999.

Langley, Travis. "Westworld, the Holocaust, and the Filter of Fiction." *Psychology Today*, July 13, 2018. https://www.psychologytoday.com/us/blog/beyond-heroes-and-villains/201807/westworld-the-holocaust-and-the-filter-fiction.

Langley, Travis, and Wind Goodfriend, eds. *Westworld Psychology: Violent Delights*. New York: Sterling, 2018.

Lanzmann, Claude. *The Patagonian Hare: A Memoir*. New York: Farrar, Strauss & Giroux, 2009.

———. *Shoah: An Oral History of the Holocaust*. New York: Pantheon Books, 1985.

Leiser, Erwin. *Nazi Cinema*. New York: Collier Books, 1974.

Levi, Primo. *The Drowned and the Saved*. Translated by Michael F. Moore, in Ann Goldstein, ed. *The Complete Works of Primo Levi*. Vol. III. New York: Liverlight, 2015.

———. *Survival in Auschwitz*. New York: Touchstone, 1996.

Libbey, Dirk. "Stephen King's Biggest Problem with Stanley Kubrick's Version of The Shining." *Cinemablend*. Accessed January 10, 2019. https://www.cinemablend.com/new/Stephen-King-Biggest-Problem-With-Stanley-Kubrick-Version-Shining-110157.html.

Liebman, Stuart, ed. *Claude Lanzmann's Shoah: Key Essays*. Oxford: Oxford University Press, 2007.

Lifton, Robert Jay. *The Nazi Doctors: Medical Killing and the Psychology of Genocide*. New York: Basic Books, 2017.

Liulevicius, Vejas Gabriel. *The German Myth of the East: 1800 to the Present*. Oxford, UK: University Press, 2011.

———. *War Land on the Eastern Front: Culture, National Identity, and German Occupation in World War I*. Cambridge: Cambridge University Press, 2005.

Lopate, Philip. *Portrait of My Body*. New York: Anchor, 1997.

Loshitzky, Yosafa, ed. *Spielberg's Holocaust: Critical Perspectives on Schindler's List*. Bloomington: Indiana University Press, 1997.

Lowder, James, ed. *Triumph of the Walking Dead: Robert Kirkman's Zombie Epic on Page and Screen*. Dallas: Smart Pop, 2011.

Lowenstein, Adam. *Shocking Representation: Historical Trauma, National Cinema, and the Modern Horror Film*. New York: Columbia University Press, 2005.

Lueckel, Wolfgang. "Atomic Apocalypse: 'Nuclear Fiction' in German Literature and Culture." PhD Dissertation, University of Cincinnati, 2010.

Lukacs, John. *The Hitler of History*. New York: Vintage Books, 1998.

MacFarlane, Kit. "Stooges from Space: Iron Sky and the Pursuit of Lowbrow Propaganda." *Metro* 173 (Winter 2012): 34–37.

Magilow, Daniel H., Kristina T. Vander Lugt, and Elizabeth Bridges, eds. *Nazisploitation! The Nazi Image in Low-Brow Cinema and Culture*. New York: Continuum, 2012.

Maio, Kathie. "Ken and Barbie in the House of Buggin'." *Fantasy & Science Fiction* 94, no. 4 (April 1998).

Mazierska, Ewa. *Roman Polanski: The Cinema of a Cultural Traveler.* New York: I.B. Tauris, 2007.

McDonald, Keith, and Roger Clark. *Guillermo del Toro: Film as Alchemic Art.* New York: Bloomsbury, 2014.

McGary, Feaghal, and Des Bel, eds. *Film, History and Public Memory.* Basingstoke, UK: Palgrave Macmillan, 2015.

Miller, Cynthia J., and A. Bowdoin van Riper, eds. *The Undead on the Battlefield: Horrors of War.* Lanham, Md.: Rowman & Littlefield, 2015.

———, eds. *Undead in the West: Vampires, Zombies, Mummies, and Ghosts on the Cinematic Frontier.* Lanham, Md.: Scarecrow Press, 2012.

Milner, Andrew. *Locating Science Fiction.* Liverpool, UK: Liverpool University Press, 2012.

Minden, Michael, and Holger Bachmann, eds. *Fritz Lang's Metropolis: Cinematic Visions of Technology and Fear.* Rochester, N.Y.: Camden House, 2000.

Mintz, Alan. *Popular Culture and the Shaping of Holocaust Memory in America.* Seattle: University of Washington Press, 2001.

Morehead, John W., ed. *The Supernatural Cinema of Guillermo del Toro.* Jefferson, N.C.: McFarland, 2015.

Moreman, Christopher R., and Cory James Rushton, eds. *Race, Oppression and the Zombie: Essays on Cross-Cultural Appropriations of the Caribbean Tradition.* Jefferson, N.C.: McFarland, 2011.

Mosse, George L. *Towards the Final Solution: A History of European Racism.* New York: Harper & Row, 1980.

Murphy, Cason. "Augusto Boal Is Alive and Well and Living in Mapleton: The Guilty Remnant in HBO's *The Leftovers.*" *Journal of Film and Video* 68, no. 3–4 (Fall/Winter 2016): 104–114.

Mussolini, Benito. "What Is Fascism, 1932." Modern History Sourcebook. http://www.fordham.edu/halsall/mod/mussolini-fascism.html.

"Nazi-inspired Ads for The Man in the High Castle Pulled from New York Subway." *The Guardian*, November 24, 2015. https://www.theguardian.com/us-news/2015/nov/25/nazi-inspired-ads-for-the-man-in-the-high-castle-pulled-from-new-york-subway.

Nizkor Project. The Trial of Adolf Eichmann, Session 68, June 7, 1961. http://www.nizkor.org/hweb/people/e/eichmann-adolf/transcripts/Sessions/Session-068-01.html.

Novick, Peter. *The Holocaust in American Life.* New York: Mariner Books, 2000.

Nussbaum, Emily. "Depression Modern: The Existential Risk-Taking of 'The Leftovers.'" *The New Yorker*, November 2, 2015. http://www.newyorker.com/magazine/2015/11/02/depression-modern.

Oberhaus, Daniel. "Fake News About a Secret Nazi UFO Base in Antarctica Refuses to Die." *Motherboard*, *Vice*, March 12, 2017. https://motherboard.vice.com/en_us/article/nz53eq/fake-news-about-a-secret-nazi-ufo-base-in-antarctica-refuses-to-die.

O'Keefe, Meghan. "'Star Wars' and Space Nazis: Hasn't Evil Evolved by Now?" *Decider*, November 30, 2015. https://decider.com/2015/11/30/star-wars-and-space-nazis/.

Ozick, Cynthia. "Who Owns Anne Frank?" *New Yorker*, September 8, 1997. https://www.newyorker.com/magazine/1997/10/06/who-owns-anne-frank.

Pardon, Joshua. "Revisiting a Science Fiction Classic: Interpreting *The Day the Earth Stood Still* for Contemporary Film Audiences." *Journal of Popular Film and Television* 36, no. 3 (September 2008): 141–149.

Patterson, David. *Genocide in Jewish Thought*. Cambridge, UK: Cambridge University Press, 2012.

Paxton, Robert O. *Anatomy of Fascism*. New York: Vintage Books, 2005.

Percival, Jesse. "Nazi Iconography in Star Wars and Modern Day Art." *Overture*, December 30, 2015. https://medium.com/overture-magazine/nazi-iconography-in-star-wars-and-modern-day-media-8d179925d23a.

Perry, Ted, ed. *Masterpieces of Modernist Cinema*. Bloomington: Indiana University Press, 2006.

Picart, Caroline Joan "Kay" S., and David A. Frank. *Frames of Evil: The Holocaust as Horror in American Film*. Carbondale: Southern Illinois University Press, 2006.

Polanski, Roman. *Roman by Polanski*. New York: William Morrow, 1984.

Poole, W. Scott. *Wasteland: The Great War and the Origins of Modern Horror*. Berkeley, Calif.: Counterpoint, 2018.

Prince, Stephen, ed. *The Horror Film*. New Brunswick, N.J.: Rutgers University Press, 2004.

Pulliam, June Michelle, and Anthony J. Fonseca, eds. *Encyclopedia of the Zombie: The Walking Dead in Popular Culture and Myth*. Santa Barbara, Calif.: Greenwood Press, 2014.

Quinn, Karl. "The Walking Dead Season 5 Opener Shows There's Plenty of Life in the Undead Yet." *Sunday Morning Herald*, October 14, 2014. http://www.smh.com.au/entertainment/tv-and-radio/the-walking-dead-season-5-opener-shows-theres-plenty-of-life-in-the-undead-yet-20141014-115qyl.html.

Rau, Petra. *Our Nazis: Representations of Fascism in Contemporary Literature and Film*. Edinburgh, UK: Edinburgh University Press, 2013.

"'Raumschiff Enterprise': ZDF neo zeigt umstrittene Nazi-Folge." *Das Bild*, November 4, 2011. https://www.bild.de/unterhaltung/tv/raumschiff-enterprise/zdf-neo-zeigt-umstrittene-nazi-folge-20803514.bild.html.

Reagin, Nancy R. and Janice Liedl, eds. *Star Wars and History*. Hoboken, N.J.: John Wiley & Sons, 2013.

Redhead, Steve, ed. *The Jean Baudrillard Reader*. New York: Columbia University Press, 2008.

Rentschler, Eric. *The Ministry of Illusion: Nazi Cinema and Its Afterlife*. Cambridge, Mass.: Harvard University Press, 1996.

———. *The Use and Abuse of Cinema: German Legacies from the Weimar Era to the Present*. New York: Columbia University Press, 2015.

Rieder, John. "The Metafictive World of the 'The Man in the High Castle': Hermeneutics, Ethics, and Political Ideology." *Science-Fiction Studies* 15, no. 2 (1988): 214–225.

Ritzenhoff, Karen A., and Catriona McAvoy, eds. *Selling Sex on Screen: From Weimar Cinema to Zombie Porn*. Lanham, Md.: Rowman & Littlefield, 2015.

Roberts, Adams. *Science Fiction*. New York: Routledge, 2000.

Rogers, Brett, and Benjamin Stevens, eds. *Classical Traditions in Science Fiction*. Oxford: Oxford University Press, 2015.

Rogovoy, Seth. "The Secret Jewish History of Blade Runner." *Forward*, October 5, 2017. https://forward.com/culture/384383/the-secret-jewish-history-of-blade-runner/.

Rosenberg, Joel. "The Soul of Catastrophe: On the 1937 Film of S. An-sky's *The Dybbuk*." *Jewish Social Studies, Culture, Society* n.s. 17, no. 2 (Winter 2011): 1–27.

Rosenfeld, Gavriel D. *The Fourth Reich: The Specter of Nazism from World War II to the Present*. Cambridge: Cambridge University Press, 2019.

———. *Hi Hitler! How the Nazi Past Is Being Normalized in Contemporary Culture*. Cambridge: Cambridge University Press, 2015.

———. *The World Hitler Never Made*. Cambridge: Cambridge University Press, 2005.

Rosenstone, Robert A., ed. *Revisioning History: Film and the Construction of a New Past*. Princeton, N.J.: Princeton University Press, 1995.

———. *Visions of the Past: The Challenge of Film to Our Idea of History*. Cambridge, Mass.: Harvard University Press, 1995.

Roth, Lane. "Dracula Meets the Zeitgeist: Nosferatu (1922) as Film Adaptation." *Literature/Film Quarterly* 7, no. 4 (1979): 309.

Rothberg, Michael. *Traumatic Realism: The Demands of Holocaust Representation*. Minneapolis: University of Minnesota Press, 2000.

Rozof, Vadim. "The Memory Thief: The Least Sentimental Holocaust Film Ever." *The Village Voice*, May 6, 2008. https://www.villagevoice.com/2008/05/06/the-memory-thief-the-least-sentimental-holocaust-film-ever/.

Ryn, Zdziław, and Stanisław Kłodziński. "An der Grenze zwischen Leben und Tod. Eine Studie über die Erscheinung des 'Muselmanns' im Konzentrationslager" Warszawa: GKBZHwP, 1983.

Sammon, Paul M. *The Making of Blade Runner*. New York: Harper Prism, 1996.

———. *The Making of Starship Troopers*. New York: Boulevard Books, 1997.

Santner, Eric L. *Stranded Objects: Mourning, Memory, and Film in Postwar Germany*. Ithaca, N.Y.: Cornell University Press, 1990.

Saxton, Libby. *Haunted Images: Film, Ethics, Testimony and the Holocaust*. London: Wallflower, 2008.

Scahill, Andrew, and Debbie C. Olsen, eds. *Lost and Othered Children in Contemporary Cinema*. Lanham, Md.: Lexington Books, 2012.

Schwarz, Daniel R. *Imagining the Holocaust*. New York: St. Martin's Press, 1999.

Shandler, Jeffrey. *While America Watches: Televising the Holocaust*. New York: Oxford University Press, 1999.

Simpson, Philip L., and Marcus Mallard, eds. *The Walking Dead Live!: Essays on the Television Show*. Lanham, Md.: Rowman & Littlefield, 2016.

Skitolsky, Lissa. "Tracing Theory on the Body of the 'Walking Dead': Der Muselmann and the Course on Holocaust Studies." *Shofar: An Interdisciplinary Journal of Jewish Studies* 30, no. 2 (Winter 2012): 74–90.

Slane, Andrea. *A Not So Foreign Affair: Fascism, Sexuality and the Cultural Rhetoric of American Democracy*. Durham, N.C.: Duke University Press, 2001.

Smith, Richard G., and David B. Clarke, eds. *Jean Baudrillard: From Hyperreality to Disappearance, Uncollected Interviews*. Edinburgh, UK: Edinburgh University Press, 2015.

Sobchack, Vivian, ed. *The Persistence of History: Cinema, Television, and the Modern Event* New York: Routledge, 1996.

———. *Screening Space: The American Science Fiction Film*. New Brunswick, N.J.: Rutgers University Press, 2004.

Sofsky, Wolfgang. *The Order of Terror: The Concentration Camp*. Princeton, N.J.: Princeton University Press, 2013.

Sontag, Susan. "Fascinating Fascism." *New York Review of Books*, February 6, 1975. http://www.nybooks.com/articles/1975/02/06/fascinating-fascism/.

———. *On Photography*. New York: Delta Books, 1977.

———. *Regarding the Pain of Others*. New York: Picador, 2003.

South, James B., and Kimberly S. Engels, eds. *Westworld and Philosophy*. Hoboken, N.J.: Wiley Blackwell, 2018.

Stack, Tim. "'American Horror Story': Ryan Murphy on Anne Frank Debut—EXCLUSIVE." *EW.com*, November 8, 2012. https://ew.com/article/2012/11/08/american-horror-story-ryan-murphy-anne-frank/.

Staiger, Janet. *Media Reception Studies*. New York: New York University Press, 2005.

———. *Perverse Spectators: The Practices of Film Reception*. New York: New York University Press, 2000.

"Starship Troopers." *Sight & Sound* 8, no. 1 (1998): 53–54.

Steiff, Josef, and Tristan D. Tamplin, eds. *Battlestar Galactica and Philosophy: Mission Accomplished or Mission Frakked Up?* Chicago: Open Court, 2008.

Steinacher, Gerald. *Nazis on the Run: How Hitler's Henchmen Fled Justice*. New York: Oxford University Press, 2012.

Stratton, Jon. "Zombie Trouble: Zombie Texts, Bare Life and Displaced People." *European Journal of Cultural Studies* 14, no. 3 (2011): 265–281.

Strong, Jeremy R. "Transformative Technology and Posthuman Futurity: The Psychosocial Cartography of Zombie Narratives." *Imagining the End: Interdisciplinary Perspectives on the Apocalypse*. London, UK: The Inter-Disciplinary Press, 2015: 209–36.

Strzelczyk, Florentine. "Our Future—Our Past: Fascism, Postmodernism, and Starship Troopers (1997)." *Modernism/Modernity* 15, no. 1 (2008): 87–99.

Svetkey, Benjamin. "The Reich Stuff." *Entertainment Weekly*, November 21, 1997. https://ew.com/article/1997/11/21/starship-troopers-relys-nazi-imagery/.

Telotte, J. P. "The Seductive Text of Metropolis." *South Atlantic Review* 55, no. 4 (1990).

———. "Verhoeven, Virilio, and 'Cinematic Derealization.'" *Film Quarterly* 53, no. 2 (Winter, 1999–2000): 30–38.

Thomson, David. *The Big Screen: The Story of the Movies*. New York: Farrar, Straus & Giroux, 2012.

van Scheers, Rob. *Paul Verhoeven*. Translated by Aletta Stevens. London: Faber & Faber, 1997.

von Bernhardi, Friedrich. "The Next War, 1914." Accessed July 18, 2008. http://www.h-net.org/~german/g-text/kaiserreich/bernhardi.html.

Waller, Gregory A. *The Living and the Undead: Slaying Vampires, Exterminating Vampires.* Urbana: University of Illinois Press, 2010.

Ward, Janet. "Holocaust Film in the Post-9/11 Era: New Directions in Staging and Emplotment." *Pacific Coast Philology* 39 (2004): 29–41.

Wasson, Sara, and Emily Alder, eds. *Gothic Science Fiction, 1980-2010.* Liverpool, UK: Liverpool University Press, 2011.

Weissman, Gary. *Fantasies of Witnessing: Postwar Efforts to Experience the Holocaust.* Ithaca, N.Y.: Cornell University Press, 2004.

Weitz, Eric D. *A Century of Genocide: Utopias of Race and Nation.* Princeton, N.J.: Princeton University Press, 2003.

Welch, David. "Nazi Propaganda and Volksgemeinschaft: Constructing a People's Community." *Journal of Contemporary History* 39, no. 2 (2004): 213–238.

Wetmore, Kevin J. Jr. *The Empire Triumphant: Race, Religion and Rebellion in the Star Wars Films.* Jefferson, N.C.: McFarland, 2005.

Whitman, James Q. *Hitler's American Model: The United States and the Making of Nazi Race Law.* Princeton, N.J.: Princeton University Press, 2017.

Wievikorka, Annette. *The Era of Witness.* Translated by Jared Stark. Ithaca, N.Y.: Cornell University Press, 2006.

Wilford, Lauren. "Death is the Curator: An Interview with Guillermo del Toro." *Bright Wall Dark Room* 44, 2017. https://www.brightwalldarkroom.com/2017/02/15/death-is-the-curator-an-interview-with-guillermo-del-toro/.

Wills, Adam. "Galactica Taps Holocaust for Occupation Inspiration." *Jewish Journal,* November 2, 2006. https://jewishjournal.com/culture/arts/13951/.

———. "'Terminator' traps Yelchin in Sci-Fi Shoah." *Jewish Journal,* May 22, 2009. https://jewishjournal.com/uncategorized/70498/.

Wilson, Kristi M., and Tomas F. Crowder-Taraborrelli. *Film & Genocide.* Madison: University of Wisconsin Press, 2012.

Wittkower, D. E., and Lucinda Rush. *Ender's Game and Philosophy: Genocide Is Child's Play.* Chicago: Open Court, 2013.

Woerner, Meredith. "We Toured the Gruesome Set of Guillermo del Toro's *The Strain.*" *GIZMODO,* July 11, 2014. https://io9.gizmodo.com/we-toured-the-gruesome-world-of-guillermo-del-toros-the-1603035324.

Wood, Robin. *Hitchcock's Films Revisited.* Revised ed. New York: Columbia University Press, 2002.

Yarborough, Nick. "The Apartment Trilogy by Roman Polanski." http://nickyarborough.com/on-polanskis-apartment-trilogy/. Accessed January 15, 2019.

Youngquist, Paul. "Life after Empathy: On Philip K. Dick and *Blade Runner 2049.*" *The Paris Review,* October 23, 2017. https://www.theparisreview.org/blog/2017/10/23/life-after-empathy-on-blade-runner-2049/.

Filmography

Abrams, J. J., dir. *Star Wars: Episode VII—The Force Awakens.* United States, 2015.

Alcalá, Félix Enríquez, dir. *Battlestar Galactica: Razor.* United States, 2007.

Aldrich, Robert, dir. *The Dirty Dozen.* United States, 1967.

Avery, Julius, dir. *Overlord.* United States, 2018.

Baker, Graham, dir. *Omen III: The Final Conflict*. United States, 1981.
Barker, Steve, dir. *Outpost*. United Kingdom, 2008.
———, dir. *Outpost: Black Sun*. United Kingdom, 2012.
Boese, Carl, and Paul Wegener, dirs. *The Golem*. Germany, 1920.
Boll, Uwe, dir. *BloodRayne: The Third Reich*. United States, 2002.
Boyle, Danny, dir. *28 Days Later*. United Kingdom, 2002.
Browning, Tod, and Karl Freund, dirs. *Dracula*. United States, 1931.
Cameron, James, dir. *The Terminator*. United States, 1984.
———, dir. *Terminator 2: Judgment Day*. United States, 1991.
Cavani, Liliana, dir. *The Night Porter*. United States, 1974.
Chaplin, Charles, dir. *The Great Dictator*. United States, 1940.
Cohen, Eli, dir. *The Quarrel*. Canada, 1991.
Crichton, Michael, dir. *Westworld*. United States, 1973.
Demme, Jonathan, dir. *The Silence of the Lambs*. United States, 1991.
Donner, Richard, dir. *The Omen*. United States, 1976.
Edmonds, Don, dir. *Ilsa: She-Wolf of the SS*. United States, 1977.
Edwards, Gareth, dir. *Rogue One: A Star Wars Story*. United States, 2016.
Friedkin, William, dir. *The Exorcist*. United States, 1973.
Gance, Abel, dir. *J'accuse!* France, 1919.
Goyer, David S., dir. *The Unborn*. United States, 2009.
Green, Rob, dir. *The Bunker*. United Kingdom, 2001.
Halperin, Victor, dir. *White Zombie*. United States, 1932.
Harlan, Veit, dir. *Jud Süss*. Germany, 1940.
Hippler, Fritz, dir. *The Eternal Jew*. Germany, 1940.
Hitchcock, Alfred, dir. *The Birds*. United States, 1963.
———, dir. *Psycho*. United States, 1960.
Hutton, Brian G., dir. *Where Eagles Dare*. United States, 1968.
Jakubowska, Wanda, dir. *The Last Stage*. Poland, 1948.
Johnson, Rian, dir. *Star Wars: Episode VIII—The Last Jedi*. United States, 2017.
Kofman, Gil, dir. *The Memory Thief*. United States, 2007.
Kubrick, Stanley, dir. *The Shining*. United States, 1980.
Lang, Fritz, dir. *Dr. Mabuse: The Gambler*. Germany, 1922.
———, dir. *M*. United States, 1931.
———, dir. *Metropolis*. Germany, 1927.
———, dir. *The Testament of Dr. Mabuse*. Germany, 1933.
Lanzmann, Claude, dir. *Shoah*. France, 1985.
Lucas, George, dir. *Star Wars: Episode I—The Phantom Menace*. United States, 1999.
———, dir. *Star Wars: Episode III—Revenge of the Sith*. United States, 2005.
———, dir. *Star Wars: Episode IV—A New Hope*. United States, 1977.
Lumet, Sidney, dir. *The Pawnbroker*. United States, 1964.
Mann, Michael, dir. *The Keep*. United States, 1983.
Marquand, Richard, dir. *Star Wars: Episode VI—Return of the Jedi*. United States, 1983.
McG, dir. *Terminator Salvation*. United States, 2009.
Mostow, Jonathan, dir. *Terminator 3: Rise of the Machines*. United States, 2003.
Murnau, F. W., dir. *Nosferatu*. Germany, 1922.

Myrick, Daniel, and Eduardo Sánchez, dirs. *The Blair Witch Project*. United States, 1999.
Polanski, Roman, dir. *The Pianist*. United States, 2002.
———, dir. *Repulsion*. United Kingdom, 1965.
———, dir. *Rosemary's Baby*. United States, 1968.
———, dir. *The Tenant*. France, 1976.
Raaphorst, Richard, dir. *Frankenstein's Army*. Netherlands, 2013.
Reed, Joel M., dir. *Night of the Zombies*. United States, 1981.
Reeves, Matt, dir. *Cloverfield*. United States, 2008.
Reitz, Edgar, dir. *Heimat: A Chronicle of Germany*. Germany, 1984.
Resnais, Alain, dir. *Night and Fog*. France, 1955.
Riefenstahl, Leni, dir. *Triumph of the Will*. Germany, 1935.
Rippert, Otto, dir. *Homunculus*. Germany, 1917.
Rollin, Jean, and Julian de Laserna, dirs. *Zombie Lake*. France, 1981.
Romero, George, dir. *Dawn of the Dead*. United States, 1978.
———, dir. *Land of the Dead*. United States, 2005.
———, dir. *The Night of the Living Dead*. United States, 1968.
Ross, Peter John, and John Whitney, dirs. *Horrors of War*. United States, 2006.
Roth, Eli, dir. *Hostel*. United States, 2005.
———, dir. *Hostel: Part II*. United States, 2007.
Schaffner, Franklin J., dir. *The Boys from Brazil*. United States, 1978.
Schrader, Paul, dir. *Dominion: Prequel to the Exorcist*. United Kingdom, 2005.
Schumacher, Joel, dir. *Blood Creek*. United States, 2009.
———, dir. *The Lost Boys*. United States, 1987.
Scott, Ridley, dir. *Blade Runner*. United States, 1982.
Spielberg, Steven, dir. *Saving Private Ryan*. United States, 1998.
———, dir. *Schindler's List*. United States, 1993.
Steinhoff, Hans, dir. *Hitlerjunge Quex*. Germany, 1933.
Tarantino, Quentin, dir. *Inglourious Basterds*. United States, 2009.
Taylor, Don, and Mike Hodges, dirs. *Damien: Omen II*. United States, 1978.
Tourneur, Jacques, dir. *I Walked with a Zombie*. United States, 1943.
Verhoeven, Paul, dir. *Starship Troopers*. United States, 1997.
Villenueve, Denis, dir. *Blade Runner 2049*. United States, 2017.
Vuorensola, Timo, dir. *Iron Sky*. Finland, Germany, Australia, 2012.
Waschneck, Erich, dir. *The Rothschilds*. Germany, 1940.
Waszynski, Michal, dir. *The Dybbuk*. Poland, 1937.
Wiederhorn, Ken, dir. *Shock Waves*. United States, 1977.
Wiene, Robert, dir. *The Cabinet of Caligari*. Germany, 1920.
Wirkola, Tommy, dir. *Dead Snow*. Norway, 2009.
Wise, Robert, dir. *The Day the Earth Stood Still*. United States, 1951.

Television and Other Media

American Horror Story: Asylum (2012)
Band of Brothers (2001)
Battlestar Galactica (1978–1979)
Battlestar Galactica Miniseries (2003)

Battlestar Galactica (2004–2009)
Beverly Hills 90210 (1990–2000)
Fear the Walking Dead (2015–)
Holocaust (1978)
The Leftovers (2014–2017)
Lost (2004–2010)
The Man in the High Castle (2015–)
Melrose Place (1992–1999)
Perfect Strangers (1986–1993)
Star Trek (1966–1969)
The Strain (2014–2017)
Terminator: The Sarah Connor Chronicles (2008–2009)
Twilight Zone (1959–1964)
V (2009–2011)
V: The Complete Series (1984–1985)
V: The Original Miniseries (1983)
The Walking Dead (2010–)
Westworld (2016–)

INDEX

Note: Figures are indicated by italicized page numbers.

ABOUT THE AUTHOR

BRIAN E. CRIM is professor of history at the University of Lynchburg where he teaches courses in modern European history, the Holocaust, and film and history. He is author of *Our Germans: Project Paperclip and the National Security State* and *Antisemitism in the German Military Community and the Jewish Response, 1914-1938*.